DEVELOPING YOUR SPEAKING VOICE

Under the Advisory Editorship of J. Jeffery Auer

developing
your
speaking
voice

SECOND EDITION

JOHN P. MONCUR
University of Michigan
and
HARRISON M. KARR

HARPER & ROW, PUBLISHERS

New York
Evanston
San Francisco
London

DEVELOPING YOUR SPEAKING VOICE, 2nd edition

Copyright © 1972 by John P. Moncur and Harrison M. Karr

Standard Book Number: 06-044568-8

Library of Congress Catalog Card Number: 77-170622

To our wives, Eva Beryl and Shirley

contents

preface

THE FIRST EDITION of *Developing Your Speaking Voice* was the outgrowth of over twenty years of teaching in the field of the speaking voice by Professor Harrison M. Karr, my former esteemed colleague and close friend. My revision of his fine text has attempted to retain the best of the original work—the Karr wit, literary taste, didactic skills, and sense of organization—and to carefully integrate them with a wealth of new ideas and materials made available through the remarkable advances of the past two decades.

The last decade in particular has seen a marked change in several areas of human endeavor—in the attitudes and behaviors of the members of our society, in the tremendous scientific advances, which have had a direct bearing upon the teaching of voice and diction, and in a new expression of our age in current prose and poetry. These changes, coupled with over twenty years of professional experience in the area of voice and articulation by the present reviser, have been responsible for the many alterations made in the original text.

The advances in the field of behavioral science have had a profound effect upon learning in general; the impact has been so great that one can hardly turn to a discipline that has not adopted the most usable of available learning models and procedures for training purposes. The application of operant conditioning and programmatic instruction to voice and diction, perhaps for the first time in any text treating this subject, was felt to be both wise and imperative. These procedures are not only very effective in producing results, they are enjoyable and should prove valuable to both instructor and student.

The original text had a wealth of selections in both prose and poetry, most of which have been retained. A few selections, particularly dated political speeches, have been deleted to make room for current selections featuring dramatic readings from well-known plays, poetry by black authors, and current public speeches. A cross index of authors and selections is provided in the back of the book for easy access to favorite material. Students are encouraged to use the lists of suggested selections which follow main divisions or chapters.

The overall organization of the revised text differs from the original somewhat in order to simplify and tighten the developmental sequence used by Dr. Karr. For example, I felt that breathing should be studied before phonation, and that rate, pitch, and force should be incorporated into a larger chapter treating vocal variety. Therefore, we commence our training program with breathing, and move systematically through tone production, resonation, articulation, pronunciation, vocal variety, and the integration of vocal skills. Many of the drill exercises are spliced into the text to provide day-to-day materials for practice. Typically, the longer selections of prose and poetry follow main divisions or chapters. Background information has been condensed and placed in the first part of functional chapters and may be assigned for outside study in order to provide more time for class drill. We make this comment to emphasize the importance of having each student perform as much as possible in large and small groups and individually. It is important to recognize that behavioral changes take place when a student is *actively* engaged in exercises, rather than in listening passively while others perform.

In order to obtain maximum results from this text, we highly recommend careful study of Chapter Two, which provides background information regarding operant conditioning, programmatic instruction, and phonetics.

The present writer was most pleased to be invited by Harper & Row, Publishers, at Dr. Karr's request, to undertake the revision of *Developing Your Speaking Voice*. It has been a rewarding and challenging experience to rework this fine text.

The author is most grateful to his wife, Mrs. Eva Beryl Moncur, who wrote many of the sentences in the original text, for her many contributions to the present edition—namely, writing new sentences for drills, reading the manuscript, checking continuity and grammar, and proofreading endlessly the typed manuscript.

I wish to express my deep appreciation to Professor J. Jeffery Auer, my consulting editor at Harper & Row, for his extensive review of each chapter. His wisdom and insight along with his fine editorial skill combined to make a major contribution to the finished product.

I wish to thank Professors Edward Stasheff and L. LaMont Okey, Speech Department, The University of Michigan, for their very helpful suggestions with regard to the poetry and prose selections and other matters included in this book.

To Mrs. Nancy Martin, the Executive Secretary, Callier Hearing and Speech Center, I owe a debt of gratitude. Her ability to turn out top-quality typing under the constant pressure of early deadlines deserves a special note of thanks.

John P. Moncur

DEVELOPING YOUR SPEAKING VOICE

CHAPTER ONE

you and your voice

WHAT IS GOOD voice and speech? Is it a gift, or is it acquired? Can good voice and speech be learned systematically?

Speech is learned behavior, not a gift, per se. It is true that we are endowed with anatomical structures and physiological processes that are inherited from our ancestors, accounting, at least in part, for similarities among family members. Imagine, for example, what your voice and speech would be like if you had been reared by an Asiatic family with all the traditions, language, and speech of that culture! Obviously, the very elements of your voice, i.e., pitch, rate, quality, and force, would be markedly different from those of your American English speech, as would be marked differences in articulation, language, and communication mores. Even within the context of American English there are also differences derived from the traditions, language, and speech of the subculture, and revealed by differences in pitch, rate, quality, and force: ghetto speech, Appalachian area speech, New England dialect, etc. Your speech behavior today, then, has been molded by the sum total of the personal interactions you have had from infancy to maturity.

From the very beginning of time man has been aware of the great importance of speech. The Roman writer Phaedrus once said, "Nothing is more useful than to speak clearly," stressing the need for good articulation.

Quintilian, the renowned Roman rhetorician, felt that perfect eloquence was "the noblest of human attainments," emphasizing that good speech is a lofty goal.

Psychologists have taught for years that our personalities are primarily revealed through our speech and voice. Very often, we are judged by our voices alone. In admiring a speaker, Mark Twain once said, "Lord, what an organ is the human voice when played on by a master."

The power of voice and speech has been demonstrated by leaders throughout time. In the nineteenth century Lord Salisbury recognized the importance of speech as a great mediator in politics when he said, "In these days, whether we like it or not, power is with the tongue; power is with the man who can speak." In our own century we need only refer back a few decades to assess the tremendous impact speakers had upon vast audiences—Adolf Hitler, Benito Mussolini, Winston Churchill, and Franklin D. Roosevelt. In more recent times the course of history has been changed by the speeches of John F. Kennedy and Martin Luther King.

Students should ask the question, "What are the benefits to be derived from voice and diction training for the person who does not plan to engage in public speaking?" There are many benefits covering a wide range of human activities. The powerful, nineteenth-century Prime Minister of Great Britain, William Gladstone, once said, "All time and money spent in the training of speech and voice is an investment that pays a greater dividend than any other."

Probably the most obvious benefit is economic success. An aspirant may be given a better job or greater financial return on the basis of effective communication; or conversely, he might be deprived of a good position because of inadequate speech. Many executives and successful salesmen have attributed their success to formal training in voice and diction.

Voice and diction training often has a pronounced effect on personality structure, particularly if we accept the premise stated earlier that personality is revealed primarily through speech. People have a strong tendency to judge a person by his manner of speaking. For example, the careless speaker who mumbles and mispronounces words often gives the impression of being slovenly, unsure of himself, and not very bright.

Voice and diction training develops in an individual latent abilities which may otherwise lie fallow throughout life. In the social realm, a speaker who has developed his ability to express himself to the fullest extent through training will probably attract more friends, be more fully understood and esteemed, and may even be more fortunate in attracting a member of the opposite sex.

Flexibility in expression is vitally important to the actor who is called upon to portray a wide range of characterizations and to make them credible. Legitimate theatre demands the ultimate from actors and actresses in the matter of voice and diction, for not only must they portray another person, they must be heard distinctly in the last row of the balcony. The American actor who is untrained in voice and diction lacks the vocal skills necessary to assume roles in Greek and Roman dramas, Elizabethan drama, the comedies of the seventeenth and eighteenth centuries, and many other period plays calling for a wide range of vocal ability. Undeniably, the rewards for the vocally able professional actor are indeed great.

Nor should we overlook the motion picture industry, television, and radio ; they may not require as much projection of the voice but most assuredly demand crisp, clear, and effective speech. Radio and television announcers must have not only a good voice but also superior articulation and pronunciation.

Voice and diction training can be extremely valuable to other professional areas—law, the ministry, and teaching. A lawyer may be prepared in law and schooled in the art of persuasion and still be ineffective in pleading his case before judge and jury because of poor vocal skills. For one seeking to inspire —be he priest, rabbi, or minister—the ability to use the voice is a priceless asset. A teacher owes it to his class to be heard and to be understood regardless of whether the teaching situation is kindergarten or the university.

CHANGING YOUR SPEECH BEHAVIOR

To the question raised earlier, "Can good voice and speech be learned systematically?" The answer is a resounding, "yes," provided, of course, that a suitable program of training is available and the student applies himself with some degree of motivation and drive. In recent years a wealth of knowledge has been made available to us by behavioral scientists, who have been perfecting their learning models and technology, and have applied these to many instructional situations. The present text has incorporated some of the most effective and successful of these techniques into many of the drill exercises, as will be explained more fully in the next chapter.

GOALS IN VOICE AND DICTION

In taking a behavioral approach to voice and diction, it is necessary prior to commencing work to establish the goals one wishes to achieve. Once these have been identified, and they will differ for each student, both the instructor and the student can begin work on highly specific aspects of human speech behavior in a systematic fashion.

There are a number of general goals that all students should seek in a beginning voice and diction course. These goals form the basic minimum for good speech and include adequate: (a) voice quality, (b) loudness, (c) pitch, (d) rate, (e) articulation, (f) pronunciation, and (g) variety.

Voice quality. A good speaking voice has a pleasing quality that is based upon efficient tone production and resonation. It should also be free from any unpleasant voice quality, such as nasality, hoarseness, etc.

Loudness. It is the duty of every speaker to be heard, and this may entail adaptation to size of audience, size of room, and quality of the acoustics.

Pitch. Pitch refers to both the habitual, overall level employed by a speaker as well as the many inflections he uses to express his thoughts and emotions. Every person, as we shall see later in the course, has a basic pitch level that is best suited for his voice.

Rate. The good speaker must adjust his rate to both his material and audience; it, of course, can vary from one situation to another. Rate also has to do with the duration one gives to sounds, words, phrases, sentences, paragraphs, etc., to achieve maximum communication.

Articulation. A speaker must be understood as well as heard. The need for good articulation should be stressed. Good articulation is not ostentatious nor overly precise. Varying situations often call for different degrees of articulatory precision.

Pronunciation. Good pronunciation calls for the ability to pronounce correctly a large body of words that comprise the expressive vocabulary of the educated, cultured people of a given dialectal area. "Correctly" has a special connotation in that in some instances more than one pronunciation of a given word is acceptable, while in other cases it is not.

Variety. Good speech requires vocal variety, which includes variety of rate, pitch, force, and quality. Care in the selection and presentation of materials is also important in achieving variety.

ANALYZING ENTERING BEHAVIORS

We recommend that an analysis of each student be made before beginning work on voice and diction skills. Such an analysis will serve to identify the "entering behaviors," which are those speech behaviors that the student possesses at the beginning of the course. After identifying the entering speech behaviors, it is then possible to state the "terminal behaviors," or the behaviors each student should possess after completing the course. The basic minimums for good speech as stated in the preceding paragraphs should be the terminal behaviors attained. Some students will be able to achieve more than others; therefore, their goals should be set correspondingly higher than those for less talented students.

EXERCISES

1. Each student is to prepare and deliver in class a three-minute reading. Include both prose and poetry. Students should be assigned to rate each speaker, using the following "Voice and Diction Analysis Form."

2. Make a tape recording of your voice. In addition to reading both prose and poetry, add at least one minute or so of conversational speech. Listen to the recording and fill out a *Voice and Diction Analysis Form.*

4

VOICE AND DICTION ANALYSIS FORM

Scale

Excellent   Poor
|————|————|————|————|
1   2   3   4   5

1. Rate:
   a. Too fast———
   b. Too slow———
   c. Monotonous———
   d. Appropriate———
   e. Other———

Excellent   Poor
|————|————|————|————|
1   2   3   4   5

2. Pitch and Pitch Patterns:
   a. Habitual level too low———
   b. Habitual level too high———
   c. Habitual level appropriate———
   d. Pitch monotone present———
   e. Repetitious patterns———
   f. Appropriate use of pitch———
   g. Other———

Excellent   Poor
|————|————|————|————|
1   2   3   4   5

3. Loudness and Stress:
   a. Too loud———
   b. Too weak———
   c. Appropriate loudness———
   d. Lacking in stress———
   e. Too much stress———
   f. Other———

Excellent   Poor
|————|————|————|————|
1   2   3   4   5

4. Quality:
   a. Tone quality poor———
   b. Tone quality good———
   c. Faulty quality present———
   d. Other———

Excellent   Poor
|————|————|————|————|
1   2   3   4   5

5. Articulation:
   a. Articulation poor———
   b. Articulation appropriate———
   c. Faulty sound production———
   d. Poor use of strong and weak forms———
   e. Other———

Excellent   Poor
|————|————|————|————|
1   2   3   4   5

6. Pronunciation:
   a. Words pronounced correctly———
   b. Words pronounced incorrectly———
   c. Other———

Rating of performance as a whole, including interpretation of meaning and emotional details:

Excellent   Poor
|————|————|————|————|
1   2   3   4   5

5

CHAPTER
TWO

backgrounds
for
instruction

THE APPLICATION OF some of the simplest principles and techniques of behavior modification and programmatic instruction to a wide range of instructional situations has : (a) made the learning process involved more clearly understood, (b) required better organization of instructional materials, and (c) speeded up the learning of tasks. It is our belief that this type of learning can be applied to voice and diction and can both be efficacious and enjoyable.

BEHAVIOR MODIFICATION AND PROGRAMMATIC INSTRUCTION

The present text has attempted to blend the traditional treatment of voice and diction materials with a behavioral approach to acquiring skills. We should like to stress this point : The programmatic exercises can also be presented in a traditional manner. Indeed, the majority of exercises have *not* been cast into the programmatic mold simply because many of them can be presented better in the dynamic, traditional manner.

Inasmuch as exercises designed for programmatic instruction utilizing an operant conditioning model are simple and powerful, we recommend

6

performing them in the manner prescribed. In this way we feel maximum results will be obtained from this type of exercise.

Many of the exercises, both traditional and programmatic, employ phonetic symbols. Rather than postpone the study of rudimentary phonetic concepts until reaching the section on articulation, Chapters 7 and 8, we recommend that the exercises on acquiring the use of phonetic symbols, found in the last portion of this chapter, be completed before starting Chapter 3.

The sections that follow—Learning, Programmatic Instruction, and the Use of Phonetic Symbols—serve as background information for many of the exercises in the text. These materials have been greatly simplified and systematized for quick assimilation.

DEFINITION OF TERMS

The following definitions of terms are applicable to the learning and programmatic concepts used in this text.

LEARNING TERMS

Stimulus. Something that rouses or incites to action or increased action.

Response. Any behavior resulting from the application of a stimulus.

Reward. Something which serves as a positive reinforcement given in return for accomplishing a desired behavior.

Punishment. A penalty imposed for failure to produce a given form of behavior. For example, an instructor may say "no" as a form of punishment if a subject fails to produce the desired behavior.

Reinforcement. Rewarding a form of behavior, thereby increasing the likelihood that it will occur again.

Shaping. Term used in behavior modification to indicate an intermediate step that will help the subject reach his goal. For example, if a dog trainer wishes to have a dog put out his paw after sitting up, he has the dog sit up ; then he grasps his paw and pulls it forward and rewards him. This intermediate step (shaping) helps the dog to achieve the final step of putting out his paw automatically. Shaping is often used as an intermediate step in acquiring voice and diction skills.

PROGRAMMATIC INSTRUCTION TERMS

Entering behaviors. The forms of behavior exhibited by the subject prior to undertaking an instructional program.

Terminal behaviors. The forms of behavior the instructor wishes the subject to possess after completing the instructional program.

Target. The given behavior selected for modification. For example, if, the [s] sound is faulty, the instructor will choose the [s] sound, as in *say*, to be worked on for improvement ; it becomes the target or behavior to be changed.

7

Goal. The stated form of behavior that it is desirable for the subject to possess (within reason) at the conclusion of the program. In the example above the student may be expected to say the [s] sound correctly in a given set of words dictated to him by the instructor. Goals may be stated according to what behavior is desired. For example, the above goal could be made more difficult by insisting that the subject produce the [s] sound correctly in conversational speech.

Instructional objective. A statement stipulating the intention of the instructional program. For example, if an instructor wants all students to be able to pronounce a given list of words correctly, he so states his objective. The examples below explain how important it is in behavior modification to state objectives properly before beginning work.

> *Correct*: All students must be able to pronounce correctly all words in List A.
> *Incorrect*: I want you to know the words in List A.
> "To know" is not to pronounce and is therefore incorrect.
> *Incorrect*: I would like you to be able to pronounce the words in List A. "Like" is not precise enough and won't get the job done.
> Instructors must make the instructional objective clear.

Program. A prearranged series of events leading to a specified goal. Programs are written by behavioral specialists in such a way as to implement learning. Generally, the program starts with steps or frames that range from easy to difficult and are within the ability of the individual to perform successfully.

Frame. The smallest unit of a program. Each frame in a program must be specified and may not be improvised.

Phase. Several related programs written to accomplish an instructional objective. One program may not be sufficient to accomplish the acquisition of a desired behavior; therefore, several related programs may be necessary to achieve the goal. For example, if a subject is to learn to discriminate between a little tension in a muscle and no tension, it may be necessary to start with a program to determine the difference between a state of tension and that of no tension.

Criterion. A precise method of evaluation that determines whether or not the goal has been reached. For example, the criterion of success in reaching the goal of pronouncing a basic pool of difficult words correctly can be stipulated in terms of numbers, i.e., 20 out of 20, 19 out of 20, 18 out of 20, etc. A criterion may be made more stringent as one progresses from one program to the next. A criterion is usually stated in concrete terms of action, such as "to produce," "to say," "to pronounce," "to write," "to read," etc., and rarely in abstractions, such as "to understand," "to know," or "to appreciate," which are not specific terms of behavior.

8

LEARNING

Gagne identifies eight types of learning: (1) signal learning, (2) stimulus-response learning, (3) chaining, (4) verbal association, (5) multiple discrimination, (6) concept learning, (7) principle learning, and (8) problem solving. The present text will be concerned primarily with the second type, stimulus-response learning. By far the most useful kind of stimulus-response learning that is available to us in voice and diction is *operant conditioning*.

OPERANT CONDITIONING

The work of Skinner has given rise to the widespread use of the operant conditioning model or paradigm, which may be diagrammed thus: S_D—R—R_f, where S_D is the discriminating stimulus, R is the response, and R_f is the reinforcement. The following example will explain the above symbols and their relationships to each other.

Let us assume an instructor wishes to correct a persistent nasality problem exhibited by a student. Using operant conditioning he might proceed in the following manner:

1. First, he gives these instructions: "Before I can correct your nasality problem you must be able to tell the difference between nasal and nonnasal speech. I am going to say one word, *play*, several times. Most of the samples will be said correctly, but occasionally, I will say *play* with nasality. I want you to raise your hand (R, or response) when you hear *play* said with nasality." The instructor says *play* several times without nasality (S's or stimuli) and once with nasality (S_D, or a discriminating stimulus—a special stimulus that calls for a response).

2. Let's say that the student raised his hand correctly, which is a response (R), and that the instructor rewarded him by giving him a dollar, which in this case is positive reinforcement (R_f). This powerful reinforcer tells the student that he was correct, and, of course, will encourage him to respond again when he hears the discriminating stimulus, the nasally produced *play*. The likelihood of a dollar per trial being the reinforcer is a little remote, but it does serve to stress the idea that rewards should be appropriate and sufficient to reinforce behavior. In voice and diction classes, an affirmative reply, "yes," or a nod of the head should be all that is necessary for sophisticated and motivated students. In other words, the approbation of the instructor should be reward enough for students.

3. Suppose the student had been incorrect. Let's say that he raised his hand when the instructor had said *play* without nasality. His response would have been incorrect because he was told to raise his hand only when he heard the nasal version. The instructor has two paths open to him: (a) he may simply decide to do nothing, which is a condition of no reward when the student is looking for a reward, or (b) he may say, "No, that's not right," which is a negative reinforcer. Negative reinforcement decreases the

likelihood that the student will respond again to that particular stimulus. Of the two courses of action, we prefer the former (no action) chiefly because of the confusion that might ensue in using two types of action.

In summary, if an instructor wants to bring out a form of behavior in a respondent, he rewards the behavior he wants when the student displays it. Such a reward is reinforcing in the sense that it increases the likelihood that the respondent will produce that behavior again when the discriminating stimulus occurs.

We purposely did not stress the use of an aversive or punishing stimulus following an incorrect response in order again to avoid confusion. Supposing the student had been given a sharp electrical shock upon producing the incorrect response. The fear of being shocked again would remind him not to respond to that particular stimulus again but to seek a more appropriate behavior, such as remaining silent. In the interest of students, we do not recommend the use of aversive or punishing stimuli in voice and diction work.

PROGRAMMATIC INSTRUCTION

The operant conditioning model is both simple in design and powerful in obtaining results. We feel that operant conditioning can be easily incorporated into programmatic instruction, which further facilitates the acquisition of voice and diction skills. Many of the exercises contained in this book are designed for programmatic instruction using an operant model.

Programmatic instruction differs from dynamic or traditional instruction in several respects. First, the programs are designed ahead of time, goals are highly specified, materials are carefully selected and graded, and a criterion is established for each program. The instructor must adhere to the rules governing the execution of the programs; i.e., he must present stimuli in a prescribed manner, reinforce correct responses, remain silent when necessary, and determine whether or not the subject has achieved the goal according to the criterion established. Programmatic instruction does not permit the instructor to improvise within the program. In a very real sense, he is "locked into" the system, which is as it should be, particularly if he wishes to obtain maximum results *from this system*.

Dynamic or traditional instruction depends upon the instructor's having the needed information and skills ready for the instructional task. Unlike the programmatic method, dynamic instruction is very flexible and permits a wide range of learning techniques to be employed. Some of the finest moments of dynamic instruction come when the instructor has an insight or hunch that serves him on the spur of the moment, and in that moment he shifts to a new technique or idea that gives him the desired results. For this reason, we have endorsed both approaches to instruction.

Please note: *all exercises in this book can be done without using the programmatic approach*. However, if you elect to do an exercise programmatically, we suggest you abide by the rules in order to get maximum results from this method.

EXAMPLE OF PROGRAMMATIC METHOD

The following exercise illustrates how to proceed with the programmatic method as used in this text. This example is typical of many exercises you will encounter later on.

Program in Pronunciation

Frames	Frames	Frames	Frames
1 actually	11 chasm	21 era	31 longevity
2 amateur	12 chiropodist	22 err	32 mischievous
3 Arctic	13 comptroller	23 forehead	33 neither
4 Arkansas	14 corps	24 gesture	34 ocean
5 bade	15 cynosure	25 Himalaya	35 pianist
6 been	16 deaf	26 Illinois	36 piano
7 blackguard	17 decade	27 Italian	37 precious
8 bouquet	18 education	28 lichen	38 pretty
9 brochure	19 either	29 literature	39 quay
10 capsule	20 envelope	30 lounge	40 quixotic

Procedure

1. The instructor pronounces each word aloud, and the student echoes him, attempting to pronounce the word in the same way.

2. The instructor signals if the response is correct by giving a reward, which can be any of the following: making a click with a clicker-counter,[1] nodding the head, raising a finger or hand, flashing a light, or using any other device that indicates that the student has given a correct response.

3. If the student gives an incorrect response, the instructor does not signal, indicating a condition of no reward.

4. The instructor goes on to the next item regardless of whether an answer is correct or not.

5. About 3 to 4 seconds are required for each frame; the process should not be slowed down, as a normal pace is best for the average student.

6. The instructor continues until all frames are completed. In long programs, such as the one above, he may elect to designate each column as a

[1] It is possible to purchase an inexpensive clicker-counter for $1.00 at a hardware store. The clicker-counter is used in taking inventories and not only makes a click sound, but keeps track of the number of times the subject has responded (up to 1000).

program, thus dividing up the longer sequence. This may be desirable for classroom drill.

7. The criterion of success is determined by the instructor. He may wish to be more lenient at first and call 8 out of 10 responses correct; later, he may raise the criterion to 10 out of 10. It is important that students reach the criterion level set by the instructor. Repetition of short programs is usually the quickest way to achieve success. If a student cannot reach the criterion after several trials, laboratory drill outside of class may be indicated.

In the foregoing procedure, the following elements of programmatic instruction and operant conditioning took place.

Entering behavior. The behavior of the student with regard to the words before the exercise began.

Terminal behavior. The behavior the instructor wished him to possess after the exercise was completed. It is entirely possible that some students may fail to achieve the terminal behaviors stipulated. More drill is needed.

Instructional objective. To teach the student how to pronounce correctly a pool of commonly mispronounced words.

Program. The structured list of items contained in the pool. The program might have been more highly structured if knowledge of word difficulty had permitted going from easy to difficult words.

Frame. One step in the program; one word constitutes a frame.

Phase. Not applicable in this sequence. However, an earlier phase might have been a number of programs organized as a phase of ear training, in which case it would have been the task of the student merely to identify whether the word was correct or not rather than to have to repeat the word.

Goal. To achieve the instructional objective, which was to pronounce all of the words correctly on the list.

Criterion. The establishment by the instructor of the number of correct responses for success in the program, i.e., 35 out of 40, 37 out of 40, etc.

Target. Pronunciation in general and the items selected in particular.

THE USE OF PHONETIC SYMBOLS

The consonants, vowels, and diphthongs that comprise the spoken sounds of our language are treated in detail in Chapters 7 and 8. Many of the exercises in earlier chapters, particularly 3 through 6, utilize phonetic symbols to represent speech sounds. In order to perform these exercises with ease, a working familiarity with phonetic transcription is desirable.

THE INTERNATIONAL PHONETIC ALPHABET

The International Phonetic Alphabet (IPA) is an alphabet sponsored by the International Phonetic Association (founded in 1886), consisting of letters to symbolize the position of the articulating organs, and therefore has the same symbol for the same sound[2] irrespective of the language in which the sound occurs. The phonetic alphabet is thus much more accurate and definitive than any system of diacritical marks, the code of dots and bars which dictionary editors use to indicate pronunciation. When the phonetic alphabet is used as a guide to the study of the muscular adjustments of the articulatory organs as well as an aid to ear training, it can become a highly valuable tool to the student of diction.

Rules Governing the Use of IPA

1. Each symbol represents one sound (see footnote 2). Since we all make *e* in *let* in a slightly different manner, there is some variation in the sound, but not enough to warrant different symbols.[3]

2. IPA is used thoughout the world; therefore, the symbols and corresponding sounds that languages share are the same. Often a language will require additional symbols for sounds that do not occur in other languages.

3. IPA is used to represent the spoken word, and it is therefore improper to use IPA for writing alone. A speaker must first say that which is recorded.

4. IPA utilizes all of the regular letters of the English alphabet, with a few exceptions: (a) in cases where a single letter in English represents more than one sound, e.g., *e* in *err*, *let*, etc., additional symbols have been added, and (b) in cases where two or more letters represent one sound, e.g., *th* in *that*, new symbols have been added.

Phonetic symbols

The majority of letters in the English alphabet are also used in IPA. In the example below, note the relationship between the two systems.

English Alphabet: a b c d e f g h i j k l m n o p q r s t u v w x y z

IPA: a b   d e f g h i j k l m n o p   r s t u v w   z

In addition to the letters indicated above, IPA uses five new consonants and nine new vowels.

---

[2] Actually, this goal has never been fully achieved because of the minute differences in pronouncing a given sound in various letter combinations. For example, the long *a* sound in *name* differs from the long *a* sound in *ate*. The difference, however, is not great enough to use two different symbols.

[3] Broad transcription differs from narrow transcription in that the latter attempts to characterize the minute differences or modifications that occur in spoken dialects. The linguistic geographer, for example, relies upon the additional notations of narrow transcription to capture the subtle nuances of a given dialect. The study of narrow transcription is beyond the scope of the present text.

Consonants

IPA Symbol	Example Words	Reason for New Symbols
[p]	put, happy, sip	
[b]	boy, above, cab	
[t]	toil, letter, bet	
[d]	day, handy, mad	
[k]	cat, picnic, book	k and c are often pronounced the same; c is eliminated.
[g]	good, buggy, bug	
[f]	five, sift, golf	
[v]	vow, wives, live	
[θ]	thin, author, bath	The letters t and h are used for other phonetic sounds.
[ð]	this, either, bathe	Same as above.
[s]	sit, mister, miss	
[z]	zebra, busy, was	
[ʃ]	she, fishing, dish	s and h are used for other phonetic symbols.
[ʒ]	beige, leisure	g and s are used for other phonetic symbols.
[h]	hot, behave	
[w]	with, away	
[j]	yes, value	
[l]	let, willing, well	
[r]	red, around, bar	
[m]	moon, among, hem	
[n]	no, went, scene	
[ŋ]	finger, hang	n and g are used for other phonetic symbols.

Vowels

The vowel diagram on p. 15 is helpful in locating the approximate position of the tongue during the production of pure vowels. The terms, *front, mid,* and *back,* refer to the position in the mouth of the high portion or apex of the tongue. The apex of the tongue, for example, is forward in the mouth for [i], but backward for [u]. The vertical dimensions depict the position of the tongue and lower jaw, which remain relatively stable during the production of pure vowels. For example, the tongue and jaw should be low (moved to their lowest position) during the production of [ɑ], but should be high (just barely lowered) for [i]. In summary, the lower line of the chart represents the position of the tongue, and the upper line represents the roof of the mouth. The vowels at the left of the diagram are called *front* vowels; those at the right are called *back* vowels; those near the top are called *high* vowels, and those near the bottom, *low* vowels. The vowels in the center of the chart are called *mid*-vowels. For example, [i] is a high, front vowel, and [ɑ] is a low, back vowel.

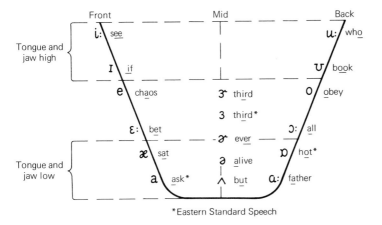

*Eastern Standard Speech

Figure 2.1. The approximate focal positions at which the vowels are formed in the mouth.

EXERCISES

1. Operant conditioning exercise: drill on the following programs to speed up easy identification.

[ʃ] Frames		[ʒ] Frames		[θ] Frames		[ð] Frames		[ŋ] Frames		[k] Frames	
1	where	17	barrage	33	psyche	49	mother	65	lent	81	pig
2	fresh	18	pleasure	34	thin	50	shirk	66	length	82	cat
3	bushel	19	mirror	35	soon	51	marsh	67	many	83	flag
4	same	20	usurer	36	method	52	teeth	68	song	84	occur
5	shirk	21	short	37	frog	53	feel	69	tongue	85	gain
6	around	22	genre	38	thimble	54	that	70	might	86	acute
7	diction	23	history	39	this	55	mist	71	finger	87	pork
8	break	24	Joffre	40	mirth	56	bathe	72	hinder	88	clean
9	cash	25	bushel	41	myth	57	thin	73	ping	89	finger
10	shell	26	derision	42	soot	58	either	74	plane	90	picked
11	sister	27	basket	43	hot	59	will	75	hanger	91	gas
12	farce	28	mirage	44	ether	60	thine	76	soon	92	clipper
13	sheen	29	major	45	thou	61	same	77	ringlet	93	bigger
14	sauce	30	Jacques	46	theory	62	weather	78	brow	94	lock
15	seashell	31	occasion	47	thumb	63	thistle	79	king	95	acute
16	thin	32	instruct	48	zoo	64	though	80	home	96	future

15

    a. Not all frames contain the target sound. The student is to identify words with the target sound in it.

    b. The instructor selects a student and dictates the words aloud. The student must close his book; the rest of the class listens.

    c. If the student hears a word with the target sound in it, he raises his hand.

    d. If the student is correct, the instructor nods his head.

    e. The instructor should use 3 seconds per frame and not repeat. If the student does not understand the procedure or misses five in a row, reinstruct and continue.

    f. The criterion for success should be established by the instructor, e.g., six out of eight correct responses.

    g. The instructor repeats the program a second time, raising the criterion.

    h. The instructor selects another student and does a second program, then a third, etc.

2. Have the students pair off into drill teams. One student dictates to the other, using the same procedure as above.

3. Make up a random list of syllables containing ten consonants and the vowel [ɑ], e.g., [kɑ], [jɑ], [rɑ], [ʃɑ], [ðɑ], [ʒɑ], [ŋɑ], [lɑ], [mɑ], and [bɑ]. Dictate the list to the class and have each student record them in phonetic transcription on a scoresheet. Continue until the students can write the symbols with ease.

4. Draw the vowel diagram (Figure 2.1) on the blackboard; be sure to include all example words, i.e., *see, if, chaos*.

    a. The instructor is to say each vowel clearly, using a pointer to indicate which vowel is being dictated. The students are to respond in unison, trying to duplicate the same placement as the instructor.

    b. The vowels may be dictated in order, i.e., from high to low, etc., then in random order.

    c. The instructor is to call on individual students following group drill.

    d. The instructor removes all example words from the diagram and continues drilling. After this series is complete, he designates a student to serve as an instructor on this series.

5. Dictate the following vowels to the class. Be sure to put the vowel diagram (Figure 2.1) with the example words on the board. Have the students record the dictation using the appropriate phonetic symbols. Correct the results. After completing several lists, remove the example words from the diagram to increase the level of difficulty.

Frames	Frames	Frames	Frames	Frames	Frames
1 [u]	15 [ɔ]	29 [ʊ]	43 [ɝ]	57 [ɑ]	71 [ɪ]
2 [e]	16 [æ]	30 [ɝ]	44 [ɔ]	58 [i]	72 [ʊ]
3 [ʌ]	17 [u]	31 [u]	45 [o]	59 [e]	73 [ɛ]
4 [i]	18 [ɪ]	32 [ɛ]	46 [e]	60 [o]	74 [ɔ]
5 [o]	19 [ɛ]	33 [o]	47 [ʌ]	61 [ɪ]	75 [ɑ]
6 [ɪ]	20 [ʊ]	34 [æ]	48 [ɛ]	62 [ɝ]	76 [ɚ]
7 [æ]	21 [e]	35 [ɚ]	49 [ɪ]	63 [ʊ]	77 [ə]
8 [ɝ]	22 [ɑ]	36 [ɪ]	50 [ɚ]	64 [ɔ]	78 [ʌ]
9 [ɛ]	23 [ɝ]	37 [ɔ]	51 [ə]	65 [ɚ]	79 [u]
10 [ʊ]	24 [i]	38 [ʌ]	52 [u]	66 [ɛ]	80 [æ]
11 [ɑ]	25 [ə]	39 [e]	53 [æ]	67 [u]	81 [ɝ]
12 [ɔ]	26 [ɚ]	40 [i]	54 [ʊ]	68 [ə]	82 [e]
13 [ɚ]	27 [o]	41 [ə]	55 [i]	69 [ʌ]	83 [i]
14 [ə]	28 [ʌ]	42 [ɑ]	56 [ɑ]	70 [æ]	84 [o]

6. Have students make up their own lists and dictate them to the class. Each student is to put his list on the board following dictation. Correct the results; clarify errors or disputes.

7. Dictate the following words; have the students write down the vowel sound for each column. Correct the results.

Frames	Frames	Frames	Frames	Frames
1 who	11 met	21 put	31 if	41 mother
2 sit	12 law	22 see	32 bend	42 obey
3 but	13 cat	23 loot	33 need	43 call
4 omen	14 soon	24 curd	34 ate	44 father
5 calm	15 send	25 open	35 saw	45 third
6 belt	16 soot	26 suds	36 cud	46 cam
7 put	17 meet	27 saw	37 slab	47 let
8 burn	18 boat	28 meat	38 book	48 inch
9 mall	19 suit	29 pain	39 coat	49 me
10 the	20 dirt	30 cad	40 psalm	50 took

CHAPTER
THREE

respiration: controlled breathing

THE BASIS FOR building a strong and responsive voice lies in developing breath control. Since it is the exhaled breath stream that activates the vocal folds and thus initiates tone, it is the muscles of exhalation that are of primary importance in developing control, that is, power and control in initiating the tone come from well-developed muscles of exhalation. In the final analysis the type of voice that a person has depends largely upon the kind of tone that is initiated, which, in turn, is dependent upon the movement of the vocal folds and the controlled breath stream which activates them. For initiating the tone properly, what we seek is : (a) *ease* in phonation and (b) *strength* and *control* in exhalation.

Voice and diction teachers are in unanimous agreement that developing breath control is essential in voice training. Here are some of the reasons underlying this belief:

1. Breathing for speech is an overlaid function and in the majority of students has not been developed to its maximum efficiency. The respiratory mechanism is designed for life breathing, not speech; therefore, humans have had to learn how to override natural control for speech purposes. The degree of success of that control varies from poor to excellent among students.

18

2. The stresses of civilization often cause breathing for speech to deteriorate. When we are undergoing emotional duress, such as anxiety due to stage fright, danger, or shock, our breath control gives way to life-sustaining forces. In order to meet the emergency, respiration rate is speeded up and is more shallow. Speaking under these conditions is noticeably more difficult.

3. Belts, tight undergarments, foundations, etc., often make it difficult for the lower rib cage and abdomen to expand naturally, reducing the efficiency with which one breathes for speech.

4. The average untrained person does not possess the fine control needed to regulate pauses and phrases, loudness, pitch changes, etc., in maximum performance. Professional singers and actors have had to learn this type of control in order to achieve success, as have many politicians, teachers, radio and TV personalities, salesmen, and others. Training, in most cases, has been a means to an end.

5. The voice pathologist working with difficult cases, such as persons with vocal nodes, contact ulcers, or functional hoarseness, invariably includes breathing exercises to achieve better function.

HOW WE BREATHE

Briefly stated, breathing is a biological process by which we inhale air through the nose or mouth into the lungs. There, some of the oxygen from the fresh air is exchanged for the waste product carbon dioxide, which is exhaled.

Ordinarily the act of breathing is automatic. That is, it functions like the heartbeat, without one's conscious attention. When the oxygen in the blood stream becomes depleted, a message automatically goes out from the respiratory center of the central nervous system, the medulla, to the muscles which control breathing, and a new breath cycle is initiated. Usually we breathe in and out, the complete cycle, about 15 or 20 times a minute. However, at any time the conscious will can take over and control the rate of breathing. We can speed up from 15 or 20 respirations a minute to twice that many, or we can slow down to 5 or 6, or we can stop altogether and hold the breath for a few seconds—even up to 2 minutes or more if we are trained for it. And we can break up the cycle; that is, whereas we ordinarily take about the same amount of time on the inhalation and the exhalation, we can, if we wish, breathe in slowly and exhale quickly, or we can do the reverse. This last fact has a vital bearing upon tone production. Since tone is produced by the exhaled breath, the ability to control the rate of exhalation becomes of paramount importance.

MECHANICS OF BREATHING

The breathing apparatus consists principally of : (a) the air passages leading to the lungs, (b) the lungs themselves, (c) the chest cavity in which they are located, (d) the muscles that control the inhalation of air into the lungs, and (e) those that control the exhalation of the air.

The air is drawn into the lungs through the nose or mouth, through the glottis of the larynx, thence into the trachea. The trachea divides into the right and left bronchial tubes. These in turn subdivide into smaller and smaller tubes called bronchioles. Each bronchiole ends in numerous minute air sacs, which are porous and elastic. Embedded in the thin walls of these air sacs are tiny blood vessels, or capillaries. Through these thin walls oxygen is exchanged for carbon dioxide. The bronchial tubes, air sacs, and blood vessels, together with their connective tissue, constitute the lungs. The chest cavity is surrounded by the rib cage, or thorax.

The lungs nearly fill the chest cavity, being large, spongy, and cone shaped. Their broad bases rest upon the diaphragm, and their narrow, rounded tops extend above the first rib.

Nasal Cavity Versus Oral Cavity

There are two pathways available for breathing (Figure 3.1), either through the mouth or through the nasal passageways. A combination of both is also possible. Because the nasal cavity is restricted, the mouth or oral cavity is best suited in breathing for speech and singing, even though

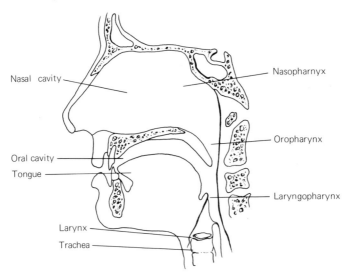

Figure 3.1. Diagrammatic median section of the head and throat, showing the position of the human larynx in relation to the nose, mouth, trachea, and the three divisions of the pharynx—the nasopharynx, the oropharynx, and the laryngopharynx.

the nasal passages are better designed for warming incoming air and removing foreign particles, such as dust and smoke.

The Pharynx as a Passageway

Note in Figure 3.1 how the pharynx is divided into three areas—the nasopharynx, or the section behind the nasal passages, the oropharynx, or the section behind the mouth, and the laryngopharynx, or the section above the larynx. The nasopharynx can be shut off from the rest of the pharynx by action of the soft palate. The pharynx also warms the incoming air.

The Larynx and Trachea as Passageways

The larynx serves as a valve and can seal off the lower respiratory system from the upper, as it does in swallowing food, drinking, or holding the breath. The trachea (Figure 3.2) is 4 inches long and has a bore of approximately 1 inch, which tapers somewhat (is smaller at the top than the bottom) ; therefore, the size of the trachea has a bearing on how fast air can be inhaled and exhaled. Test the speed with which you can inhale. Now, exhale.

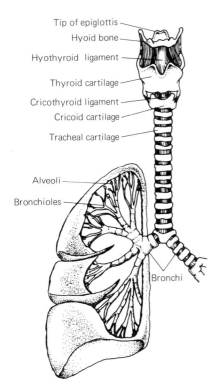

Tip of epiglottis
Hyoid bone
Hyothyroid ligament
Thyroid cartilage
Cricothyroid ligament
Cricoid cartilage
Tracheal cartilage
Alveoli
Bronchioles
Bronchi

Figure 3.2. Portion of the respiratory tract showing larynx, trachea, bronchi, bronchioles, and alveoli.

The exhalation took just a fraction longer, did it not? The air passageways get smaller as the trachea divides off into the bronchi and then into the bronchioles. You are probably quite familiar with the term bronchitis, an inflamation of the lining in the bronchial tubes, which reduces the air passageway considerably and makes breathing much more difficult.

The Rib Cage

Inasmuch as the rib cage or *thorax* is manipulated by two systems of muscles, some attention to its structure may help you to understand the breathing exercises to follow. The chest cavity is conical in shape (Figure 3.3). There are 12 pairs of ribs, 10 of which are attached in the back by a ball and socket arrangement in the spinal column, and in the front by varying lengths of cartilage to the breastbone or *sternum*. The floating ribs, the 11th and 12th pairs, are attached in the back and are of minor importance in breathing. The 6th through the 10th pairs are attached to two extensions of cartilage, permitting more extensive movement and flexibility than exist for the 1st to the 5th pairs.

THE MUSCLES CONTROLLING BREATHING

The increase and decrease of the volume of the chest cavity is the means by which air is brought into and expelled from the lungs. Enlarging or decreasing the size of this cavity is brought about by two forces: (a) the manipulation of the structure by two systems of muscles,[1] and (b) by the structure itself, through elastic recoil and gravity pull.

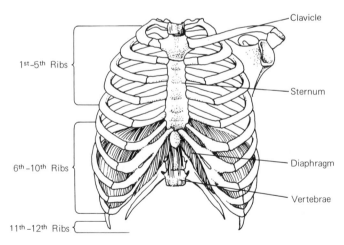

Figure 3.3. Diagram of the rib cage showing rib arrangement, left clavicle, sternum, diaphragm, and vertebrae.

[1] Bear in mind that a muscle can only contract, thereby exerting a pull between two points, usually the origin and insertion. Muscles often work in opposition or antagonism to each other in order to move a structure in opposite directions, e.g., up-down, out-in, etc.

22

Inhalation

The most important muscle of inhalation is the *diaphragm*. It is a broad, leaflike sheet of muscle and fiber, attached at the sides and back to the ribs and spinal column, and in front to the breastbone. Extending traversely across the body, the diaphragm is a partition separating the heart and lungs from the digestive system (it has been facetiously described as separating the victuals from the vitals). In its relaxed state it is highly arched and dome-shaped. When the diaphragm contracts, the dome descends downward and flattens out, losing most of its convexity. This downward movement exerts pressure on the viscera and causes the walls of the abdomen to protrude.

The *external intercostals* also play a part in inhalation. These muscles are attached between the ribs at the upper and lower margins. When certain fibers of these muscles contract, the rib cage is both lifted up and expanded laterally. As we pointed out in the discussion of its structure, the rib cage is ideally designed to expand in the area of the sixth through the tenth rib pairs.

Exhalation

During inhalation several structures of the rib cage undergo increased tension, particularly the cartilages, linings, ligaments, and lung tissues. When the diaphragm and the external intercostals are suddenly relaxed, the elastic recoil of the rib cage, along with gravity pull, quickly snaps the cage back to its unexpanded position. For example, take a breath, hold it for a moment, then quickly relax. Notice how easily air is expelled when the rib cage returns to its original position. This type of exhalation is typical of life breathing.

In controlled breathing we do not relax quickly, but rather we meter the air out slowly. This action is actually quite subtle and has caused some confusion to voice and diction teachers for years. Previously, it was felt that the diaphragm was the chief antagonist of the *abdominal* muscles, and that the diaphragm under contraction was increasingly overcome or shoved back into its high-domed position by the steady driving force of the abdominal wall. Experimental evidence has revealed that at least a part of the external intercostals remains under contraction and is also antagonistic to the inward thrust of the abdominals. Take a deep breath, hold it, then gradually release it. Did you feel that your lower rib cage was gradually being relaxed? It seems apparent that sensitive control of the outgoing breath stream requires coordination between the abdominal muscles, the internal intercostal muscles, the diaphragm, and the external intercostals.

Figure 3.4 illustrates the three types of abdominal muscles that enclose the abdominal cavity and serve as the major source of power for controlled exhalation. As these muscles contract, they exert an inward squeezing pressure on the viscera, which in turn puts an upward pressure on the

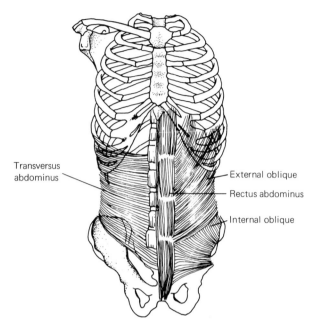

Transversus
abdominus

External oblique

Rectus abdominus

Internal oblique

Figure 3.4. Abdominal muscles of respiration.

diaphragm. The *internal intercostals* have fibers that are responsible for a downward pull on the rib cage and thus aid in exhalation. Other fibers are said to extend the rib cage laterally and contribute in a small degree to inhalation. Two other pairs of muscles in the back play a minor role in exhalation but need not concern us here.

An understanding of the process of breathing may be obtained by observing the action of a laboratory device known as Hering's apparatus (Figure 3.5). This consists of a widemouthed glass bottle with a sheet of rubber stretched across the bottom in place of the glass; to it is attached a ring by which the sheet may be pulled down. From the cork of the bottle is suspended a tube which divides into two branches, and to each of these a rubber bag is attached.

In part (a) of Figure 3.5, the rubber bags hang deflated in an airtight cavity. In (b), the rubber sheet has been pulled downward, thus increasing the volume of the bottle. The air pressure in the bottle is thereby decreased, creating a low-pressure area. Because of the greater pressure of the atmosphere outside, air rushes in through the tube to equalize the pressure, and the rubber bags are inflated.

If the rubber sheet is allowed to return to its normal position, the process is reversed—the volume of the bottle is decreased, pressure within the bottle is correspondingly increased, air is forced from the bags, and they again become deflated.

24

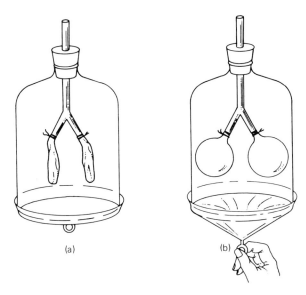

(a) (b)

Figure 3.5. Hering's apparatus illustrating the breathing process.

This is roughly comparable to the process of human breathing. The neck of the bottle may be compared to the human throat, the walls to the rib cage that houses the lungs, the rubber bags to the lungs, and the sheet of rubber to the muscles, particularly the diaphragm.

There are differences between Hering's apparatus and the human breathing mechanism which should be noted: (a) the ribs, being less rigid than the bottle walls, can and do move slightly; (b) the lungs, unlike the rubber bags, fill the chest cavity; (c) instead of consisting of a single bag, each lung consists of great clusters of tiny sacs; (d) the diaphragm, being a muscle, is not pulled down by an outside force, but descends by its own contraction; and (e) instead of changing from a flat to a concave position, it changes from its normal dome-like position to one slightly less arched.

The schematic drawing in Figure 3.6 shows changes in the position of the diaphragm and the abdominal walls in inhalation and exhalation.

BREATHING FOR SPEECH

The passive breathing carried on for normal life processes described in the preceding paragraphs is not adequate to provide the controlled breath stream necessary for tone production. Control must be active and precise. This is true to some extent in inhalation, but much more so in exhalation. The following comparative chart emphasizes the differences between life and speech breathing.[2]

[2] Human capacities vary, i.e., male-female, large-small, etc., as do demands for air in each type of breathing.

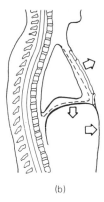

(a)   (b)

Figure 3.6. The position of the diaphragm, lungs, abdomen, and chest in breathing. (a) Exhalation: note decreased chest size, relaxed dome-shaped diaphragm, and taut, indrawn abdominal wall. (b) Inhalation: note increased chest size, contracted and flattened diaphragm, and relaxed and distended abdominal wall.

A COMPARISON OF BREATHING FOR SPEECH AND LIFE

Function	Life	Speech
1. Air intake	Nose	Mouth
2. Control	Unconscious (medulla)	Conscious (cortex)
3. Cycle	Even (inhalation and exhalation same length)	Uneven (inhalation, short; exhalation, long)
4. Rate	12–20 cycles per minute (approx.)	8–12 cycles per minute (approx.)
5. Depth	500 cc of air (approx.)	750 cc of air (approx.)

There is an old saying that is applicable to breathing, "It isn't how much breath you use but how you use it." This is particularly true when it comes to depth of breathing: *It is not important to breathe deeply for speech.* Actually, you have a reserve of air available that you seldom touch amounting to almost one-half of the air that you breathe. The number of inhalations per minute is not especially important either, simply because you can increase the number per minute without interfering with the speech process as long as the inspirations are timed properly. Figure 3.7 further illustrates some of the differences between breathing for life and speech, as well as giving an indication of capacities.

From Figure 3.7 we may conclude: (a) the inhalation time for speech is much shorter than exhalation; (b) inhalation is deeper in speech than in life, but a far greater capacity is still available, though usually not needed; (c) exhalation may go *beyond* the level inhaled by forcing some of the

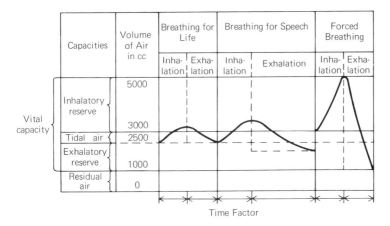

Capacities	Volume of Air in cc	Breathing for Life		Breathing for Speech		Forced Breathing	
		Inhalation	Exhalation	Inhalation	Exhalation	Inhalation	Exhalation
Vital capacity { Inhalatory reserve	5000						
	3000						
Tidal air {	2500						
Exhalatory reserve	1000						
Residual air {	0						

Time Factor

Figure 3.7. Cycles and capacities of breathing.

exhalatory reserve air out. This is a common practice in speech; (d) forced inhalation and exhalation far exceed that which is required in speech; and (e) about 1000 cc of residual air can never be expelled from the lungs.

TYPES OF BREATHING, GOOD AND BAD

Breathing habits vary from speaker to speaker and may, from a standpoint of speech, range all the way from poor to excellent. You have unconsciously adjusted your breathing habits to meet your speech needs. At least four distinct types of breathing are identifiable, (a) clavicular breathing, (b) upper-thoracic breathing, (c) medial breathing, and (d) diaphragmatic-abdominal. It is possible to use combinations of any two or three, or all of these types of breathing at one time.

Clavicular Breathing

In clavicular breathing the rib cage is elevated by raising the shoulders and clavicles (collarbones), which enlarges the volume of the chest cavity. Since the rib cage is not designed to expand easily in the upper portion, the amount of air available is small and control of exhalation is difficult. Actually, this type of breathing provides for additional volume at the bottom of the cavity rather than the top.

Probably the greatest liability of this type of breathing lies in the amount of tension and pressure created at the base of the neck and upper chest and shoulders. The tension and pressure can easily impinge upon the area of the larynx and interfere with voice production. Furthermore, tension in the neck can be unsightly. With the aid of a mirror, lift your rib cage by raising your shoulders and collarbones. Observe how much air is inhaled. Ask a fellow student to attempt this type of breathing; notice how his neck becomes tense as he reaches the limit of inhalation.

27

Of all the types of breath control, clavicular breathing is considered by authorities to be the most unsatisfactory for good voice and is to be avoided.

Upper-Thoracic (Chest) Breathing

Upper-thoracic breathing is accomplished by expanding and lifting the upper rib cage, but not in the exaggerated manner of clavicular breathing. The sternum or breastbone rises as do the shoulders. For the amount of air obtained the effort is great. Control is not as sensitive as in types of breathing using a lower region of the rib cage for expansion. We should stress here that upper-thoracic breathing permits maximum expansion beyond the capacity of the other methods of breathing and may be considered a supplementary method of breath control. Inhale by expanding the lower part of your rib cage and abdomen. When you have expanded as far as you can go, expand the upper rib cage to the limit. You probably managed to increase the amount of air inhaled by approximately one-third.

The use of predominantly upper-thoracic breathing for speech is questionable when compared to lower-control methods for several reasons: (a) the effort involved is greater, (b) the sensitivity of control is less precise, (c) the possibility of impinging upon the larynx is greater, and (d) the additional supply actually is not needed in speech.

Medial Breathing

So-called medial breathing, also called intercostal breathing, derives its identity from the fact that control is predominantly accomplished by the diaphragm and the expansion of the lower perimeter of the rib cage without involving any appreciable expansion of the frontal abdomen. As discussed earlier in this chapter, the lower ribs are very flexible and can with ease be moved by muscle systems both laterally and upward. If this method of breathing is properly executed, the amount of air inhaled is satisfactory for speech, and control of exhalation is good. Many speakers rated "superior" use this type of breathing. Medial breathing is also readily combined with diaphragmatic-abdominal breathing with excellent results.

Diaphragmatic-Abdominal Breathing

Diaphragmatic-abdominal breathing is chiefly characterized by the interaction between the diaphragm and the abdominal wall. Stated simply, as the diaphragm contracts and descends, the abdominal wall is literally pushed out to relieve pressure on the viscera. On the other hand, when the abdominal wall contracts and exerts a greater pressure on the viscera than the diaphragm, the latter is pushed back into its high-domed position.

Attempt to inhale without expanding the rib cage laterally. Notice the frontal protrusion of the abdomen. Now, slowly exhale; notice how the abdominal wall gently pushes in on the viscera.

You will note that throughout our discussion of breathing we have purposely used the words *predominantly* or *chiefly* to emphasize a region of breath control. We fully recognize that any one type of breathing does not exist to the exclusion of the others, but rather exists as the type in primary use. Scientific investigation has revealed that a wide range of involvement of various muscles is possible. We can, however, extract from both scientific investigation and experience goals and criteria that can be helpful in obtaining better habits of breathing for speech.

GOALS AND CRITERIA

Goals	Criterion
1. To avoid tension in the neck and upper chest while speaking.	Read a paragraph of at least 100 words in front of the class without observable neck tension.
2. To achieve breath control through medial and/or diaphragmatic-abdominal breathing.	Complete successfully Exercises 1 and 2 on page 31.
3. To regulate successfully the amount of breath needed to support breath groups varying from short to long.	Complete successfully Exercise 4d, on page 33.
4. To use "catch breaths" whenever needed (see p. 32).	Read a selection marked for "catch breaths" and achieve success on 80 percent of the items marked. Choose your own selection and mark it.
5. To regulate breath control to suit good pauses and phrases for meaning.	Mark a prose passage of 100 words or more indicating your pauses and phrases and deliver this passage successfully in front of the class according to your marks.

CENTER OF BREATHING

EXERCISES TO ACHIEVE ABDOMINAL-DIAPHRAGMATIC/MEDIAL BREATHING

1. Place one hand on your abdominal wall just below your breastbone. Place the other hand to one side slightly above the hip and partly on the lower ribs. Spread your fingers slightly to feel any movement that takes place in this area. Now inhale slowly through your mouth. Be sure that your upper rib cage does not expand or rise. Observe the lateral movement of the lower ribs as well as the frontal expansion of the abdomen. Repeat, attempting to exceed the expansion achieved on the first trial.

2. Any device that can indicate the amount of expansion laterally and frontally can be put to good use at this time. One such device that has been used successfully is a leather belt altered as follows: (a) cut the belt in

half and (b) join the severed ends by sewing in a piece of white elastic; be sure the ends of the belt abut.

Procedure: Strap the belt on with the buckle at the back and the elastic in front. Place the belt over the area covered by your hands in Exercise 1, and be sure it is tight enough to permit expansion of the elastic the instant you begin to inhale. Inhale slowly. Observe the amount of expansion of the elastic. Repeat, attempting to increase the amount of expansion.

The same exercise can be done with a tailor's soft tape measure. If you overlap the tape measure in front, you can observe the exact amount of expansion in inches and fractions of inches. Attempt to improve upon your best performance. If you do not have a belt or tailor's tape measure, use a piece of string or cord and measure the amount of expansion on a straight ruler.

3. Stand in an erect position using good posture. Press a book against your abdominal wall. Inhale slowly without raising your shoulders or upper chest. Observe the forward movement of the book. Note: This exercise does not account for lateral movement. Repeat, attempting to achieve greater forward movement of the book.

4. The classic version of the foregoing exercise is as follows: Lie in a supine position (on your back) on a rug or firm bed. Place at least five heavy books on your abdomen. Raise the books slowly by inhaling. Balance the books and do not let them fall. Attempt to increase the amount you can raise the books. Concert and opera singers and actors have used this exercise not only to locate the center of breathing, but to strengthen the breathing muscles as well.

You may explore your breathing center and capacity by lying on your back at home. Breathe regularly—easily—deeply. Note that in this position it is difficult to move the shoulders and upper chest; thus, it is quite likely that abdominal or medial breathing will take place. Try to increase your capacity.

5. Several forms of popular physical exercise will develop natural breathing habits. The key to all of these exercises is to put pressure on the respiratory system to supply more oxygen to the blood stream to meet the demands of the muscular activity of the exercises. In all of these forms, the action of the legs is of prime importance. The exercises most commonly used are walking, jogging, running in place, cycling, and swimming. In all of these activities, you must keep up a steady pace for a given period of time. A complete list of all programs leading up to 100 percent fitness is available in Kenneth Cooper's *The New Aerobics*.[3]

As a class exercise, run in place for one minute at a steady pace of seventy (left-foot counts). Observe the action of the medial-abdominal areas.

[3] Kenneth Cooper, *The New Aerobics*, New York: M. Evans, 1970, pp. 52–114.

CONTROL AND DEPTH OF BREATHING

After becoming aware of the proper site for efficient breathing for speech, you should now work for greater control and depth of breathing. The following exercises will help you attain two goals: (a) an adequate breath supply for all single breath groups, and (b) the control necessary to supply breath for all voice demands within the breath group.

EXERCISES FOR CONTROL AND DEPTH OF BREATHING

1. The "Cycle of Breathing" exercise is probably the most valuable exercise for gaining depth and control. Many professional actors and singers have relied only upon this exercise to gain mastery of breathing.

    a. Inhale slowly through your mouth over a count of six. Be sure you draw in your breath evenly on all counts. To insure evenness, purse your lips so that you can hear the air rushing in.

    b. Hold the air in your lungs for a count of six. Be sure you do not close your glottis.[4] This will require the breath to be held by the muscles of inhalation.

    c. Exhale slowly over a count of six. Be sure you do so evenly and that all air is out by the last count. Again, purse your lips so you can hear and monitor the outgoing breath stream.

    d. Hold in the exhale position for a count of six without closing your glottis. This is accomplished by keeping the muscles of exhalation under contraction.

    e. Repeat the cycle at least one more time.

Steps (a) through (d) above are the nucleus for this exercise and serve as a beginning. When you have mastered each step thoroughly, you may vary the exercise in three different ways: (1) increasing the count for each step, (2) decreasing the speed of counting, and (3) doing the exercise when walking, a step for each count. Each of these three variations puts additional pressure and demand upon the respiratory system. You can easily practice this exercise when walking or riding to school or work.

2. The following exercise is particularly good for developing depth of breathing:

    a. Inhale to one-third of your total capacity. Release a small amount of air, but not more than one-third of the amount you just inhaled. Hold your breath for three seconds, but do not close the glottis—use your muscles of inhalation to hold it.

    b. Inhale to two-thirds of your total capacity and release a small amount. Hold for three seconds. Again, do not close the glottis.

    c. Now inhale to your total capacity, but this time do not release any air and hold your breath with your muscles of inhalation only. Do not close the glottis. Hold for three seconds and release.

---

[4] For all practical purposes, the *glottis* is the airspace between the vocal folds. However, marginal structures are also considered to be the *glottis* by anatomists.

In this step you will need to expand your upper chest for maximum capacity.

d. Repeat the exercise one more time. Caution: Do not do this exercise more than twice, as you can easily overoxygenate your blood stream and become dizzy.

BREATH CONTROL FOR PAUSES AND PHRASES

Breathing for speech not only requires the speaker to inhale and control sufficient air for speaking, but demands concern with the speed and timing of both inhalation and exhalation as well. Generally the pauses between major breath groups or after end-stopped punctuation, e.g., period, semicolon, question mark, and exclamation mark, permit ample time for inhalation for the next breath group. However, there are many times when one is required to speed up inhalation to accommodate good timing.

Professionals have had to master the so-called catch breath technique in order to sustain tone without a pronounced break, or to quickly move from one phrase to another at a time when more breath is needed. These catch breaths typically occur between phrases within compound or complex sentences. In order to exemplify the catch breath technique, visualize the dome-shaped diaphragm at its rest position, e.g., vaulted like an inverted bowl. Now picture this muscle in its fully contracted position, e.g., like an inverted pancake suddenly gone flat. The increase in the volume of the thoracic cavity is great, and the quicker the movement, naturally, the faster the air is drawn into the lungs. You may wish to refer back to Figure 3.6, to study the before and after positions of inhalation. Demonstrate this action to yourself by forming an inverted bowl with your hands. Lace your fingers lightly and turn your palms down. Now, snap your hands flat with a downward motion. See if you can accomplish this in less than half of a second.

EXERCISES FOR PHRASING

In the following exercises attempt to achieve speed of action of your diaphragm:

1. Place the palm of one hand on your abdomen just below the breastbone. On a silent count of one inhale rapidly. Check the amount of air exhaled by blowing on the finger tips of the other hand. Repeat until you have an adequate supply. If you canot demonstrate success, inhale a little more slowly at first and gradually speed up the action.

2. Place one hand on your abdomen as in the foregoing exercise and put the other one in front of your mouth to check the outgoing breath stream. Inhale quickly; now exhale over a silent count of one to five. Inhale immediately at the end of the silent count and exhale again for another count of five. Repeat this exercise until you demonstrate a satisfactory catch breath.

32

3. Modify Exercise 2 as follows, always using a silent count. Inhale quickly, exhale over a count of five, then pause, holding your breath but without closing your glottis. After a silent count of one, continue to exhale for an additional count of five.

4. When you have succeeded in mastering the first three exercises and can demonstrate a good catch breath, you are ready to add voice to this exercise.

    a. Inhale quickly ; now count one to five aloud. Repeat three times.

    b. Inhale quickly ; count one to five and pause for one second without closing the glottis and continue counting six to ten, e.g., inhale, one, two, three, four, five, pause, six, seven, eight, nine, ten.

    c. Inhale quickly ; count one to five and pause, but do not inhale or close your glottis ; now count six to ten and pause briefly for a catch breath ; continue counting eleven to fifteen and pause, but do not inhale ; now finish counting sixteen to twenty. Repeat this exercise until you can do it smoothly. This exercise demonstrates a typical breathing pattern for a compound sentence.

    d. Practice the material below using the following marks for guides : (/ /) usual, unhurried inhalation for speech ; (/) pause without inhalation ; and (√) catch breath.

    / / 1-2-3-4-5-6-7-8-9-10 √ 11-12-13-14-15-16-17-18-19-20.

    / / 1-2-3-4-5-6-7 √ 8-9-10-11-12-13-14 √ 15-16-17-18-19-20-21-22.

    / / 1-2-3-4-5-6-7-8-9-10-11-12 / / 13-14-15-16-17-18-19-20.

    / / 1-2-3-4 / 5-6-7-8-9-10-11 √ 12-13-14-15-16 / 17-18-19-20.

    / / 1-2-3-4-5-6 √ 7-8-9-10-11-12 √ 13-14-15-16-17-18 √ 19-20-21-22-23-24.

The most important rule to remember in breath control for pauses and phrases is that there are no rules, only guidelines. Pauses and phrases are determined by the meaning and emotional content a speaker wishes to communicate. In this chapter we will be concerned with the relationship of breath control to pauses and phrases ; in Chapter 9, Achieving Vocal Variety, we will study pauses and phrases for meaning and emotion. The guidelines that may be applied are as follows :

1. Pausing and phrasing must be tailored to your interpretation and capacities.

2. Punctuation, particularly the end-stopped type, can be used for both pauses and phrasing.

3. Syntax (the sequence of words and phrases in a sentence) may often be used as a guide to phrasing.

4. Sentences are usually phrased into their most meaningful components.

5. Long sentences are often divided into convenient breath groups.

EXERCISES COMBINING PHRASING AND BREATHING

1. Practice phrasing Lincoln's well-known sentence:

> Fourscore and seven years ago, our fathers brought forth on this continent a new nation, conceived in liberty, and dedicated to the proposition that all men are created equal.

It would be possible, of course, to say this sentence in two phrases, pausing for breath only at the comma in the middle of the sentence, but this would not be wise for getting full meaning from the sentence. There are a dozen different ways the above sentence can be phrased. Try some of them, and at the appropriate places for pauses for phrasing, take a catch breath to keep your supply of air replenished. Try it this way, for example:

> / / Fourscore and seven years ago / our fathers brought forth on this continent / a new nation / conceived in liberty / and dedicated to the proposition √ that all men are created equal.

Now, imagine you are talking to a very large audience requiring much shorter phrasing and greater breath support and control:

> / / Fourscore / and seven / years / ago / / our fathers / brought forth / on this continent / a new nation / / conceived in liberty / and dedicated / to the proposition / / that all men / are created equal.

2. Try different lengths of phrases with the following sentence by Dwight D. Eisenhower:

> For me, there is something almost shocking in the realization that, though many millions have been voluntarily donated for research in cancer of the individual body, nothing similar has been done with respect to the most malignant cancer of the world body, war.

3. Using the symbols (/ /), (/), and (√) indicating, respectively, normal breath for speech, phrase without inhalation, and catch breath; mark the following passage and read it aloud:

REMEMBER

Remember me when I am gone away,
    Gone far away into the silent land;
    When you can no more hold me by the hand,
Nor I half turn to go, yet turning stay.
Remember me when no more, day by day,
    You tell me of our future that you planned:
    Only remember me; you understand
It will be late to counsel then or pray.
Yet if you should forget me for a while
    And afterwards remember, do not grieve:
    For if the darkness and corruption leave
    A vestige of the thoughts that once I had,
Better by far you should forget and smile
    Than that you should remember and be sad.

                   —Christina Rossetti

4. Mark at least two additional selections of both prose and poetry from the selections included in this chapter.

BREATH CONTROL AND FORCE, EMPHASIS AND STRESS

Trained speakers use breath control as a means of varying amplitude of the voice for different sizes of audience, for emphasis of certain phrases and sentences, and for stress of a given word. Projection as a speaking technique is covered more fully in Chapter 6, "Developing Vocal Resonance."

EXERCISES FOR LOUDNESS

1. Practice exhalation on five distinct puffs. Did you feel your abdominal wall suddenly contract on each one? Repeat until all five puffs are of equal force and duration.

2. Tear off a corner of a piece of paper and place it on a table at least two feet away from your mouth. Can you move it with one puff? Try it again, attempting to gain greater force.

3. Pretend you are blowing out the candles on a birthday cake—all in one breath. Now pretend you are attempting to get the smouldering coals of a barbecue fire going. Lastly, pretend you have a sticky feather on each finger tip—blow each one off, one at a time.

4. Practice the following words, first with normal loudness, then in a loud voice, and finally in a very loud voice.

yes	high	now	may
hold	ho	boy	my
key	one	fall	man

5. Practice the following sentences using *five* levels of loudness for each one.

    a. Who are you?

    b. Romans, countrymen, and lovers.

    c. How do you know it's true?

    d. Give me liberty, or give me death!

    e. In these days, whether we like it or not, power is with the tongue, power is with the man who can talk.

SELECTIONS

The following selections place many demands upon the performer in terms of catch breaths, breath groups, and breath support.

VOICES

Now I make a leaf of Voices—for I have found nothing mightier
than they are,
And I have found that no word spoken, but is beautiful, in its
place.

O what is it in me that makes me tremble so at voices?
Surely, whoever speaks to me in the right voice, him or her I
shall follow,
As the water follows the moon, silently, with fluid steps,
anywhere around the globe.
All waits for the right voices;

Where is the practis'd and perfect organ? Where is the
develop'd Soul?
For I see every word utter'd thence has deeper, sweeter, new
sounds, impossible on less terms.

I see brains and lips closed—tympans and temples unstruck,
Until that comes which has the quality to strike and to unclose,
Until that comes which has the quality to bring forth what lies
slumbering, forever ready, in all words.
—Walt Whitman

Lord Henry stroked his pointed brown beard, and tapped the toe of his patent-leather boot with a tasseled ebony cane. "How English you are, Basil! That is the second time you have made that observation. If one puts forward an idea to a true Englishman—always a rash thing to do—he never dreams of considering whether the idea is right or wrong. The only thing

36

he considers of any importance is whether one believes it one's self. Now, the value of an idea has nothing whatsoever to do with the sincerity of the man who expresses it. Indeed, the probabilities are that the more insincere the man is, the more purely intellectual will the idea be, as in that case it will not be colored by either his wants, his desires, or his prejudices."

—Oscar Wilde

There's a barrel-organ carolling across a golden street
    In the City as the sun sinks low;
And the music's not immortal; but the world has made it sweet
    And fulfilled it with the sunset glow;
And it pulses through the pleasures of the City and the pain
    That surround the singing organ like a large eternal light;
And they've given it a glory and a part to play again
    In the Symphony that rules the day and night.[5]

—Alfred Noyes

As a fond mother, when the day is o'er,
    Leads by the hand her little child to bed,
    Half willing, half reluctant to be led,
    And leave his broken playthings on the floor,
Still gazing at them through the open door,
    Nor wholly reassured and comforted
    By promises of others in their stead,
    Which, though more splendid, may not please him more;
So Nature deals with us, and takes away
    Our playthings one by one, and by the hand
    Leads us to rest so gently, that we go
Scarce knowing if we wish to go or stay,
    Being too full of sleep to understand
    How far the unknown transcends the what we know.

—Henry W. Longfellow

To myself, mountains are the beginning and the end of all natural scenery; in them, and in the forms of inferior landscape that lead to them, my affections are wholly bound up; and though I can look with happy admiration at the lowland flowers, and woods, and open skies, the happiness is tranquil and cold, like that of examining detached flowers in a conservatory, or reading a pleasant book; and if the scenery be resolutely level, insisting upon the declaration of its own flatness

[5] Reprinted by permission of the publishers, J. B. Lippincott Company, from *Collected Poems in One Volume* by Alfred Noyes. Copyright, 1906, 1934, 1947, by Alfred Noyes.

37

in all the detail of it . . . it appears to me like a prison, and I cannot long endure it. But the slightest rise and fall in the road —a mossy bank at the side of a crag of chalk, with brambles at its brow, overhanging it, a ripple over three or four stones in the stream by the bridge, above all, a wild bit of ferny ground under a fir or two, looking as if, possibly, one might see a hill if one got to the other side of the trees—will instantly give me intense delight, because the shadow, or the hope, of the hills is in them.

—John Ruskin

O wind, that is so strong and cold,
O blower, are you young or old?
Are you a beast of field and tree,
Or just a stronger child than me?
    O wind, a-blowing all day long,
    O wind, that sings so loud a song!

I saw the different things you did,
But always you yourself you hid,
I felt you push, I heard you call,
I could not see yourself at all—
    O wind, a-blowing all day long,
    O wind, that sings so loud a song!

—Robert Louis Stevenson

HOME-THOUGHTS, FROM ABROAD

Oh, to be in England
Now that April's there,
And whoever wakes in England
Sees, some morning, unaware,
That the lowest boughs and the brush-wood sheaf
Round the elm-tree bole are in tiny leaf,
While the chaffinch sings on the orchard bough
In England—now!

And after April, when May follows,
And the white-throat builds, and all the swallows!
Hark, where my blossomed pear-tree in the hedge
Leans to the field and scatters on the clover
Blossoms and dewdrops—at the bent spray's edge—
That's the wise thrush: he sings each song twice over,
Lest you should think he never could recapture
The first fine careless rapture!

And, though the fields look rough with hoary dew,
All will be gay when noontide wakes anew
The buttercups, the little children's dower—
Far brighter than this gaudy melon-flower !

—Robert Browning

These are the times that try men's souls. The summer soldier
and the sunshine patriot will in this crisis, shrink from the
service of his country ; but he that stands it NOW, deserves the
love and thanks of man and woman. Tyranny, like hell, is not
easily conquered. . . .

—Tom Paine

From MACBETH

MACBETH : If it were done when 'tis done, then 'twere well
It were done quickly. If the assassination
Could trammel up the consequence, and catch
With his surcease success ; that but this blow
Might be the be-all and the end-all here,
But here, upon this bank and shoal of time,
We'd jump the life to come. But in these cases
We still have judgment here ; that we but teach
Bloody instructions, which, being taught, return
To plague the inventor : this even-handed justice
Commends the ingredients of our poison'd chalice
To our own lips. He's here in double trust ;
First, as I am his kinsman and his subject,
Strong both against the deed ; then, as his host,
Who should against his murderer shut the door,
Not bear the knife myself. Besides, this Duncan
Hath borne his faculties so meek, hath been
So clear in his great office, that his virtues
Will plead like angels, trumpet-tongu'd, against
The deep damnation of his taking-off ;
And pity, like a naked new-born babe,
Striding the blast, or heaven's cherubim, hors'd
Upon the sightless couriers of the air,
Shall blow the horrid deed in every eye,
That tears shall drown the wind. I have no spur
To prick the sides of my intent, but only
Vaulting ambition.

—William Shakespeare

From APOLOGY

SOCRATES: And now, O men who have condemned me, I would fain prophesy to you; for I am about to die, and in the hour of death men are gifted with prophetic power. And I prophesy to you who are my murderers, that immediately after my departure punishment far heavier than you have inflicted on me will surely await you. Me you have killed because you wanted to escape the accuser, and not to give an account of your lives. But that will not be as you suppose: far otherwise. For I say that there will be more accusers of you than there are now; accusers whom hitherto I have restrained: and as they are younger they will be more inconsiderate with you, and you will be more offended at them. If you think that by killing men you can prevent some one from censuring your evil lives, you are mistaken; that is not a way of escape which is either possible or honourable; the easiest and the noblest way is not to be disabling others, but to be improving yourselves. This is the prophecy which I utter before my departure to the judges who have condemned me.

—Plato

How amazing is this spirit of man! In spite of innumerable failings, man, throughout the ages, has sacrificed his life and all he held dear for an ideal, for truth, for faith, for country and honor. That ideal may change, but that capacity for self-sacrifice continues, and because of that, much may be forgiven to man, and it is impossible to lose hope for him. In the midst of disaster he has not lost his dignity or his faith in the values he cherished. Plaything of nature's mighty forces, less than the speck of dust in this vast universe, he has hurled defiance at the elemental powers, and with his mind, cradle of revolution, sought to master them. Whatever gods there be, there is something godlike in man, as there is also something of the devil in him.

—Jawaharlal Nehru

From THE IMPORTANCE OF BEING EARNEST

ALGERNON: I am engaged to be married to Cecily, Aunt Augusta.
LADY BRACKNELL: I beg your pardon?

40

CECILY: Mr. Moncrieff and I are engaged to be married, Lady Bracknell.

LADY BRACKNELL (*with a shiver, crossing to the sofa and sitting down*): I do not know whether there is anything peculiarly exciting in the air of this particular part of Hertfordshire, but the number of engagements that go on seems to me considerably above the proper average that statistics have laid down for our guidance. I think some preliminary enquiry on my part would not be out of place. Mr. Worthing, is Miss Cardew at all connected with any of the larger railway stations in London? I merely desire information. Until yesterday I had no idea that there were any families or persons whose origin was a Terminus. (JACK *looks perfectly furious, but restrains himself.*)

JACK (*in a clear, cold voice*): Miss Cardew is the granddaughter of the late Mr. Thomas Cardew of 149, Belgrave Square, S.W.; Gervase Park, Dorking, Surrey; and the Sporran, Fifeshire, N.B.

LADY BRACKNELL: That sounds not unsatisfactory. Three addresses always inspire confidence, even in tradesmen. But what proof have I of their authenticity?

JACK: I have carefully preserved the Court Guide of the period. They are open to your inspection, Lady Bracknell.

LADY BRACKNELL (*grimly*): I have known strange errors in that publication.

JACK: Miss Cardew's family solicitors are Messrs. Markby, Markby, and Markby.

LADY BRACKNELL: Markby, Markby, and Markby? A firm of the very highest position in their profession. Indeed I am told that one of the Mr. Markbys is occasionally to be seen at dinner parties. So far I am satisfied.

JACK (*very irritably*): How extremely kind of you, Lady Bracknell. I have also in my possession, you will be pleased to hear, cerificates of Miss Cardew's birth, baptism, whooping cough, registration, vaccination, confirmation, and the measles; both the German and the English variety.

LADY BRACKNELL: Ah! A life crowded with incident, I see; though perhaps somewhat too exciting for a young girl. I am not myself in favor of premature experiences. (*Rises, looks at her watch.*) Gwendolen! the time approaches for our departure. We have not a moment to lose. As a matter of form, Mr. Worthing, I had better ask you if Miss Cardew has any little fortune?

JACK: Oh, about a hundred and thirty thousand pounds in the

Funds. That is all. Goodbye, Lady Bracknell. So pleased to have seen you.

LADY BRACKNELL (*sitting down again*) : A moment, Mr. Worthing. A hundred and thirty thousand pounds! And in the Funds! Miss Cardew seems to me a most attractive young lady, now that I look at her. Few girls of the present day have any real solid qualities, any of the qualities that last, and improve with time. We live, I regret to say, in an age of surfaces. (*To* CECILY.) Come over here, dear. (CECILY *goes across*.) Pretty child! Your dress is sadly simple, and your hair seems almost as Nature might have left it. But we can soon alter all that. A thoroughly experienced French maid produces a really marvellous result in a very brief space of time. I remember recommending one to young Lady Lancing, and after three months her own husband did not know her.

JACK (*aside*) : And after six months nobody knew her.

LADY BRACKNELL (*glares at JACK for a few moments. Then bends, with a practiced smile, to* CECILY) : Kindly turn round, sweet child. (CECILY *turns completely round*.) No, the side view is what I want. (CECILY *presents her profile*.) Yes, quite as I expected. There are distinct social possibilities in your profile. The two weak points in our age are its want of principle and its want of profile. The chin a little higher, dear. Style largely depends on the way the chin is worn. They are worn very high, just at present.

—Oscar Wilde

SUPPLEMENTARY SELECTIONS FOR CLASS PRESENTATION

The Bear, William Faulkner, *prose.*

The Charge of the Light Brigade, Alfred, Lord Tennyson, *poetry.*

Evangeline, Henry Wadsworth Longfellow, *poetry.*

Fern Hill, Dylan Thomas, *poetry.*

Hiawatha, Henry Wadsworth Longfellow, *poetry.*

Kubla Khan, Samuel Taylor Coleridge, *poetry.*

Ode on a Grecian Urn, John Keat, *poetry.*

Ozymandias, Percy Bysshe Shelley, *poetry.*

Portrait of a Cog, Kenneth Fearing, *poetry.*

There Was a Child Went Forth, Walt Whitman, *poetry.*

Ulysses, James Joyce, *prose.*

The Veteran, Stephen Crane, *prose.*

You Can't Go Home Again, Thomas Wolfe, *prose.*

Note: In oral presentations consideration should be given to the selection of contemporary materials such as sports commentaries, editorials, plays, speeches, and volumes of poetry.

CHAPTER FOUR

how the voice is produced

IN ORDER TO produce good vocal tones, some knowledge of the anatomy and physiology of the larynx is not only desirable but necessary. The average person does not use his voice properly in all the speaking situations in which he is involved, and therefore, must be taught some of the basic principles underlying good tone production. The purpose of this chapter is to present basic background information regarding the anatomy and physiology of the tone-producing mechanism, the larynx, to aid the student in voice exercises.

Students may ask, "Why do I need to know about the structure and function of the larynx to produce a good tone?" There are several good reasons. Many of the exercises are concerned with making fine adjustments of the muscles of the larynx. These adjustments are obtained by both listening to the voice and monitoring the kinesthetic sense. Instructions are often given in terms of the structures involved, such as, "I want you to bring your vocal folds together very lightly and produce an [ɑ] sound," or "Close your glottis and build up pressure before producing the sound." Specific instructions, such as these, require some knowledge on the part of the student in order that he may visualize and understand the process properly. A student is often asked to relax the extrinsic muscles of the larynx during phonation; if he doesn't know where these muscles are located, he may have difficulty in following instructions.

The following true story illustrates our point of view. A young golfer once became a national champion at the age of 19. He had perfect form and needed no formal instruction, even though he admitted later that he did not know the mechanics of the golf swing. Shortly after he achieved national prominence, his game began to deteriorate, and within a year, he had difficulty maintaining his position as a professional golfer. After several years of study with some of the finest teachers and with rigorous self-analysis, he regained his form. He commented that he had had to learn everything about the golf swing, i.e., the muscles involved, relaxation, mental attitude, etc., before he could achieve his goal. Basic knowledge, then, in any highly coordinated physical activity, is important in gaining appropriate skills and in correcting problems when they arise.

Although the basic information concerning the larynx is presented as simply as possible, it should be kept in mind that the act of speaking is not simple; it is an extremely complicated process. From the time we are born, the process of developing voice and speech begins, first as undifferentiated crying, then through a progression of differentiated crying, babbling, lalling, echoing, and finally symbolizing. These early efforts involve much experimentation with the voice and the articulators, and eventually lead to the conditioning of habits that characterize the voice and speech for the rest of one's life. In spite of the fact that human beings develop their voices spontaneously, very few understand the processes that are involved.

THE PURPOSE OF THE LARYNX

It is well to keep in mind that the biological function of the larynx is to serve as a valve (Figure 4.1). The valve actually has several purposes, namely to keep food, drink, and any other ingested material out of the respiratory system, to aid in the expulsion of any foreign matter from the respiratory tract (sneezing, coughing), and to seal off the system below the valve when undertaking strenuous activities such as lifting, striking, and pushing. As man evolved as an organism, he found that he could utilize certain structures and functions for communication. Inasmuch as all of the structures used in the speech process have their primary biological function, such as eating, breathing, etc., speech is an overlaid function.

To produce sound we need a source of energy and a vibrator. Later we shall discuss amplifying, transmitting, and receiving the sound, but for the moment let us consider the first factor, sound production. The source of energy or power available to man was the controlled breath stream, and the best vibrator was in the larynx. Other structures, such as the tongue, lips, and palate, can be used as sound sources, but they lack the flexibility and range of the structures of the larynx.

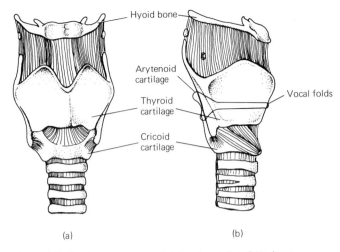

Figure 4.1. The human larynx: (a) front and (b) side views.

STRUCTURE OF THE LARYNX

THE CARTILAGES

The vocal folds are housed in a cartilaginous frame rigid enough to hold the air passageway open when we want to breathe, but flexible enough to permit minor adjustments when we want to speak or swallow. The chief cartilages of the larynx (Figure 4.2) are as follows:

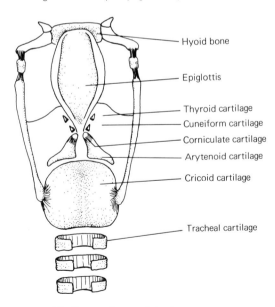

Figure 4.2. The cartilages of the larynx.

The Cricoid Cartilage. This cartilage serves as the base of the larynx. It is circular in shape, similar to a signet ring, and located just above the top ring of the trachea. The enlarged, or signet portion of the ring, is at the back. The name comes from the Greek work *krikos,* meaning ringlike.

The Thyroid Cartilage. This large cartilage is at the front of the larynx, directly above the cricoid cartilage. It is composed of two plates joined together at about a ninety degree angle to form what is often referred to as the Adam's apple. The name *thyroid* comes from the Greek word meaning shield. This cartilage actually shields the larynx as well as housing and accommodating other structures. The plates do not join in the back; the front (anterior) wall of the esophagus serves as the rear (posterior) wall of the larynx.

The Arytenoid Cartilages. These two upright cartilages lie above the back part (the signet portion) of the cricoid. They are like little pyramids. The vocal folds attach to the front processes of these cartilages and to the thyroid cartilage just below and inside the notch.

The Corniculate Cartilages. These are the horn-like tips atop the arytenoid cartilages. To them are attached the various fibres of aryepiglottic folds which traverse the larynx superiorly and insert behind the epiglottis.

The Cunieform Cartilages (when present). Found within the aryepiglottic folds, these cartilages serve as stiffeners.

The Epiglottis. Large and leaflike, this structure is attached to the front, inside part of the thyroid cartilage. This vestigial structure plays little or no part in speech production.

THE MUSCLES

Two groups of muscles control the movements of the larynx, the *intrinsic* (inside) muscles, and the *extrinsic* (outside) muscles (Figure 4.3). The latter group of muscles lift and tilt the larynx in swallowing and to an extent aid in producing high-pitched tones. It is well to keep in mind that certain external muscles can impinge upon the intrinsic muscles and seriously hamper good tone production. The intrinsic muscles are involved in the movement of the cartilages of the larynx and provide the necessary actions for both biologic functions and tone production for speech. It is with these muscles that we are primarily concerned in the study of voice.

The muscles that are responsible for moving the vocal folds together to permit phonation are named *adductors* (move toward), and those that pull them apart are called *abductors* (take away). The critical event in phonation is the complex action of the adductors in making fine adjustments to breath pressure in order to determine: (a) the frequency or rate of vibration (pitch), (b) the amplitude of the tone, and (c) the timbre (quality) of the tone produced. In reality, when the adductors are relaxed, the vocal folds return to the open or quiet breathing position. This action is aided in part by the elastic recoil of the ligaments and the muscles

46

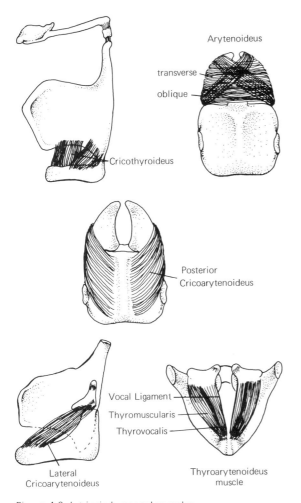

Figure 4.3. Intrinsic laryngeal muscles.

themselves. Abduction takes place when the bore of the larynx needs to be widened as in forced inhalation.

The Individual Muscles

Thyroarytenoideus. This wedge-shaped muscle is paired and serves as the vibrator in human phonation. Various synonyms are used to label this muscle, such as vocal folds, vocal lips, vocal cords, and vocal bands; however, we shall refer to them only as vocal folds in our discussion. A tough, fibrous vocal ligament covers the rounded margins of the vocal folds, which probably accounts for the terms *bands* or *cords*. The vocal folds are attached in front to the thyroid cartilage and insert into the vocal

47

processes of the arytenoid cartilages. The thyroarytenoideus has several interrelated functions that have a direct bearing on rate and amplitude of vibration. They help pull themselves together by contracting. The closed, tensed vocal folds resist the breath pressure building up beneath and are blown quickly apart. The folds can selectively relax under contraction to alter the degree of resistance to the outgoing breath stream and thus change the tone created. One must also bear in mind that the thickness of this muscle is changed by its own contraction, which alters rate of vibration. Additionally, the folds can be tensed and elongated under contraction by the action of other muscles.

Arytenoideus. The unpaired arytenoid muscle is attached to the posterior surfaces of the two arytenoid cartilages, which are separated when this muscle is at rest. The contraction of the arytenoideus pulls these little cartilages together and thus aids in the adduction of the vocal folds.

Lateral Cricoarytenoideus. This fan-shaped muscle originates at the upper border of the cricoid cartilage and attaches laterally to the arytenoid cartilages. This muscle rotates the arytenoid cartilages inward, bringing the vocal folds together at the midline.

Cricothyroideus. The paired elements of the cricothyroid muscle originate on the upper-front and lateral surface of the cricoid cartilage and fan upward and backward to insert on the lower border of the thyroid cartilage. When this muscle contracts, it pulls the thyroid cartilage forward and down, elongating and tensing the vocal folds.

MUSCLES OF THE LARYNX

Muscle	Origin	Insertion	Function
Thyroarytenoideus	Thyroid cartilage (front, inside)	Arytenoid cartilages (vocal processes)	Adducts, tenses, selectively relaxes, shortens, and thickens vocal folds.
Arytenoideus (oblique and transverse)	Arytenoid cartilages (from one arytenoid to the other)	Arytenoid cartilages (from one arytenoid to the other)	Adducts vocal folds by pulling arytenoid cartilages together. Helps to resist forward pull on arytenoid cartilages by other muscles.
Lateral cricoarytenoideus	Cricoid cartilage (side, back, upper margin)	Arytenoid cartilages (front, side)	Adducts vocal folds, aids in resisting subglottic air pressure.
Cricothyroideus	Cricoid cartilage (upper front, side)	Thyroid cartilage (lower side)	Adducts vocal folds (pulls thyroid cartilages forward and down).
Posterior cricoarytenoideus	Cricoid cartilage (posterior plate)	Arytenoid cartilage (lateral margins)	Abducts vocal folds (rotates arytenoid cartilages outward). Said by some to tilt arytenoid cartilages backward, increasing length and tension of vocal folds.

Posterior Cricoarytenoideus. The posterior cricoarytenoideus is a fan-shaped pair of muscles that originates on the posterior surface of the cricoid cartilage (signet part of the ring) and inserts on the outer rear processes of the arytenoid cartilages. The chief function of this muscle is to rotate the arytenoid cartilages outwardly to abduct the vocal folds in forced exhalation. Some specialists feel that the posterior cricoarytenoideus tilts the arytenoid cartilages backward exerting tension on the vocal folds and therefore is involved in phonation.

The chart summarizing the muscles of the larynx is necessarily brief, but may help in reviewing this section.

PRODUCING THE TONE

In normal breathing the vocal folds are relaxed and lie close to the inner walls of the larynx. They are apart at the back, but are always together at the front. This triangular opening, which may be observed during quiet breathing, is called the *glottis,* a term that will be used throughout the book. Figure 4.4 shows the vocal folds during quiet breathing, whispering,

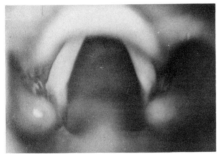

Forced inhalation

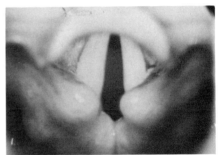

Quiet breathing

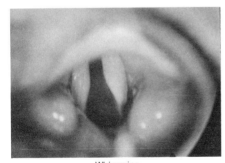

Whispering

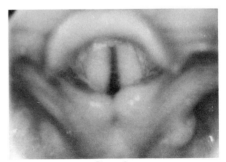

Phonation

Figure 4.4. Position of the vocal folds during forced inhalation, quiet breathing, whispering, and phonation.

Source: Courtesy of Professor Willard R. Zemlin, Director, Speech and Hearing Laboratory, University of Illinois.

phonation, and forced inhalation. When one gets an impulse to speak, he initiates action by bringing the vocal folds together at the midline to seal off the outgoing air flow that is initiated at the same time. The impounded air builds up pressure beneath the tensed vocal folds and literally blows them apart. As the impounded air is released, there is an immediate decrease in the subglottic pressure, and the still-tensed vocal folds snap shut. Some scientists have applied Bernoulli's law to vocal fold action, holding that the rush of air over the vocal fold structure is similar to air rushing over an air foil (wing) of an airplane. The resultant drop in pressure at the surface

Start

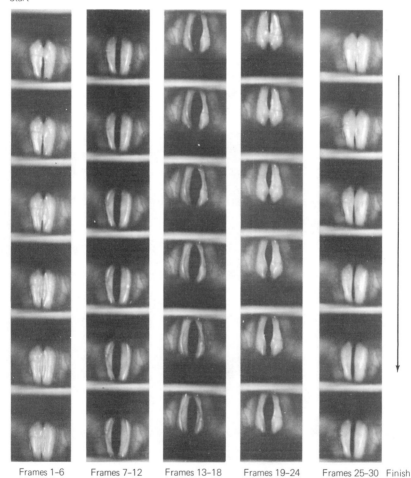

Frames 1–6   Frames 7–12   Frames 13–18   Frames 19–24   Frames 25–30 Finish

Figure 4.5. The cycle of a normal vocal fold vibration as seen by high-speed photography.
Source: Courtesy of Professor Willard R. Zemlin, Director, Speech and Hearing Laboratory, University of Illinois.

gives rise to "lift." In a sense, then, the vocal folds are literally sucked together by the drop in pressure, since the lift is in the direction of the approximated position of the folds. Another cycle begins with the building up of pressure.

In this manner, then, cycles of pressure and pressure release are maintained as long as the force (breath) and the vibrator (vocal folds) are kept in play. These cycles are unbelievably fast, so fast indeed that they cannot be seen with the naked eye. High-speed photography, however, has captured the movement of the vocal folds in great detail (Figure 4.5). In the average male at fundamental frequency the rate is 130 hertz (cycles per second) and in the female, 260 hertz. The human voice is capable of pitch change, of course, in which case the rate of vibration changes.

PITCH AND PITCH CHANGES

Pitch, i.e., the highness or lowness of the tone with regard to a musical scale, is determined by the number of double vibrations of the vocal folds per second—the faster the rate of vibration, the higher the pitch, and conversely the slower the rate of vibration, the lower the pitch.

Two factors are involved in determining the rate of vibration: (a) the structure of the vocal folds, including the length, thickness, and density, and (b) the degree of tenseness of the vocal folds while the tone is being made.

Length and Thickness

The length and thickness of the vocal folds vary greatly among individuals, and largely determine whether one is to be a tenor, baritone, basso, soprano, or alto. The length varies from $\frac{3}{8}$ to $\frac{7}{8}$ of an inch, depending upon age, sex, and general physical structure of the individual. Women's voices are normally higher pitched than men's because their vocal folds are thinner and shorter (roughly three-quarters as long). The average voice is capable of producing approximately two octaves on a musical scale. While range may be extended somewhat by exercise, which increases flexibility, pitch, range, and voice type (i.e., soprano, tenor, etc.) are determined by the structures an individual possesses. We should emphasize that in speaking one usually does not utilize all of his speaking range, while in singing the entire range is frequently employed. Figure 4.6 may be helpful in locating various types and ranges of voice in relation to a musical scale.

Tension

The tenseness of the vocal folds also helps to determine pitch, for with a given length a tense vocal fold will vibrate faster than a less tense one. Tenseness varies not only among different individuals, but within the same individual according to his changing thoughts and moods and how he

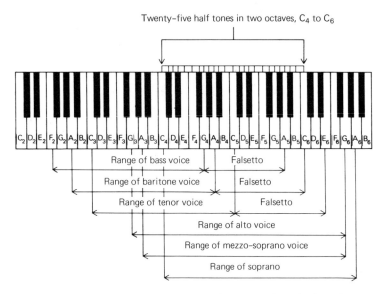

Figure 4.6. Voice types and ranges in relation to the piano keyboard.

wishes to express them. Pitch changes are made possible by varying the degree of tenseness of the folds, which is accomplished by the muscles of the larynx in the manner previously discussed.

INTENSITY OR LOUDNESS

Intensity of tone is determined by two factors: (a) *amplitude* of vibration, and (b) *resonance*. In the determination of the intensity of sound, it is not the rate but the extent of the vocal fold activity while vibrating that is the critical factor. The more extensive the movement of the vocal folds, the more intense or loud the sound. In viewing the action of the folds by high-speed photography, one may observe that as the folds are blown apart, they move laterally to the sides in a rippling action. Very little upward movement takes place as was previously believed. To increase intensity of tone, the vocal folds must build up more tension to resist breath pressure; thus, a larger "explosion" takes place and a larger rippling action may be observed in the vocal folds as they open to release the pressure. As each cycle of pressure and pressure release increases in extremity, the resultant wave of compression and rarifaction is likewise more compressed and rarified in the outgoing air flow. The changes in the sound wave structure are perceived by an auditor as a change in loudness. Resonance has much to do with the amplification of tone produced at the laryngeal level, which in itself is quite small. We shall present the phenomena of resonance in greater detail in Chapter 6.

QUALITY

Voice quality, or *timbre*, is still another factor that is influenced and largely controlled by the vibration of the vocal folds. Again, resonance plays an important part in determining quality, but at this point we are considering only the manner in which the tone is initiated. In this respect the vibration of the folds is basically important.

Sounds may have individual qualities that distinguish them from each other. When we listen to an orchestra tuning up, we have little difficulty in identifying the tones of many different instruments, even though they are all playing the same key. The full round tone of the bass viol is quite different from the thinner tone of the violin, and the rich full tone of the organ contrasts markedly with the piping tone of the fife or piccolo. The same difference is apparent, though to a lesser degree, in the quality of the voices of different persons. It is not difficult to distinguish individual voice quality among our friends and acquaintances.

Voice quality is directly related to the kind of tone produced in the larynx. The vocal folds produce a fundamental tone by the vibration of these structures as a whole. However, within the rippling movement of the folds many oscillations are observable which are the physical movements that give rise to harmonics or overtones. The violin or piano string, for example, vibrates both as a whole and in segments. The vibration of the entire string gives rise to what we call the fundamental tone. The segmental vibrations produce the harmonics or overtones. If these overtones bear a fortunate harmonic relationship to the fundamental, the tone is labelled good. If there is a poor harmonic relationship, as in the sound of a fingernail scratching across a blackboard, the resultant product is called noise. A continuum of laryngeal tones from good to poor exists among speakers.

The amplification of the complex laryngeal tone will be discussed more fully in the chapter on resonance. One should bear in mind, however, that if we were to hear the laryngeal tone only, it would sound very much like a buzz of low intensity. The tiny oscillations within the total movement of the vocal folds vary among individuals and in part account for differences in voices of the same pitch and pitch range. The effective resonation of the laryngeal tone also has much to do with a pleasing voice.

Training, then, can modify the tone produced by the larynx and can do much to enable one to use the voice effectively in speech.

CHAPTER
FIVE

tone
production

TONE PRODUCTION SHOULD be easy. A good vocal tone is made with little effort in and around the larynx. The best voices come from larynxes which are most free from strain. Conversely, it is virtually impossible to develop a pleasing and effective voice quality as long as there is tension in the muscles of the larynx.

One might ask, "If producing the tone is easy, why is it that relatively few people have good voices?" The answer lies in the realm of the habits we have acquired in producing tone from the very beginnings of our lives. Developing good vocal tone may be compared with the development of a good, basic swing in golf—the end product looks very easy, but the path leading to the end product may be very difficult, particularly when an individual receives no formal training along the way. True, the golf swing is a very natural action. The body is relaxed and only those muscles that are needed are used. Timing has to be perfect. The average person starts by trying to overpower the ball, and before long he is swinging at the ball as though it weighed ten pounds rather than a mere ounce and a half. The poor muscle habits acquired in this process become learned and difficult to eradicate. So it is with voice. One may have been producing it with inefficient motor patterns for years, and retraining, therefore, becomes more difficult than starting with no prior experience.

In order to set the stage for good work in tone production, one should: (a) study the nature of physiological interference with tone production, and (b) learn how to relax.

PHYSIOLOGICAL INTERFERENCE WITH TONE PRODUCTION

It is essential that the extrinsic muscles of the larynx remain relaxed during phonation. If they are not, their contraction may hamper the free movement of the vocal folds which is necessary for good tone production. Many beginning students of voice have unwanted tension in the muscles of the jaw, neck, and larynx. Before undertaking phonation exercises to develop better tone quality, they should attempt to relax the muscles in these areas that are not involved in producing voice. An extreme form of this problem is often seen in voice pathology cases where unwanted tension in the extrinsic muscles of the larynx is especially visible.

Physiologically, the extrinsic muscles (as well as others) are involved in the process of swallowing. This is what happens when they contract:

1. The larynx is lifted and pressed against the base of the tongue to protect the trachea from the admission of food.

2. The false vocal folds, which are located above the true vocal folds, serve as a valve and close.[1]

3. The soft palate seals off the oropharynx from the nasopharynx.

4. The tongue moves food or drink to the esophagus.

The biologic function of swallowing, naturally, is a much older process in humans than phonation, and the latter yields readily to the former during a moment of incoordination. Place the tip of your finger on the notch of the thyroid and swallow. Now try to phonate at the same time! It is obvious that relaxation of the extrinsic muscles is imperative if good phonation is to be achieved. Developing good phonation with selective relaxation is analagous to a golfer attempting to develop an effective swing—if he contracts muscles in the arms and body that are not involved, he will not only lose distance and control, he will spend the better part of his time looking for his ball.

RELAXATION DURING PHONATION

Relaxation is not easy. The noise, hurry, and strain of our competitive living are all against it. Add to this the psychological effect of world problems upon humanity and it is little wonder that the average person just is not relaxed, even during periods of relative quiet. The constant striving to cope with our environment gives rise to hypertension—a condition that has become

---

[1] In extreme cases of tension (pathologic voice cases) the false vocal folds have been known to produce the tone in phonation. The tone produced is hoarse and very unsatisfactory. Any false vocal fold activity seriously hampers true vocal fold action.

all too prevalent in recent decades. In learning how to relax we are taking the first steps toward not only an improved method of tone production, but an improved way of living. Unhampered judgment, undisturbed thinking, calmer nerves, improved poise—all these should and will come to him who learns to combat nervous tension.

METHODS OF RELAXATION

There are many widely used methods of relaxation in voice training, each involving a slightly different set of principles and approach: (a) progressive relaxation, (b) direct suggestion, (c) autosuggestion, (d) hypnosis, and (e) manipulative relaxation.

Progressive Relaxation

One of the best known writers on the subject of relaxation is the medical authority Dr. Edmund Jacobson, whose techniques of relaxation have been used extensively in treating medical problems, particularly those arising from hypertension. Jacobson uses the term "differential relaxation" to indicate that there should be a minimum of tension in the muscles required for an act along with the relaxation of other muscles. Only those muscles are used which are needed for the performance of the act, and there should be *no excess* tension in them. Jacobson stresses the development of what he terms "muscle sense."

While it is not possible to review the Jacobson method with justice in the space of a paragraph or two, the following points will orient the student to his techniques. The patient is asked to lie supine to immobilize major muscle groups. A set of antagonistic muscles—those that work in opposition to one another—is selected, such as the set that flexes and extends the arm. The patient is asked to tense *both* muscles evenly (so one does not overcome the other). Then, progressing in a series, the patient is asked to "feel" the difference between several degrees of contraction and relaxation, starting with the easiest—the contrast between extreme contraction and relaxation—and working toward sensing the more subtle difference between very little contraction and complete, deep relaxation. Eventually a person should be able to sense the difference between "thinking contraction" and deep relaxation. An end product, then, is for a person to "think" relaxation, i.e., reconstruct the kinesthetic "feel" of relaxation, and in the moments that follow he will actually release contraction in hypertense muscles.

In summarizing this method, four points should be stressed: (a) muscle sense helps us locate tension areas in the body, (b) muscle sense allows us to discriminate between muscle states along a continuum from no muscle contraction (relaxation) to extreme muscle contraction, (c) muscle sense (and control) permits us to voluntarily relax muscles in specific areas,

and (d) muscle sense permits us to achieve relaxation of one set of an-
tagonists, which generally seems to spread relaxation to other nearby
muscle groups and eventually to the body as a whole.

Direct Suggestion and Autosuggestion

Direct Suggestion. Voice teachers often use direct suggestion to
achieve relaxation. Usually, an instructor gives directions to one or more
subjects. It is also possible to instruct oneself. The manner in which the
instructions are given may vary from a direct imperative statement, "Relax!",
to the recommendation that the subject assume the substance and quality
of an entity embodying relaxation, such as a rag doll. Direct suggestion to
relax often follows an instruction to undergo some form of exercise calling
for tension. Many variations of the same idea can be found in every standard
text on the subject. Here are but a few:

> (After tensing) Now let go. Relax all over, to the point where
> you have barely enough "starch" in your muscles . . . let them
> all sag."
>
> (After stretching) Slump! Let go! Think of a cat stretching,
> then curling up to snooze before a warm fire.
>
> Take a deep breath and sigh. Be sure you fully relax on the
> sigh; "give up" to it.
>
> Go limp. Let everything go. . . .

In a sense this type of exercise exhorts the subject simply to relax,
assuming that he knows how. Unfortunately, too many people do not know
how to relax and have to be instructed *systematically*.

Autosuggestion. This method may be defined as a "suggestion to
oneself arising within oneself and having effects on one's thinking and
bodily functions." In hypnosis the hypnotist suggests to the subject who in
turn suggests to himself, and in this sense two people are involved. Auto-
suggestion in one form or another appears to be involved in all methods of
relaxation.

Hypnosis

Hypnosis is widely used in therapy to achieve deep relaxation, and in
the hands of a qualified professional (trained and certified) it may produce
good results in a very short period of time. The deep relaxation achieved
through hypnosis has often been used to good effect as a substitute response
for anxiety in reciprocal inhibition therapy. Voice cases in particular have
been successfully treated in this way. Hypnosis, as such, should not be
used in voice and diction classes, but many of the techniques typically
employed in this process can be used by themselves or in combinations to

good effect. Some of the most useful of these are : (a) creation of a peaceful environment, (b) utilization of sensory stimuli to induce relaxation, and (c) creation of mental concepts inducing relaxation.

Hypnosis requires that the operator (hypnotist) have the complete confidence and cooperation of the subject. The subject normally will not place his confidence in the hyponotist unless he wants to. In other words, the subject only does what he thinks is right, ethically and morally. Usually a form of distraction is used to control the visual sense, particularly at the outset. Such devices as an oscillating coin, a moving wheel, or a swinging key are routinely used. The hypnotist then begins a running monologue involving concepts of warmth, comfort, relaxation, drowsiness, and bodily sensations ; eventually, he may create verbally for the subject scenes of pastoral beauty involving all of the senses. The subject is often told to follow simple instructions such as "When I say, 'one,' you will close your eyes," or "I want you to open your eyes and look at the wheel." During this process the subject is often told that his eyelids or his arms are getting heavy ; these instructions are tantamount to telling him to relax. Often he is told, "You are very relaxed now," and usually he is. Eventually, he is told that he will awaken on a given signal, refreshed, relaxed, and happy. He may even be told that he will feel relaxed for a long time—a form of auto-suggestion that invariably works. The effects of hypnotism ordinarily do not last very long ; for this reason the process is more useful as an adjunct to training the voice rather than as an end in itself.

Manipulative Relaxation

This type of relaxation is achieved by stretching and limbering up tense muscles before attempting phonation. The student is instructed to rotate his head slowly to one side or the other and stretch. The movement is calculated to reduce or eliminate any residual tension that might exist in the neck muscles. Several variations of this type of exercise are presented in this chapter.

Manipulative relaxation also implies relaxation achieved through massage. This method of relaxation is used more frequently in speech pathology practice than in voice and diction classes.

EXERCISES FOR DEVELOPING RELAXATION

1. Progressive relaxation requires you to become highly aware of the states of tension and relaxation in your muscles. The following series is adapted from techniques commonly used in behavior therapy :[2]

    a. Settle comfortably in your chair.

    b. Clench your right fist, tighter, tighter.

[2] Exercise 1 can be done on any set of antagonistic muscles—for example the extensor and flexor muscles of the arm. Usually a complete program of relaxation is given. The following muscle sets are commonly used. It is probably easiest to start with the hands or arms.

c. Now relax, allowing the fingers of your right hand to become more loose. Concentrate on relaxation for 10 seconds.

d. Repeat the two steps of tension and relaxation, attempting to increase the feeling of relaxation of your hand and fingers.

e. Now clench both of your fists, tighter, tighter. Hold for more than 5 seconds, but less than 10 seconds.

f. Now relax, deeper, deeper. Notice how the relaxation seems to extend to the rest of your body.

Relaxation of the arms:

a. Clench your fists, tighter, relax, etc.

b. Tense the flexors and extensors of the arms. Relax. Concentrate on the difference.

Relaxation of the head, neck, and shoulders:

a. Tense the muscles of your forehead and raise your eyebrows, tighter, etc. Relax. Feel the difference.

b. Widen and tense the muscles of your eyes. Relax.

c. Tense the masseter muscles of your jaw (the chewing muscles). Relax.

d. Tense the tongue by pressing against the gum ridge of the lower teeth. Relax, deeper, deeper.

e. Tense the muscles involved in a pout, mouth closed. Relax, etc.

f. Tense the muscles of your neck by placing the palm of your hand against your forehead and pressing. Relax.

g. Tense the muscles of your neck by rolling your head straight back. Relax.

h. Tense the shoulders by an extreme shrug. Relax.

i. Open your mouth and thrust your lower jaw forward under hard tension. Relax.

Relaxation of chest, stomach, and back:

a. Tense both muscles of inhalation and exhalation. Relax.

b. Tense the upper rib cage. Relax.

c. Tense the lower abdominal muscles. Relax.

d. Tense the muscles of the upper legs and lower back. Relax.

Relaxation of legs and feet:

a. Tense the muscles of the feet much the same as in clenching your fist. Relax.

b. Flex and tense your toes and feet upward toward your shins as far as they can go. Relax.

c. Tense all muscles above and below the knees. Relax.

2. A variation of the above procedure that the authors have used extensively employs a more graded series of steps of tension and relaxation.

a. Tense your fist, tighter, tighter. Hold clenched for 10 seconds.

b. Now relax. Feel the difference, which is extreme. Concentrate on the feeling of relaxation for 10 seconds.

c. Tense your fist, but not as much. Hold the tension constant for 10 seconds.

d. Now relax. Feel the difference and try to obtain a greater feeling of relaxation—let the hand go limp, allowing the fingers to straighten. Concentrate on relaxation for 10 seconds.

e. Close your fist lightly. Hold it for 10 seconds. Concentrate on the feeling in the muscles. Hold for 10 seconds.

f. Now relax your hand, more, more. Feel the difference in your hand. Try to relax even further—let all the muscle fibres go. Hold for 10 seconds.

g. Now close your eyes and pretend you are clenching your fist without actually doing so. Tighter, tighter. You should be able to feel some tension in the muscles. Hold for 10 seconds.

h. Now relax, deeper, deeper. Let it go, let it go.

The last step develops a *feel* for relaxation. In a short time you will be able to command various parts or all of your body to relax as you gain complete control over the relaxation process.

ADDITIONAL EXERCISES FOR RELAXATION

There are a number of time-honored relaxation exercises which are useful ; we present some of them here :

1. Elephant walk. Let your body flop over at the waist like a rag doll. Let your arms be the elephant's trunk. Now move forward slowly, head down and arms loose, shaking your body slightly. Attempt to loosen the muscles of your spine, rib cage and shoulders. Walk about 10 feet.

2. Take a deep breath and yawn, stretching your arms and upper body like a giant cat. S-t-r-e-t-c-h.

3. Standing erect with your feet parted, drop your head on your chest. Now slump your shoulders forward in an arch. Next drop your head, shoulders, and body at the waist. Gently shake your upper body loose from left to right and back again. Repeat.

4. A number of rotation exercises have been used to loosen up the head and neck. These should be performed slowly in order to avoid pinching the nerves or straining the muscles.

a. Drop your head forward to your chest. Move it slowly to the right shoulder, stretch, and return. Now move it slowly to the left shoulder, stretch, and return.

b. Drop your head forward to your chest and to a slow count of three, rotate it to the left shoulder. Instead of stopping, continue to move your head, slowly letting it drop backward of its own weight and letting your mouth fall open. Keep moving it in a circle to the right shoulder to another count of three. Now complete the circle on a final count of three. This exercise may be a little difficult at first because of stiffness. Reverse the direction of roll and do three more complete rolls in the other direction. Do not rotate your head more than three times in one direction.

c. If you feel energetic, Exercise 4b can be extended to the entire body. Roll from the waist and let the arms and upper torso follow loosely while remaining completely relaxed.

5. Stand erect. Tense your jaw and neck muscles. Tighter, tighter. Now begin to relax. Release the tension a little more, and more, and more. Keep striving for a deeper and deeper state of relaxation.

6. Drop your head to your chest. Let your jaw fall slack. Now gently shake your jaw loose, letting your lips and facial muscles go limp. Shake gently until you achieve freedom from tension and rigidity.

7. Repeat the following syllable chains slowly, attempting to get a full jaw swing, openness of mouth, and relaxation of the facial muscles :

a. suh-suh-suh-suh-suh-suh-suh-suh-suh-suh

b. fuh-fuh-fuh-fuh-fuh-fuh-fuh-fuh-fuh-fuh

c. shuh-shuh-shuh-shuh-shuh-shuh-shuh-shuh-shuh-shuh

d. puh-puh-puh-puh-puh-puh-puh-puh-puh-puh

e. kuh-kuh-kuh-kuh-kuh-kuh-kuh-kuh-kuh-kuh

8. Try the following words, attempting to get more jaw swing on the vowel in each succeeding word : see   sit   say   sat   saw.

HOW TO PRODUCE TONE

Good voice quality is based upon producing a good laryngeal tone. If the laryngeal tone itself is less than satisfactory, little if anything can be done by the resonating process to improve it, and poor voice quality results. For example, if anything decreases the efficiency with which you vibrate your vocal folds, such as slight swelling due to abuse or a cold, or the presence of phlegm from nasal discharge, the results are immediately apparent—it is evident that the voice is muffled or hoarse and is definitely not as good as it usually is.

Before starting tone production exercises, keep in mind the following points, which will help in achieving maximum results :

1. Begin all tone production work with at least a minimum of relaxation exercises to limber up and get rid of undue tension in the neck.

2. Inasmuch as good tone production requires adequate breath support, include preliminary breathing exercises to reestablish proper supply and support.

3. Keep in mind that the tone produced in the larynx involves a complicated physiological process involving several sets of muscles, none of which can be independently manipulated. You adjust your tone by *listening* to the results. *Your own judgment of what you will accept or*

reject becomes critical. An experienced teacher can do much to help to develop good critical listening and judgment.

4. In the beginning, *easy does it.* The best results are usually attained by initiating tones that are relatively low in intensity. Work for clarity of tone even though you may spend some time in achieving it. Remember: Learning theory requires the attainment of the goal of a particular program before going on. In this instance achievement of a satisfactory tone is the goal of the first program. Establish a criterion for each program. What is *your* criterion for going on? Eight out of ten good tone productions on the vowel *ah* would serve when judged by an experienced coach.

5. In producing tone use the vowels *ah* [ɑ], *aw* [ɔ], and *oh* [oʊ]. These are the most powerful speech sounds in American English. Furthermore, the air passageway is less occluded on the production of these vowels than on most of the others.

6. The student should practice using a pitch level that is *best* for him. There are within everyone's pitch range two or three tones that are approximately 25 percent up from the bottom of one's range. Usually, these are the tones around which we habitually vary all of our pitch changes. Find them. See, "Optimum Pitch and Habitual Pitch," pp. 71–74.

7. In developing tone, the student will be asked to move from easy to difficult material. The chief reason for this progression is to enable him to carry on to the next step the good phonatory results of the last step. Movement from step to step can go at a pace suited to his needs. Again, a *criterion* of success for each step should be set up. The basic plan uses the following progression: (a) back vowels, (b) vowel-consonant combinations, (c) consonant-vowel combinations, (d) consonant-vowel-consonant combinations, (e) meaningful words, (f) meaningful word combinations, (g) phrases, (h) sentences, and (i) passages.

GOALS AND CRITERIA FOR PHONATION

Goal	Criterion
1. To achieve easy initiation of tone.	Perform Exercise 2, page 63, successfully.
2. To be able to exhibit good tone production in front of class.	Perform Exercise 8, page 66, successfully.
3. To eliminate faulty voice quality from tone production.	Perform Exercise, 3, page 64, successfully.
4. To learn how to determine optimum pitch.	Perform Exercises 1, 2, 3, 4, or 5 correctly, pages 71–72.
5. To learn how to determine modal or habitual pitch.	Perform Exercise 1 or 4, page 74, successfully.
6. To be able to determine your pitch range.	Perform Exercise 1 (a–e), page 72, successfully.

Exercises for specific vocal faults such as breathiness, hoarseness, etc., follow this section. Material to develop voice power is contained in the chapter on resonance.

Easy Initiation of Tone

Two approaches are presented to initiate tone easily, the traditional method, which typically uses a breathy tonal attack, and the operant, programmatic method.

EXERCISES FOR TONE PRODUCTION

1. Initiate tone as follows:
   a. Hum lightly at a comfortable pitch level about one-fourth up from the bottom of your total range. Repeat, attempting to attain an easy, clear tone. This step, while not absolutely necessary, will place the tone.
   b. Intone an easy, somewhat breathy *ah* sound. Repeat several times, attempting to improve upon the quality of the sound.
   c. Repeat the syllable *ha* in an easy, effortless way, prolonging both the *h* and the *a*, again using a monotone.
   d. Prolong both elements of *ha*, only this time use a falling inflection. Diminish the volume of *ha* at the end of the inflection. Repeat, until you are able to do this smoothly and with good quality.
   e. Repeat step *d*, but use a rising inflection this time. Do not become tense at the end of the rising inflection. Rather, attempt to diminish the tone to extinction.
   f. Repeat steps *a* through *e* using *oh* instead of *ah*. Repeat steps *a* through *e* using the vowel *aw*.
2. Operant conditioning exercise:

Frames	Frames	Frames	Frames	Frames
1 ha	11 ho	21 ho	31 haw	41 who
2 haw	12 high	22 high	32 how	42 he
3 ho	13 how	23 haw	33 high	43 ho
4 high	14 ha	24 ha	34 ho	44 hey
5 how	15 haw	25 how	35 ha	45 ha
6 ha	16 high	26 high	36 how	46 hoy
7 haw	17 haw	27 haw	37 ho	47 how
8 ho	18 ha	28 ha	38 high	48 ho
9 how	19 ho	29 how	39 haw	49 ha
10 high	20 how	30 ho	40 ha	50 high

Instructions: [3] The instructor or the person in charge should: (a) use three to four seconds per frame, (b) present the word and have the student echo it after him, (c) signal if the student does the frame correctly using a clicker, light, or raised hand (finger), (d) do not repeat the frame if incorrectly done, unless there are five misses in a row; after five misses, reinstruct, go back five frames, and continue, (e) slightly prolong the phonemic elements, e.g., [h] and [ɑ], (f) use a downward inflection, and (g) do the entire program of 50 frames, working for at least 80 percent success as a minimum.

3. Adjusting the tone. Very often a tone will be satisfactory, but not ideal. You should be able to produce tone over a range of qualities from breathy to strident. Choose five degrees of contraction of the muscles of phonation as follows: (a) level one, breathy, little tone, (b) level two, more tone than in one but still breathy (c) level three, tone easy, slight breathiness, (d) level four, tone easy, resonant, not strident, and (e) level five, tone hard, quality strident or metallic.

Instructions: (a) do the material in Exercise 2, but only ten frames at a time, (b) do each word with all five levels of contraction, (c) use all other instructions in Exercise 2, and (d) work for at least 80 percent success as your minimum criterion.

Note: Level four is the goal toward which all students should strive. If students are paired for practice, judges should be consistent in their judgments; they should not be strict on one series and lenient on another. If a student has poor voice quality, the reinforcement level may have to be lowered, i.e., the best of the poor performance is accepted at first, then gradually the standards are raised.

4. Exercise for consonant-vowel production:

Frames		Frames		Frames		Frames		Frames	
1	ma	11	raw	21	know	31	know	41	know
2	ma	12	raw	22	know	32	row	42	ma
3	ma	13	woe	23	ma	33	ma	43	law
4	low	14	woe	24	law	34	show	44	sow
5	low	15	la	25	fa	35	fa	45	fa
6	low	16	la	26	raw	36	row	46	maw
7	fa	17	maw	27	woe	37	law	47	woe
8	fa	18	maw	28	la	38	saw	48	ma
9	fa	19	row	29	maw	39	row	49	show
10	row	20	row	30	row	40	ma	50	low

Instructions are the same as for Exercise 2, p. 64.

[3] The instructor may elect to have the class break up into pairs, in which case the student-instructor assumes responsibility for carrying out the instructions.

5. Exercise for vowel-consonant production :

Frames		Frames		Frames		Frames		Frames	
1	our	11	on	21	own	31	arm	41	old
2	our	12	on	22	awe	32	ohm	42	on
3	our	13	all	23	are	33	own	43	our
4	all	14	all	24	ought	34	are	44	awe
5	all	15	ohm	25	all	35	old	45	are
6	all	16	ohm	26	on	36	our	46	on
7	arm	17	our	27	old	37	all	47	own
8	arm	18	all	28	awe	38	awe	48	ought
9	arm	19	arm	29	ought	39	arm	49	arm
10	on	20	on	30	our	40	own	50	all

Instructions are the same as for Exercise 2, p. 64.

6. Exercise for consonant-vowel-consonant production :

Frames		Frames		Frames		Frames		Frames	
1	main	11	yarn	21	roam	31	yarn	41	lawn
2	main	12	yarn	22	loan	32	lamb	42	balm
3	main	13	lamb	23	loan	33	balm	43	loan
4	lawn	14	lamb	24	yawn	34	roam	44	wore
5	lawn	15	lamb	25	yawn	35	loan	45	warm
6	lawn	16	balm	26	wore	36	yawn	46	yarn
7	warm	17	balm	27	wore	37	wore	47	roam
8	warm	18	balm	28	main	38	maim	48	yawn
9	warm	19	roam	29	lawn	39	yarn	49	maim
10	yarn	20	roam	30	warm	40	loan	50	lamb

Instructions are the same as for Exercise 2, p. 64.

7. Word combinations :

Frames		Frames		Frames		Frames		Frames	
1	how high	11	your lawn	21	you wore	31	you yawn	41	I know
2	how high	12	your lawn	22	you wore	32	you wore	42	I roam
3	how high	13	I know	23	how warm	33	how warm	43	how high
4	you roll	14	I know	24	how warm	34	how high	44	I wore
5	you roll	15	I know	25	how high	35	you yawn	45	your lawn
6	you roll	16	I loan	26	you roll	36	your lawn	46	blue yarn
7	blue yarn	17	I loan	27	blue yarn	37	blue yarn	47	I loan
8	blue yarn	18	I roam	28	your lawn	38	I know	48	how warm
9	blue yarn	19	I roam	29	I know	39	you wore	49	you roll
10	your lawn	20	you yawn	30	I loan	40	I roam	50	how high

Instructions are the same as for Exercise 2, p. 64.

8. Developmental sentences : [4]

Frames		Frames		Frames		Frames	
1	ocean	11	how far away	21	it hangs over your head	31	right
2	the ocean	12	know how far away	22	green	32	is right
3	see the ocean	13	now	23	is green	33	he is right
4	I see the ocean	14	gone now	24	the lawn is green	34	know he is right
5	now	15	is gone now	25	your lawn is green	35	I know he is right
6	go now	16	fog is gone now	26	thee	36	me
7	may go now	17	the fog is gone now	27	for thee	37	to me
8	you may go now	18	head	28	tolls for thee	38	here to me
9	away	19	your head	29	bell tolls for thee	39	over here to me
10	far away	20	over your head	30	the bell tolls for thee	40	come over here to me

Instructions are the same for Exercise 2, p. 64.

VOICE QUALITY PROBLEMS RELATED TO TONE PRODUCTION

Hoarse Voice Quality

The hoarse voice has three characteristics that are identifiable : (a) the voice is lacking in tone or sonority ; the tone is more like a noise band than a sonorous tone, (b) breathiness is invariably present, and (c) the voice is low in volume for the amount of effort expended. All of us have experienced hoarse voice quality at one time or another, usually when we have an inflammation of the larynx. The most common causes of hoarseness are acute or chronic abuse, colds or viral infections, and interference of the vocal folds by secretions, such as phlegm. Chronic abuse can lead to vocal nodes or contact ulcers which give rise to hoarseness. Other laryngeal pathologies such as cancer and tuberculosis can also cause hoarseness.

If a person suffers from chronic hoarseness, it is urgent that he first be examined by a physician to determine the cause, as it is dangerous to start voice work without knowing whether or not the vocal folds are in condition to do exercises. If the cause of hoarseness is vocal abuse, such as screaming at football games, talking for long periods under tension, and the like, vocal rest is the best remedy. If the problem is chronic, vocal exercises to improve

---

[4] Attempt to develop good tone production on a single word, then carry this into the word combination, and finally, into an entire sentence.

tone production are advisable. One should precede the easy initiation of tone exercises with discrimination exercises to identify the problem for the student.

EXERCISES FOR HOARSENESS

1. Practice exercises 1 and 2 on page 63 until you are able to produce tone in isolation satisfactorily. Do not be in a hurry to proceed to Exercises 3–7.

2. After you have accomplished Exercises 1 and 2 successfully, go on to Exercises 3–7.

Harsh Voice Quality

Harsh voice may be characterized as : (a) an unpleasant grating type of voice that has both tonal and noise components present, (b) a hard or metallic secondary quality, and (c) being too loud. The causes of harsh voice quality appear to be more functional than pathological. Tension in the larynx as well as in the walls of the resonators makes harshness a problem of both phonation and resonation. According to speech scientists, the vocal folds of a person with a harsh voice vibrate asymmetrically.

To eradicate harsh voice quality, the following steps should be followed : (a) eliminate the causes of excess tension, (b) work on relaxation exercises, (c) precede all voice production exercises with ear training, that is, discrimination exercises to differentiate varying degrees of harshness from normal voice quality, and (d) practice tone production exercises.

EXERCISES FOR HARSHNESS

1. Practice relaxation Exercise 1 on page 59.
2. Practice the following discrimination exercises :
   a. Have a good model[5], who can imitate harsh quality easily, read the following word pairs, simulating harsh voice quality randomly on one word of each pair. Use a hand signal to indicate the harsh word. The model should pause between words.

keen—complete	exit—end	mantle—brass
street—peel	center—never	jam—rang
ego—edict	betting—renter	sank—crank
tree—spree	engine—enter	fraternize—attribute
conceal—agree	together—forever	ham—mat

---

[5] Usually, the instructor will serve as the model. If the class is divided into small groups, a student who is able to demonstrate harsh quality can serve as the model.

b. Have a good model, who can imitate harsh quality easily, read the following passage. Signal when he uses harshness.

I can hardly imagine any man who would be ungrateful to receive thanks for a deed well done. Helpfulness is a virtue that many men lack. We should strive to preserve this attribute in our culture.

c. Observe speakers in your daily life who exhibit harsh quality. Attempt to identify the characteristics of the problem as listed in the opening paragraph on harshness. Watch the harsh speaker carefully to observe tension of the jaw and neck. Report your findings to your instructor.

d. Use negative practice to increase your awareness of harshness. In the three-word series below say the first word with breathiness, the second without harshness if possible, and the third word with harshness. In a second series demonstrate three degrees of harshness, doing the first word with the least tension and the last word with the most.

complete—spree—see	ebb—exit—help
each—Easter—easy	end—exude—forever
eel—Egypt—easy	elk—center—exquisite
flea—eager—ego	enter—engine—never
elect—street—agree	edible—ever—betting
add—abduct—fan	aspire—mat—manner
attribute—atom—act	angle—rang—clang

3. Practice the initiating of tone exercises commencing on p. 63.

Breathy Voice Quality

Breathiness is a voice quality that is characterized by: (a) an excessive escape of air during tone production that results in reduced sonority, (b) the presence of the noise component caused by the excessive escape, and (c) a loss of vocal power resulting from the reduction in the sonority of the tone. Actually, the person with a breathy voice does not suffer from having an unpleasant voice quality as much as from the inefficiency of the tone produced. All of us have experienced breathiness at one time or another, such as when we were asked to talk right after strenuous physical activity that placed demands upon the respiratory system (running, for example). Take a deep, deep breath; now try to talk as you allow an excess of air to escape—the result should be breathy speech. There are many causes for breathiness, such as muscular weakness, swelling of the vocal folds, etc. Again, in order to rule out pathology, one should consult a laryngologist before commencing exercises to overcome this problem.

EXERCISES FOR BREATHINESS

1. Read one of the selections at the end of this chapter. Have at least three judges listen to your voice. Do they detect undue escapage of air during phonation? Lack of volume? A voice quality lacking in tonality?

2. Attempt to develop good tone on the initial vowels in the following word pairs. Be sure to conserve breath on the [h] by shortening it somewhat.

air—hair	odd—hod	ail—hail	elm—helm
ear—hear	opal—hope	add—had	eat—heat
every—heavy	arm—harm	and—hand	own—hone
eel—heel	apt—hap	ail—hail	eight—hey
ate—hate	act—hacked	empty—hem	am—ham

3. Practice the words beginning with a vowel in the above pairs from a closed position, that is, adduct the vocal folds before initiating tone. Try to avoid a plosive attack.

4. Concentrate on Exercise 3 on page 64. Attempt to move from level two to level three by the accepted criterion. Now, see if you can succeed in getting 80 percent on level four. This last step should be your ultimate goal.

5. The entire tone production program is good for breathiness.

Juvenile Voice

Juvenile voice quality may be characterized as: (a) a voice that is inappropriately high for the speaker, i.e., males speaking in the range normal for females, (b) a falsetto voice, (c) an effeminate sounding male voice as a result of (a) and (b), (d) a voice that lacks resonance because of the falsetto tone, and (e) a voice that breaks when the speaker attempts to lower it.

This rare voice quality is abnormal and usually comes about when a young man passing through puberty attempts to retain his childhood voice pitch and quality by resorting to falsetto. The author has worked with a number of juvenile voice cases and has found that the problem has psychological as well as physiological bases. The juvenile voice can be corrected by a voice therapist; therefore, such cases should be referred for treatment.

Glottal Shock

While not a fault in overall voice quality, glottal shock is a specific problem that should be studied as a fault occurring at the vocal fold level. Glottal shock occurs when one attempts to stress a word beginning with a vowel. The chief characteristics are that: (a) the vocal folds are adducted and held under tension prior to the initiation of tone, (b) breath pressure is released in an explosion, and (c) an audible "click" is heard as the tone is initiated. The sudden release of air gives the vowel a plosivelike character. Because of the undue tension in the vocal folds and the often strident quality of the following vowel, glottal shock should be avoided. One should be able to say words with stressed vowels in the initial position smoothly. Most students are not aware that they use the glottal shock in their speech.

EXERCISES TO ELIMINATE GLOTTAL SHOCK

1. Say each of the following words two ways, first with a glottal shock and then without it. Observe the "click" as another student performs the exercise. Can you hear it in your own voice?

itch	any	eight	act	ant
each	engine	aid	atom	am
ignore	etch	ace	attempt	ad
index	every	April	ample	angry
insult	else	aim	account	adze

2. Say each of the following word pairs, attempting to get the same easy initiation of tone on the second word as you do on the first. Use a slight pause between words in the pairs.

hair—air	hap—apt	hod—odd	hope—opal
hear—ear	harm—arm	hate—ate	heat—eat
heavy—every	hem—empty	hat—at	hail—ail
hone—own	ham—am	helm—elm	heel—eel
hamper—ample	hay—eight	high—eye	hit—it
heap—each	hack—action	hand—and	had—add

3. Perform the following sentences, attempting to eliminate glottal shock from all initial stressed vowels.
   a. "Aim! Aim! Aim!" Aram yelled, as he stood with his arms jammed into his armpits.
   b. Each and every one of us ought to do it.
   c. Eighty-eight percent own their own home.
   d. Eat what you can—act as though you enjoy it.
   e. Ace's engine failed—everybody yelled, "watch out!"

PITCH CONSIDERATIONS

In this section we shall concern ourselves with three goals with regard to pitch: (a) determination of pitch range, (b) determination of optimum pitch, and (c) determination of habitual or modal pitch. In Chapter 9 we shall explore methods of using pitch to vary meaning and emotional expression.

Several terms and concepts should be thoroughly understood in order to analyze the use of pitch in everyday speech:

Optimum Pitch. There is an ideal modal pitch for every voice. According to this concept, there are two or three half-tones in an individual's range that are ideal for the location of the habitual or modal level. These tones can be produced with greater intensity per effort than tones above and below this level. They are easier to produce than other tone levels in one's pitch range. They are located at a fortunate place in the pitch range that allows for maximum variation in pitch patterns for meaning.

Habitual (Modal) Pitch. This is a range of pitch patterns habitually used by a speaker in his everyday speech. These levels *may* coincide with the optimum levels, but often they do not because the stress and strain of every day living may cause undue tension in the laryngeal area with a resultant or unconscious raising of pitch level. Some speakers, in an attempt to sound more mature or pontifical, use a lower modal pitch level than the optimum. Voice strain can result from either extreme.

Falsetto. This quality of voice is produced by relaxing the deeper muscle fibres of the vocal folds, thus thinning out the margins or those portions of the folds nearest the midline in phonation. Resistance to subglottic breath pressure is markedly decreased. Thus, amplitude of the tone is substantially less than a fully supported tone. The falsetto range overlaps the middle and upper range of fully supported phonation (in most bassos and baritones) and usually extends the upper range several full notes above the last normally supported tone. Falsetto is frequently used in diminishing tone and in creating special tonal effects in speech. The quality of falsetto is also perceived as higher in pitch than it may actually be, and is commonly used by males to impersonate females. In a few rare cases, young men may attempt to retain the same habitual pitch after puberty as they had before the vocal folds began growing in length. In order to achieve a habitual level consistent with their prepurberty voice, these lads utilize falsetto.

HOW TO DETERMINE OPTIMUM PITCH

There are several methods of determining optimum pitch. Before the exercise is attempted, a piano keyboard should be drawn on the blackboard. Include at least four octaves and label as shown in Figure 5.1.

1. Use of singing to determine optimum pitch.
   a. The instructor, using a pitch pipe (or piano), will help students locate C in the lower part of their range. (They should try to stay away from the bottom of their range.) The instructor will have the class as a whole hum this note lightly. The men will hopefully choose a level one octave below the women.

71

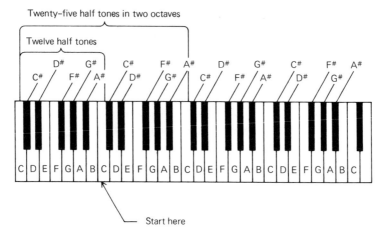

Figure 5.1. Diagram of the piano keyboard.

b. The instructor, using a pointer to indicate the notes, will guide individuals or the entire class up the scale one note at a time (singing *ah*). Each student should identify the last note he can comfortably perform without strain. Repeat several times if necessary.

c. Now, trying the same process again, this time students should lapse into falsetto and extend the upper limit as far as they can go. Make notations of the location of both the last fully supported tone and the last falsetto tone.

d. Now the class returns to the starting point again, and this time descends slowly until a tone can no longer be produced. The last true tone that each one produces should be noted.

e. The total number of tones produced *including* falsetto, should be counted.

f. The number of tones found in the preceding step is then divided by four.

g. Each student should count up from the bottom of his range by the number derived in step f. The note located and the half tones bordering it designate optimum pitch.

2. Use of notes or numbers to determine optimum pitch. This method is a slight variation of Exercise 1 above.

a. Instead of singing *ah* up the scale, the class intones the traditional *do* (on the starting note), *re, mi, fa, sol, la, ti, do.* Notations are made in the same manner as in Exercise 1, and the same method for calculation should be used.

b. Numbers may be used in place of notes, e.g., one (C), two (D), etc. These may be spoken rather than sung, although it it more difficult to do.

72

c. Since sustaining full notes in progression, i.e., C, D, E, etc., is admittedly a difficult task when one is trying to reach the highest note in his range, many singing teachers prefer to use major intervals in an effort to determine a student's highest note. The exercise is then modified as follows: An open vowel *ah, aw,* or *oh,* C–E–G–C[6] is sung, then quickly sung back down, reversing from the top C to G, E, and C. The next step in this procedure is that the same is done with the key of C♯. The teacher can locate each progressively higher key on the chromatic scale by use of his pitch pipe. Notations can be derived as in the other exercises.

TESTING THE STRENGTH AND EFFICIENCY OF OPTIMUM PITCH

1. Test the strength and efficiency of your new-found optimum pitch.
   a. Locate your optimum pitch with a pitch pipe or piano.
   b. Phonate an *ah* without attempting to force it in any way.
   c. Without varying your force move up the scale two or three half notes. Theoretically you will have just moved away from the central area of the optimum and a slight decrease in the tone should be perceptible—the highest tone should not be as easy to produce nor as great in amplitude.
   d. Return to your optimum pitch and descend down the scale. Listen carefully to the tone. Did the last tone decrease in power, ease, or quality? Try this procedure several times. If you cannot detect a difference, have someone listen who has a good "ear" for tone to help you judge. You may even wish to stop up one ear by placing your forefinger over the part of your ear covering the canal (the tip called the tragus) in order to hear yourself better. If you cannot tell the difference, it may well be that the tones produced at the optimum level are *not* efficient and you are in need of voice training.

2. Using your optimum pitch, count one-two-three-four-five on a monotone. You may intone slightly (prolong vowel sounds) or even sing. Does the level seem higher or lower than the one you habitually use to initiate tone? Repeat the count. Now simply count one to five in your normal manner. Did the second trial seem higher or lower in pitch than the first? If the habitual level is higher than the optimum, it could well be that the vicissitudes of life are such that they have produced excess tension which has caused you to use a slightly higher modal pitch than your optimum pitch and that the optimum actually sounds low to you.

[6] C–E–G–C refer to notes on the chromatic scale as found on the piano keyboard. C–E–G–C are major intervals of the key of C major (see Figure 4.6).

DETERMINING YOUR HABITUAL PITCH

1. Read the following prose passage in a conversational voice:

> The boy called out, "Wolf, Wolf!"
> and the villagers came out to help him.
> A few days afterward he tried the same
> trick, and again they came to his help.
> Shortly after this a Wolf actually came,
> but this time the villagers thought the
> boy was deceiving them again and nobody
> came to his help.... A liar will
> not be believed, even when he speaks the
> truth.
>
> —Aesop

    a. As you read; the instructor will select several words from the passage that seem to be representative of your habitual level. Underline these words and proceed to step b.

    b. Read the passage again. Prolong the stressed vowels of the underlined words on a steady pitch level. Your instructor will then check the level of this pitch with a pitch pipe or a piano. Continue until all the words that are underlined have been checked. If the pitch levels of the words vary, average them to one level. The result will be your habitual pitch.

2. Repeat Exercise 1, using a fellow student with a good "ear" to locate the pitch levels for you (if you have not been called upon).

3. Using a pitch pipe, select a pitch level within the range found in Exercise 1. If you have not completed this exercise, use your optimum pitch level. Count on a monotone at the pitch level. Now vary your pitch pattern very slightly while counting, but do not change the base level. Does the general level seem consistent with your everyday use? Move to the next note higher on the scale (use half notes, e.g., F to F sharp, etc.). Does the higher one seem more natural? If you still seem to be lower than normal, continue by half notes until you reach a level you feel you use habitually. Now count in a natural manner. Locate the base level. Does this level coincide with the level established in raising by half notes?

4. While you are reading the passage in Exercise 1, the instructor or a classmate will hum the general key you are using. This can be done without difficulty. To check the accuracy of this procedure, the instructor or the classmate will hum slightly above the general level—a difference between his level and yours will be apparent. He may also hum a half or whole note below your general level to demonstrate a disparity. If your classmates are somewhat timid about performing in this manner, have the class as a whole

lightly hum your general level as you read. Use a pitch pipe to check this level just the same as you would do if an individual were doing the checking.

5. Read the following sentences in a conversational manner as follows: (a) at your optimum level (using a pitch pipe to establish), (b) the next higher pitch level, (c) the next higher level, and so on. Stop when you have reached a level that feels high for you. Repeat this exercise but this time descend the scale until you feel the level is low for you. What were the levels that seemed most natural? Actually a whole-note change should make an appreciable difference in your voice.

> a. I don't think it is possible for me to go to the game next week.
> b. I don't think my voice is pitched too high, do you?
> c. The midterm exam didn't cover all of the material presented in class.
> d. I worked for over a month this summer, but didn't make much money.
> e. How do you arrange for tickets when more than one airline is involved?

WHEN TO CHANGE YOUR HABITUAL OR MODAL PITCH

1. If your modal pitch is more than two half notes above or below your optimum pitch, a change may result in a more pleasing and more efficient general level.

2. If your modal pitch is high (more than two half notes), you may have difficulty developing pitch changes in the middle and upper part of your pitch range.

3. If your habitual pitch is below your optimum by more than two half notes, you may not be able to develop adequate downglides at the end of simple, declarative sentences, or complete segments within compound or complex sentences. A range of four notes below the modal pitch is necessary for downglides. If these are not available to you, you will not be able to sustain tone and you will either lapse into a glottal fry (rasping sound), or the ends of your sentences will remain indefinite and sound monotonous.

SELECTIONS

The following selections are particularly good for tone production practice. It is best to work on the shorter selections first before attempting the longer, more demanding ones.

> The curfew tolls the knell of parting day,
>   The lowing herd winds slowly o'er the lea,
> The plowman homeward plods his weary way
>   And leaves the world to darkness and to me.

Now fades the glimmering landscape on the sight,
    And all the air a solemn stillness holds,
Save where the beetle wheels his droning flight,
    And drowsy tinklings lull the distant folds;

Save that from yonder ivy-mantled tower
    The moping owl does to the moon complain
Of such as, wandering near her secret bower,
    Molest her ancient solitary reign.

                    —Thomas Gray

Here, where the world is quiet;
    Here, where all trouble seems
Dead winds' and spent waves' riot
    In doubtful dreams of dreams;
I watch the green field growing
For reaping folk and sowing,
For harvest-time and mowing,
    A sleepy world of streams.

I am tired of tears and laughter,
    And men that laugh and weep,
Of what may come hereafter
    For men that sow to reap;
I am weary of days and hours,
Blown buds of barren flowers,
Desires and dreams and powers,
    And everything but sleep.

           —Algernon Charles Swinburne

The ocean old,
Centuries old,
Strong as youth, and as uncontrolled,
Paces restless to and fro,
Up and down the sands of gold.

His beating heart is not at rest;
And far and wide,
With ceaseless flow,
His beard of snow
Heaves with the heaving of his breast.

           —Henry W. Longfellow

    I then turned toward the Wingdam Temperance Hotel.... It might have been called the "Total Abstinence" Hotel, from the lack of anything to intoxicate or inthrall the senses. It was designed with an eye to artistic dreariness. It was so much large for settlement, that it appeared to be a very slight improvement on out-doors. It was unpleasantly new.

—Bret Harte

Not far from this village, perhaps about two miles, there is a little valley, or rather lap of land, among the hills, which is one of the quietest places in the whole world. A small brook glides through it, with just murmur enough to lull one to repose.... this sequestered glen has long been known by the name of *Sleepy Hollow*.

—Washington Irving

TO SLEEP

A flock of sheep that leisurely pass by,
One after one; the sound of rain, and bees
Murmuring; the fall of rivers, winds and seas,
Smooth fields, white sheets of water, and pure sky;
I've thought of all by turns, and yet do lie
Sleepless! and soon the small birds' melodies
Must hear, first uttered from my orchard trees,
And the first cuckoo's melancholy cry.
Even thus last night, and two nights more, I lay,
And could not win thee, Sleep! by any stealth:
So do not let me wear tonight away:
Without Thee what is all the morning's wealth?
Come, blessed barrier between day and day,
Dear mother of fresh thoughts and joyous health!

—William Wordsworth

SWEET AND LOW

Sweet and low, sweet and low,
  Wind of the western sea,
Low, low, breathe and blow,
  Wind of the western sea!
Over the rolling waters go,
Come from the dying moon, and blow,
  Blow him again to me;

While my little one, while my pretty one, sleeps.
Sleep and rest, sleep and rest,
  Father will come to thee soon;
Rest, rest, on mother's breast,
  Father will come to thee soon;
Father will come to his babe in the nest
Silver sails all out of the west
  Under the silver moon;
Sleep, my little one, sleep, my pretty one, sleep.

—Alfred, Lord Tennyson

A RED, RED ROSE

O my Luve's like a red, red rose
  That's newly sprung in June:
O my Luve's like the melodie
  That's sweetly played in tune.

As fair art thou, my bonnie lass,
  So deep in luve am I;
And I will luve thee still, my dear,
  Till a' the seas gang dry.

Till a' the seas gang dry, my dear,
  And the rocks melt wi' the sun;
I will luve thee still, my dear,
  While the sands o' life shall run.

And fare thee weel, my only Luve!
  And fare thee weel awhile!
And I will come again, my Luve,
  Tho' it were ten thousand mile.

—Robert Burns

THE DAFFODILS

I wandered lonely as a cloud
That floats on high o'er vales and hills,
When all at once I saw a crowd,
A host, of golden daffodils,
Beside the lake, beneath the trees,
Fluttering and dancing in the breeze.

78

Continuous as the stars that shine
And twinkle on the milky way,
They stretched in never-ending line
Along the margin of a bay :
Ten thousand saw I at a glance,
Tossing their heads in sprightly dance.

The waves beside them danced, but they
Outdid the sparkling waves in glee—
A poet could not but be gay
In such a jocund company.
I gazed—and gazed—but little thought
What wealth the show to me had brought.

For oft when on my couch I lie
In vacant or in pensive mood,
They flash upon that inward eye
Which is the bliss of solitude,
And then my heart with pleasure fills,
And dances with the daffodils.

—William Wordsworth

SONNET 29

When, in disgrace with fortune and men's eyes,
I all alone beweep my outcast state,
And trouble deaf heaven with my bootless cries,
And look upon myself and curse my fate,
Wishing me like to one more rich in hope,
Featured like him, like him with friends possessed,
Desiring this man's art and that man's scope,
With what I most enjoy contented least ;
Yet in these thoughts myself almost despising—
Haply I think on thee ; and then my state,
Like to the lark at break of day arising
From sullen earth, sings hymns at heaven's gate ;
    For thy sweet love remembered such wealth brings
    That then I scorn to change my state with kings.

—William Shakespeare

DOVER BEACH

The sea is calm tonight.
The tide is full, the moon lies fair
Upon the straits,—on the French coast the light
Gleams and is gone; the cliffs of England stand,
Glimmering and vast, out in the tranquil bay.
Come to the window, sweet is the night air!
Only, from the long line of spray
Where the sea meets the moon-blanched land,
Listen! you hear the grating roar
Of pebbles which the waves draw back, and fling,
At their return, up the high strand,
Begin, and cease, and then again begin,
With tremulous cadence slow, and bring
The eternal note of sadness in.

Sophocles, long ago,
Heard it on the Aegean, and it brought
Into his mind the turbid ebb and flow
Of human misery; we
Find also in the sound a thought,
Hearing it by this distant northern sea.

The Sea of Faith
Was once, too, at the full, and round earth's shore
Lay like the folds of a bright girdle furled.
But now I only hear
Its melancholy, long, withdrawing roar,
Retreating, to the breath
Of the night-wind, down the vast edges drear
And naked shingles of the world.

Ah, love, let us be true
To one another! for the world, which seems
To lie before us like a land of dreams,
So various, so beautiful, so new,
Hath really neither joy, nor love, nor light,
Nor certitude, nor peace, nor help for pain;
And we are here as on a darkling plain,
Swept with confused alarms of struggle and flight,
Where ignorant armies clash by night.

—Matthew Arnold

From PEER GYNT

(*Scene—Crossroads*. PEER GYNT *is confronted by the* BUTTON MOULDER.)

BUTTON MOULDER: Good morning, Peer Gynt! Where's your list of sins?

PEER GYNT: I assure you that I have shouted and whistled for all I knew!

BUTTON MOULDER: But you found no one?

PEER GYNT: Only a travelling photographer.

BUTTON MOULDER: Well, your time is up.

PEER GYNT: Everything's up. The owl smells a rat. Do you hear him hooting?

BUTTON MOULDER: That's the matins bell—

PEER GYNT (*pointing*): What's that, that's shining?

BUTTON MOULDER: Only a light in a house.

PEER GYNT: That sound like wailing?

BUTTON MOULDER: Only a woman's song.

PEER GYNT: 'Tis there—there I shall find my list of sins!

BUTTON MOULDER (*grasping him by the arm*): Come, set your house in order. (*They have come out of the wood, and are standing near* SOLVEIG'S *hut. Day is dawning.*)

PEER GYNT: Set my house in order? That's it!—Go! Be off! Were your ladle as big as a coffin, I tell you 'twould not hold me and my list!

BUTTON MOULDER: To the third crossroads, Peer; but *then*—! (*Moves aside and disappears.*)

PEER GYNT (*approaching the hut*): Backward or forward, it's just as far; out or in, the way's as narrow. (*Stops.*) No! Like a wild unceasing cry I seem to hear a voice that bids me go in— go back—back to my home. (*Takes a few steps, then stops again.*) "Round about," said the Boyg! (*Hears the sound of singing from the hut*). No; this time it's straight ahead in spite of all, however narrow be the way! (*Runs towards the hut. At the same time* SOLVEIG *comes to the door, guiding her steps with a stick* [*for she is nearly blind*]. *She is dressed for church and carries a prayer-book wrapped up in a handkerchief. She stands still, erect and gentle.*)

PEER GYNT (*throwing himself down on the threshold*): Pronounce the sentence of a sinner!

SOLVEIG: 'Tis he! 'Tis he! Thanks be to God. (*Gropes for him.*)

PEER GYNT: Tell me how sinfully I have offended!

81

SOLVEIG: You have sinned in nothing, my own dear lad! (*Gropes for him again, and finds him.*)

BUTTON MOULDER (*from behind the hut*): Where is that list of sins, Peer Gynt?

PEER GYNT: Cry out, cry out my sins aloud!

SOLVEIG (*sitting down beside him*): You have made my life a beautiful song. Bless you for having come back to me! And blest be this morn of Pentecost!

PEER GYNT: Then I am lost!

SOLVEIG: There is One who will help.

PEER GYNT (*with a laugh*): Lost! Unless you can solve a riddle!

SOLVEIG: What is it?

PEER GYNT: What is it? You shall hear. Can you tell me where Peer Gynt has been since last we met?

SOLVEIG: Where he has been?

PEER GYNT: With the mark of destiny on his brow—the man that he was when a thought of God's created him! Can you tell me that? If not, I must go to my last home in the land of shadows.

SOLVEIG (*smiling*): That riddle's easy.

PEER GYNT: Tell me, then—where was my real self, complete and true—the Peer who bore the stamp of God upon his brow?

SOLVEIG: In my faith, in my hope and in my love.

PEER GYNT: What are you saying? It is a riddle that you are speaking now. So speaks a mother of her child.

SOLVEIG: Ah, yes; and that is what I am; but He who grants a pardon for the sake of a mother's prayers, He is his father. (*A ray of light seems to flash on* PEER GYNT. *He cries out.*)

PEER GYNT: Mother and wife! You stainless woman! Oh, hide me, hide me in your love! (*Clings to her and buries his face in her lap. There is a long silence. The sun rises.*)

SOLVEIG (singing softly):

Sleep, my boy, my dearest boy!
I will rock you to sleep and guard you.

The boy has sat on his mother's lap.
The two have played the livelong day.

The boy has lain on his mother's breast
The livelong day. God bless you, my sweet!

The boy has lain so close to my heart
The livelong day. He is weary now.

Sleep, my boy, my dearest boy!
I will rock you to sleep and guard you.

(*The* BUTTON MOULDER's *voice is heard from behind the hut.*)
BUTTON MOULDER: At the last crossroads I shall meet you,
Peer; *then* we'll see—whether——! I say no more.
SOLVEIG (*singing louder in the sunshine*): I will rock you
to sleep and guard you! Sleep and dream, my dearest boy!

—Henrik Ibsen

SUPPLEMENTARY SELECTIONS FOR CLASS PRESENTATION
The Ballad of Reading Gaol, Oscard Wilde, *poetry.*
Blowin' in the Wind, Bob Dylan, *poetry.*
The Rime of the Ancient Mariner, Samuel Taylor Coleridge, *poetry.*
The Rubaiyat of Omar Khayyam, Edward Fitzgerald, *poetry.*

CHAPTER
SIX

developing vocal resonance

IN THE LAST chapter we were concerned primarily with producing and manipulating an efficient laryngeal tone. This tone, when it lacks resonation, is very low in intensity and sounds more like a buzz than a human voice. The process of enlarging and modifying the laryngeal tone is known as resonation.

RESONATION DEFINED

The word resonance comes from the Latin word, *resonantia,* meaning echo, and may be simply defined as "the quality or state of being resonant." Resonance can be further defined as the reinforcement and prolongation of a sound by reflection or by the vibration of other bodies. Keep in mind that resonance has nothing to do with the production of sound energy, but it has everything to do with the amplifying and moulding of this energy into the sounds we hear in speech. Resonation is a process in which there is typically a concentration and reflection of sound waves in a confined volume. In order to grasp the full meaning of resonance, we must study this phenomenon in its various components.

SYMPATHETIC VIBRATION, FORCED VIBRATION, AND CAVITY RESONANCE

In the study of the process of resonance, three concepts are of importance, since all three play a part in human resonance; they are sympathetic vibration, forced vibration, and cavity resonance.

SYMPATHETIC VIBRATION

When the sound source and the resonator are in close agreement because of their physical properties, maximum amplification occurs. This principle can be explained by the following analogy. If a child on a swing is being pushed by her father, the latter waits until the youngster has reached the top of the backswing before giving her the next push. If he repeats this act without increasing force, he can easily attain and maintain the maximum amplitude of swing. Literally, the energy source, the father, is in sympathy with the swing of the child. If, however, the father's timing is poor, he might partly reduce the swing by catching it too soon, on the backswing before the top is reached, thereby losing some of his force. In this case he is not in sympathy with the swing.

The principle of sympathetic vibration is used extensively in musical instruments, particularly the xylophone, which has a sound source and resonator in sharp tuning to each other. Old parlor tricks often use this same principle. For example, a famous tenor used to fill a wine glass to a given level and then hum high C. He kept adding wine until the airspace in the goblet was in sharp tuning with his note. After his guests arrived, he volunteered to sing an aria. As you might guess, when he sang the high C, the wine glass shattered and the guests were overcome with admiration for the tenor's tremendous power. You too can experiment with this principle by filling a water glass to a given level and making it whine by circling your forefinger vigorously over the moistened lip.

FORCED VIBRATION

The principle of forced vibration is perhaps a little easier to understand, for it is exactly what the term implies. If the source of energy is great enough, it can cause a given body to vibrate regardless of tuning, i.e., the source in this case need not be in tuning with the vibrating object. If you strike a table top with your hand, you create a sound because the table is forced to vibrate even though it is not sharply tuned to the energy source, the blow of your hand. The resultant sound of a plucked tuning fork will be amplified if held to a table top simply because the energy imparted by the fork is great enough to cause the table to vibrate. The table top in this case is definitely not in tune with the tuning fork. A resonator can be constructed in such a way as to function as a broad resonator; that is, it may be responsive in a general way to a broad range of frequencies without being sharply tuned to any particular one. The piano sounding board, which is comprised of many pieces of wood of different sizes, is a good example of a broad resonator.

CAVITY RESONANCE

Part of our definition of resonance includes the concept of the "concentration and reflection of sound waves in a confined volume." In order to demonstrate cavity resonance, try the following experiment. Either in a group or individually, initiate an *ah* sound. Do not vary your level of intensity while you are producing the tone. Now, cup your hands around your mouth like a megaphone. Your voice becomes much louder does it not? The size, shape, wall construction, openings, and coupling of any given cavity govern its function as a resonator. The following principles explain these factors:

Size or Volume. The greater the volume of a cavity, the lower is the frequency at which it will resonate efficiently.

Size of Opening. The larger the opening of a cavity, the higher the frequency at which it will resonate.

Passageway or Neck of Opening. The longer the passageway, the lower the frequency at which it will resonate.

Construction of Walls. The harder and the more dense the walls of a resonator, the more efficiently it will reflect the energy contained in the higher overtones. Much energy can be absorbed into the wall of a cavity if it is made of a soft, deep spongy material. A reverberation or echo chamber has very hard walls made of a special cement, while an anechoic chamber has wedgelike projections of its walls stuffed with highly absorbent materials.

With these principles in mind, study the models in Figure 6.1.

COUPLING OF RESONATORS

Each resonator in the same system of amplification, i.e., amplifying the same sound source, has an effect upon the end product one hears. The

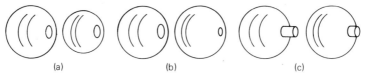

Condition:	Volume		Opening		Neck	
Size:	Large	Small	Large	Small	Long	Short
Frequency:	Lower	Higher	Higher	Lower	Lower	Higher

Figure 6.1. Relationship of size and openings of a resonator to frequency.

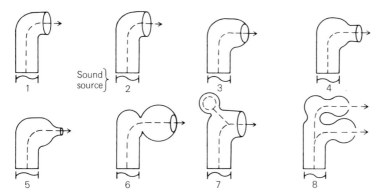

Figure 6.2. Modification of resonance by manipulation of size, coupling, and openings.

examples in Figure 6.2 illustrate how adding or modifying resonators in the same system can change the quality of the sound heard.

Assume in the above models that the sound source is a broad band buzz similar to a laryngeal tone.

1. Resonator 1 is a simple, single resonating system. The frequency it will amplify is determined by its size, shape, walls, and opening.

2. Resonator 2, because it is larger than resonator 1, will sound lower in pitch.

3. Resonator 3 has a smaller opening than resonator 2 and will consequently sound lower in pitch.

4. Even though resonator 4 has the same size opening as resonator 3, it will modify the tone to a lower level because of its neck.

5. Resonator 5 has a smaller neck than resonator 4, which will make the tone higher, but the smaller opening will lower the tone.

6. In resonator 6 two resonators have been placed in series. Since one resonator is smaller than the other in this system, the modification of the tone is more complex than in the single-resonator system.

7. A side resonator or cul-de-sac has been added in model 7. Provided the neck is not too long or the opening too restrictive, the side resonator can modify the tone produced by the main resonating passageway considerably.

8. The strange looking resonator 8 has been devised to illustrate a system with two pathways for the passage of sound waves. Human resonation may be related to this model with one notable exception, that the openings can be manipulated, changing the simple model depicted here.

The above models help us to understand human resonance better and will be referred to in the following discussion.

RESONANCE IN THE HUMAN VOICE

Resonance in the human voice is provided principally by three cavities, the *pharynx*, which is the chamber back of the nose and mouth and above the larynx, the *oral cavity* or mouth, and the *nasal cavity*. The factor of greatest importance about the pharynx and the oral cavity is their marvelous ability to adjust. They can be lengthened or shortened, widened or narrowed, made to have soft or hard walls, and can be modified to exclude part or all of certain cavities. The ability to change the characteristics of these two cavities is utilized in human speech to resonate tones with a great variety of quality and pitch, thus forming the different sounds of our spoken language—the vowels, consonants, and diphthongs.

To illustrate just how this principle works with our voices in forming the various sounds of speech, try the following experiments:

1. Initiate an easy tone, *ah*, as in *father*. While producing the tone, form an *ee* sound as in *see*. Repeat, *ah-ee*. Note how radically you change the shape of your mouth to accomplish this feat. You might have recognized the personal pronoun "I" in the process. Not only did the cavity change shape, but the opening was also considerably altered.

2. Prolong the sound *l* as in *low*. Notice how you have partly shut off the front part of your mouth and sent the voiced breath stream around your tongue. The change from the cavities created in Exercise 1 is marked. Contrast the difference between the shape of this cavity and the two you created in Exercise 1.

3. Now prolong the *n* in *no*. Notice now that you have completely shut off the front part of your mouth and have sent the voiced breath stream through your nose, thus creating an entirely different sound from the *l* in Exercise 2. Contrast *l* and *n* on one voiced breath stream. Analyze the changes taking place in the resonators.

4. As a last experiment, whisper the word *how*. Notice that the intensity is greatly decreased in spite of the fact that the sound source is being resonated. The laryngeal tone with its wealth of overtones is much more powerful and easier to resonate than is the relatively weak noise band of a whisper.

If we are to manipulate the human resonators in order to improve our voices, it is desirable to analyze the structure and function of them in sufficient detail to permit understanding.

THE MOUTH AS A RESONATOR

Of all the resonators the mouth is the most flexible and adaptable for amplifying the laryngeal tone. The size may vary from small to large, depending on the position of the tongue and jaw. The wall construction of the mouth likewise varies from hard to soft. The teeth, the hard palate, and the gums are hard, while the side walls and tongue are made up of muscles and linings which are relatively soft. The latter walls may vary (soft-hard), depending upon the degree of contraction of the muscles. The oral cavity varies in shape in speech production depending upon the position of the tongue and lower jaw. The oral cavity has two openings—one at the front, the lips, and one at the back, the opening to the oropharynx; both openings are highly adjustable. The oral cavity is coupled with the pharynx.

THE PHARYNX AS A RESONATOR

The pharynx is the large cavity which extends from the top of the larynx up to and including the cavity back of the nasal vault (see Figure 3.1). As the chapter on respiration explains, the pharynx is divided into three sections: the laryngopharynx, the part of the pharynx just above the larynx; the oropharynx, the part back of the mouth; and the nasopharynx, the part back of the nasal cavity. Taken as a whole, the pharynx is second to the mouth in the number of adjustment possibilities. The adjustments are controlled by the action of the muscles of the larynx, the soft palate, and the tongue.

The *laryngopharynx* varies in size and shape during the production of speech sounds. By the upward and downward movement of the larynx, plus the contracting and relaxing of the muscles of the pharyngeal wall, the diameter and length of the laryngopharynx can be changed easily and speedily to modify resonance. The varying degree of tension of the muscular walls of this resonator makes different values possible. The resonator is coupled below to the larynx and above to the oropharynx.

The *oropharynx* is a fairly large, highly adjustable resonator located behind the oral cavity. The walls are chiefly made up of muscles which may vary in tension. The tongue and soft palate are of key importance in modifying the size and shape of this resonator. When the soft palate moves upward and backward to seal off the nasopharynx, the oropharynx is not only enlarged but the nasal cavity as well as the nasopharynx is excluded from the system. As the tongue moves forward or backward or is placed high or low in the mouth, the oropharynx is changed in size and shape. The oropharynx may be joined with other resonators such as (a) the laryngopharynx, (b) the oral cavity, and (c) the nasopharynx (see Figure 3.1). The size of the opening between the oropharynx and the oral cavity can be manipulated to good effect in voice training, as it can by the judicious use of the nasopharynx on nonnasal sounds.

The *nasopharynx*, or upper part of the pharynx, is located behind the nasal cavity. The walls vary in hardness and softness, as the bony structure of the head is hard, while the muscles of the soft palate and upper pharynx are relatively soft. Normally the nasopharynx is sealed off from the main passageway for speech on all sounds except *m*, *n*, and *ng*. The size and shape of this cavity does not vary to any extent on the production of

nasal sounds. The action of sealing off the nasopharynx from the oropharynx is known as velopharyngeal valving. If the timing of the closure
is poor or incomplete, nasality on nonnasal sounds results.

THE NASAL CAVITY AS RESONATOR

The nasal passages are relatively large, vault-shaped, and almost inflexible.
The cavity is divided into two separate chambers by the nasal septum. The
septum extends from the cartilaginous portion readily felt and seen in
the nose to the bony plate, which extends backward to the posterior openings
leading to the nasopharynx. Because the walls are fixed, nothing can be
done during speech to change their size and alter resonation. The only
possible means of changing nasal resonation is to pinch the nostrils and
occlude the opening, an unlikely procedure for normal behavior during
speech.

In spite of the size of the nasal vault, its resonating volume is greatly
reduced because of the three sets of turbinate bones, membranous linings,
and hair projections, which nearly fill the two chambers. Because of the
occlusion of the nasal passageways by these structures, it is often difficult
to keep them open and clear of obstructions, particularly as so many people
are susceptible to colds, infections, and allergies, which swell the linings,
and to sinus discharges, not to mention growths, deviations, and other
problems. When the nasal vault is closed, denasality, or "cold-in-the-head"
speech results.

In order to understand nasal resonance better, study the three models
depicted in Figure 6.3. Notice that the mouth functions as a side resonator
for the main resonating pathway, which emits the voiced breath stream out
of the nose on *m, n,* and *ng.* On each of the first two sounds, *m,* and *n,* the
tongue assumes a different position, changing the size and shape of the
mouth, which is the side resonator. The mouth is blocked off entirely on *ng.*

Reinforcement of Nonnasal Sounds by Nasal Emission

Some voice teachers think that vibrations from the oropharynx and
mouth actually pass through the closed stretched soft palate and the thin

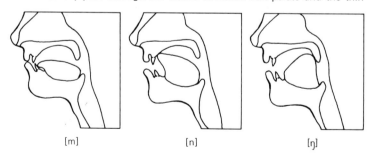

Figure 6.3. Positions of tongue and soft palate for [m], [n], and [ŋ].

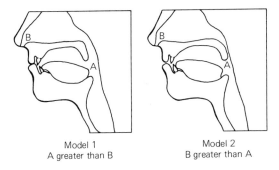

Model 1
A greater than B

Model 2
B greater than A

Figure 6.4. Relationship of opening at soft palate and pharynx to anterior nares.

bony floor of the nasal vault and have sufficient energy to concentrate and reflect sound waves in the nasopharynx and the nasal cavity, giving a degree of reinforcement to nonnasal sounds. While this may possibly be true, experimental evidence is lacking to verify this point of view.

There is a strong belief among successful voice teachers that nonnasal sounds can be reinforced by the nasopharynx and nasal cavities if done properly. The crux of the argument lies in the amount of opening used to couple the oropharynx with the nasopharynx. Observe the two models in Figure 6.4.

In Model 1, the opening between the oropharynx and nasopharynx A is greater than the opening at the nostrils B, and a cul-de-sac is created in the nose, causing unwanted nasality. In Model 2, the opening at the nostrils B is greater than at the opening at the nasopharynx and oropharynx A, and desirable reinforcement of the main passageway resonance is attained. The conclusion one may reach with this line of reasoning is that it is possible to obtain reinforcement of the tone by carefully adjusting the velopharyngeal valve to an opening slightly less than that of the nostrils. This would have to be done by training one's sense of hearing to detect the difference between a properly reinforced tone and unwanted nasality. The great danger lies in the possibility that one could overdo it and unwittingly develop nasal speech.

THE SINUSES

The part played by the sinuses as resonators is not entirely known. The majority of voice scientists feel that the tubes connecting the sinuses with the nasal cavities are too small to admit sound waves for resonation. The sinuses adversely affect both resonation and tone production by becoming infected and sending a discharge into the nasal passageways and posteriorly to the pharynx. The argument that *mask* or *face* resonance is attributable to the sinuses seems to be both anatomically and physiologically unlikely.

TYPES OF VOICE QUALITY

The quality of a person's voice is usually judged subjectively rather than objectively. We do not have a scientific standard to which all voices can be compared, hence we listen to a voice and judge it favorably or unfavorably, ranging from good to bad. However, most people can do an able job of selecting good voices from bad. What, then, is the basis for our judgment?

The concept of the normal voice is deeply embedded in our linguistic habits and culture. We are attuned by our environment to the way we use our voice, and deviations are quicky spotted and rejected. For example, strident, nasal, harsh, or guttural voices are easily identified as different from normally resonated voices. Therefore, we know what we do not like— at least in others. On the other hand we admire a full, rich voice.

Several identifiable voice qualities that are directly related to faulty resonation will be briefly discussed in this section. These are voices that are nasal, denasal, strident, guttural, or thin. Three other voice quality types, the hoarse, harsh, and juvenile voice, were discussed in the previous chapter dealing with tone production.

NORMAL AND OROTUND VOICE QUALITY

Normal voice quality is usually available to a large majority of speakers, provided of course that no problems of structure or function exist. As an experiment, pretend your pharynx and oral cavities are like a megaphone. Take a deep breath, open your mouth and throat, and sigh *ah*. Repeat, but this time make it a little louder; do not get tense in any way. The result should be a somewhat breathy tone on the first trial, then a more resonant tone on the second attempt. Repeat until you are convinced that you have a capacity for greater resonance than you are now using.

Speech sounds require a wide range of adjustments of the articulators which modify the sizes and shapes of the resonators and change the resonance values. Two of the best ways to improve vocal resonance are: (a) learning how to get maximum results on the more sonorous speech sounds, and (b) learning how to link sounds and build up resonance within the phrase to greater advantage.

The majority of exercises in this chapter provide specific techniques for developing better vocal resonance in speech. As one becomes successful in developing a full, resonant voice, which is often labeled "orotund" in its extreme form, he must heed the advice of the professionals, "Don't fall in love with the sound of your own voice." In other words do not intone or manipulate your voice while you are talking to someone else or you will sound artificial.

NASALITY

Nasality as a speech problem refers to an undesirable voice quality on non-nasal speech sounds as a result of nasal emission of the voiced breath stream. The causes of nasality are too broad and complex to warrant treatment here. If one has a chronic problem of nasality, he should consult a speech pathologist.

The borderline nasality problems encountered in basic voice classes usually are learned behaviors and can be eradicated with practice. The person with incipient nasality must recognize that he has a problem, for in most cases of this sort, he may not be aware that his speech is slightly nasal. Discrimination exercises are usually needed before correction of the problem can begin. These should be followed by drill on the exercises for faulty nasal resonance, which are contained in this chapter. Working with another person to help him judge whether or not he is succeeding is highly advisable.

All of us should be aware that certain conditions sometimes prevail that may cause us to be nasal:

1. Nasality is most apt to occur on speech sounds that immediately precede or follow the nasal sounds, *m, n,* and *ng.* The nasal port is either opened too soon or is closed too late, and nasal emission is heard on the sounds adjacent to the nasal. The condition is known as assimilation nasality. To demonstrate this point, try the sentence, "Many men met at the music center," permitting the vowels adjacent to the nasal consonants to become nasalized.

2. Mid-vowels, such as the *a* in *father,* the *a* in *cat,* and the *a* in *law,* are prone to becoming nasalized. Speech scientists point out that as the tongue and jaw descend to produce these sounds, the soft palate, which is connected to the tongue by the anterior pillars of fauces, is pulled downward and forward at a time when it is attempting to move backwards to effect a closure of the nasal port.

3. The vowel *ee* as in *see* is often nasalized, particularly when coupled with a nasal consonant. The belief is that the high, front position of the apex of the tongue has a tendency to occlude the oral cavity somewhat and drive the voiced breath stream through the nasal passageways.

DENASALITY

Denasality has already been described as a voice lacking nasal resonance on the nasal sounds *m, n,* and *ng.* These sounds end up being pronounced *b, d,* and *g,* respectively, or left out altogether. Most of us have experienced this type of speech at one time or another when suffering from a head cold. The nasal passages are either blocked or are seriously reduced in size, and nasal resonance is either muffled or blocked. To demonstrate this quality, pinch your nostrils slightly and say the following sentence aloud: "Marie sang many songs." Do you detect a difference in your voice? Now, pinch your nostrils firmly, blocking the air passageways completely. The result this time should be both amusing and nearly unintelligible.

If the blockage of the nasal passageways is chronic, the problem should be handled by a physician. Functionally, one can decrease the amount of nasality by shortening the length of the nasal consonants somewhat, making the problem less noticeable. One might also work on voice placement.

STRIDENT VOICE QUALITY

The strident voice is characterized by a certain hard quality that makes the voice seem a little higher in pitch than it actually is and louder than is needed for the situation. There are times when all of us have strident voices. For example, contrast the difference between your voice quality in a heated argument and in a quiet conversation with a friend.

If the voice is habitually strident, relaxation exercises of the head and neck are helpful as a first-aid measure. The best way to solve this problem is to work on the negative emotional states that give rise to tension. Normal resonation exercises, if needed, should then follow.

GUTTURAL VOICE QUALITY

The guttural voice is characterized by a predominance of lower pharyngeal resonance, which is often accompanied by a harsh or "gravelly" voice quality. During the production of a guttural tone, the posterior portion of the tongue tends to occlude the lower pharynx, and the intrinsic muscles of the larynx are poorly coordinated. Tension is also evident in the lower pharyngeal walls and in the extrinsic muscles of the larynx. The end result is a poorly placed, unpleasant voice quality often associated with the "tough" or "heavy" in the acting profession.

To eliminate any tendency in this direction, open up the pharyngeal resonators by moving the tongue forward, relax the uninvolved muscles in the neck and jaw, work on tone production, and attempt forward placement of the tone. A good voice therapist can materially help the person with a habitually guttural voice.

THIN OR WEAK VOICE QUALITY

Many voices simply do not have enough resonance, and for lack of a better term, we call the voice quality "thin" or "weak." This type of voice is easily recognized in the classroom as being flat, lacking in vitality or interest, and insufficiently loud.

While the problem is chiefly one of resonance, tone production may also be involved, as we need sound energy to be concentrated and reflected in the resonators. The weak voice may also be directly linked with vitality or personality, as a person having this voice quality may be physically weak, introverted, unduly fearful, anxious, or shy. Assuming that the underlying causes can be overcome, those with weak voices need to work on the entire vocal process, starting with adequate breath support and control, and continuing on with tone production and resonation exercises.

94

GOALS AND CRITERIA FOR RESONANCE

Goal	Criterion
1. To develop the ability to analyze voice for resonance.	Make a successful analysis of another student's voice.
2. To achieve good resonance of the sonorous speech sounds.	Perform exercises 5 and 6 on pages 99–100 successfully.
3. To achieve good resonance by duration and run-on resonance.	Read 20 frames of Exercise 3, on page 102, getting a score of 80 percent of the frames judged correctly done.
4. To develop the ability to use four levels of loudness with ease.	Perform Exercise 2 on page 104 successfully.
5. To eliminate poor voice quality because of nasality.	Read a selection in front of the class that is judged free from nasality.
6. To be able to change voice quality to suit meaning.	Demonstrate ability by successfully performing the two stanzas of Poe's "The Bells" on page 97.

PHONETIC POWER

When working on resonation exercises be aware that the sounds of American English vary in acoustic power when effort is held constant. The most powerful sound [ɔ] as in *saw*, for example, is 680 times as loud as [θ] in *thin*. A chart of the phonetic power of speech sounds is useful in determining the power of one sound to another, and can be helpful in locating the best place to develop resonance in words.

CHART OF PHONETIC POWER RATIOS

Phoneme[1]	Ratio to [θ]	Phoneme	Ratio to [θ]	Phoneme	Ratio to [θ]
[ɔ]	680	[r]	210	[t]	15
[a]	600	[l]	100	[g]	15
[ʌ]	510	[ʃ]	80	[k]	13
[æ]	490	[ŋ]	73	[v]	12
[oʊ]	470	[m]	52	[ð]	11
[ʊ]	460	[tʃ]	42	[b]	7
[eɪ]	370	[n]	36	[d]	7
[ɛ]	350	[j]	23	[p]	6
[u]	310	[dʒ]	20	[f]	5
[ɪ]	260	[z]	16	[θ]	1
[i]	220	[s]	16		

[1] *The phonemes are arranged in this chart according to their phonetic power. The values are expressed in terms of a ratio, e.g., [f] is 5 times more powerful than [θ]; [ɔ] is 680 times more powerful than [θ].*

SUMMARY

1. Most vowels and diphthongs are easily resonated. Notable exceptions are the short and indefinite vowels [ɪ], [ʊ], [ə], and [ɚ], as in thin, put, the, and father.

2. The consonantal glides and nasals, [w], [j], [l], [r], [m], [n], and [ŋ], are easily resonated.

3. Other voiced consonants are not as resonant as those indicated above chiefly because the resonators are either occluded or partly occluded during production; these are [v], [ð], [z], [ʒ], and [b], [d], and [g].

4. The voiceless consonants are not sonorous, and thus are not suitable for resonation. These are [f], [s], [ʃ], [h], [p], [t], and [k].

ANALYSIS OF VOICE FOR VOCAL RESONANCE

Choose one of the three selections below for presentation to the class using the following rating scale in judging class performances for resonance. A perfect score of 5 points for each of the four items judged will yield 20 points. The lowest score possible is 4. At least three persons should judge each performance; scores should be averaged. Interpret each score according to the following ratings: 18–20 points, Excellent; 15–17 points, Good; 12–14, Average; 9–11, Fair; below 9, Poor.

RESONANCE RATING CHART

Item	Poor 1	Fair 2	Points Average 3	Good 4	Excellent 5	Score[1]:
Achieves resonance on key words.						
Loudness suits material, class size.						
Ability to change resonance to suit material.						
Freedom from faulty voice quality						
					Grand Total:	

[1] Check appropriate column and place score in the right hand column; total scores when complete.

THE BELLS

Hear the sledges with the bells—
    Silver bells !
What a world of merriment their melody foretells !
How they tinkle, tinkle, tinkle,
    In the icy air of night !
    While the stars that oversprinkle
    All the heavens, seem to twinkle
        With a crystalline delight ;
    Keeping time, time, time,
    In a sort of Runic rhyme,
To the tintinnabulation that so musically wells
    From the bells. . . .

Hear the mellow wedding bells—
    Golden bells !
What a world of happiness their harmony foretells !
    Through the balmy air of night
    How they ring out their delight !—
        From the molten-golden notes,
        And all in tune,
        What a liquid ditty floats
To the turtle-dove that listens, while she gloats
        On the moon. . . .

                                —Edgar Allan Poe

ROLL ON

Roll on, thou deep and dark blue Ocean—roll !
Ten thousand fleets sweep over thee in vain ;
Man marks the earth with ruin—his control
Stops with the shore ;—upon the watery plain
The wrecks are all thy deed, nor doth remain
A shadow of man's ravage, save his own,
When, for a moment, like a drop of rain,
He sinks into thy depths with bubbling groan,
Without a grave, unknelled, uncoffined, and unknown.

                                —George Gordon, Lord Byron

97

OZYMANDIAS

I met a traveller from an antique land
Who said : "Two vast and trunkless legs of stone
Stand in the desert. Near them, on the sand,
Half sunk, a shattered visage lies, whose frown,
And wrinkled lip, and sneer of cold command,
Tell that its sculptor well those passions read
Which yet survive, stamped on these lifeless things,
The hand that mocked them, and the heart that fed :
And on the pedestal these words appear :
'My name is Ozymandias, king of kings :
Look on my works, ye Mighty, and despair !'
Nothing beside remains. Round the decay
Of that colossal wreck, boundless and bare,
The lone and level sands stretch far away."

—Percy Bysshe Shelley

EXERCISES FOR DEVELOPING ORAL AND PHARYNGEAL RESONANCE

1. Practice the following syllable chains to develop better resonance. Instructions: (a) use good breath support, (b) relax the lower jaw and tongue, (c) open oral and pharyngeal passageways, (d) use a downward inflection, and (e) pause slightly between each syllable in the breath group.

[ɑ]	yah-yah-yah-yah-yah-yah-yah-yah.
[ɔ]	yaw-yaw-yaw-yaw-yaw-yaw-yaw-yaw.
[oʊ]	yo-yo-yo-yo-yo-yo-yo-yo.
[ɑ]	mah-mah-mah-mah-mah-mah-mah-mah.
[ɔ]	maw-maw-maw-maw-maw-maw-maw-maw.
[oʊ]	mow-mow-mow-mow-mow-mow-mow-mow.
[ɑ]	rah-rah-rah-rah-rah-rah-rah-rah.
[ɔ]	raw-raw-raw-raw-raw-raw-raw-raw.
[oʊ]	row-row-row-row-row-row-row-row.

2. Try the following syllable chains, only this time begin from a wide open position :

[ɑ]	ahm-ahm-ahm-ahm-ahm-ahm-ahm-ahm-ahm.
[ɔ]	awm-awm-awm-awm-awm-awm-awm-awm-awm.
[oʊ]	ohm-ohm-ohm-ohm-ohm-ohm-ohm-ohm-ohm-ohm.
[ɑ]	are-are-are-are-are-are-are-are-are-are-are.
[ɔ]	or-or-or-or-or-or-or-or-or-or-or.
[oʊ]	ore-ore-ore-ore-ore-ore-ore-ore-ore-ore-ore.
[ɑ]	ahl-ahl-ahl-ahl-ahl-ahl-ahl-ahl-ahl-ahl-ahl.
[ɔ]	all-all-all-all-all-all-all-all-all-all-all.
[oʊ]	ole-ole-ole-ole-ole-ole-ole-ole-ole-ole-ole.

3. Try to bring the pharynx into greater use on the following syllable chains. Imagine you are making a megaphone out of your throat and mouth. If you can remain relaxed, use a little more force without raising your voice.

[ɑ]	ha-ha-ha-ha-ha-ha-ha-ha-ha-ha.
[oʊ]	ho-ho-ho-ho-ho-ho-ho-ho-ho-ho.
[ɔ]	haw-haw-haw-haw-haw-haw-haw-haw-haw-haw.
[ɔ]	caw-caw-caw-caw-caw-caw-caw-caw-caw-caw.
[ɑ]	bah-bah-bah-bah-bah-bah-bah-bah-bah-bah.
[ɔ]	gaw-gaw-gaw-gaw-gaw-gaw-gaw-gaw-gaw-gaw.
[oʊ]	go-go-go-go-go-go-go-go-go-go.

4. Diphthongs, which are made up of two sounds, the first stressed and the second unstressed, always start from an open position and move toward a more closed one. Be sure to get good opening of the mouth on the first element, and be sure to give it plenty of power and duration. These sounds are excellent for developing additional force in speech. The last five chains start with a plosive in order to make the exercise more difficult; try to retain good voice quality.

[aʊ]	how-how-how-how-how-how-how-how-how-how.
[aɪ]	my-my-my-my-my-my-my-my-my-my.
[eɪ]	aim-aim-aim-aim-aim-aim-aim-aim-aim-aim.
[oʊ]	know-know-know-know-know-know-know-know.
[ɔɪ]	boy-boy-boy-boy-boy-boy-boy-boy-boy-boy.
[iɚ]	dear-dear-dear-dear-dear-dear-dear-dear-dear-dear.
[ɛɚ]	pair-pair-pair-pair-pair-pair-pair-pair-pair-pair.
[ʊɚ]	poor-poor-poor-poor-poor-poor-poor-poor-poor-poor.
[oɚ]	door-door-door-door-door-door-door-door-door-door.

5. Practice the following sentences, attempting to achieve good oral and pharyngeal resonance:
  a. It's a seemly and Christian-like custom indeed this casting a so-called memorial glance in charity over the life that is ended.
  b. He is like a wine-skin that perishes or a garment that moths have eaten.
  c. All autumn we sought the haunts of the deer.
  d. Low on the ground creeps the Irish moss.
  e. I know thou hast spoken wisely.
  f. The old boat groaned and moaned as forty boarded her.
  g. Annoy, deploy, decoy, destroy are the artifices used in ambush.
  h. The smoke hung like a pall over the mall.
  i. The donkey balked as the old man talked.
  j. Caw, caw, caw, called the crow from the live oak's bough.

6. Practice oral and pharyngeal resonance on the following short selections:

How sweet the moonlight sleeps upon this bank!
Here will we sit, and let the sounds of music
Creep in our ears; soft stillness and the night
Become the touches of sweet harmony.
Sit, Jessica; look how the floor of heaven
Is thick inlaid with patines of bright gold;
There's not the smallest orb which thou behold'st,
But in his motion like an angel sings,
Still quiring to the young-eyed cherubins;
Such harmony is in immortal souls,
But whilst this muddy vesture of decay
Doth grossly close it in, we cannot hear it. . . .

—William Shakespeare

OUT IN THE FIELDS

The little cares that fretted me,
    I lost them yesterday
Among the fields above the seas,
    Among the winds at play,
Among the lowing of the herds,
    The rustling of the trees,
Among the singing of the birds,
    The humming of the bees.
The foolish fears of what might happen,—
    I cast them all away
Among the clover-scented grass,
    Among the new-mown hay;
Among the husking of the corn,
    Where drowsy poppies nod,
Where ill thoughts die and good are born,
    Out in the fields with God.

—Elizabeth Barrett Browning

In the Fir Cone Tavern a merry group was gathered, drinking and dicing. The door swung noisily open and a strange figure entered, a man of middle height, spare and slight. His face was bronzed by sun and wind, his dark hair long and unkempt, his eyes bright and quick. . . . He was dressed in faded finery.

100

His ruined cloak was tilted by a long sword and in his leathern belt a vellum-bound book of verse kept company with a dagger. It was François Villon, scholar.

—Justin Huntley McCarthy

DURATION AND RUN-ON RESONANCE

The use of greater duration and run-on resonance can be particularly effective in developing vocal power if done properly. Duration refers to the time element involved in producing a sound or word while run-on resonance refers to eliding words in order to prevent loss of energy due to cessation of phonation between words.

Man speaks primarily in sound sequences made up of many syllables and words. True, we pause and often repeat, but for the most part we utter consecutive syllables. We obtain meaning by decoding the consecutive bombardment of articulated sounds. For example, try the two sound sequences, *Constantinople* and *Can't stand the opal.* Phonemically, they are almost the same, and it is only the meaning we assign instantaneously to the latter that divides the sentences into discrete words. Many speakers have a tendency to utter words individually with little elision with the next word. This tendency may well be a throwback to an earlier time when they were taught to read—one word at a time!

EXERCISES

1. Practice the following sentences, attempting to vary duration and words as marked:

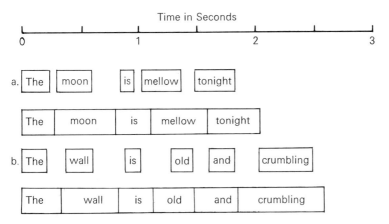

2. Study the sonogram (sound energy) of sentence *a*, "The moon is mellow tonight"; the upper sonogram shows the sentence done without run-on resonance, while the lower depicts this type of resonance (Figure 6.5).

THE   MOON   IS   MELLOW   TONIGHT

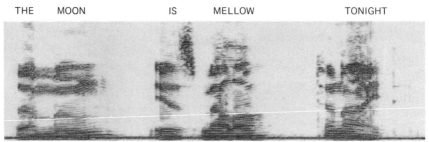

(a) Short duration to "run-on" resonance.

THE   MOON   IS   MELLOW   TONIGHT

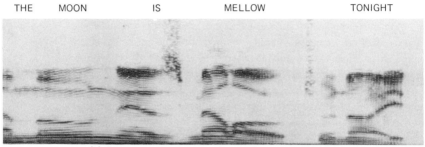

(b) Greater duration than in a; "run-on" resonance apparent.

Figure 6.5. Sonograms of "The moon is mellow tonight."

3. Optional operant conditioning exercise:

Frames		Frames		Frames	
1	moon	17	I want to go home	33	sand
2	the moon	18	ghost	34	the sand
3	on the moon	19	the ghost	35	to the sand
4	man on the moon	20	saw the ghost	36	falls to the sand
5	him	21	I saw the ghost	37	ball falls to the sand
6	to him	22	haul	38	the ball falls to the sand
7	give it to him	23	may haul	39	years
8	I give it to him	24	you may haul	40	future years
9	calm	25	now you may haul	41	of future years
10	is calm	26	soon	42	hopes of future years
11	sea is calm	27	how soon	43	thunder
12	the sea is calm	28	know how soon	44	the thunder
13	home	29	you know how soon	45	of the thunder
14	go home	30	fun	46	roar of the thunder
15	to go home	31	much fun	47	the roar of the thunder
16	want to go home	32	know how much fun	48	dreams

Frames		Frames		Frames	
49	their dreams	53	sail	57	yourself
50	for their dreams	54	the sail	58	like yourself
51	paid for their dreams	55	of the sail	59	exactly like yourself
52	they paid for their dreams	56	flapping of the sail	60	be exactly like yourself

Instructions: Procedure (a) : The instructor says each frame and the class echoes the word or phrase presented. If the response is not adequate, the instructor repeats until each step is done to his satisfaction. This exercise can also be done with different groups, i.e., instructor to one student, instructor to small group, one student to another, etc.

Procedure (b), operant conditioning :[1] (1) three to four seconds are used for each frame; (2) the instructor presents the words and the student echoes him; (3) the student is rewarded with a signal if he responds correctly (clicker, light, hand signal) ; on an incorrect response no signal is given and the next frame is presented; (4) if a student misses many trials consecutively, he should be stopped and reinstructed before continuing; and (5) count number of successful frames in the program (if a counter-clicker is used) and compare to the class average. If the student is below the class average he should continue to practice until he can reach the mean average. Outside help or laboratory work may be necessary.

4. Nasal consonants can be used to develop additional resonance if given greater duration. This must be done judiciously, as exaggeration is to be avoided.

Instructions: (a) slightly prolong the nasal consonants in the following words and sentences without sounding artificial, (b) carry-over the achievement of additional resonance on single words to the longer phrases.

1.	might	he might	he might move
2.	novice	the novice	the novice knows
3.	ring	ring no	ring no more
4.	remember	I remember	I remember him
5.	annoy	may annoy ·	you may annoy him
6.	anger	your anger	know your anger
7.	lamb	the lamb	the lamb is merry
8.	loan	the loan	the mortgage loan matured
9.	Cambrian	the Cambrian	it came from the Cambrian age
10.	finger	on my finger	the ring on my finger fell

[1] The person in charge of the class may assign responsibility for administering the sequence to a student teacher, especially if the class breaks up into pairs.

EXERCISES FOR LEVELS OF LOUDNESS

Very often we are asked to speak in situations requiring different levels of loudness. Resonation, particularly on the sonorous speech sounds, is the best means for projecting the voice. The factors governing how much power to use are: (a) the number of persons or size of audience, (b) size of the room or space, (c) the acoustical characteristics of the room or auditorium, i.e., reverberant versus dead room, (d) availability of amplification, and (e) background noise present.

While we may create an infinite number of situations and places, use the four listed below as a guide for practice:

Type	Description
Level one	Living room, quiet, speaking to one person quietly.
Level two	Living room, some background music, speaking to four other persons seated around rhe room.
Level three	Classroom, some outside noise, speaking to a class of 30 students.
Level four	Auditorium, no amplification, some background noise, speaking to 300—500 students.

Instructions: (a) use good diaphragmatic-abdominal-medial breathing, (b) concentrate on developing power on the sonorous sounds, (c) use longer duration of sonorous sounds, greater stress, shorter phrasing, and better articulation on levels three and four, (d) do not raise your basic pitch level more than a note or two, and (e) try to remain relatively relaxed during each exercise, avoiding tension in the neck and jaw.

1. Try all levels on the following words, one at a time: Fire! Halt! Whoa! Ouch! Wait!

2. Practice each sentence at all four levels of loudness, going from level one to the next level, etc.
    a. Ready, set, go.
    b. I know you do.
    c. Who goes there?
    d. They will never come back.
    e. Gold! Gold! Gold!

3. Use four levels of loudness for the following sentences.
    a. The roar of the thunder could be heard in the distance.
    b. We want the team to go all the way to the Rose Bowl.
    c. I believe that the rights of man should not be abridged in a democracy.
    d. Do you know when the next bus will leave the terminal?
    e. First he walked, then he jogged, and finally he ran.

4. Practice the two selections below at various levels of loudness, the men using Brutus' speech and the women Portia's speech.

From JULIUS CAESAR

BRUTUS: Be patient till the last. Romans, countrymen, and lovers! hear me for my cause; and be silent, that you may hear: believe me for mine honor, and have respect to mine honor, that you may believe: censure me in your wisdom, and awake your senses, that you may the better judge. If there be any in this assembly, any dear friend of Caesar's, to him I say that Brutus' love to Caesar was no less than his. If then that friend demand why Brutus rose against Caesar, this is my answer: Not that I loved Caesar less, but that I loved Rome more....

—William Shakespeare

From THE MERCHANT OF VENICE

PORTIA: The quality of mercy is not strain'd,
It droppeth as the gentle rain from heaven
Upon the place beneath: it is twice bless'd;
It blesseth him that gives and him that takes:
'Tis mightiest in the mightiest; it becomes
The throned monarch better than his crown;
His sceptre shows the force of temporal power,
The attribute to awe and majesty,
Wherein doth sit the dread and fear of kings;
But mercy is above this sceptred sway,
It is enthroned in the hearts of kings,
It is an attribute to God himself,
And earthly power doth then show likest God's
When mercy seasons justice.

—William Shakespeare

EXERCISES TO ELIMINATE NASALITY

1. Place your forefinger on the side of the bridge of your nose in order to feel the vibration of nasal sounds. Attempt to reduce or eliminate vibration on the nonnasal sounds in the following exercise on [m, n, and ŋ].

Instructions: Use the following markings carefully: the dash (—) indicates a pause; the colon (:) indicates a long prolongation; the single dot (·) indicates short prolongation. All material is in phonetic transcription. Note that [ŋ] does not occur initially; use this exercise for control only.

105

Initial

[m]

[m—ɑ]	[m : ɑ]	[m · ɑ, mɑ]
[m—ɔ]	[m : ɔ]	[m · ɔ, mɔ]
[m—oʊ]	[m : oʊ]	[m · oʊ, moʊ]
[m—u]	[m : u]	[m · u, mu]
[m—i]	[m : i]	[m · i, mi]

[n]

[n—ɑ]	[n : ɑ]	[n · ɑ, nɑ]
[n—ɔ]	[n : ɔ]	[n · ɔ, nɔ]
[n—oʊ]	[n : oʊ]	[n · oʊ, noʊ]
[n—u]	[n : u]	[n · u, nu]
[n—i]	[n : i]	[n · i, ni]

[ŋ]

[ŋ—ɑ]	[ŋ : ɑ]	[ŋ · ɑ, ŋɑ]
[ŋ—ɔ]	[ŋ : ɔ]	[ŋ · ɔ, ŋɔ]
[ŋ—oʊ]	[ŋ : oʊ]	[ŋ · oʊ, ŋoʊ]
[ŋ—u]	[ŋ : u]	[ŋ · u, ŋu]
[ŋ—i]	[ŋ : i]	[ŋ · i, ŋi]

Medial

[m]

[ɑ—m—ɑ]	[ɑ : m : ɑ]	[ɑ · m · ɑ, ɑmɑ]
[ɔ—m—ɔ]	[ɔ : m : ɔ]	[ɔ · m · ɔ, ɔmɔ]
[oʊ—m—oʊ]	[oʊ : m : oʊ]	[oʊ · m · oʊ, oʊmoʊ]
[u—m—u]	[u : m : u]	[u · m · u, umu]
[i—m—i]	[i : m : i]	[i · m · i, imi]

[n]

[ɑ—n—ɑ]	[ɑ : n : ɑ]	[ɑ · n · ɑ, ɑnɑ]
[ɔ—n—ɔ]	[ɔ : n : ɔ]	[ɔ · n · ɔ, ɔnɔ]
[oʊ—m—oʊ]	[oʊ : n : oʊ]	[oʊ · oʊ ·, oʊmoʊ]
[u—n—u]	[u: n : u]	[u · n · n, unu]
[i—n—i]	[i : n : i]	[i · n · i, ini]

[ŋ]

[ɑ—ŋ—ɑ]	[ɑ : ŋ : ɑ]	[ɑ · ŋ · ɑ, ɑŋɑ]
[ɔ—ŋ—ɔ]	[ɔ : ŋ : ɔ]	[ɔ · ŋ · ɔ, ɔŋɔ]
[oʊ—ŋ—oʊ]	[oʊ : ŋ : oʊ]	[oʊŋ · oʊ, oʊŋoʊ]
[u—ŋ—u]	[u : ŋ : u]	[i · ŋ · u, uŋu]
[i—ŋ—i]	[i : ŋ : i]	[i · ŋ · i, iŋi]

	Final	
[m]		
[ɑ—m]	[ɑ : m]	[ɑ · m, ɑm]
[ɔ—m]	[ɔ : m]	[ɔ · m, ɔm]
[oʊ—m]	[oʊ : m]	[oʊ · m, oʊm]
[u—m]	[u : m]	[u · m, um]
[i—m]	[i : m]	[i · m, im]
[n]		
[ɑ—n]	[ɑ : n]	[ɑ · n, ɑn]
[ɔ—n]	[ɔ : n]	[ɔ · n, ɔn]
[oʊ—n]	[oʊ : n]	[oʊ · n, oʊn]
[u—n]	[u : n]	[u · n, un]
[i—n]	[i : n]	[i · n, in]
[ŋ]		
[ɑ—ŋ]	[ɑ : ŋ]	[ɑ · ŋ · ɑŋ]
[ɔ—ŋ]	[ɔ : ŋ]	[ɔ · ŋ, ɔŋ]
[oʊ—ŋ]	[oʊ : ŋ]	[oʊ · ŋ, oʊŋ]
[u—ŋ]	[u : ŋ]	[u · ŋ, uŋ]
[i—ŋ]	[i : ŋ]	[i · ŋ, iŋ]

2. Two methods have been used widely to detect nasality on nonnasal sounds: (a) pinching the nostrils firmly during speech production, and (b) placing a mirror under the nostrils during production; if nasal emission of the voiced breath stream occurs, clouding of the mirror will be evident.

    a. Pinch your nostrils on the first word of the following word pairs, and release them on the second word. Listen carefully, or have a skilled listener judge for you. Do you detect a difference in vowel quality between the two words?

see—see	father—father	coat—coat
hit—hit	third—third	tight—tight
air—air	call—call	bowl—bowl
eight—eight	school—school	boy—boy
bat—bat	put—put	how—how

    b. Using the same word pairs, place a small mirror beneath your nostrils and say the word pairs. Look at the mirror after each pair to see if clouding occurs.

107

3. Practice the following sentences, which do not contain nasal consonants. You should be able to pinch your nostrils and retain the same voice
quality. Alternate reading with your nostrils unpinched and pinched.

    a. Her corsage was beautiful but costly.
    b. He leapt deftly over the high wall.
    c. The basket was filled with the fruits of the harvest.
    d. Hate breeds war while love begets peace.
    e. The obstacle course was very hazardous.
    f. The roses, heavy with dew, bowed their heads.
    g. The salt flats stretched before us—white, bright, stark.
    h. Whatever you do, try to do well.
    i. The hackberry grew by the great oak's side.
    j. To ride to the top of Pikes Peak is a tourist's delight.

SELECTIONS

The prose selections in the last pages of this chapter should be undertaken after good resonance has been established on the poetry.

SEA-FEVER

I must do down to the seas again, to the lonely sea and the sky,
And all I ask is a tall ship and a star to steer her by,
And the wheel's kick and the wind's song and the white sail's
    shaking,
And a grey mist on the sea's face and a grey dawn breaking.
I must go down to the seas again, for the call of the running tide
Is a wild call and a clear call that may not be denied;
And all I ask is a windy day with the white clouds flying,
And the flung spray and the blown spume, and the sea-gulls
    crying.
I must go down to the seas again, to the vagrant gypsy life,
To the gull's way, and the whale's way, where the wind's like
    a whetted knife,
And all I ask is a merry yarn from a laughing fellow-rover,
And a quiet sleep and a sweet dream when the long trick's over.[2]
    —John Masefield

She left the web, she left the loom,
She made three paces through the room,
She saw the water-lily bloom,
She saw the helmet and the plume....

    —Alfred, Lord Tennyson

[2] From John Masefield, *Selected Poems*, copyright 1938 by John Masefield and used with
The Macmillan Company's permission.

Clear and cool, clear and cool,
By laughing shallow and dreaming pool;
Cool and clear, cool and clear,
By shining shingle and foaming weir;
Under the crag where the ouzel sings,
And the ivied wall where the church bell rings....

—Charles Kingsley

I am the daughter of earth and water,
    And the nursling of the sky;
I pass through the pores of the ocean and shores;
    I change, but I cannot die.
For after the rain, when with never a stain
    The pavilion of heaven is bare,
And the winds and sunbeams with their convex gleams
    Build up the blue dome of air,
I silently laugh at my own cenotaph,
    And out of the caverns of rain,
Like a child from the womb, like a ghost from the tomb,
    I arise and unbuild it again.

—Percy Bysshe Shelley

My heart leaps up when I behold
    A rainbow in the sky:
So was it when my life began;
So is it now I am a man;
So be it when I shall grow old,
    Or let me die!
The Child is father of the Man;
And I could wish my days to be
Bound each to each by natural piety.

—William Wordsworth

We are the music-makers,
    And we are the dreamers of dreams,
Wandering by lone sea-breakers,
    And sitting by desolate streams—
World-losers and world-forsakers,
    On whom the pale moon gleams—
Yet we are the movers and shakers
    Of the world forever, it seems.

109

With wonderful deathless ditties
We build up the world's great cities,
    And out of a fabulous story
    We fashion an empire's glory;
One man with a dream, at pleasure,
    Shall go forth and conquer a crown;
And three with a new song's measure
    Can trample a kingdom down.

              —Arthur O'Shaughnessy

Oh, joyous boon! oh, mad delight;
Oh, sun and moon! oh, day and night!
    Rejoice, rejoice with me!
Proclaim our joy, ye birds above—
Ye brooklets, murmur forth our love
    In choral ecstasy:
Oh, joyous boon!
    Oh, mad delight!
Oh, sun and moon!
    Oh, day and night!
Ye birds, and brooks, and fruitful trees,
With choral joy delight the breeze—
    Rejoice, rejoice with me!

              —W. S. Gilbert

Gold! Gold! Gold! Gold!
Bright and yellow, hard and cold,
Molten, graven, hammered, and rolled;
Hard to get and heavy to hold;
Hoarded, bartered, bought and sold,
Stolen, borrowed, squandered, doled:
Spurned by the young, but hugged by the old
To the very verge of the church-yard mould;
Gold! Gold! Gold! Gold!
Good or bad a thousand-fold!
    How widely its agencies vary—
To save—to ruin—to curse—to bless—
As even its minted coins express,
Now stamped with the image of good Queen Bess,
    And now of a Bloody Mary.

              —Thomas Hood

110

From THE CREATION
_____

And God looked around
On all that he had made.
He looked at his sun,
And he looked at his moon,
And he looked at his little stars ;
He looked on his world
With all its living things,
And God said : I'm lonely still.

Then God sat down—
On the side of a hill where he could think ;
By a deep, wide river he sat down ;
With his head in his hands,
God thought and thought,
Till he thought : I'll make me a man !

Up from the bed of the river
God scooped the clay ;
And by the bank of the river
He kneeled him down ;
And there the great God Almighty
Who lit the sun and fixed it in the sky,
Who flung the stars to the most far corner of the night,
Who rounded the earth in the middle of his hand ;
This Great God,
Like a mammy bending over her baby,
Kneeled down in the dust
Toiling over a lump of clay
Till he shaped it in his own image ;

Then into it he blew the breath of life,
And man became a living soul.
Amen. Amen.[3]

—James Weldon Johnson

A WET SHEET AND A FLOWING SEA
_____

A wet sheet and a flowing sea,
   A wind that follows fast
And fills the white and rustling sail
   And bends the gallant mast ;

[3] From *God's Trombones* by James Weldon Johnson. Copyright 1927 by The Viking Press, Inc. Reprinted by permission of The Viking Press, Inc., New York.

And bends the gallant mast, my boys,
    While like the eagle free
Away the good ship flies, and leaves
    Old England on the lee.

O for a soft and gentle wind!
    I heard a fair one cry;
But give to me the snoring breeze
    And white waves heaving high;
And white waves heaving high, my lads,
    The good ship tight and free—
The world of waters is our home
    And merry men are we.

There's tempest in yon horned moon,
    And lightning in yon cloud;
But hark the music, mariners!
    The wind is piping loud,
The wind is piping loud, my boys,
    The lightning flashes free—
While the hollow oak our palace is,
    Our heritage the sea.

                        —Allan Cunningham

FOREBODING

Zoom, zoom, zoom!
That is the sound of the surf,
As the great green waves rush up the shore
With a murderous, thundering, ominous roar;
And leave drowned dead things by my door.
Zoom, zoom, zoom!
Sh-wsh-wsh! Sh-wsh-wsh! Sh-wsh-wsh!
That is the sound of the tow
As it slips and slithers along the sands
Like terrible, groping, formless hands,
That drag at my beach house where it stands.
Sh-wsh-wsh! Sh-wsh-wsh! Sh-wsh-wsh!
Ee-oh-i-oo! Ee-oh-i-oo! Ee-oh-i-oo!
That is the sound of the wind.
It wails like a banshee adrift in space.
It threatens to scatter my driftwood place.
It splashes the sand like spite in my face.

112

Ee-oh-i-oo! Ee-oh-i-oo! Ee-oh-i-oo!
Surf?
Tow?
Or the wind?
Which of the three will it be?
The surf, will it bludgeon and beat me dead?
Or the tow drag me down to the ocean bed?
Or the wind wail a dirge above my head?
Zoom!
Sh-wsh-wsh!
Ee-oh-i-oo![4]

—Don Blanding

From JULIUS CAESAR

CASSIUS: For once, upon a raw and gusty day,
The troubled Tiber chafing with her shores,
Caesar said to me, "Dar'st thou, Cassius, now
Leap in with me into this angry flood,
And swim to yonder point?" Upon the word,
Accoutred as I was, I plunged in
And bade him follow; so indeed he did.
The torrent roar'd, and we did buffet it
With lusty sinews, throwing it aside
And stemming it with hearts of controversy;
But ere we could arrive the point propos'd,
Caesar cried, "Help me, Cassius, or I sink!"
I, as Aeneas, our great ancestor,
Did from the flames of Troy upon his shoulder
The old Anchises bear, so from the waves of Tiber
Did I the tired Caesar. And this man
Is now become a god, and Cassius is
A wretched creature, and must bend his body
If Caesar carelessly but nod on him.
He had a fever when he was in Spain,
And when the fit was on him, I did mark
How he did shake—'tis true, this god did shake,
His coward lips did from their colour fly,
And that same eye whose bend doth awe the world
Did lose his lustre; I did hear him groan.

[4] Reprinted by permission of Dodd, Mead & Company from *Vagabond's House* by Don Blanding. Copyright 1928 by Don Blanding.

Ay, and that tongue of his that bade the Romans
Mark him and write his speeches in their books,
Alas, it cried, "Give me some drink, Titinius,"
As a sick girl. Ye gods, it doth amaze me
A man of such a feeble temper should
So get the start of the majestic world
And bear the palm alone.

—William Shakespeare

ECHO

I asked of Echo, t'other day
    (Whose words are often few and funny)
What to a novice she could say
    Of courtship, love and matrimony.
    Quoth Echo plainly,—"Matter-o'-money!"

Whom should I marry? Should it be
    A dashing damsel, gay and pert,
A pattern of inconstancy;
    Or selfish, mercenary flirt?
    Quoth Echo sharply,—"Nary flirt!"

What if, aweary of the strife
    That long has lured the dear deceiver,
She promise to amend her life,
    And sin no more; can I believe her?
    Quoth Echo, very promptly,—"Leave her!"

But if some maiden with a heart
    On me should venture to bestow it,
Pray, should I act the wiser part
    To take the treasure or forego it?
    Quoth Echo, with decision,—"Go it!"

What if, in spite of her disdain,
    I find my heart entwined about
With Cupid's dear delicious chain
    So closely that I can't get out?
    Quoth Echo, laughingly,—"Get out!"

But if some maid with beauty blest,
    As pure and fair as Heaven can make her,
Will share my labor and my rest
    Till envious Death shall overtake her?
    Quoth Echo (SOTTO VOCE),—"Take her!"

—John G. Saxe

From MACBETH

FIRST WITCH : Round about the cauldron go ;
In the poison'd entrails throw.
Toad, that under cold stone
Days and nights has thirty-one
Swelt'red venom sleeping got,
Boil thou first i' the charmed pot.
ALL : Double, double, toil and trouble ;
Fire burn and cauldron bubble.
SECOND WITCH : Fillet of a fenny snake,
In the cauldron boil and bake ;
Eye of newt and toe of frog,
Wool of bat and tongue of dog,
Adder's fork and blind-worm's sting,
Lizard's leg and howlet's wing,
For a charm of powerful trouble,
Like a hell-broth boil and bubble.
ALL : Double, double, toil and trouble ;
Fire burn and cauldron bubble.

—William Shakespeare

There was a sound of revelry by night,
    And Belgium's capital had gathered then
Her beauty and her chivalry, and bright
    The lamps shone o'er fair women and brave men.
    A thousand hearts beat happily ; and when
Music arose with its voluptuous swell,
    Soft eyes looked love to eyes which spake again,
And all went merry as a marriage bell ;
But hush ! hark ! a deep sound strikes like a rising knell.

Did you not hear it ?—No : 'twas but the wind,
    Or the car rattling o'er the stony street ;
On with the dance ! Let joy be unconfined ;
    No sleep till morn, when youth and pleasure meet
    To chase the glowing hours with flying feet—
But, hark !—that heavy sound breaks in once more,
    As if the clouds its echo would repeat
And nearer, clearer, deadlier than before !
Arm ! Arm ! it is—it is the cannon's opening roar.

Ah! then and there was hurrying to and fro,
    And gathering tears, and tremblings of distress,
And cheeks all pale, which but an hour ago
    Blush'd at the praise of their own loveliness;
    And there were sudden partings, such as press
The life from out young hearts, and choking sighs
    Which ne'er might be repeated: who could guess
If ever more should meet those mutual eyes,
Since upon night so sweet such awful morn could rise!

And there was mounting in hot haste; the steed,
    The mustering squadron, and the clattering car
Went pouring forward with impetuous speed,
    And swiftly forming in the ranks of war;
    And the deep thunder, peal on peal afar;
And, near, the beat of the alarming drum
    Roused up the soldier ere the morning star:
While thronged the citizens with terror dumb,
—Or whispering with white lips, "The foe! they come!
                                        they come!"

                            —George Gordon, Lord Byron

O Thou vast Ocean! ever sounding sea!
Thou vast symbol of drear immensity!
Thou thing that windest round the solid world,
Like a huge animal, which, downward hurled
From the black clouds, lies weltering alone,
Lashing and writhing till its strength is gone.
Thy voice is like the thunder, and thy sleep
Is as a giant's slumber, loud and deep.

                            —Bryan Waller Proctor

Thou, too, sail on, O Ship of State!
Sail on, O Union, strong and great!
Humanity with all its fears,
With all the hopes of future years,
Is hanging breathless on thy fate!
We know what Master laid thy keel,
What Workmen wrought thy ribs of steel,
Who made each mast, and sail, and rope,

What anvils rang, what hammers beat,
In what a forge and what a heat
Were shaped the anchors of thy hope!
Fear not each sudden sound and shock,
'T is of the wave and not the rock;
'T is but the flapping of the sail,
And not a rent made by the gale!
In spite of rock and tempest's roar,
In spite of false lights on the shore,
Sail on, nor fear to breast the sea!
Our hearts, our hopes, are all with thee,
Our hearts, our hopes, our prayers, our tears,
Our faith triumphant o'er our fears,
Are all with thee,—are all with thee!

—Henry W. Longfellow

I was born an American; I live an American; I shall die an American; and I intend to perform the duties incumbent upon me in that character to the end of my career. I mean to do this with absolute disregard of personal consequences. What are the personal consequences? What is the individual man, with all the good or evil that may betide him, in comparison with the good or evil which may befall a great country, and in the midst of great transactions which concern that country's fate? Let the consequences be what they will, I am careless. No man can suffer too much, and no man can fall too soon, if he suffer or if he fall in the defense of the liberties and constitution of his country.

—Daniel Webster

DECLARATION OF WAR SPEECH

Yesterday, December 7, 1941—a date which will live in infamy—the United States of America was suddenly and deliberately attacked by naval and air forces of the Empire of Japan.

The United States was at peace with that nation and, at the solicitation of Japan, was still in conversation with its Government and its Emperor looking toward the maintenance of peace in the Pacific.

Indeed, one hour after Japanese air squadrons had commenced bombing Oahu, the Japanese Ambassador to the United States and his colleague delivered to the Secretary of

117

State a formal reply to a recent American message. While this reply stated that it seemed useless to continue the existing diplomatic negotiations, it contained no threat or hint of war or armed attack.

It will be recorded that the distance of Hawaii from Japan makes it obvious that the attack was deliberately planned many days or even weeks ago. During the intervening time, the Japanese Government had deliberately sought to deceive the United States by false statements and expressions of hope for continued peace.

The attack yesterday on the Hawaiian Islands has caused severe damage to American naval and military forces. Very many American lives have been lost. In addition, American ships have been reported torpedoed on the high seas between San Francisco and Honolulu.

Yesterday the Japanese Government also launched an attack against Malaya.

Last night Japanese forces attacked Hong Kong.

Last night Japanese forces attacked Guam.

Last night Japanese forces attacked the Philippine Islands.

Last night the Japanese attacked Wake Island.

This morning the Japanese attacked Midway Island.

Japan has, therefore, undertaken a surprise offensive extending throughout the Pacific area. The facts of yesterday speak for themselves. The people of the United States have already formed their opinions and well understand the implications to the very life and safety of out nation.

As Commander-in-Chief of the Army and Navy I have directed that all measures be taken for our defense.

Always will we remember the character of the onslaught against us.

No matter how long it may take us to overcome this premeditated invasion, the American people in their righteous might will win through to absolute victory.

I believe I interpret the will of the Congress and of the people when I assert that we will not only defend ourselves to the uttermost but will make very certain that this form of treachery shall never endanger us again.

Hostilities exist. There is no blinking at the fact that our people, our territory and our interests are in grave danger.

With confidence in our armed forces—with the unbounding determination of our people—we will gain the inevitable triumph—so help us God.

—Franklin Delano Roosevelt

EULOGY AT HIS BROTHER'S GRAVE

This brave and tender man in every storm of life was oak and rock, but in the sunshine he was vine and flower. He was the friend of all heroic souls. He climbed the heights and left all superstitions here below, while on his forehead fell the golden dawning of a grander day. He loved the beautiful, and was with color, form, and music touched to tears. He sided with the weak, the poor, the wronged, and lovingly gave alms. With loyal heart and with purest hands he faithfully discharged all public trusts. He was a worshipper of liberty and a friend of the oppressed. A thousand times I have heard him quote these words : "For justice, all place a temple, and all season, summer." He believed that happiness was the only good, reason the only torch, justice the only worship, humanity the only religion, and love the only priest. He added to the sum of human joy, and were everyone for whom he did some loving service to bring a blossom to his grave, he would sleep to-night beneath a wilderness of flowers.

Life is a narrow vale between the cold and barren peaks of two eternities. We strive in vain to look beyond the heights. We cry aloud, and the only answer is the echo of our wailing cry. From the voiceless lips of the unreplying dead, there comes no word ; but in the night of death, hope sees a star, and listening love can hear the rustle of a wing.

He who sleeps here, when dying, mistaking the approach of death for the return of health, whispered with his latest breath : "I am better now." Let us believe, in spite of doubts and dogmas, of fears and tears, these dear words are true of all the countless dead.

—Robert G. Ingersoll

From THE TAMING OF THE SHREW

PETRUCHIO : Good-morrow, Kate ; for that's your name, I hear.
KATHARINA : Well have you heard, but something hard of hearing :
They call me Katharine that do talk of me.
PETRUCHIO : You lie, in faith ; for you are call'd plain Kate,
And bonny Kate, and sometimes Kate the curst ;
But, Kate, the prettiest Kate in Christendom ;
Kate of Kate-Hall, my super-dainty Kate,

119

For dainties are all cates : and therefore, Kate,
Take this of me, Kate of my consolation ;
Hearing thy mildness prais'd in every town,
Thy virtues spoke of, and thy beauty sounded,—
Yet not so deeply as to thee belongs,—
Myself am mov'd to woo thee for my wife.
KATHARINA : Mov'd ! in good time : let him that mov'd you hither
Remove you hence. I knew you at the first,
You were a moveable.
PETRUCHIO : Why, what's a moveable ?
KATHARINA : A joint-stool.
PETRUCHIO : Thou hast hit it : come, sit on me.
KATHARINA : Asses are made to bear, and so are you.
PETRUCHIO : Women are made to bear, and so are you.
KATHARINA : No such jade as bear you, if me you mean.
PETRUCHIO : Alas ! good Kate, I will not burden thee ;
For, knowing thee to be but young and light,—
KATHARINA : Too light for such a swain as you to catch,
And yet as heavy as my weight should be.
PETRUCHIO : Should be ! should buzz !
KATHARINA : Well ta'en, and like a buzzard.
PETRUCHIO : O slow-wing'd turtle ! shall a buzzard take thee ?
KATHARINA : Ay, for a turtle, as he takes a buzzard.
PETRUCHIO : Come, come, you wasp ; i' faith you are too angry.
KATHARINA : If I be waspish, best beware my sting.
PETRUCHIO : My remedy is, then, to pluck it out.
KATHARINA : Ay, if the fool could find where it lies.
PETRUCHIO : Who knows not where a wasp does wear his sting ?
In his tail.
KATHARINA : In his tongue.
PETRUCHIO : Whose tongue ?
KATHARINA : Yours, if you talk of tails ; and so farewell.
PETRUCHIO : What ! with my tongue in your tail ? nay, come again.
Good Kate, I am a gentleman.
KATHARINA : That I'll try (*striking him*).
PETRUCHIO : I swear I'll cuff you if you strike again.
KATHARINA : So may you lose your arms :
If you strike me, you are no gentleman ;
And if no gentleman, why then no arms.

PETRUCHIO : A herald, Kate ? O ! put me in thy books.

KATHARINA : What is your crest ? a coxcomb ?

PETRUCHIO : A combless cock, so Kate will be my hen.

KATHARINA : No cock of mine ; you crow too like a craven.

PETRUCHIO : Nay, come, Kate, come ; you must not look so sour.

KATHARINA : It is my fashion when I see a crab.

PETRUCHIO : Why, here's no crab, and therefore look not sour.

KATHARINA : There is, there is.

PETRUCHIO : Then show it me.

KATHARINA : Had I a glass, I would.

PETRUCHIO : What, you mean my face ?

KATHARINA : Well aim'd of such a young one.

PETRUCHIO : Now, by Saint George, I am too young for you.

KATHARINA : Yet you are wither'd.

PETRUCHIO : 'Tis with cares.

KATHARINA : I care not.

PETRUCHIO : Nay, hear you, Kate : in sooth, you 'scape not so.

KATHARINA : I chafe you, if I tarry : let me go.

PETRUCHIO : No, not a whit : I find you passing gentle.
'Twas told me you were rough and coy and sullen,
And now I find report a very liar ;
For thou art pleasant, gamesome, passing courteous,
But slow in speech, yet sweet as spring-time flowers :
Thou canst not frown, thou canst not look askance,
Nor bite the lip, as angry wenches will ;
Nor hast thou pleasure to be cross in talk ;
But thou with mildness entertain'st thy wooers,
With gentle conference, soft and affable.
Why does the world report that Kate doth limp ?
O slanderous world ! Kate, like the hazel-twig.
Is straight and slender, and as brown in hue
As hazel-nuts, and sweeter than the kernels.
O ! let me see thee walk : thou dost not halt.

KATHARINA : Go, fool, and whom thou keep'st command.

PETRUCHIO : Did ever Dian so become a grove
As Kate this chamber with her princely gait ?
O ! be thou Dian, and let her be Kate,
And then let Kate be chaste, and Dian sportful !

KATHARINA : Where did you study all this goodly speech ?

PETRUCHIO : It is extempore, from my mother-wit.

KATHARINA : A witty mother ! witless else her son.

PETRUCHIO : Am I not wise ?

KATHARINA : Yes ; keep you warm.
PETRUCHIO : Marry, so I mean, sweet Katharine, in thy bed :
And therefore, setting all this chat aside,
Thus in plain terms : your father hath consented
That you shall be my wife ; your dowry 'greed on ;
And will you, nill you, I will marry you.
Now, Kate, I am a husband for your turn ;
For, by this light, whereby I see thy beauty,—
Thy beauty that doth make me like thee well,—
Thou must be married to no man but me :
For I am he am born to tame you, Kate ;
And bring you from a wild Kate to a Kate
Comfortable as other household Kates.
Here comes your father : never make denial ;
I must and will have Katharine to my wife.

—William Shakespeare

When in the course of human events, it becomes necessary for one people to dissolve the political bands which have connected them with one another, and to assume among the powers of the earth the separate and equal station to which the Laws of Nature and of Nature's God entitle them, a decent respect to the opinions of mankind requires that they should declare the causes which impel them to the separation.

We hold these truths to be self-evident, that all men are created equal, that they are endowed by their Creator with certain inalienable Rights, that among these are Life, Liberty and the pursuit of happiness.—That to secure these rights, Governments are instituted among Men, deriving their just powers from the consent of the governed.—That whenever any Form of Government becomes destructive of these ends, it is the Right of the People to alter or to abolish it, and to institute new Government, laying its foundation on such principles and organizing its powers in such form, as to them shall seem most likely to effect their Safety and Happiness. Prudence, indeed, will dictate that Governments long established should not be changed for light and transient causes ; and accordingly all experience hath shewn, that mankind are more disposed to suffer, while evils are sufferable, than to right themselves by abolishing the forms to which they are accustomed. But when a long train of abuses and usurpations, begun at a distinguished period, pursuing invariably the same Object, evinces a design to reduce them under absolute Despotism, it is their right, it is their duty, to throw off such Government, and to provide new Guards for their future security.

—Thomas Jefferson

SUPPLEMENTARY SELECTIONS FOR CLASS PRESENTATION
I Corinthians, Chapter 13, *The Bible.*
Lord God of Hosts, Rudyard Kipling, *poetry.*
Ode to the West Wind, Percy Bysshe Shelley, *poetry.*
The Speeches of Winston Churchill.
The Starlight Night, Gerard Manley Hopkins, *poetry.*
Stopping by Woods on a Snowy Evening, Robert Frost, *poetry.*

CHAPTER SEVEN

articulation: the consonants

THUS FAR WE have been primarily concerned with the control, production, and amplification of the voice, and have not stressed the importance of speaking distinctly. All the benefits of mastering good voice production will avail us little unless we also master good articulation. The contrast is great between two speakers with basically good voices, one with poor articulation and the other with good articulation. The former's speech is characterized by slurring, mumbling, and oral inaccuracy, while the latter's speech has appropriate preciseness and is easy to understand at any level of loudness.

With most people who garble their words, poor articulation is simply a matter of habit and can be overcome by a little serious attention and conscious effort continuously applied. But whatever the cause and however severe the malady, it must be overcome by anyone who aspires to success in any field involving communication with others.

ARTICULATION DEFINED

In phonetics articulation may be defined as the movement of the speech organs, e.g., lips, tongue, soft palate, etc., in the forming of discrete speech sounds. It is interesting to note that most dictionaries add ''a spoken sound, especially a consonant.''

124

APPROACHES TO THE STUDY OF ARTICULATION

Before we get into the technical discussion of articulation, let us stress an important point: *articulation should not be ostentatious*. Our listeners should not be aware of the fact that we are striving for good articulation. The desired goal is speech that is clear and easy to understand, but also free from an exaggerated precision that calls attention to itself.

How can we overcome long habits of careless speaking? How can we be sure that we are speaking clearly, distinctly, and accurately? First of all, we must have an intimate awareness of the sounds of the English language and how they occur in their many sound combinations.

SPELLING AND PRONUNCIATION

As we have seen, spelling is not a reliable guide to pronunciation. The lack of consistency between the way our words are spelled and the way they are pronounced is illustrated by noting the silent letters in such common words as *gnaw, gnat, thumb, debt, palm, almond, salmon, though, through*, and many other words. We should also be aware of the different pronunciations of the same spellings in such words as ar*ch*—ar*ch*itect and *gesture*—*g*arter—rou*g*e.

Observe the numerous ways some common English sounds may be spelled. For example, the italicized letters in the following words illustrate variant spellings of the sound [aɪ] as in *ice*: *i*re, he*i*ght, h*i*gh, t*ie*, *ai*sle, *aye*, *eye*, m*y*, bu*y*, and l*y*e. Similarly, the sound [eɪ] as in *ale* is spelled in many ways: *a*te, r*ai*n, g*ao*l, g*au*ge, r*ay*, st*ea*k, v*ei*l, ob*ey*, and f*e*te. And note some of the spellings for the [k] sound: *k*ite, hi*ck*, *c*at, *ch*orus, *q*uilt, and *kh*aki. Note also some of the various sounds which may be given to a single letter, for example, the *i* in *mice, it, pique, Sioux, sirloin*; the *a* in *ate, art, at, all, dare, alone*; and the *e* in *he, ebb, sergeant* (note both the first and last *e*), *sedan, fete*, and *there*.

Daniel Jones, a renowned British scholar, has been reported as illustrating the absurdities of our spelling by claiming that the word *fish* could be spelled *ghoti*, simply by taking the *gh* from *cough*, the *o* from *women*, and the *ti* from any word ending in *tion* such as *tuition*.

It is not strange that children find so much difficulty in learning to spell, nor that foreigners, as well as persons from different parts of our own country, can consult the same dictionary and get quite different concepts of the way a given word should be pronounced.

PHONETIC SYMBOLS AND DIACRITICAL MARKS

If we seek a tool to help us in pronunciation, we have three alternatives open to us: (1) diacritical marks, (2) phonetic symbols, or (3) a combination of both systems.[1] We feel that the last alternative is best because these

---

[1] If you have not yet acquired a basic knowledge of the phonetic symbols, we highly recommend that you turn to the last section of Chapter 2 dealing with the use of phonetics.

systems are often used both in dictionaries and in voice and diction texts. The relationship of phonetic symbols to diacritical marks is presented in the chart that follows.

CHART OF PHONETIC SYMBOLS—CONSONANTS

Phonetic Symbol	Key Word	Phonetic Transcription	Various Spellings	Examples
[p]	pet	[pɛt]	p, pp	pen, stopper
[b]	bet	[bɛt]	b, bb	bed, hobby
[t]	tip	[tɪp]	ed, ght, t, th, tt	talked, bought, toe, thyme, bottom
[d]	did	[dɪd]	d, dd, ed	do, ladder, pulled
[k]	cat	[kæt]	c, cc, cch, ch, ck, cq, cque, cu, k, qu	car, account, bacchanal, character, back, acquaint, sacque, biscuit, kill, liquor
[g]	give	[gɪv]	g, gg, gh, gu, gue	give, egg, ghost, guard, demagogue
[h]	hat	[hæt]	h, wh	hit, who
[f]	fill	[fɪl]	f, ff, gh, ph	feed, muffin, tough, physics
[v]	very	[ˈvɛrɪ]	f, ph, v, vv	of, Stephen, visit, flivver
[θ]	thin	[θɪn]	th	thin
[ð]	this	[ðɪs]	th, the	then, bathe
[s]	sea	[si]	c, ce, s, sc, sch, ss	city, mice, see, scene, schism, loss
[z]	zoo	[zu]	s, sc, ss, x, z, zz	has, discern, scissors, Xerxes, zone, dazzle
[ʃ]	show	[ʃoʊ]	ce, ch, ci, psh, s, sch, sci, se, sh, si, ss, ssi, ti	ocean, machine, special, pshaw, sugar, schist, conscience, nauseous, ship, mansion, tissue, mission, mention
[ʒ]	measure	[ˈmɛʒɤ]	g, s, si, z, zi	garage, measure, division, azure, brazier
[tʃ]	chief	[tʃif]	ch, tch, te, ti, tu	chief, catch, righteous, question, natural
[dʒ]	judge	[ˈdʒʌdʒ]	ch, d, dg, dge, di, g, gg, j	Greenwich, graduate, judgment, bridge, soldier, magic, exaggerate, just
[m]	man	[mæn]	chm, gm, lm, m, mb, mm, mn	drachm, paradigm, calm, more, limb, hammer, hymn
[n]	now	[naʊ]	gn, kn, n, nn, pn	gnat, knife, not, runner, pneumatic
[ŋ]	going	[ˈgoʊɪŋ]	n, ng, ngue	pink, ring, tongue
[l]	let	[lɛt]	l, ll	live, call
[r]	run	[rʌn]	r, rh, rr	red, rhythm, carrot
[j]	yes	[jɛs]	g, i, j, y	lorgnette, union, hallelujah, yet
[w]	word	[wɝd]	o, u, w	choir, quiet, well

CHART OF PHONETIC SYMBOLS—VOWELS

Phonetic Symbol	Key Word	Phonetic Transcription	Various Spellings	Examples
[i]	see	[si]	ae, ay, e, ea, ee, ei, eo, ey, i, ie, oe	Caesar, quay, equal, team, see, deceive, people, key, machine, field, amoeba
[ɪ]	if	[ɪf]	e, ee, i, ie, o, u, ui, y	England, been, if, sieve, women, busy, build, hymn
[e]	ate	[et]	a, ai, ao, au, ay, ea, eh, ei, ey	ate, rain, gaol, gauge, ray, steak, eh, veil, obey
[ɛ]	bet	[bɛt]	a, ae, ai, ay, e, ea, ei, eo, ie, oe, u	any, aesthetic, said, says, ebb, leather, heifer, leopard, friend, foetid, bury
[æ]	sat	[sæt]	a, ai	hat, plaid
[a]¹	ask	[ask]	a	
[u]	who	[hu]	eu, ew, o, oe, oo, ou, u, ue, ui	maneuver, grew, move, canoe, ooze, troupe, rule, flue, fruit
[ʊ]	could	[kʊd]	o, oo, ou, u	wolf, look, should, pull
[o]²	omit	[o'mɪt]	o	
[ɔ]	all	[ɔl]	a, ah, al, au, aw, o, oa, ou	tall, Utah, talk, fault, raw, order, broad, fought
[ɒ]³	stop	[stɒp]	a, o	wander, box
[ɑ]	father	['fɑðɚ]	a, e, ea	father, sergeant, hearth
[ɜ], [ɝ]⁴	bird	[bɜd] [bɝd]	er, ear, ir, or, our, ur, yr	term, learn, thirst, worm, courage, hurt, myrtle
[ɚ]⁵	ever	['ɛvə] ['ɛvɚ]	ar, er, ir, or, our, ur, yr	liar, father, elixir, labor, labour, augur, martyr
[ə]⁵	above	[ə'bʌv]	a, ai, e, ei, eo, i, ia, o, oi, ou, u	alone, mountain, system, mullein, dungeon, easily, parliament, gallop, porpoise, curious, circus
[ʌ]	but	[bʌt]	o, oe, oo, ou, u	son, does, flood, couple, cup

¹ *This vowel appears primarily in Eastern Standard Speech.*

² *Except in unstressed syllables, as in* obey, omit, *this sound in English is usually a diphthong. See* [oʊ].

³ *Dialectal differences occur on this vowel. In General American speech* [ɑ] *is frequently substituted for* [ɒ].

⁴ *General American speech differs from both Eastern Standard and Southern Standard on this vowel.*

⁵ *These symbols are used primarily in unstressed syllables.*

CHART OF PHONETIC SYMBOLS—DIPHTHONGS

Phonetic Symbol	Key Word	Phonetic Transcription	Various Spellings	Examples
[aɪ]	by	[baɪ]	ai, ay, ei, ey, i, ie, uy, y, ye	aisle, aye, height, eye, ice, tie, buy, sky, lye
[ɔɪ]	boy	[bɔɪ]	oi, oy	oil, toy
[aʊ]	now	[naʊ]	ou, ough, ow	out, bough, brow
[eɪ]	lay	[leɪ]	a, ai, ao, au, ay, ea, eh, ei, ey	ate, rain, gaol, gauge, ray, steak, eh, veil, obey
[oʊ]	old	[oʊld]	au, eau, oe, ew, o, oa, oe, oh, oo, ou, ow	hautboy, beau, yeoman, sew, note, road, toe, oh, brooch, soul, flow
[ju]	beauty	['bjutɪ]	eau, eu, eue, ew, ieu, iew, u, ue, ui, yu, yew, you	beauty, feud, queue, few, adieu, view, use, cue, suit, yule, yew, you

:   *Indicates prolongation of the vowel which it follows.*
ı   *When placed beneath a consonant, indicates that the consonant is used syllabically, i.e., to form a syllable without an accompanying vowel.*
′   *When placed above and to the left of a syllable, indicates that this syllable is to receive primary accent.*
,   *When placed to the left and below the syllable, indicates secondary accent.*
[ʔ] *Symbol used to indicate the glottal stop.*

CONSONANTS DISTINGUISHED FROM VOWELS

Although the old and often-quoted maxim, "Take care of the consonants and the vowels will take care of themselves," is an exaggeration, most articulation problems, as far as they relate to distinctness, are associated with consonants. Problems related to good tone quality, loudness, pitch change, and rate are more concerned with vowels than with consonants. Being understood is the attribute of the speaker who takes care of his consonants, particularly since much more movement of the articulators is required for producing consonants than vowels.

Imagine for a moment the very beginnings of language and speech in primitive man. By opening his mouth and bellowing forth a sound, he probably produced what we today would call a vowel. This is not unlike a 3-month-old baby today experimenting with a new found plaything—his voice. He experiments over a wide range of mouth openings and tongue positions, and quite without trying to categorize them produces many more vowels than are found in American English. Primitive man no doubt realized that by manipulating his lips, tongue and soft palate he could add great variability to the utterances of the voiced breath stream. He was thus able to form many units of language, known as morphemes, which led to the development of language as he matured in civilization. We simply want to stress this point: The voice was used primarily to project speech various distances, while the consonants were employed to carry the burden of meaning. To demonstrate this point, try the following experiment: Say the sentence, "She can not trim down," two ways. First remove all the consonants and say the vowels only, and second, remove all the vowels and say the consonants only. The first version should be totally unintelligible, though loud, while the latter should be roughly intelligible but greatly reduced in power.

If you utter the vowel sounds [u, o, ɔ, ɑ, and æ] on a continuous exhalation while looking into the mirror, you will observe that at all times the mouth is partly open so that the tone is relatively unobstructed. Now utter on a continuous breath the consonants [s, t, f, d, and g], and you will see that each of the sounds either partly or completely checks the flow of the outgoing breath stream. That is essentially the difference between vowels and consonants. In vowels the mouth is open and the flow of sound relatively unobstructed, whereas in consonants the flow of sound is restricted or temporarily stopped. The accompanying chart comparing vowels and consonants will further clarify some of their differences.

COMPARISON OF VOWELS AND CONSONANTS

Vowels	Consonants
1. Vowels are sonorous speech sounds and are relatively open and unobstructed.	Consonants on the whole are less sonorous, have more noise elements, and are generally more obstructed.
2. Vowels make possible good carrying power for the voice.	Consonants have less phonetic power and in many instances detract from good voice quality.
3. Vowels, with few exceptions, have little specific meaning in themselves.	Consonants are chiefly responsible for clearness in diction; they are the chief agent for making words understandable.
4. Vowels depend upon certain pitch and resonance characteristics as well as duration for their identification.	Consonants depend upon specific movements of the articulators (i.e., tongue, lips, jaw, and soft palate) for their identity.
5. All vowels are voiced, except in whispering.	Many consonants are unvoiced.

CLASSIFICATION OF CONSONANTS

For convenience of study, consonants are classified in various ways, depending upon physical characteristics of the sounds or on manner of articulation.

Perhaps the simplest and most clear-cut of these classifications is based on whether they are voiced or voiceless. In many instances, for each

129

adjustment of the articulators we have two different sounds. The following pairs demonstrate this point: [p-b], [t-d][k-g], [f-v], [ʃ-ʒ]. In each pair the second sound is differentiated from the first only in that the vocal folds are brought together and the breath stream is voiced. In order to demonstrate this difference, place your finger on your larynx during the production of [f], holding it for a few seconds; then without interrupting the steady flow of breath bring your vocal folds together. The added vibration of the vocal folds changes the [f] to [v]. Note, however, that all consonants are not paired in this manner.

A second classification, popular in the study of phonetics, is based on the arrangement of consonants according to their physical characteristics: (a) *plosives* [p, b, t, d, k, and g]; (b) *fricatives* [f, v, θ, ð, s, z, ʃ, ʒ, and h]; (c) *nasals* [m, n, and ŋ]; (d) *glides* [r, j, w, and l]; and (e) *affricates* [tʃ and dʒ].

A third classification is based upon the placement of tongue, lips, jaw, and palate during the production of the sounds: (a) *labial* [p, b, m, and w]; (b) *labiodental* [f and v]; (c) *lingua-dental* [θ and ð]; (d) *lingua-alveolar* [t, d, n, l, s, and z]; (e) *lingua-palatal* [ʃ, ʒ, r, and j]; (f) *lingua-velar* [k, g, and ŋ]; and (g) *glottal* [h]. Figure 7.1 shows the articulatory mechanism.

We should think of these classifications not as being mutually exclusive, but rather as being interrelated and sometimes overlapping. They should, however, aid the student in gaining a better understanding of the sounds. The accompanying chart shows the interrelationship of the three classifications.

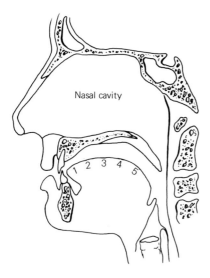

Nasal cavity

Figure 7.1. The articulatory mechanism, showing the different parts of the tongue: 1, tip; 2, blade; 3, front; 4, middle; 5, back.

130

CONSONANT CLASSIFICATION CHART (vs = voiceless; v = voiced)

	Bilabial		Labio-Dental		Lingua-Dental		Lingua-Alveolar		Lingua-Palatal		Lingua-Velar		Glottal	
	vs	v	vs	v	vs	v	vs	v	vs	v	vs	v	vs	v
Plosives	p	b					t	d			k	g		
Fricatives			f	v	θ	ð	s	z	ʃ	ʒ			h	
Nasals		m						n				ŋ		
Glides		w						l		r j				
Affricates									tʃ	dʒ				

THE PLOSIVES

The *plosives*, or *stops*, as they are sometimes called, are a group of consonants formed by momentarily halting the outward passage of the breath stream, building up pressure, then suddenly releasing the breath in a little explosion. There are three sets of plosives, bilabial, [p] and [b]; lingua-alveolar, [t] and [d]; and lingua-palatal, [k] and [g]; these are determined by the site of occlusion of the breath stream. Three of the plosives are voiced, [b, d, and g], and three are voiceless, [p, t, and k].

Plosives will differ in articulation depending upon their position in a word, phrase, or sentence. In a stressed syllable, the impounding of air is more pronounced as is the release; consequently, the plosives in this position have greater phonetic power. If these sounds occur in the middle of a word or syllable chain, more than likely they will have to be articulated much more quickly and with greater crispness to sustain their character. In the final position of a word or sentence, the plosives almost disappear, yet one must go through the proper articulatory movements in order to insure correct enunciation of the word.

THE CONSONANTS [p] AND [b]

The consonants [p] and [b] are called *bilabial, stop plosives*. They are made by stopping the breath stream at the firmly closed lips, while the soft palate is elevated at the same time so that no breath escapes through the nose. Then suddenly the lips are opened releasing the impounded breath stream with a perceptible explosion. The sound [p] is voiceless, and the [b] is voiced.

Common Errors

1. The plosives, when well articulated, give crispness and precision to speech; therefore, it is important to master the correct movements before drilling on meaningful material. Be sure to complete Exercise 1 before going on to the words and sentences in exercises 2 and 3.

2. Very often speakers do not develop sufficient breath pressure buildup and release to achieve the needed explosion for plosives, in which case the plosives take on a fricative quality. This is a fault that is typical of lip-lazy, careless, or weak speakers.

3. In common with the other plosives, weakness in articulation becomes especially evident when the [p] and [b] occur in conjunction with other consonants as in *caps, cabs, flapjacks, abduction*, etc. In these cases one of the consonants is likely to be seriously slighted or even dropped entirely.

4. Persons with a foreign language background, particularly German, often substitute the voiceless [p] for the voiced [b]. Thus, *tub* may become *tup*, *shrub* may become *shrup*, *slab* may become *slap*, etc.

EXERCISES

1. Practice the frames of the following operant conditioning exercise for [p] and [b]:

Initial		Medial		Final	
Frames	Frames	Frames	Frames	Frames	Frames
1 i	11 i	21 i	31 i	41 i	51 i
2 pi	12 bi	22 ipi	32 ibi	42 ip	52 ib
3 ε	13 ε	23 ε	33 ε	43 ε	53 ε
4 pε	14 bε	24 εpε	34 εbε	44 εp	54 εb
5 ɑ	15 ɑ	25 ɑ	35 ɑ	45 ɑ	55 ɑ
6 pɑ	16 bɑ	26 ɑpɑ	36 ɑbɑ	46 ɑp	56 ɑb
7 u	17 u	27 u	37 u	47 u	57 u
8 pu	18 bu	28 upu	38 ubu	48 up	58 ub
9 ɔ	19 ɔ	29 ɔ	39 ɔ	49 ɔ	59 ɔ
10 pɔ	20 bɔ	30 ɔpɔ	40 ɔbɔ	50 ɔp	60 ɔb

Instructions: (a) the instructor (or other good model) says the sound or syllable unit, and the student echoes in response, (b) the instructor signals if the response is correct (hand, clicker, light, etc.), (c) the instructor continues until all frames are done in the program, (d) if the percentage of correct responses falls below 80 percent, the instructor reinstructs the student and repeats the program. If a student is unable to complete the programs with 80 percent success, outside help may be necessary.

2. Practice the following words either as frames in an operant conditioning sequence or individually.

Initial		Medial		Final	
Frames	Frames	Frames	Frames	Frames	Frames
1 pretty	11 balm	21 sharply	31 table	41 harp	51 diatribe
2 proud	12 been	22 nuptials	32 sherbet	42 clasp	52 probe
3 plural	13 bill	23 topmast	33 cabal	43 yelp	53 tribe
4 principle	14 beat	24 aptly	34 rabbit	44 warp	54 drab
5 plenty	15 bet	25 capital	35 rubble	45 sloop	55 absorb
6 pot	16 bargain	26 happy	36 substitute	46 hop	56 cherub
7 power	17 basket	27 supper	37 submarine	47 catnip	57 crib
8 puff	18 bright	28 pamper	38 cabbage	48 tulip	58 rob
9 pan	19 blend	29 poppy	39 cupboard	49 pulp	59 describe
10 political	20 brown	30 pepper	40 fabricate	50 gap	60 bribe

3. Practice the following sentences:

    a. Power politics involves principles that are apt to keep the world in suspense.

    b. Popcorn and peanuts are a happy combination.

    c. Please pass the pepper, Peter.

    d. Stopgap legislation may precipitate unhappy results.

    e. Apparently the people at the pageant were pleased with the players.

    f. The babbling brook broke its boundaries near the Arab tents.

    g. The basket on the table was filled with cabbages.

    h. The baby's bib is not on the table but in his crib.

    i. His job was to probe for microbes.

    j. Benjamin Franklin could not be bribed by foreign cabals.

4. Work on the following lines of poetry and tongue twisters:

    a. I bubble into eddying bays,
      I babble on the pebbles.

    b. I sing of brooks, of blossoms, of birds, and bowers.

    c. Boots, boots, boots, boots,
      Moving up and down again!

    d. A tap at the pane, the quick sharp scratch
      And blue spurt of a lighted match.

    e. Beat, beat, beat, beat, beat upon the tom-tom.[2]

    f. Baa, baa, black sheep, have you any wool?

    g. Peter Prangle, the prickly prangly pear picker, picked a peck of prickly, prangly pears from the prickly, prangly pear trees on the pleasant prairies.

[2] From *Covenant with Earth* by Lew Sarett. Edited and copyrighted, 1956, by Alma Johnson Sarett, and published, 1956, by University of Florida Press. Reprinted by permission of Mrs. Sarett.

h. Peter Piper, the pepper picker, picked a peck of pickled peppers. A peck of pickled peppers did Peter Piper, the pepper picker pick. If Peter Piper, the pepper picker, picked a peck of pickled peppers, where is the peck of pickled peppers that Peter Piper, the pepper picker, picked?

i. Betty Botta bought a bit of butter, but, she said, "This butter's bitter. If I put it in my batter, it will make my batter bitter. But a bit of better butter will make my bitter batter better."

j. Algy met a bear. The bear was bulgy. The bulge was Algy.

k. Two bootblacks, one white and one black, were standing at the corner doing nothing, when the white bootblack agreed to black the black bootblack's boots. The black bootblack was willing to have his boots blacked by his fellow bootblack, and the bootblack who had agreed to black the black bootblack's boots went to work.

THE CONSONANTS [t] AND [d]

The consonants [t] and [d] are called *lingua-alveolar stop plosives*. On these sounds the breath stream is impounded by applying the firm pressure of the tip of the tongue against the upper teeth ridge, closing the nasal port so that no breath can escape through the nose, then quickly releasing the tongue tip and letting the breath escape in a small explosion. The sound [d] is voiced, the [t] unvoiced.

Common Errors

1. If the tongue tip is allowed to fall too low, so that it rests against the teeth rather than the gum ridge, the sound resembles a lisp. Thus *cat* [kæt] becomes *cath* [kæθ], *fate* [feɪt] becomes *faith* [feɪθ].

2. When either of these sounds occurs at the end of a word, careless speakers may drop the sound completely. Thus *asked* [æskt] becomes *ask* [æsk], *apt* [æpt] becomes *ap* [æp].

3. The above problem becomes a special hazard when one of these sounds follows another in successive words as in *cold day* [koʊld deɪ] and *sit down* [sɪt daʊn]; these phrases are likely to sound like *col' day* [koʊldeɪ] and *si' down* [sɪdaʊn]. In correcting this fault, do not go to the opposite extreme and make these sounds too conspicuous. Experiment with the above two phrases and with others in the following exercises, trying to make the words distinct but not pedantic.

4. When one of these plosives is followed by [l], [m], [n], or [ŋ], one of two things may happen:

   a. Being too difficult for a lazy speaker to bother with, it may simply be left out. Thus *little* ['lɪtl̩] may become *lil* [lɪl], and *middle* ['mɪdl̩] may become *mil* [mɪl].

b. The glottal stop may be substituted. Thus *bottle* ['bɑtl̩], may become ['bɑʔl̩] and *battle* ['bætl̩] may become ['bæʔl̩].

5. In the difficult combination of sounds where [t] occurs between two [s] sounds, care and practice are often required to make these sounds distinct, so that *lists* [lɪsts] does not become [lɪs], and *chests* [tʃɛsts] does not become *ches* [tʃɛs].

6. Some persons fail to realize that the *-ed* past tense of verbs is pronounced sometimes as [t] and sometimes as [d], depending upon whether it follows a voiced or an unvoiced sound. Following a voiced sound the *ed* is pronounced [d], and following an unvoiced sound it is pronounced [t]. For example, *clipped* is pronounced [klɪpt], *tabbed* is pronounced [tæbd], *tripped* is pronounced [trɪpt], and *cribbed* is pronounced [krɪbd].

7. One other fault, rare but still common enough to merit being mentioned, is the adding of a final [t] where it does not belong on such words as *once* [wʌns] and *twice* [twaɪs], making them [wʌnst] and [twaɪst].

EXERCISES

1. Practice the frames in the following operant conditioning exercise for [t] and [d] :

Initial				Medial				Final			
Frames		Frames		Frames		Frames		Frames		Frames	
1	i	11	i	21	i	31	i	41	i	51	i
2	ti	12	di	22	iti	32	idi	42	it	52	id
3	ɛ	13	ɛ	23	ɛ	33	ɛ	43	ɛ	53	ɛ
4	tɛ	14	dɛ	24	ɛtɛ	34	ɛdɛ	44	ɛt	54	ɛd
5	ɑ	15	ɑ	25	ɑ	35	ɑ	45	ɑ	55	ɑ
6	tɑ	16	dɑ	26	ɑtɑ	36	ɑdɑ	46	ɑt	56	ɑd
7	u	17	u	27	u	37	u	47	u	57	u
8	tu	18	du	28	utu	38	udu	48	ut	58	ud
9	ɔ	19	ɔ	29	ɔ	39	ɔ	49	ɔ	59	ɔ
10	tɔ	20	dɔ	30	ɔtɔ	40	ɔdɔ	50	ɔt	60	ɔd

Instructions are the same as for Exercise 1, p. 132.

2. Practice the following words either as frames in an operant conditioning sequence or individually :

Initial		Medial		Final	
Frames	Frames	Frames	Frames	Frames	Frames
1 tie	11 dimple	21 bitter	31 peddle	41 bucket	51 pod
2 time	12 dentist	22 quantity	32 saddle	42 pit	52 pride
3 taught	13 dare	23 patter	33 today	43 part	53 afraid
4 tooth	14 dart	24 little	34 Sunday	44 sot	54 crowed
5 team	15 dog	25 battle	35 haddock	45 mat	55 deride
6 trip	16 delve	26 butter	36 madame	46 debt	56 shade
7 trowel	17 drown	27 pretty	37 pardon	47 straight	57 occurred
8 trite	18 drab	28 plenty	38 middle	48 strident	58 bleed
9 trouble	19 drought	29 turtle	39 quandary	49 fright	59 allude
10 trombone	20 dress	30 bestial	40 hardy	50 boast	60 approved

3. Practice the following [t, d] sentences:
   a. Terry bit the tip of his tongue.
   b. The pitter-patter of the rain frightened the little children.
   c. The bestial act caused twenty-two thousand heretics to be held suspect.
   d. The strident tones of the soprano were apparent from the outset.
   e. The pretty little girl encountered trouble with her front teeth.
   f. Madame, afraid of the dentist, darted past his door.
   g. The hardy haddock defied the daring fisherman.
   h. Mad dogs go out in the noonday sun.
   i. On Sunday people drive out of the crowded city into the open fields.
   j. To meddle in somebody else's business is unpardonable.

4. Try the following paired words over in rapid succession, working for clear and distinct but easy articulation:

bold—bolt had—hat nod—not paid—pate
cold—colt cod—cot found—fount feed—feet
mold—molt send—sent pod—pot wad—watt
heed—heat code—coat road—rote moat—coat

5. Try words in the difficult [ts] combination:

hats—cats clots—blots shots—Scots skates—mates
cents—rents coats—floats brutes—shoots hates—rates

6. Work on the following tongue twisters and lines of poetry:
   a. A tree toad loved a she-toad
      That lived up in a tree.
      She was a three-toed she-toad.

136

But a two-toed tree toad tried to win
The she-toad's friendly nod,
For the two-toed tree toad loved the ground
That the three-toed she-toad trod.

b. Amidst the mists and coldest frosts,
With stoutest wrists and loudest boasts,
He thrusts his fists against the posts,
And still insists he sees the ghosts.

c. And darest thou then
To beard the lion in his den,
The Douglas in his hall ?

d. Dust thou art, to dust returnest,
Was not spoken of the soul.

e. I dare do all that doth become a man ;
Who dares do more is none.

f. Into the street the piper stept,
Smiling first a little smile,
As if he knew what magic slept,
In his quiet pipe the while.

THE CONSONANTS [k] AND [g]

The [k] and [g] sounds are called *lingua-palatal* or *lingua-velar, stop plo-sives*. In forming them the back of the tongue is pressed firmly against the tensed soft palate to impound the breath stream, and the compressed air is then released in a small explosion by the quick withdrawal of the tongue. The [g] is voiced, [k] is unvoiced.

Common Errors

1. If the lingua-palatal closure is not tight enough, insufficient breath pressure to produce a plosive effect results. Be sure that the breath stream is sufficiently impounded to produce an appropriate explosion.

2. Many speakers do not develop enough voice production on [g] during the impounding stage, resulting in a clipped version of [g]. Practice voicing during the impounding phase until adequate duration of voicing takes place.

3. Care must be taken to prevent the final [k] and [g] from being almost omitted, as frequently happens with all final plosives. In substandard speech, it is typical for a speaker to weaken these final sounds until they are almost inaudible.

EXERCISES

1. Practice the frames in the following operant conditioning exercise for [k] and [g] :

137

Initial		Medial		Final	
Frames	Frames	Frames	Frames	Frames	Frames
1 i	11 i	21 i	31 i	41 i	51 i
2 ki	12 gi	22 iki	32 igi	42 ik	52 ig
3 ɛ	13 ɛ	23 ɛ	33 ɛ	43 ɛ	53 ɛ
4 kɛ	14 gɛ	24 ɛkɛ	34 ɛgɛ	44 ɛk	54 ɛg
5 ɑ	15 ɑ	25 ɑ	35 ɑ	45 ɑ	55 ɑ
6 kɑ	16 gɑ	26 ɑkɑ	36 ɑgɑ	46 ɑk	56 ɑg
7 u	17 u	27 u	37 u	47 u	57 u
8 ku	18 gu	28 uku	38 ugu	48 uk	58 ug
9 ɔ	19 ɔ	29 ɔ	39 ɔ	49 ɔ	59 ɔ
10 kɔ	20 gɔ	30 ɔkɔ	40 ɔgɔ	50 ɔk	60 ɔg

Instructions are the same as for Exercise 1, p. 132.

2. Practice the following words either as frames in an operant conditioning sequence or individually:

Initial		Medial		Final	
Frames	Frames	Frames	Frames	Frames	Frames
1 cat	11 gas	21 packed	31 doggerel	41 medic	51 peg
2 caught	12 get	22 uncle	32 dogma	42 static	52 pig
3 cure	13 gone	23 accompanist	33 beggar	43 peak	53 hug
4 culinary	14 gust	24 plucked	34 bigger	44 bleak	54 flag
5 kine	15 gain	25 instruct	35 buggy	45 pork	55 cog
6 crop	16 gravel	26 occur	36 plagued	46 music	56 brig
7 clean	17 gloom	27 accurate	37 flogged	47 lock	57 rag
8 crime	18 grimace	28 oracle	38 finger	48 flick	58 plague
9 crystal	19 gleam	29 acute	39 figure	49 opaque	59 agog
10 clipper	20 grammar	30 anchor	40 trigger	50 oblique	60 prig

3. Practice the following sentences:

    a. The music instructor could accompany his students as well as conduct the orchestra.

    b. The crystal was packed carefully into a clean crate.

    c. The cat cleaned her kittens with incredible care.

    d. The oracle at Delphi could not always be considered accurate in forecasting world conditions.

    e. Uncooked pork may cause trichinosis.

f. If gas gets scarce, the horse and buggy of bygone days may gain in popularity.
g. Goodness and greatness often go hand in hand.
h. The ghastly green light cast a ghostly shadow across the grass.
i. The Hungarian linguist could not conquer the English language.
j. The dog growled at the beggar.

4. Avoid guttural or glottal sounds in the following words and syllables. Keep them as *light* as possible and as far forward in the mouth as is consistent with proper articulation of the sounds. Repeat them many times in order to develop the desired kinesthetic sense.

a. *bag* [bæg], *flag* ([flæg], *sag* [sæg].
b. *darken* ['dɑɚkn̩], *garden* ['gɑɚdn̩], *taken* ['teɪkn̩].
c. *carpet* ['kɑɚpɪt], *market* ['mɑɚkɪt], *sparklet* ['spɑɚklɪt].

5. Articulate the following jingles carefully:

a. The king was in the counting house,
counting out his money.
b. Eight gray geese in a green field grazing;
Gray were the geese and green was the grazing.
c. There was a crooked man
And he walked a crooked mile,
He found a crooked sixpence
Against a crooked stile.

6. The following selections afford excellent drill in the [k] and [g] sounds, as well as in many other consonant combinations:

a. "Lying Awake," p. 174.
b. "Jabberwocky," p. 175.

THE FRICATIVE CONTINUANTS

The classification of phonemes known as fricatives or fricative continuants is based upon both the place of articulation and their acoustic characteristics. As the label implies, there are both friction and continuation components in all of these sounds. In all fricatives [f, v, θ, ð, s, z, ʃ, ʒ, and h], the main resonating tube is narrowed at a specific place of articulation, depending upon the phoneme pair involved, and the outgoing breath stream is greatly restricted. However, the breath stream is not blocked, as it is in plosives, and a *hissing* or *buzzing* sound quality is created. The aperture or place of restriction remains constant, as does the position of articulators throughout the production of fricatives, giving them the durational and quality characteristics by which they are identified. Each voiceless fricative except [h] has its voiced cognate.

THE CONSONANTS [f] AND [v]

The sounds [f] and [v] are *labiodental fricative continuants.* The lower lip is brought into light contact with the upper front teeth and the voiced or voiceless airstream is forced through this restricted area. Note that the adjustment is quite specific and that most of the air escapes frontally.

Common Errors

1. Insufficient force and duration of these sounds result in their not being heard accurately by the listener. *Five* becomes [faɪ], *fifth* becomes [fɪθ], and so forth.

2. If the lower lip does not make a satisfactory adjustment, because of lack of adequate pressure, the resultant phoneme can easily be confused with other continuants, e.g., [f] for [θ].

3. Many speakers encounter difficulty in articulation when continuants occur one after the other, as in *fifths, proofs, cuff that.*

4. The [f] and [v] are often omitted through carelessness when they occur in the final position in words.

EXERCISES

1. Practice the frames in the following operant conditioning exercise for [f] and [v] :

Initial		Medial		Final	
Frames	Frames	Frames	Frames	Frames	Frames
1 i	11 i	21 i	31 i	41 i	51 i
2 fi	12 vi	22 ifi	32 ivi	42 if	52 iv
3 ɛ	13 ɛ	23 ɛ	33 ɛ	43 ɛ	53 ɛ
4 fɛ	14 vɛ	24 ɛfɛ	34 ɛvɛ	44 ɛf	54 ɛv
5 ɑ	15 ɑ	25 ɑ	35 ɑ	45 ɑ	55 ɑ
6 fɑ	16 vɑ	26 ɑfɑ	36 ɑvɑ	46 ɑf	56 ɑv
7 u	17 u	27 u	37 u	47 u	57 u
8 fu	18 vu	28 ufu	38 uvu	48 uf	58 uv
9 ɔ	19 ɔ	29 ɔ	39 ɔ	49 ɔ	59 ɔ
10 fɔ	20 vɔ	30 ɔfɔ	40 ɔvɔ	50 ɔf	60 ɔv

Instructions are the same as for Exercise 1, p.132.

2. Practice the following words either as frames in an operant conditioning sequence or individually :

Initial		Medial		Final	
Frames	Frames	Frames	Frames	Frames	Frames
1 fur	11 vile	21 awful	31 invincible	41 half	51 strive
2 finish	12 vary	22 draught	32 universal	42 laugh	52 hive
3 foggy	13 vanish	23 gopher	33 event	43 rough	53 save
4 fen	14 vital	24 effect	34 uvula	44 enough	54 sleeve
5 foam	15 verse	25 traffic	35 heaven	45 cuff	55 love
6 fun	16 valuable	26 afraid	36 trivial	46 proof	56 perceive
7 frank	11 voracious	27 affluent	37 revise	47 staff	57 suave
8 face	18 vulnerable	28 baffle	38 evident	48 bluff	58 twelve
9 fright	19 vest	29 different	39 alleviate	49 whiff	59 retrieve
10 philosophy	20 vinegar	30 buffer	40 prevalent	50 tough	60 brave

3. Practice the following sentences:
   a. The tough traffic officer felt that a fine of fifteen dollars was insufficient for the offense.
   b. The gopher baffled the furious housewife.
   c. Fred and Frank fought furiously over Florence.
   d. The far-flung effects of Christian philosophy have never been fully explored.
   e. He offered fifty-five dollars for finding his flea-bitten fox terrier.
   f. The visible universe is trivial in comparison to the vast infinity of time and space.
   g. The storm hovered over the village, obstructing the view of the visitor.
   h. Vera and Eva vied for valedictorian honors.
   i. Viking victories have been recorded in various verse forms by the medieval writers.
   j. The uvular muscle of the velum has very nearly lost its function.

4. While articulating the following words, observe your lip action in a mirror, at the same time touching your larynx to determine whether or not the sound is voiced:

velvet ['vɛlvɪt]   wife [waɪf]   selves [sɛlvz]
value ['vælju]   wives [waɪvz]   shelf [ʃɛlf]
vaudeville ['voudvɪl]   life [laɪf]   shelves [ʃɛlvz]
revolver ([rɪ'vɑlvɚ]   lives [laɪvz]   fain [feɪn]
fife [faɪf]   self [sɛlf]   vain [veɪn]

141

5. Practice the following combinations:

off—of	waifs—waves
fifty—fifth	shuffle—shovel
fear—veer	fine—vines
safe—saves	think—over—my—offer

6. Work for both accuracy and ease on the following lines:
   a. Fair is foul and foul is fair.
   b. The fair breeze blew, the white foam flew,
      The furrow followed free.
   c. False face must hide what false heart doth know.

THE CONSONANTS [θ] AND [ð]

The [θ] and [ð] are *lingua-dental fricatives*. They are made by lightly touching the tip of the tongue to the edge of the upper front teeth and forcing the breath stream between the teeth and the tip of the tongue. The sides of the tongue back of the tip are pressed lightly against the teeth laterally to direct the breath stream centrally. The [ð] is voiced, the [θ] voiceless.

Common Errors

1. Some persons fail to make a clear distinction between [θ] and [ð], often substituting one for the other. A word like *frothing* ['frɔθɪŋ) is likely to sound more like ['frɔðɪŋ], *oath* [oʊθ] like [oʊð].

2. Occasionally, people with foreign accents have difficulty in distinguishing between these two sounds and the [d] and [t]. Since the [θ] and [ð] do not appear in most other languages, it is necessary to teach these persons the proper positions for the sounds.

Bite the tip of your tongue lightly, retract the lower teeth and emit the breath stream between the tongue tip and the upper front teeth. A properly placed [θ] should result. Another way of approximating this sound is to extend the tongue tip well beyond the upper front teeth, and emit the breath stream while keeping the tongue blade in contact with the upper front teeth. Now slowly retract the tongue until the tip reaches the upper front teeth. If the tongue is not too tense and the friction of the outgoing breath stream is sufficient, a good [θ] sound should result.

3. Faulty production of these sounds may often be attributed to carelessness in placement of the tongue or to poor muscular coordination.

EXERCISES

1. Practice the frames in the following operant conditioning exercise for [θ] and [ð]:

Initial		Medial		Final	
Frames	Frames	Frames	Frames	Frames	Frames
1 i	11 i	21 i	31 i	41 i	51 i
2 θi	12 ði	22 iθi	32 iði	42 iθ	52 ið
3 ε	13 ε	23 ε	33 ε	43 ε	53 ε
4 θε	14 ðε	24 εθε	34 εðε	44 εθ	54 εð
5 ɑ	15 ɑ	25 ɑ	35 ɑ	45 ɑ	55 ɑ
6 θɑ	16 ðɑ	36 ɑθɑ	36 ɑðɑ	46 ɑθ	56 ɑð
7 u	17 u	27 u	37 u	47 u	57 u
8 θu	18 ðu	28 uθu	38 uðu	48 uθ	58 uð
9 ɔ	19 ɔ	29 ɔ	39 ɔ	49 ɔ	59 ɔ
10 θɔ	20 ðɔ	30 ɔθɔ	40 ɔðɔ	50 ɔθ	60 ɔð

Instructions are the same as for Exercise 1, p. 132.

2. Practice the following words either as frames in an operant conditioning sequence or individually:

Initial		Medial		Final	
Frames	Frames	Frames	Frames	Frames	Frames
1 thin	11 that	21 catholic	31 another	41 width	51 soothe
2 thick	12 this	22 healthy	32 either	42 hearth	52 smooth
3 thought	13 those	23 birthday	33 neither	43 mirth	53 blithe
4 thaw	14 thou	24 method	34 although	44 wealth	54 clothe
5 thousand	15 there	25 mythical	35 mother	45 death	55 teethe
6 three	16 the	26 pathology	36 southern	46 myth	56 tithe
7 thigh	17 thus	27 ether	37 smoother	47 wreath	57 loathe
8 thimble	18 then	28 atheist	38 whither	48 teeth	58 breathe
9 thumb	19 thine	29 ethical	39 weather	49 mouth	59 bathe
10 theory	20 though	30 author	40 lather	50 fifth	60 sheathe

3. Practice the following difficult [θ-ð] combinations:

thread	furthered	thousandth	bathes	growths
throw	weathered	faiths	clothes	fourths
three	bothered	widths	breathes	whether
thrice	tethered	myths	lathes	through
thrive	mothered	breadths	writhes	forthwith

143

4. Practice the following sentences:

  a. Three thousand Christians thought death no threat to their faith.

  b. The author may not have been wealthy, but he was ethical.

  c. The youth spoke the truth concerning his pathological methods.

  d. Thirty-three thugs hid in the thatched hut.

  e. Through the thicket the stealthy panther crept.

  f. Another Southerner seethed and writhed at the smothered legislation, but was loath to leave.

  g. The blithe spirit then pointed to the sheathed sword.

  h. This is the mother rather than the grandmother.

  i. Although there may be those who tithe, there are those who are loath to do so.

  j. My brother was not bothered with his teething, but the weather withered him.

5. Practice before the mirror to observe the tongue action on such words as *death, hearth, dearth, thud, thing, Thaddeus,* etc.

6. Distinguish between [θ] and [ð] in the following word pairs:

thing—thou	thought—those	fifth—mouthed
thirst—that	thumb—wither	sixth—though
theatre—there	twelfth—worthy	wealth—farthing

7. Carefully distinguish between the following paired words:

ether—either	cloth—clothe	moth—mother
south—southern	north—northern	breath—breathe

8. Work on the following tongue twisters and other passages:

  a. The sea ceaseth and sufficeth us.

  b. Theophilus Thistle, the successful thistle sifter, in sifting a sieve full of unsifted thistles, thrust three thousand thistles through the thick of his thumb. Now, if Theophilus Thistle, the successful thistle sifter, in sifting a sieve full of unsifted thistles, thrust three thousand thistles through the thick of his thumb, see that thou in sifting a sieve full of unsifted thistles, thrust not three thousand thistles through the thick of thy thumb. Success to the successful thistle sifter!

  c. The wind bloweth where it listeth, and thou hearest the sound thereof, but canst not tell whence it cometh or whither it goeth.

  d. Breathes there the man with soul so dead
    Who never to himself hath said:
    This is my own, my native land!

  e. As feud-seeking foemen afore-time assailed thee, a thousand thanes to thee did I bring, heroes to help thee.

THE CONSONANTS [s] AND [z]

Probably, for the majority of people, the *postdental fricatives* [s] and [z] afford more difficulty than any of the other English sounds. The proper production of these sounds requires not only keen hearing, but an extremely delicate adjustment of the articulators. The sides of the tongue must be kept in contact (laterally) with the teeth, yet raised and grooved sufficiently to force the air along the midline of the tongue. The tip of the tongue must not come in contact with either the upper front teeth or the gum ridge, and the breath stream must be directed across the cutting edges of the teeth. A second method of producing this sound involves placing the tip of the tongue behind the lower front teeth, and arching, grooving, and bringing the tongue laterally into contact with the teeth in much the same way as was described above. These two methods are known respectively as *up* and *down* techniques of tongue placement. The [z] is voiced, the [s] unvoiced.

Common Errors

1. The *central lisp* (also called the *frontal* or *dental lisp*) is made by the substitution of [θ] for [s], and [ð] for [z]. This substitution results from allowing the tongue tip to touch the upper teeth as in the formation of [θ] or [ð]. The correction lies primarily in properly retracting the tongue tip and redirecting the breath stream between the slightly parted teeth. Test this on words like *sick* [sɪk], *snow* [snoʊ], *Suzy* ['suzɪ], and the like.

2. The *lateral lisp* is caused by allowing the air to escape at the sides of the tongue over the bicuspids or canine teeth. Firm contact must be maintained between the sides of the tongue and the upper gum and teeth as far forward in the mouth as the canines to prevent this leakage.

3. One of the most common faults is overemphasis of [s] so that it is either too prominent or whistled. This can be corrected in various ways.

Perhaps the simplest means of correcting this fault is to reduce breath pressure or the duration of the sound itself. Do not breathe too heavily; do not force the sound. "Gently, brother, gently, pray!"

Occasionally the whistle is caused by too wide an aperture between certain teeth, or poor occlusion of the upper and lower teeth, or some other condition which defies even the most skillful efforts at compensation. In such a case you will be wise to consult your dentist or orthodontist.

4. Another common fault in the production of [s] and [z] is the occurrence of too high or too low frequency. The first condition results from having the tongue elevated too high, and the latter from having the tongue placed too low.

EXERCISES

1. Practice the frames in the following operant conditioning exercise for [s] and [z]:

Initial		Medial		Final	
Frames	Frames	Frames	Frames	Frames	Frames
1 i	11 i	21 i	31 i	41 i	51 i
2 si	12 zi	22 isi	32 izi	42 is	52 iz
3 ɛ	13 ɛ	23 ɛ	33 ɛ	43 ɛ	53 ɛ
4 sɛ	14 zɛ	24 ɛsɛ	34 ɛzɛ	44 ɛs	54 ɛz
5 ɑ	15 ɑ	25 ɑ	35 ɑ	45 ɑ	55 ɑ
6 sɑ	16 zɑ	26 ɑsɑ	36 ɑzɑ	46 ɑs	56 ɑz
7 u	17 u	27 u	37 u	47 u	57 u
8 su	18 zu	28 usu	38 uzu	48 us	58 uz
9 ɔ	19 ɔ	29 ɔ	39 ɔ	49 ɔ	59 ɔ
10 sɔ	20 zɔ	30 ɔsɔ	40 ɔzɔ	50 ɔs	60 ɔz

Instructions are the same as for Exercise 1, p. 132.

2. Practice the following words either as frames in an operant conditioning sequence or individually:

Initial		Medial		Final	
Frames	Frames	Frames	Frames	Frames	Frames
1 sit	11 zone	21 distinguish	31 lazy	41 fuss	51 gaze
2 soothe	12 zeal	22 decimal	32 prizes	42 press	52 goes
3 sartorial	13 zip	23 dastardly	33 razor	43 crass	53 was
4 saint	14 zoo	24 absolute	34 cousin	44 numerous	54 choose
5 settle	15 zephyr	25 classify	35 museum	45 gloss	55 cruise
6 string	16 zenith	26 Christmas	36 amused	46 flecks	56 trees
7 street	11 Zion	27 system	37 scissors	47 confess	57 always
8 slide	18 zinc	28 drastic	38 imposing	48 address	58 knives
9 slope	11 zany	29 dorsal	39 closet	49 superstitious	59 arise
10 sweet	20 zero	30 destitute	40 crazed	50 across	60 chives

3. Practice the following sentences:

    a. Saint Nicholas, the patron saint of the Christmas season, is synonymous with Santa Claus.

    b. The sun rises in the east and sets in the west.

    c. Our distinguished senator rose to his feet to address us.

    d. Sulfur and molasses were used as a spring tonic.

    e. The street lights glistened on the glossy pavement.

    f. My cousin was amused by the zebras in the zoo.

g. Knives and razors should be used with caution.

h. Lazy, hazy days are dog days.

i. I gazed at the imposing trees which lined the horizon.

j. A zany zephyr zipped through the trees.

4. Practice [s] and [z] in the following words:

skip	steam	stroke	grasps
scow	steep	strip	wasps
scatter	start	stream	lisps
scout	stunt	strewn	crisps
sleep	sweet	ships	blasts
slight	swell	stops	fasts
slow	swim	mops	lists
slap	swing	helps	bests
smite	split	pats	masks
smart	splendor	mitts	asks
smirk	spring	puts	casks
smell	spray	bets	husks
snout	squeal	ticks	spar
snip	square	kicks	spent
sneeze	squire	looks	scream
sneer	squint	lacks	scrape
spite	script	staffs	stiffs
spout	scratch	muffs	ifs

5. Practice words which contain both [s] and [z], such as *signs, suppose, sausages, solos, business, saws, saves,* and *softens.*

6. Practice the following phrases and sentences:

a. Sit in solemn silence.

b. Snort several times.

c. Ships, seven ships sailing.

d. Seasons of mists.

e. Steps of passing ghosts.

f. Silver shoes.

g. The assassin suddenly stepped into the street.

h. Seas and shoals and seasons.

7. Say the following jingles and tongue twisters rapidly:

a. The sixth sheik's sixth sheep is sick.

b. Some shun sunshine; do you shun sunshine?

c. Sister Susie's sewing shirts for soldiers.

d. Esau saw the sheep and the sheep saw Esau.

e. Sheila sells sea shells on the sea shore.

147

    f. Six slim, slick, slender saplings.

    g. Two twin-screw steel cruisers steamed up the Thames.

    h. Sing a song of sixpence
       A pocket full of rye
       Four and twenty blackbirds
       Baked in a pie.

    i. Swan swim over the sea;
       Swim, swan, swim.
       Swan swim back again;
       Well swam, swan.

    j. To sit in solemn silence in a dull, dark dock,
       In a pestilential prison, with a life-long lock.
       Awaiting the sensation of a short, sharp shock.
       From a cheap and chippy chopper, on a big, black block.

8. Work on the following lines of poetry:

    a. Silver sails all out of the west
       Under the silver moon.

    b. . . . Go not like a quarry-slave at night,
       Scourged to his dungeon, but sustained and soothed
       By an unfaltering trust.

    c. The setting sun, and music at the close,
       As the last taste of sweets, is sweetest last.

    d. Marching along, fifty-score strong,
       Great-hearted gentlemen, singing this song.

    e. Round the cape of a sudden came the sea,
       And the sun looked over the mountain's rim. . . .

    f. Sleep is a reconciling,
       A rest that peace begets;
       Shall not the sun rise smiling
       When fair at even it sets?

    g. Hail to thee, blithe Spirit!
       Bird thou never wert,
       That from heaven, or near it
       Pourest thy full heart
       In profuse strains of unpremeditated art.

9. Practice the following selection:

       My soul today
       Is far away,
       Sailing the Vesuvian Bay;
       My wingéd boat,
       A bird afloat,
       Swims round the purple peaks remote.

Round purple peaks
It sails and seeks
Blue inlets, and their crystal creeks,
Where high rocks throw,
Through deeps below,
A duplicated golden glow.

Oh, happy ship,
To rise and dip,
With the blue crystal at your lip!
Oh, happy crew,
My heart with you
Sails, and sails, and sings anew!

—Thomas Buchanan Read

THE CONSONANTS [ʃ] AND [ʒ]

[ʃ] and [ʒ] are *lingua-palatal fricatives* and are articulated with the tongue drawn slightly farther back and lower than it is for the [s] and [z] sounds. Note also that the blade of the tongue is spread laterally, so that the breath emerges over a broad surface rather than in a narrow stream. The [ʒ] is voiced, the [ʃ] unvoiced.

Common Errors

1. Occasionally these sounds become defective when the tongue is allowed to rise too high toward the palate; the resultant [ʃ] and [ʒ] are too high in frequency, somewhat resembling the German *ich*. Lowering of the blade of the tongue and thorough ear training will eliminate this fault.

2. A second fault arises in allowing the tongue to be lowered and retracted to such an extent that too large a resonating chamber is formed in the front of the mouth. Particularly is this true when the [ʃ] sound follows a back vowel, as in *gauche* [goʊʃ] and *emotion* [i'moʊʃn]. This fault is often associated with lateral lisps.

149

EXERCISES

1. Practice the frames of the following operant conditioning exercises for [ʃ] and [ʒ] :

Initial		Medial		Final	
Frames	Frames	Frames	Frames	Frames	Frames
1 i	11 i	21 i	31 i	41 i	51 i
2 ʃi	12 ʒi	22 iʃi	32 iʒi	42 iʃ	52 iʒ
3 ɛ	13 ɛ	23 ɛ	33 ɛ	43 ɛ	53 ɛ
4 ʃɛ	14 ʒɛ	24 ɛʃɛ	34 ɛʒɛ	44 ɛʃ	54 ɛʒ
5 a	15 a	25 a	35 a	45 a	55 a
6 ʃa	16 ʒa	26 aʃa	36 aʒa	46 aʃ	56 aʒ
7 u	17 u	27 u	37 u	47 u	57 u
8 ʃu	18 ʒu	28 uʃu	38 uʒu	48 uʃ	58 uʒ
9 ɔ	19 ɔ	29 ɔ	39 ɔ	49 ɔ	59 ɔ
10 ʃɔ	20 ʒɔ	30 ɔʃɔ	40 ɔʒɔ	50 ɔʃ	60 ɔʒ

Instructions are the same as for Exercise 1, p. 132.

2. Practice the following words either as frames in an operant conditioning sequence or individually :

Initial		Medial		Final	
Frames	Frames	Frames	Frames	Frames	Frames
1 shell	11 jabot	21 seashell	31 usual	41 crush	51 mirage
2 shingle	12 genre	22 description	32 pleasure	42 cash	52 barrage
3 sharp	13 gendarme	23 diction	33 regime	43 wish	53 corsage
4 should	14 Jeanne	24 sachet	34 usurer	44 fresh	54 sabotage
5 shirk	15 Gireaux	25 direction	35 derision	45 clash	55 rouge
6 shrimp	16 Gironde	26 patience	36 composure	46 radish	56 prestige
7 shake	17 Gide	27 emotion	37 illusion	47 finish	57 beige
8 shadow	18 Giraud	28 bushel	38 collision	48 gauche	58 garage
9 sheen	19 Jacques	29 profession	39 casual	49 fetish	59 menage
10 shallow	20 Joffre	30 anxious	40 occasion	50 astonish	60 persiflage

3. Practice the following sentences :
   a. She became anxious when sharks surrounded the ship.
   b. The roof of the mansion was finished with shake shingles.
   c. The shad is a fish, while the shrimp is a crustacean.

d. She shaded her shoulders with a mesh shawl.
e. The sun shone on the shabby shop windows.
f. The plans for invasion by the Hoosier division underwent revision.
g. The usurer made his decision of seizure with composure.
h. A mirage is a visionary illusion.
i. The beige jardiniere was stored in the garage.
j. Jacques, the jongleur, entertained the gendarme.

4. Compare and contrast the following word pairs:

shell—genre	fisher—azure
sharp—Jacques	emotion—regime
anxious—pleasure	sheen—rouge
precious—prestige	sachet—casual

5. Try the following tongue twister: The Shah of Shay shouted short shrill shrieks which shattered the shadowy night.
6. Work on the following passages:
a. Better than all measures
Of delightful sound,
Better than all treasures
That in books are found,
Thy skill to poet were, thou scorner of the ground.
b. A flock of sheep that leisurely pass by,
One after one; the sound of rain and bees
Murmuring; the fall of rivers, winds and seas,
Smooth fields, white sheets of water, and pure sky.
c. Hush, ah, hush, the scythes are saying,
Hush, and heed not, and fall asleep;
Hush they say to the grasses swaying;
Hush they sing to the clover deep!

THE CONSONANT [h]

The sound [h] may be classified as a *voiceless glottal fricative.* In making this sound the vocal cords are approximated sufficiently to restrict the outgoing breath stream, thus creating a fricative sound. However, the cords are not brought close enough together to create tone, hence the sound is voiceless. This sound occurs in the initial and medial positions of words only.

151

Common Errors

Usually the [h] sound does not give Americans much trouble, except in the [hw] combination which will be discussed later. Care should be taken, however, to see that an excessive amount of air does not escape during the production of this sound.

EXERCISES

1. Practice the frames in the following operant conditioning exercise for [h] :

Initial		Medial	
Frames	Frames	Frames	Frames
1 i	7 u	13 i	19 u
2 hi	8 hu	14 ihi	20 uhu
3 ɛ	9 oʊ	15 ɛ	21 oʊ
4 hɛ	10 hoʊ	16 ɛhɛ	22 oʊhoʊ
5 ɑ	11 ɔ	17 ɑ	23 ɔ
6 hɑ	12 hɔ	18 ɑhɑ	24 ɔhɔ

2. Practice the following words either as frames in an operant sequence or individually :

Initial		Medial	
Frames	Frames	Frames	Frames
1 how	6 health	11 behalf	16 behind
2 half	7 hint	12 behead	17 uphold
3 home	8 honey	13 cohort	18 perhaps
4 hello	9 hustle	14 rehearse	19 anyhow
5 hunt	10 hazard	15 inhale	20 overhead

3. Practice the following sentences.
   a. High heels have been called a hazard to good health.
   b. Hundreds of tomahawks were held high as the hardy Mohawks hunted their prey.
   c. Hydrogen and helium have to be handled with caution.
   d. The hotel in the hollow has housed many historic figures.
   e. His humility and heroism have held him in high repute.

4. Distinguish between the words in the following pairs:

oh—hoe	err—her	ate—hate	eat—heat
you—who	eye—high	ear—hear	ale—hale
awe—haw	at—hat	them—hem	it—hit

5. Practice the following tongue twisters:
   a. The hammer, hammer, hammer of the jackhammer
      Harassed the actors' rehearsal of Hamlet.
   b. If to hoot and to toot a Hottentot tot
      Were taught by a Hottentot tutor,
      Should the tutor get hot if the Hottentot tot
      Should hoot and toot at the tutor?
6. Work on the following lines of poetry:
   a. Sing, heigh ho, the holly!
   b. Home is the sailor, home from the Sea,
      And the hunter home from the hill.
   c. Tell me where is fancy bred,
      Or in the heart, or in the head?
   d. That hour it was when heaven's first gift of sleep
      On weary hearts of men most sweetly steals.

THE GLIDES OR SEMIVOWELS

Four consonants, [r], [j], [w], and [l], defy strict classification and have been treated differently by speech specialists. We chose to classify them simply as glides, realizing they are vowel-like yet have their distinctive features. Each will be considered separately.

A glide may be described as a transitionary sound resulting from the movement of the articulators from one vowel position to another during continuous voicing. For example, prolong an [i:] sound; without stopping the vocalized breath stream, proceed quickly to an [ʌ] sound—the transitional sound should be [j]; do likewise with [u] and [ʌ], and [ɜ] and [ʌ]—the resultant sounds should approximate [w] and [r].[3] Such a demonstration also illustrates the vowel-like nature of these sounds; it is not without reason that some authorities look upon the glides as semivowels. All glides are voiced.

[3] Much of the identity of these sounds depends upon the speed of movement of the articulators from one position to another, for if the movement is not made with speed and precision, the resultant sound loses much of its identifiable character.

THE CONSONANT [r]

The [r] may be classified as a *voiced postdental, lingua-palatal glide*. The nature of [r] varies greatly, depending upon its position in the word, and actually may be at least four different sounds. Say the following words aloud and compare and contrast the [r] sounds, *right, around, here,* and *bird*. The [r] is performed in all four words with the lateral margins of the tongue against the adjacent alveolar ridge. A retroflex action of the tongue is also observable, as the tip is slightly curled up. A definite tension is built up in the tongue muscles. In the initial position the phoneme [r] is started in the retroflex position and glides vigorously to the position required for the next sound. Indeed, if the movement is not made with precision and speed, the [r] loses much of its identifiable character. In the medial position the [r] is begun from the preceding phoneme and the tongue glides quickly toward the retroflex position, and then in one continuous action moves quickly toward the following phoneme, but not without a perceptible increase in loudness and a speeding up of the glide action as the tongue leaves the retroflex position. Final [r] is not truly consonantal, since it functions more like a vowel or second element of a diphthong, i.e., *father* [faðɚ] and *here* [hɪɚ], and more often is written phonetically (after utterance) as [ɚ]. The weak and strong forms of the vowel [ɝ] and [ɚ] will be treated in the next chapter.

In sections of the East and South, the [ɚ] sound following a vowel is either greatly weakened or omitted altogether. For example, *fear* [fɪɚ] may become [fiə], poor [pʊɚ] may become [pʊə], *harbor* ['hɑrbɚ] may become ['hɑ : bə], *start* [stɑɚt] may become [stɑ : t], etc. The student of diction should use as his standard the pronunciation of the best speakers in his culture or region.

Common Errors

1. Very often an individual will curl (retroflex) the tip of his tongue backward excessively (at the same time tensing the tongue), which gives rise to a rather hard, unpleasant tone. This is especially true of certain sections of the country where General American is the regional dialect.

2. As was mentioned earlier, sluggish tongue movements do much to destroy the identifiable characteristics of the glides, particularly the [r]. In this case drill in precision and speed is indicated.

3. Various distortions, substitutions, and omissions are possible on the [r] sound. For example, trilled [r], uvular [r], and no [r] whatsoever are typical of certain types of foreign accent. Various physiological and pathological conditions also may seriously impair the proper production of [r]. In such cases the student will do well to seek the services of a competent physician or speech correctionist.

154

EXERCISES

1. Operant conditioning exercise for [r] :

Initial				Medial				Final[1]			
Frames		Frames		Frames		Frames		Frames		Frames	
1	i	11	ɪ	21	i	31	ɪ	41	i	51	ɪ
2	ri	12	rɪ	22	iri	32	ɪrɪ	42	ir	52	ɪr
3	ɛ	13	eɪ	23	eɪ	33	ɛ	43	ɛ	53	ɛɪ
4	rɛ	14	reɪ	24	eɪre	34	ɛrɛ	44	ɛr	54	eɪr
5	ɑ	15	æ	25	ɑ	35	æ	45	ɑ	55	æ
6	rɑ	16	ræ	26	ɑrɑ	36	æræ	46	ɑr	56	ær
7	u	17	ʊ	27	u	37	ʊ	47	u	57	ʊ
8	ru	18	rʊ	28	uru	38	ʊrʊ	48	ur	58	ʊr
9	ɔ	19	oʊ	29	ɔ	39	oʊ	49	ɔ	59	oʊ
10	rɔ	20	roʊ	30	ɔrɔ	40	oʊroʊ	50	ɔr	60	oʊr

[1] *[r] usually forms a diphthong* [iɚ, ɛɚ, *etc.*] *in the final position following a vowel; hence, the vowel* [ɚ] *is often used in phonetic transcription.*

Instructions are the same as for Exercise 1, p. 132.

2. Practice the following words either as frames in an operant conditioning sequence or individually :

Initial				Medial				Final			
Frames		Frames		Frames		Frames		Frames		Frames	
1	rat	6	radio	11	America	16	sparse	21	monster	26	mother
2	ripe	7	religion	12	Africa	17	around	22	fodder	27	clear
3	rogue	8	region	13	bury	18	arid	23	floor	28	pier
4	run	9	ruminate	14	barn	19	variety	24	veneer	29	creator
5	read	10	rodent	15	sparrow	20	pardon	25	sheer	30	patter

3. Practice the following sentences :

    a. America, South America, Africa, Asia, Europe, and Australia present a variety of flora and fauna.

    b. The pitter-patter of the rain on the roof interferes with our radio reception.

    c. To rid the barnyard of the variety of rodents that frequent it is a major undertaking.

    d. Arid regions of the Rockies are sparsely settled.

    e. Reading the newspaper every morning is a religion with our father.

    f. The ordinarily torpid Raisin River roils and rages when it rains.

g. The surfers on the Rinconada rest on their surf boards treading water while awaiting a propitious curl.

h. Turn to the right for Hickory Farms.

i. Numerous arguments surround instruction of the three "R's", reading, writing, and arithmetic.

j. Spring's herald, the purple crocus, brightens the fields surrounding our farm.

4. Attempt to perfect good articulation of [r] in each of the phrases below, then carry over your control to the sentence following:

Frames		Frames	
1	round room	14	Harriet was recently married.
2	The round room is attractive.	15	merrily rolling
3	rough road	16	The car went merrily rolling along.
4	The rough road turned.		
5	rare recipe	17	drowsily dreaming
6	Her mother made a rare recipe.	18	He sat drowsily dreaming.
		19	brightly burnished
7	red roses	20	The art piece was brightly burnished.
8	Red roses are pretty.		
9	reading rapidly	21	rarely recite
10	Harvey tried reading rapidly.	22	Shy persons rarely recite.
11	round robins	23	wearily running
12	Stutterers like round robins.	24	He was wearily running the marathon.
13	recently married		

5. Work on the following selections:

When a merry maiden marries,
Sorrow goes and pleasure tarries;
Every sound becomes a song.
All is right and nothing's wrong.

Over hill, over dale,
Through brush, through brier,
Over park, over pale,
Through flood, through fire,
I do wander everywhere.

Drip, drip, the rain comes falling,
Rain in the woods, rain on the sea;
Even the little waves, beaten, come crawling,
As if to find shelter here with me.

156

Our purses shall be proud, our garments poor,
For 'tis the mind that makes the body rich;
And as the sun breaks through the darkest clouds,
So honor peereth in the meanest habit.

Once upon a midnight dreary, while I pondered, weak and
weary,
Over many a quaint and curious volume of forgotten lore—
While I nodded, nearly napping, suddenly there came a
tapping,
As of someone gently rapping, rapping at my chamber door,
"Tis some visitor," I muttered, "tapping at my chamber door—
Only this and nothing more."

The rainbow comes and goes,
And lovely is the rose,
The moon doth with delight
Look round her when the heavens are bare;
Waters on a starry night
Are beautiful and fair;
The sunshine is a glorious birth;
But yet I know, where'er I go,
That there hath pass'd away a glory from the earth.

THE CONSONANT [j]

The sound [j] is often described as a *voiced, lingua-palatal glide*; however, some writers prefer to call it a palatal *semivowel*. To form [j] the tongue starts from a position approximating that for the vowel [i], then moves quickly to the position of a following vowel. To demonstrate this sound prolong an [i:] for a few seconds, then move quickly to the vowel [u]; the result should be the word *you* [ju]. The [j] sound occurs only in initial and medial positions.

Common Errors

As a general rule, the formation of [j] presents no great problem to most speakers. However, two tendencies with regard to its use should be noted:

1. There is a growing tendency, even among careful speakers to eliminate [j] in favor of a more intermediate sound in certain words. For instance, *due* [dju] is rapidly changing to [dɪu] or even [du]. Usage is the law and rule of speech; hence the student of diction should be guided by the most acceptable standards of his dialectal area for guidance in this problem.

2. Too frequently [j] is intruded where it does not belong, as in such words as *coupon* ['k(j)upɑn], *column* ['kɑl(j)əm], *escalator* ['ɛsk(j)əleɪtɚ], *percolator* ['pɝk(j)əleɪtɚ], *similar* ['sɪm(j)əlɚ], *tremendous* [trɪ'mɛnd(j)əs].

157

1. Practice the frames in the following operant conditioning exercise for [j] :

Initial				Medial			
Frames		Frames		Frames		Frames	
1	i	11	ɪ	21	i	31	ɪ
2	ji	12	jɪ	22	iji	32	ɪjɪ
3	ɛ	13	eɪ	23	ɛ	33	eɪ
4	jɛ	14	jeɪ	24	ɛjɛ	34	eɪjeɪ
5	ɑ	15	æ	25	ɑ	35	æ
6	jɑ	16	jæ	26	ɑjɑ	36	æjæ
7	u	17	ʊ	27	ʊ	37	u
8	ju	18	jʊ	28	ʊjʊ	38	uju
9	ɔ	19	oʊ	29	ɔ	39	oʊ
10	jɔ	20	joʊ	30	ɔjɔ	40	oʊjoʊ

Instructions are the same as for Exercise 1, p. 132.

2. Practice the following words either as frames in an operant conditioning sequence or individually :

Initial				Medial			
Frames		Frames		Frames		Frames	
1	yam	11	yeast	21	accuse	31	bunion
2	year	12	yesterday	22	million	32	familiar
3	yoke	13	yellow	23	onion	33	canyon
4	yet	14	yarn	24	beyond	34	civilian
5	youth	15	yacht	25	companion	35	senior
6	yawn	16	your	26	coyote	36	union
7	young	17	yule	27	cotillion	37	arroyo
8	yes	18	Yonkers	28	banyan	38	milieu
9	yank	19	yard	29	barnyard	39	vineyard
10	yowl	20	yawl	30	toyon	40	ridicule

3. Practice the following sentences :

    a. My youthful companion gazed beyond the vineyards to the yachts and yawls anchored in the Yellow Sea.

    b. Yes, he yearned for his yesterday's youth.

    c. The yams and onions in our yard are valueless.

    d. A million Brazilians yelled, "Hallelujah."

    e. My senior companion yelped when York's yak stepped on his bunions.

THE CONSONANT [w]; THE COMBINATION [hw]

[w] is a *voiced bilabial glide*. It is produced by forming the lips for [u] and moving quickly to the position of the following vowel. To illustrate this process, prolong [u:] for a few seconds, then move rapidly to [i:]; the product should be a clearly articulated *we*. Inasmuch as [hw] is a combination of [h] and [w], detailed description will not be given. Suffice it to say that this sound unit is produced by making a glottal fricative approach to [w].[4]

Common Errors

1. As is common with the other bilabial consonants, people with stiff or lazy lips articulate [w] and [hw] poorly.

2. Perhaps the most common fault with the combination sound [hw] is that some individuals have difficulty in articulating the glottal fricative approach, and fall into error by completely omitting [h]. Thus *why* [hwaɪ] becomes [waɪ], which [hwɪtʃ] becomes [wɪtʃ], *wheel* [hwil] becomes [wil], etc. This fault may cause complications in meaning, because the only distinguishing characteristic of many word pairs is the glottal fricative approach to [w]. The following word pairs illustrate this point: wail-whale, wear-where, witch-which.

3. As is true of [r] and [j], [w] very often loses much of its character if the glide is not made with speed and precision.

EXERCISES

1. Practice the frames in the following operant conditioning exercise for [w] and [hw]:

Initial		Medial	
Frames	Frames	Frames	Frames
1 i	11 i	21 i	31 i
2 wi	12 hwi	22 iwi	32 ihwi
3 ɛ	13 ɛ	23 ɛ	33 ɛ
4 wɛ	14 hwɛ	24 ɛwɛ	34 ɛhwɛ
5 ɑ	15 ɑ	25 ɑ	35 ɑ
6 wɑ	16 hwɑ	26 ɑwɑ	36 ɑhwɑ
7 u	17 u	27 u	37 u
8 wu	18 hwu	28 uwu	38 uhwu
9 ɔ	19 ɔ	29 ɔ	39 ɔ
10 wɔ	20 hwɔ	30 ɔwɔ	40 ɔhwɔ

Instructions are the same as for Exercise 1, p. 132.

---

[4] [hw] is often described by phoneticians as voiceless [w], and is represented by the symbol [ʍ].

159

2. Practice the following words either as frames in an operant conditioning sequence or individually:

Initial		Medial	
Frames	Frames	Frames	Frames
1 we	11 where	21 beware	31 meanwhile
2 wash	12 what	22 anyone	32 somewhat
3 wit	13 which	23 reward	33 somewhere
4 watch	14 whip	24 away	34 nowhere
5 one	15 while	25 awash	35 elsewhere
6 window	16 whistle	26 aware	36 anywhere
7 weather	17 whether	27 unworthy	37 overwhelm
8 worship	18 when	28 inkwell	38 awhile
9 wealth	19 whet	29 always	39 bobwhite
10 wonder	20 whirl	30 reward	40 everywhere

3. Practice the following sentences:
   a. Warren washed the windows as William watched.
   b. Twelve bewitched dwarfs were walking in our woods.
   c. To woo is not always to win.
   d. Onward the stalwart wagons wended their way to the West.
   e. The weary wanderer waded through the billowy waters.
   f. Why whip or whack a horse when a "whoa" serves better?
   g. The whippet whined and whimpered when the bobwhite whistled.
   h. We were somewhat overwhelmed when the whale whirled and whizzed by the pier.
   i. While Mr. Wherry whispered to the whippoorwill, Grandpa chortled in his whiskers.
   j. When the millwheel refused to whirl, the wheat remained unground.

4. Distinguish between the words in each of the following pairs:

were—whir	wear—where	woe—whoa
wet—whet	wight—white	way—whey
wail—whale	wine—whine	weather—whether
witch—which	wetted—whetted	watt—what

160

5. Work on the following lines:
   a. To the gull's way, and the whale's way
      Where the wind's like a whetted knife.[5]
   b. Water, water, everywhere.
   c. But whether we meet or whether we part
      (For our ways are past our knowing),
      A pledge from the heart to its fellow heart
      On the ways we all are going!
   d. Into this Universe, and Why not knowing
      Nor *Whence*, like Water willy-nilly flowing;
      And out of it, as Wind along the Waste,
      I know not *Whether*, willy-nilly blowing.

      What, without asking, hither hurried *Whence*?
      And, without asking, *Whither* hurried hence!
      Oh, many a Cup of this forbidden Wine
      Must drown the memory of that insolence!

THE CONSONANT [l]

The sound [l] is a *voiced, lingua-alveolar glide*; it is sometimes labelled a lateral continuant. The [l] is subject to great variability dependent upon its phonemic environment. On the production of this sound the tip of the tongue is placed against the alveolar ridge just above the upper front teeth. The blade of the tongue (the part behind the tip) is lowered to permit the voiced breath stream to escape around the frontal sides of the tongue. This position must be maintained long enough to establish the characteristic [l] quality, whether the sound occurs initially, medially, or finally in words. As in all glides the movement of the tongue contributes to the final product, as it must be precise in order to give the [l] sound distinctiveness in its various positions.

In certain combinations [l] assumes the value of a vowel; some phoneticians classify it as one of the vowellike consonants, along with the other glides and the nasals. The vowellike nature of [l] is especially noticeable when it is syllabicated, as in battle ['bætl̩] and saddle ['sædl̩].

Common Errors

1. As with many other sounds, there is a tendency to pronounce this sound too far back in the mouth. There are, to be sure, some differences in the position of the tongue, depending upon the type of vowel preceding or following the [l] sound; an example is the difference between *fell* and

[5] From John Masefield, *Selected Poems*, copyright 1938 by John Masefield and used with The Macmillan Company's permission.

full. The second of these sounds is sometimes called the "dark" [l] in contrast to the "light" [l] in the first word. The real danger comes in permitting all the [l] sounds to become "dark." In extreme cases this tendency results in what is called *retroflex* or *inverted* [l]. This undesirable pronunciation is indicated in dialect by spelling *wul* for *well* etc.

2. It is not uncommon to hear someone substitute [w] for [l]; in such cases, a word like *line* [laɪn] becomes [waɪn], *look* [luk] becomes [wuk], and *low* [loʊ] becomes [woʊ]. The [w] sound is formed principally with the lips, whereas in making the [l] the tongue is active.

3. Very often [l] is omitted altogether, as is common in such words as *William*, *million*, and *civilian*, which may become ['wɪjəm], ['mɪjən], and [sɪ'vɪjən].

4. Some speakers have a tendency to place both the tip of the tongue *and* the blade against the alveolar ridge, causing [l] to lose much of its distinctiveness. A variation of this fault is the same type of placement of the tongue against the upper front teeth.

5. Lack of precision in movement of the tongue either before, during, or after the continuation phase of this sound will destroy much of the glide-like distinctiveness of [l].

EXERCISES

1. Practice the frames in the following operant conditioning exercise for [l] :

Initial		Medial		Final	
Frames	Frames	Frames	Frames	Frames	Frames
1 i	11 ɪ	21 i	31 ɪ	41 i	51 ɪ
2 li	12 lɪ	22 ili	32 ɪlɪ	42 il	52 ɪl
3 ɛ	13 eɪ	23 ɛ	33 eɪ	43 ɛ	53 ɛɪ
4 lɛ	14 lɛɪ	24 ɛlɛ	34 eɪleɪ	44 ɛl	54 eɪl
5 ɑ	15 æ	25 ɑ	35 æ	45 ɑ	55 æ
6 lɑ	16 læ	26 ɑlɑ	36 ælæ	46 ɑl	56 æl
7 u	17 ʊ	27 u	37 ʊ	47 u	57 ʊ
8 lu	18 lʊ	28 ulu	38 ʊlʊ	48 ul	58 ʊl
9 ɔ	19 oʊ	29 ɔ	39 oʊ	49 ɔ	59 oʊ
10 lɔ	20 loʊ	30 ɔlɔ	40 oʊloʊ	50 ɔl	60 oʊl

Instructions are the same as for Exercise 1, p. 132.

2. Practice the following words either as frames of an operant conditioning sequence or individually :

162

Initial		Medial		Final	
Frames	Frames	Frames	Frames	Frames	Frames
1 lady	11 list	21 silence	31 chalice	41 animal	51 appeal
2 lest	12 libido	22 mildew	32 malice	42 frail	52 creel
3 love	13 length	23 million	33 cylinder	43 trial	53 vial
4 lusty	14 link	24 willing	34 palate	44 bill	54 jail
5 lure	15 locate	25 outlook	35 relate	45 conceal	55 model
6 laboratory	16 lunge	26 aloud	36 tolerate	46 ball	56 ventral
7 lawyer	17 lumber	27 highland	37 silver	47 broil	57 jell
8 lantern	18 lark	28 vermillion	38 politic	48 appall	58 mole
9 languish	19 latent	29 belong	39 bowler	49 pile	59 chill
10 ladder	20 liberate	30 pillbox	40 dolorous	50 swell	60 drill

3. Practice [l] in the following sentences:

    a. A million lanterns lighted the landscape.

    b. A violent gale swept every hill and dale of the island.

    c. Swallows, larks, and quail all love our laurel tree.

    d. My lady loves lavender, silks, and old lace.

    e. Molly fell pell-mell into the well, and Willy laughed and laughed.

    f. Luscious yellow pineapple, succulent pork, colorful flowers—all enliven the luau.

    g. Environmentalists believe our world will last only if pollution is greatly lessened.

    h. Billy's filly loped willy-nilly—silly filly!

    i. A quality of loveliness lingers o'er small friendly places.

    j. Love is a leaping flood engulfing all.

4. Practice [l] in the following consonant combinations:

[pl]	[bl]	[fl]	[sl]	[kl]	[gl]
plaque	blast	flack	slap	clack	glad
pliant	blend	fluent	sledge	clean	glow
plead	blind	florid	slick	click	glue
plow	blow	fleece	slow	cloak	glee
plod	blunt	flaunt	slaw	cluck	glint

5. Practice [l] as a syllabic consonant:

[ml̩]	[pl̩]	[bl̩]	[tl̩]
absymal	sepal	marble	petal
camel	example	cobble	battle
dismal	papal	fable	dental
formal	pimple	babble	frontal
caramel	dapple	bubble	fetal

[dḷ]	[nḷ]	[kḷ]	[gḷ]
coddle	penal	tackle	tingle
cuddle	final	pickle	single
pedal	banal	focal	waggle
cradle	panel	wrinkle	beagle
addle	zonal	fickle	toggle

6. Practice the following lines :
   a. Sail on ! Sail on ! Sail on and on !
   b. Alone, alone, all, all alone.
   c. The curfew tolls the knell of parting day,
      The lowing herd winds slowly o'er the lea.
   d. Why so pale and wan, fond lover ?
      Prithee, why so pale ?
      Will, when looking well can't move her,
      Looking ill prevail ?
   e. Across wide lotus-ponds of light,
      I marked a giant fire-fly's flight.
   f. He loves but lightly who his love can tell.
   g. Roll on, thou deep and dark blue Ocean—roll.

THE NASALS

The nasals are made by blocking the flow of air out of the mouth and emitting it through the nasal passages. In all of these sounds the soft palate is lowered so that the voiced breath stream is directed through the nasal passages. The place and type of interference in the mouth vary with each of the three nasal consonants.

THE CONSONANTS [m], [n], and [ŋ]

As was discussed under nasal resonance (pp. 90–91), the mouth serves as a side resonator for [m] and [n], giving them their distinctive resonance characteristics. Care must be taken to give [m, n, and ŋ] adequate duration in order to establish the full value due these sounds.

The [m] is a *voiced bilabial nasal.* It is made by closing the lips as for the [b] sound. However, instead of the sound being temporarily blocked as in [b], the soft palate is lowered and the sound emitted through the nasal passages.

The [n] is a *voiced postdental nasal.* Although the tongue is pressed against the gum ridge as for [d], the soft palate is lowered, and the sound directed through the nose.

The [ŋ], a *lingua-velar nasal,* is the *ng* in such words as *long, fling,* and the like. It is made by arching the back of the tongue against the soft palate,

164

relaxing the velum,[6] and directing the voiced breath stream through the nasal passages.

Common Errors

Many of the errors of nasal consonants have already been discussed in the section on nasal resonance in Chapter 6, p. 90. Several additional matters, however, deserve special mention at this time.

1. Care should be taken to avoid substituting [n] for [ŋ]. Careless speakers often are guilty of saying *runnin'* ['rʌnɪn] for ['rʌnɪŋ], *catchin'* ['kætʃɪn] for ['kætʃɪŋ], etc.

2. At the other extreme is the fault sometimes found in the speech of some foreigners as well as in that of some native-born Americans. This is the tendency to add the [g] sound after the [ŋ] when it does not belong there. Thus *singer* ['sɪŋɚ] becomes ['sɪŋgɚ], *longing* ['lɔŋɪŋ] becomes ['lɔŋgɪŋ] ; *Long Island* [lɔŋ'aɪlənd] becomes [lɔŋ'gaɪlənd].

3. Occasionally this is reversed and words that should be pronounced [ŋg] are pronounced simply [ŋ]. Thus *finger* ['fɪŋgɚ] becomes [fɪŋɚ], etc.

4. It is a matter of interest that when our nasal passages are congested, as in severe head colds, our [m], [n], and [ŋ] consonants sound more like their cognates [b], [d], and [g]. Thus *my nose is running* [maɪ'noʊz ɪz 'rʌnɪŋ] becomes [baɪ 'doʊz ɪz 'rʌdɪg]. Any obstruction of the nasal passages can give rise to denasality or typical "cold-in-the-head" speech.

EXERCISES

1. Practice the frames of the following operant conditioning exercise for [m], [n] and [ŋ] :

Initial		Medial			Final		
Frames	Frames	Frames	Frames	Frames	Frames	Frames	Frames
1 i	11 i	21 i	31 i	41 i	51 i	61 i	71 i
2 mi	12 ni	22 imi	32 ini	42 iɲi	52 im	62 in	72 iŋ
3 ɛ	13 ɛ	23 ɛ	33 ɛ	43 ɛ	53 ɛ	63 ɛ	73 ɛ
4 mɛ	14 nɛ	24 ɛmɛ	34 ɛnɛ	44 ɛɲɛ	54 ɛm	64 ɛn	74 ɛŋ
5 ɑ	15 ɑ	25 ɑ	35 ɑ	45 ɑ	55 ɑ	65 ɑ	75 ɑ
6 mɑ	16 nɑ	26 ɑmɑ	36 ɑnɑ	46 ɑɲɑ	56 ɑm	66 ɑn	76 ɑŋ
7 u	17 u	27 u	37 u	47 u	57 u	67 u	77 u
8 mu	18 nu	28 umu	38 unu	48 uɲu	58 um	68 un	78 uŋ
9 ɔ	19 ɔ	29 ɔ	39 ɔ	49 ɔ	59 ɔ	69 ɔ	79 ɔ
10 mɔ	20 nɔ	30 ɔmɔ	40 ɔnɔ	50 ɔɲɔ	60 ɔm	70 ɔn	80 ɔŋ

Instructions are the same as for Exercise 1, p. 132.

[6] The velum is the soft palate.

2. Practice the following words either as frames in an operant conditioning sequence or individually:

Initial		Medial		Final	
Frames	Frames	Frames	Frames	Frames	Frames
[m]					
1 mar	6 music	11 compose	16 common	21 swim	26 broom
2 men	7 maternal	12 companion	17 dramatic	22 same	27 perform
3 meet	8 marriage	13 summer	18 comely	23 palm	28 thumb
4 most	9 mourn	14 remember	19 tumult	24 dream	29 hymn
5 mill	10 mood	15 element	20 tamper	25 dome	30 tomb
[n]					
1 none	6 north	11 land	16 sound	21 cane	26 blown
2 know	7 near	12 many	17 pony	22 pain	27 wine
3 nest	8 neck	13 manic	18 stand	23 fine	28 vain
4 gnat	9 knit	14 penny	19 under	24 brown	29 plan
5 nine	10 pneumatic	15 funny	20 month	25 lane	30 coin
[ŋ]					
		1 longingly	6 hanger	11 young	16 tongue
		2 donkey	7 ringlet	12 hung	17 going
		3 tingle	8 wringer	13 bang	18 racing
		4 length	9 songster	14 song	19 playing
		5 strength	10 youngster	15 king	20 bring

3. Practice the following sentences:
  a. The music's mournful lament marred our homecoming.
  b. Many middle-aged men were employed for the summer harvest.
  c. Ham, yams, jam, and pumpkin pies made our Monday meeting a memorable occasion.
  d. Many men prefer feminine companionship to masculine.
  e. Hymns were hummed by the assembled multitudes at the Tomb of the Unknown Soldier.
  f. The new minister warned the congregation against nurturing sinful thoughts.
  g. Nine funny gnomes danced in the shining moonlight.
  h. An open-minded discussion contributes to an acquisition of knowledge.
  i. Ned's grandfather warned the neighbors never to frequent his manor on the plantation.

    j. Man learns, but nature knows.

    k. The Anglo-Saxons conquered the English long ago.

    l. The young ringleader of the gang was hanged for killing the distinguished congressman.

    m. The youngster was angry when the buzzing bee stung his tongue.

    n. The hungry throng stormed the stronghold of the king.

    o. Rowing, hiking, and swimming gave him outstanding strength.

4. Practice the [ŋ] sounds in the following pairs of words :

song—finger	winged—wrangle	clanging—shingle
singer—linger	cling—languor	sting—wrangle
singing—longer	clinging—jungle	stinging—tingle
long—English	king—mingle	ring—hungry
longing—wink	kingly—single	ringing—language
wing—bank	clang—bungle	bring—angry

5. Practice the following selection :

> The cataract strong
> Then plunges along,
> Striking and raging
> As if a war waging
> Its caverns and rocks among ;
> Rising and leaping,
> Sinking and creeping,
> Swelling and sweeping,
> Showering and springing,
> Flying and flinging,
> Writhing and ringing,
> Eddying and whisking,
> Spouting and frisking,
> Turning and twisting,
> Around and around
> With endless rebound.

THE CONSONANT COMBINATIONS [tʃ] AND [dʒ]

The combinations [tʃ] and [dʒ] are sometimes called affricates by phoneticians (a fricative that is begun from a closed position). Each of these combinations has a double symbol because it is in reality two sounds blended into one. Note, however, that they are truly blended, for in forming either of them you do not completely finish one sound and then begin the other ; rather, you merge the two thus : The breath stream is stopped on the first part of the blend [t] or [d], held momentarily, then released directly into

167

the second part of the sound unit [ʃ] or [ʒ]. Since each element of these sound units has already been discussed in detail, further elaboration here is unnecessary. The [dʒ] is voiced, the [tʃ] unvoiced.

Affricates also occur on several other consonant combinations, such as [ps, bs, ts, ds, ks, gs, etc.] ; however, the use of these combinations in the initial position in words is rare. On the other hand [tʃ] and [dʒ] occur regularly ; therefore, they deserve special treatment here.

Common Errors

Common errors of the consonant combinations have already been discussed under [t, d, ʃ, and ʒ] individually. However, [tʃ] and [dʒ] are often misarticulated as a combination. In addition to the errors listed under each sound, the following misarticulations occur on the combinations :

1. [tʃ] and [dʒ] require a definite explosion from the closed position [t] and [d] into the following fricative. If this event does not take place, the combination has a tendency to sound like the fricative element only, e.g., *church* [tʃɝtʃ] becomes *shursh* [ʃɝʃ], etc.

2. Hard-of-hearing persons often have great difficulty with these sounds as they cannot hear them adequately. In addition to making the error listed above, they often make substitutions of [s] and [z] for [ʃ] and [ʒ], or omit the fricative altogether.

3. Since [tʃ] and [dʒ] do not occur in many foreign languages, foreigners have difficulty acquiring adequate production of these sounds.

EXERCISES

1. Practice the frames in the following operant conditioning exercise for [tʃ] and [dʒ] :

Initial		Medial		Final	
Frames	Frames	Frames	Frames	Frames	Frames
1 i	11 i	21 i	31 i	41 i	51 i
2 tʃi	12 dʒi	22 itʃi	32 idʒi	42 itʃ	52 idʒ
3 ɛ	13 ɛ	23 ɛ	33 ɛ	43 ɛ	53 ɛ
4 tʃɛ	14 dʒɛ	24 ɛtʃɛ	34 ɛdʒɛ	44 ɛtʃ	54 ɛdʒ
5 ɑ	15 ɑ	25 ɑ	35 ɑ	45 ɑ	55 ɑ
6 tʃɑ	16 dʒɑ	26 atʃɑ	36 adʒɑ	46 atʃ	56 adʒ
7 u	17 u	27 u	37 u	47 u	57 u
8 tʃu	18 dʒu	28 utʃu	38 udʒu	48 utʃ	58 udʒ
9 ɔ	19 ɔ	29 ɔ	39 ɔ	49 ɔ	59 ɔ
10 tʃɔ	20 dʒɔ	30 ɔtʃɔ	40 ɔdʒɔ	50 ɔtʃ	60 ɔdʒ

Instructions are the same as for Exercise 1, p. 132.

168

2. Practice the following words either as frames in an operant conditioning exercise or individually:

Initial		Medial		Final	
Frames	Frames	Frames	Frames	Frames	Frames
1 church	11 joy	21 butcher	31 pigeon	41 hatch	51 badge
2 chose	12 jolly	22 satchel	32 majestic	42 batch	52 hedge
3 chair	13 gem	23 teacher	33 object	43 speech	53 orange
4 chuckle	14 jewel	24 question	34 engine	44 march	54 sage
5 churn	15 jail	25 escutcheon	35 badger	45 pitch	55 language
6 chief	16 gentle	26 concerto	36 magic	46 lunch	56 gage
7 chatter	17 journey	27 hatchet	37 manager	47 beach	57 serge
8 chest	18 judge	28 lecture	38 fragile	48 catch	58 huge
9 cherry	19 jest	29 exchange	39 agile	49 such	59 image
10 chop	20 genius	30 merchant	40 wager	50 scratch	60 strange

3. Practice the following sentences:
   a. Charlie chuckled while chopping chips from Churchill's cherry tree.
   b. The pitcher chided the churlish catcher for changing his signals.
   c. The teacher lectured on the nature and virtues of cello concertos.
   d. Chicle is used chiefly in the manufacture of chewing gum.
   e. The Chinese chieftain chastised Ching for leaving chopsticks in Chang's chop suey.
   f. John and Jerry jumped with joy when their geology major was approved.
   g. The jaunty major wagered his gems and jewels that the judge would not jail Jerome.
   h. He emerged from college an educated gentleman but not a genius.
   i. The geranium on the ridge bloomed earlier than the gentian in the gorge.
   j. Midge's fudge became a hodgepodge when George added sage and orange to her batter.
4. Practice [tʃ] combinations in such words as:

chalk—clinch	change—flinch	chase—search
chink—cinch	charge—watch	chicken—birch
champion—winch	choice—scratch	choose—spinach

5. Practice the [dʒ] combination in such words as :

jam—charge	ginger—fidget	gesture—cage
jungle—smudge	Jasper—midget	joint—conjure
general—fudge	joke—Bridget	Jack—budget

6. Distinguish clearly between the following pairs of sounds :

match—magic	chunk—junk	breeches—bridges
catch—cage	chive—jive	punch—plunge
cheer—jeer	such—smudge	puncheon—dungeon
choke—joke	choose—refuge	lunch—sludge
chest—jest	choice—rejoice	bunch—budge

GENERAL SUGGESTIONS REGARDING ARTICULATION

Now that you have studied consonants individually and are relatively sure that you can produce them correctly in all positions, the next step is to undertake a program of practice that will make good articulation habitual in all forms of communication. A few suggestions and reminders will help you to establish a successful program.

1. The nature of the speaking situation will have a bearing upon the precision with which you speak. Loudness levels are pretty much determined by the size of the listener group, acoustics, and background noise. The more power you have to use, the more precise your articulation must become. The reverse is also true. If you are speaking quietly to only one person the energy level of output is low ; there is a decrease in the various pressures involved in articulation which results in less precision, particularly on the consonants. One must then develop a sensitivity to the articulatory requirements of the speaking situation and adjust his speech accordingly.

2. We must maintain a constant effort to avoid careless speech. Almost all humans, including professionals, let their guard down when the pressure to perform is off. Good speaking habits must become second nature. It is not enough to attain good articulation, we must *maintain* the habit through constant use.

3. Remain a student of speech throughout life. You have just begun to understand some of the principles and processes governing speech. You may continue in your study by becoming increasingly aware of general speech standards, the speech behavior of others, and finally, and, most important, your speech behavior in relation to others. You may continue your study on your own in many ways—by looking up words in the dictionary, increasing your vocabulary, consciously using your best speech, practicing, and by preparing for the many speaking events in which you will participate.

170

Articulation drill may concentrate upon given consonants, such as have already been presented, or it may be upon exercises and selection demanding articulation skill on various consonants and consonant combinations over an entire work. Following are a number of exercises and selections that will help you to gain greater articulatory control and skill.

EXERCISES

1. The judicious use of strong and weak forms is the mark of a trained speaker. However, weakening the phonemic elements in articles, prepositions, and unstressed syllables in polysyllabic words to excess can lead to substandard speech. Below are a few of the words and phrases you may hear, together with translations into Standard American. Speak them first as the mutilated spellings try to indicate, then say them in Standard American speech. Avoid being overly precise or pedantic.

[nɛn]	n'nen	and then
[tɔl]	'tall	at all
[dʒu]	d'ju	did you?
[doʊntʃə'noʊ]	donchuno	don't you know?
[frʌs]	f'rus	for us
[fr'ɪnstənts]	f'instance	for instance
[gwaʊt]	g'wout	go out
[ˌhiz'aʊt]	he'zout	he is out
[ˌaɪm'goʊnə]	I'm gona	I am going to
[zæ't ʃʊ]	zat chew	is that you?
[zæt'soʊ]	zat so	is that so?
[moʊrn]	mor'n	more than
[koʊrs]	'course	of course
[ˌsæftɚ'nun]	'safternoon	this afternoon
[s'mɔrnɪn]	'smornin'	this morning
[wɪli'goʊ]	wil'ego	will he go?
[wɝsə'nɛvɚ]	worse'never	worse than ever
[jɔl]	y'all	you all
[hoʊl'ɑn]	hol'on	hold on
[dʒit]	'jeat	did you eat?
[nɔ'dʒu]	naw; d'u	no; did you?

2. Speak the following rather tricky phrases distinctly, without being too obvious in your effort to do so:

 a. An ice house, *not* a nice house.

 b. The summer school, *not* the summer's cool.

 e. Your two eyes, *not* you're too wise.

 d. Five minutes to eight, *not* five minutes to wait.

171

e. Give me some ice, *not* give me some mice.

f. His acts, *not* his axe.

g. Red's pies, *not* red spies.

3. The stage whisper is a device used by professional actors to project their voices to the back of auditoriums without perceptible use of voice. The demand placed upon good articulation is at a premium. Imagine a friend across the room to whom you whisper the italicized lines in the Shakespearian selections below.

From TWELFTH NIGHT

(*As* MALVOLIO *enters, talking to himself,* SIR TOBY BELCH, SIR ANDREW AGUECHEEK, *and* FABIAN *are partially hidden behind a hedge, whispering.*)

MAL: She uses me with a more exalted respect than any one else that follows her. What should I think on't?

SIR TO: *Here's an overwhelming rogue!*

FAB: *O, peace! Contemplation makes a rare turkey-cock of him: how he jets under his advanced plumes!*

SIR AND: *'Slight, I could so beat the rogue!*

SIR TO: *Peace, I say.*

MAL: To be Count Malvolio!

SIR TO: *Ah, rogue!*

SIR AND: *Pistol him, pistol him.*

Sir TO: *Peace, peace!*

MAL: There is example for't: the lady of the Strachy married the yeoman of the wardrobe.

SIR AND: *Fie on him, Jezebel!*

FAB: *O, peace! now he's deeply in; look how imagination blows him.*

MAL: Having been three months married to her, sitting in my state,—

SIR TO: *O, for a stone-bow, to hit him in the eye!*

MAL: Calling my officers about me, in my branched velvet gown; having come from a day-bed, where I have left Olivia sleeping,—

SIR TO: *Fire and brimstone!*

FAB: *O, peace, peace!*

MAL: And then to have the humor of state: and after a demure travel of regard, telling them I know my place, as I would they should do theirs, to ask for my kinsman Toby,—

SIR TO: *Bolts and Shackles!*

FAB: *O, peace, peace, peace! now, now.*

MAL: Seven of my people, with an obedient start, make out for him. I frown the while; and perchance wind up my watch, or play with my—some rich jewel. Toby approaches; curt'sies there to me,—

SIR TO: *Shall this fellow live?*

FAB: *Though our silence be drawn from us by th' ears, yet peace!*

MAL: I extend my hand to him thus, quenching my familiar smile with an austere regard of control,—

SIR TO: *And does not Toby take you a blow o' the lips then?*

MAL: Saying, 'Cousin Toby, my fortunes having cast me on your niece, give me this prerogative of speech,—'

SIR TO: *What, what?*

MAL: 'You must amend your drunkenness.'

SIR TO: *Out, scab!*

—William Shakespeare

From MACBETH

(*As* LADY MACBETH *descends the stairs, holding a lighted candle, the* DOCTOR *and the* GENTLEWOMAN *are standing to one side, whispering.*)

GENT: *Lo you! her she comes. This is her very guise; and, upon my life, fast asleep. Observe her; stand close.*

DOCTOR: *How came she by that light?*

GENT: *Why, it stood by her: she has light by her continually; 'tis her command.*

DOCTOR: *You see, her eyes are open.*

GENT: *Ay, but their sense is shut.*

DOCTOR: *What is it she does now? Look, how she rubs her hands.*

GENT: *It is an accustomed action with her, to seem thus washing her hands. I have known her to continue in this a quarter of an hour.*

LADY M: Yet here's a spot.

DOCTOR: *Hark! she speaks. I will set down what comes from her, to satisfy my remembrance the more strongly.*

LADY M: Out, damned spot! out, I say! One, two: why, then 'tis time to do't. Hell is murky! Fie, my lord, fie! a soldier, and afeard? What need we fear who knows it, when none can call our power to account? Yet who would have thought the old man to have had so much blood in him?

DOCTOR: *Do you mark that?*

LADY M : The thane of Fife had a wife; where is she now?
What! will these hands ne'er be clean? No more o' that, my
lord, no more o' that: you mar all with this starting.
DOCTOR : *Go to, go to; you have known what you should not.*
GENT : *She has spoke what she should not, I am sure of that:
heaven knows what she has known.*
LADY M : Here's the smell of the blood still : all the perfumes
of Arabia will not sweeten this little hand. Oh! oh! oh!
DOCTOR : *What a sigh is there! The heart is sorely charged.*
GENT : *I would not have such a heart in my bosom for the
dignity of the whole body.*
DOCTOR : *Well, well. well.*
GENT : *Pray God it be, sir.*
DOCTOR : *This disease is beyond my practice: yet I have known
those which have walked in their sleep who have died holily
in their beds.*
LADY M : Wash your hands, put on your night-gown; look not
so pale. I tell you yet again, Banquo's buried; he cannot come
out on's grave.
DOCTOR : *Even so?*
LADY M : To bed, to bed : there's knocking at the gate. Come,
come, come, come, give me your hand. What's done cannot
be undone. To bed, to bed, to bed.   (*Exit.*)

—William Shakespeare

SELECTIONS

The following selections are particularly valuable in developing greater
articulatory skill. Work for preciseness of articulation without becoming
pedantic. Many of the selections call for a light touch, and should be free
from laborious mouthing of words and phrases.

LYING AWAKE

When you're lying awake with a dismal headache, and repose
                              is taboo'd by anxiety,
I conceive you may use any language you choose to indulge in,
                              without impropriety;
For your brain is on fire—the bedclothes conspire of usual
                              slumber to plunder you:
First your counterpane goes, and uncovers your toes, and your
                              sheet slips demurely from under you;

Then the blanketing tickles—you feel like mixed pickles—so
terribly sharp is the pricking,
And you're hot, and you're cross, and you tumble and toss till
there's nothing 'twixt you and the ticking.
Then the bedclothes all creep to the ground in a heap, and you
pick 'em all up in a tangle ;
Next your pillow resigns and politely declines to remain at its
usual angle !
Well, you get some repose in the form of a doze, with hot eye-
balls and head ever aching,
But your slumbering teems with such horrible dreams that you'd
very much better be waking.
You're a regular wreck, with a crick in your neck, and no wonder
you snore, for your head's on the floor, and you've needles and
pins from your soles to your shins, and your flesh is a-creep, for
your left leg's asleep, and you've cramp in your toes, and a fly
on your nose, and some fluff in your lung, and a feverish tongue,
and a thirst that's intense, and a general sense that you haven't
been sleeping in clover ;
But the darkness has passed, and it's daylight at last, and the
night has been long—ditto ditto my song—and thank goodness
they're both of them over !

—W. S. Gilbert

I am the very model of a modern Major General,
I've information vegetable, animal, and mineral ;
I know the kings of England, and I quote the fights historical,
From Marathon to Waterloo, in order categorical ;
I'm very well acquainted, too, with matters mathematical,
I understand equations, both the simple and quadratical,
About binomial theorem I'm teeming with a lot of news,
With many cheerful facts about the square of the hypotenuse.

—W. S. Gilbert

JABBERWOCKY

'Twas brillig, and the slithy toves
    Did gyre and gimble in the wabe ;
All mimsy were the borogoves,
    And the mome raths outgrabe.

"Beware the Jabberwock, my son!
   The jaws that bite, the claws that catch!
Beware the Jubjub bird, and shun
   The frumious Bandersnatch!"

He took his vorpal sword in hand;
   Long time the manxome foe he sought—
So rested he by the Tumtum tree,
   And stood awhile in thought.

And as in uffish thought he stood,
   The Jabberwock, with eyes of flame,
Came whiffling through the tulgey wood,
   And burbled as it came!

One, two! One, two! And through and through
   The vorpal blade went snicker-snack!
He left it dead, and with its head
   He went galumphing back.

"And hast thou slain the Jabberwock?
   Come to my arms, my beamish boy!
O frabjous day! Callooh! Callay!"
   He chortled in his joy.

—Lewis Carroll

From HAMLET

HAMLET (*to the players*): Speak the Speech, I pray you, as I pronounced it to you, trippingly on the tongue; but if you mouth it, as many of your players do, I had as lief the town crier spoke my lines. Nor do not saw the air too much with your hand, thus; but use all gently: for in the very torrent, tempest, and, as I may say, whirlwind of your passion, you must acquire and beget a temperance that may give it smoothness. Oh! it offends me to the soul to hear a robustious periwig-pated fellow tear a passion to tatters, to very rags, to split the ears of the groundlings, who, for the most part, are capable of nothing but inexplicable dumb-shows and noise: I would have such a fellow whipped for o'erdoing Termagant; it out-herods Herod; pray you, avoid it.

Be not too tame, neither, but let your own discretion be your tutor : suit the action to the word, the word to the action ; with this special observance, that you o'erstep not the modesty of nature ; for anything so overdone is from the purpose of playing, whose end, both at the first and now, was and is, to hold, as 'twere, the mirror up to nature ; to show virtue her own feature, scorn her own image, and the very age and body of the time his form and pressure. Now, this overdone, or come tardy off, though it make the unskillful laugh, cannot but make the judicious grieve ; the censure of the which one must in your allowance o'erweigh a whole theatre of others. Oh ! there be players that I have seen play, and heard others praise, and that highly, not to speak it profanely, that neither having the accent of Christians, nor the gait of Christian, pagan, nor man, have so strutted and bellowed that I have thought some of nature's journeymen had made men and not made them well, they imitated humanity so abominbably.

—William Shakespeare

THE THROSTLE

"Summer is coming, summer is coming,
I know it, I know it, I know it.
Light again, leaf again, life again, love again !"
Yes, my wild little Poet.

Sing the new year in under the blue,
Last year you sang it as gladly.
"New, new, new, new !" Is it then *so* new
That you should carol so madly ?

"Love again, song again, nest again, young again,"
Never a prophet so crazy !
And hardly a daisy as yet, little friend,
See, there is hardly a daisy.

"Here again, here, here, here, happy year !"
O warble unchidden, unbidden !
Summer is coming, is coming, my dear,
And all the winters are hidden.

—Alfred, Lord Tennyson

My good blade carves the casques of men,
   My tough lance thrusteth sure,
My strength is as the strength of ten,
   Because my heart is pure.
The shattering trumpet shrilleth high,
   The hard brands shiver on the steel,
The splinter'd spear-shafts crack and fly,
   The horse and rider reel :
They reel, they roll in clanging lists,
   And when the tide of combat stands,
Perfume and flowers fall in showers,
   That lightly rain from ladies' hands.

—Alfred, Lord Tennyson

IF YOU'RE ANXIOUS FOR TO SHINE

If you're anxious for to shine in the high esthetic line as a man
     of culture rare,
You must get up all the germs of the transcendental terms, and
     plant them everywhere.
You must lie upon the daisies and discourse in novel phrases of
     your complicated state of mind,
The meaning doesn't matter if it's only idle chatter of a trans-
     scendental kind.
And everyone will say,
As you walk your mystic way,
"If this young man expresses himself in terms too deep for *me*,
Why, what a very singularly deep young man this deep young
     man must be !"
Be eloquent in praise of the very dull old days which have long
     since passed away,
And convince 'em if you can, that the reign of good Queen
     Anne was Culture's palmiest day·
Of course, you will pooh-pooh whatever's fresh and new, and
     declare it's crude and mean ;
For Art stopped short in the cultivated court of the Empress
     Josephine.
And everyone will say,
As you walk your mystic way,
"If that's not good enough for him which is good enough for
     me,
Why, what a very cultivated kind of youth this kind of youth
     must be !"

Then a sentimental passion of a vegetable fashion must excite
your languid spleen,

An attachment *à la* Plato for a bashful young potato, or a
not-too-French French bean!

Though the Philistines may jostle, you will rank as an apostle in
the high esthetic band,

If you walk down Piccadilly, with a poppy or a lily in your
medieval hand.

And everyone will say,

As you walk your flowery way,

"If he's content with a vegetable love which would certainly
not suit *me*.

Why, what a particularly pure young man this pure young man
must be!"

—W. S. Gilbert

PETER AND "SHE"

Last week after our talks, I was corrected on my enunciation, so
this week while in the process of trying to correct this bad habit,
I composed a little story of a boy and girl that I would like to
relate to you.

Once upon a time there lived in the San Fernando Valley a boy
by the name of Peter. Now Peter made his living by picking a
peck of pickled peppers each day in the fields nearby. However,
during the day's work Peter always became quite pickled
himself.

One afternoon after picking his peck of pickled peppers and
becoming quite pickled, Peter wandered down to the beach of
Santa Monica, and here he met the girl in our story. Now for
the sake of simplicity let us call this girl "She." "She" sold sea
shells by the sea shore and by the continuous purchases by
Peter, the pickled pepper picker, from "She," who sold sea
shells by the sea shore, they became quite good friends.

As time went on this friendship blossomed into love, and they
were married and moved out to Peter's, the pickled pepper
picker's home in the valley where "She" got a job in the fields
pickling pickled peppers.

Now every morning you see the two of them, "She," who used
to sell sea shells by the sea shore, and Peter the pickled pepper
picker, walking out to the fields to pick their peck of pickled
peppers, and every evening both of them pickled after a hard
day of picking pickled peppers.

179

Now, fellow students, after you graduate and are seeking for a way of making your living, if some of you should chance to become pickled pepper pickers, please remember: while you are picking your daily peck of pickled peppers, don't become pickled, for there are already too many pickled people in this pickled old world today.

—Ralph McKenzie

From THE IMPORTANCE OF BEING EARNEST

ALGERNON: What you really are is a Bunburyist. I was quite right in saying you were a Bunburyist. You are one of the most advanced Bunburyists I know.

JACK: What on earth do you mean?

ALGERNON: You have invented a very useful younger brother called Ernest, in order that you may be able to come up to town as often as you like. I have invented an invaluable permanent invalid called Bunbury, in order that I may be able to go down into the country whenever I choose. Bunbury is perfectly invaluable. If it wasn't for Bunbury's extraordinary bad health, for instance, I wouldn't be able to dine with you at Willis's tonight; for I have been really engaged to Aunt Augusta for more than a week.

JACK: I haven't asked you to dine with me anywhere tonight.

ALGERNON: I know. You are absolutely careless about sending out invitations. It is very foolish of you. Nothing annoys people so much as not receiving invitations.

JACK: You had much better dine with your Aunt Augusta.

ALGERNON: I haven't the smallest intention of doing anything of the kind. To begin with, I dined there on Monday, and once a week is quite enough to dine with one's own relatives. In the second place, whenever I do dine there I am always treated as a member of the family, and sent down with either no woman at all, or two. In the third place, I know perfectly well whom she will place me next to, to-night. She will place me next to Mary Farquhar, who always flirts with her own husband across the dinner-table. That is not very pleasant. Indeed, it is not even decent ... and that sort of thing is enormously on the increase. The amount of women in London who flirt with their own husbands is perfectly scandalous. It looks so bad. It is simply washing one's clean linen in public. Besides, now that I know you to be a confirmed Bunburyist I naturally want to talk to you about Bunburying. I want to tell you the rules.

180

JACK: I am not a Bunburyist at all. If Gwendolen accepts me, I am going to kill my brother; indeed, I think I'll kill him in any case. Cecily is a little too much interested in him. It is rather a bore. So I am going to get rid of Ernest. And I strongly advise you to do the same with Mr. . . . with your invalid friend who has the absurd name.

ALGERNON: Nothing will induce me to part with Bunbury, and if you ever get married, which seems to me extremely problematic, you will be very glad to know Bunbury. A man who marries without knowing Bunbury has a very tedious time of it.

JACK: That is nonsense. If I marry a charming girl like Gwendolen, and she is the only girl I ever saw in my life that I would marry, I certainly won't want to know Bunbury.

ALGERNON: Then your wife will. You don't seem to realize, that in married life three is company and two is none.

JACK (*sententiously*): That, my dear young friend, is the theory that the corrupt French Drama has been propounding for the last fifty years.

ALGERNON: Yes, and that the happy English home has proved in half the time.

JACK: For heaven's sake, don't try to be cynical. It's perfectly easy to be cynical.

ALGERNON: My dear fellow, it isn't easy to be anything now-a-days. There's such a lot of beastly competition about.

—Oscar Wilde

articulation: pronouncing words correctly

IN THE LAST chapter we were concerned primarily with speaking distinctly by articulating consonant sounds with precision and clarity. However, to pronounce words correctly we must master the proper use of vowels and diphthongs. In order to accomplish this goal we must: (a) know how the different vowels and diphthongs are made, (b) be able to discriminate fine shades of difference in the production of vowels and diphthongs, (c) be able to produce vowels and diphthongs with accuracy upon demand, (d) command a good working knowledge of the pronunciation tools in the dictionary, phonetics and diacritical marks, and (e) develop the capacity to pronounce correctly a basic pool of commonly mispronounced words.

STANDARDS OF PRONUNCIATION

In discussing pronunciation one hears the terms *proper*, *correct*, and *accurate*, which seem to assume that there is one standard to which we can all turn. If such were the case the student would have a relatively easy time of adapting his speech to the one standard, but, alas, no such panacea exists. In reality, we find that pronunciation is far from static—it is a dynamic, ever-changing process that requires constant study.

The student of diction should be aware of a principle that has governed pronunciation through the ages, namely, that *usage is the law and rule of speech*. Prior to the last decade this principle stressed a prescriptive approach to pronunciation. Dictionaries based pronunciation upon the usage of the most cultured, educated members of the societies of three large regional areas. The scholars who had made a lifelong study of the English language served as editors of our dictionaries and were, in fact, the guardians of pronunciation. They, in turn, depended upon other scholars to help them in the colossal task of compiling contemporary pronunciation in the regional areas of the United States. While it is true that the speech of educated and cultured persons has served as the standard, it is likewise true that a minority of speakers can influence a majority to change the pronunciation of a word; then, the new pronunciation in time will become the first or most accepted pronunciation in the dictionary. Understandably the dictionaries are slow to change, chiefly because the changes suggested must stand the test of time to prove the legitimacy of the new, popular pronunciation. These, then, are the general rules that governed standards prior to the controversy that has arisen in recent years concerning a more permissive approach to pronunciation for subcultural groups.

The controversy has not been without "fevered" discussion and differences in opinion among educators. The more conservative point of view stresses that standards should be prescriptive, as they have been in the past. Those opposing this philosophy argue that the dictionary and instruction in the classroom should be more permissive, recognizing the dialects of subcultural groups. The latter point of view has had an impact upon standards in that dictionaries reflect a degree of permissiveness not present in earlier editions.

Most educators are agreed that communication or *talking together* is of greatest importance in speech. Also it is suggested that members of subcultural groups learn a new dialect, much the same as General American speakers might learn another language, while retaining their own local dialects.

In view of the prescriptive-permissive controversy, three guidelines are suggested:

1. If students have been reared with a regional dialect and are not involved with subcultural speech, they should adhere to a prescriptive approach to pronunciation, i.e., adhere to the standards of the regional area.

2. Students reared with a subcultural dialect should be prescriptive in adhering to the best models of that dialect. A permissive approach is desirable when studying the pronunciation of a regional dialect.

3. Students should be encouraged to study a regional dialect as a new language if they now use a subcultural dialect; however, they should pursue this study without the pressure of having to change their local dialect.

183

REGIONAL STANDARDS

In the United States, in addition to many minor variations, there are three fairly well defined standards: Eastern Standard speech, Southern Standard speech, and General American Standard speech. Attempts have been made to standardize American pronunciation, but the major dialects remain relatively unchanged. Earlier in our history Eastern Standard speech was promoted by scholars and others as the true standard of American English. This notion received substantial support from the writers of standard textbooks in phonetics, who themselves were either Englishmen or graduates of New England colleges, but in spite of their efforts pronunciation in the regional areas changed little.

Despite Eastern Standard emphasis, the majority of people in the United States today, approximately 80 percent, use General American. It was felt that the communication media—television, radio, and motion pictures— would have a great leveling effect upon the regional areas; possibly it has, but regional dialects persist much the same as they have in the past, with the possible exception of the reduction in the number of persons employing local dialects within regional areas. At the present time General American is used most prevalently in communication media, while a variant of Eastern Standard, *theatre speech*, is frequently used by professional actors in legitimate theatre, but not exclusively.

CORRECT PRONUNCIATION

Correct pronunciation reflects the regional (or subcultural) area in which a speaker is born. The first rule of correct pronunciation should be that he adhere to the standard of his native area. If he moves to another regional area, he should continue to use the dialect of the area from whence he came. If he attempts to change his speech to suit the new area, chances are he will make many errors, some of which may cause him considerable embarrassment. He will be accepted in the new area regardless of the difference in regional dialect. Time will cause some modification in his speech, but older habits will prevail, perhaps throughout life. He also has the opportunity to study the dialect of the new area as a second language.

Correct pronunciation and language usage should be natural rather than ostentatious. Many speakers adopt the pronunciation or idiom of another area for effect; they can be both conspicuous and easily misunderstood. One must always strive to use language as a common denominator for good communication. Speaking either above or below the level of one's audience is a serious fault, and is usually paid for by a negative reaction from the listeners.

Standard regional pronunciation is relatively free from the pronunciation of local dialects within the area.

184

Correct pronunciation requires constant attention on the part of the speaker, as it takes time and effort to develop good speaking habits. Carelessness can erode away our hard-won achievements in a relatively short time; therefore, it is urgent that the new student develop perseverance in acquiring better speech habits.

CAUSES OF DEVIANT PRONUNCIATION

Early Environment. To those who learned to pronounce words incorrectly in their formative years, the habit patterns are deeply set and they cling tenaciously; only by constant vigilance can the incorrect pronunciations be overcome. We may even know the correct pronunciation of certain words, but find it hard to put it into actual practice. Many persons who learned to say "chimley" for *chimney* "mis-chee-vee-ous" for *mischievous*, and "tre-men-dju-ous" for *tremendous* find the incorrect pronunciations slipping into their speech in unguarded moments, much to their embarrassment. The person is as lucky as he is rare who has been reared in surroundings where words were always pronounced properly. Like table manners, good pronunciation habits come easiest by means of constant observation and practice.

Regional Dialect. Inasmuch as the United States was settled by both English-speaking and non-English-speaking people, it is not surprising that a whole host of local dialects emerged. The various backgrounds and linguistic heritages of the newcomers to this country brought a wealth of new words, interpretations of current usage, and ultimate changes in existing speech patterns. Dialects within regional areas flourished and were perpetuated by the "closeness" of the people. In time, communication through travel, public lectures, theatre, general education, and eventually, radio, motion pictures, and television, did much to level local differences. Unfortunately, much of our linguistic culture becomes lost in such a process, particularly since change is rewarded through acceptance by society as a whole.

Ethnic and Racial Differences. Throughout the country there are both small and large areas of language and speech usage variations from the regional dialect that are identified with given groups. For example, to the millions of Mexican-Americans throughout the West and Southwest, English is the second language. Indeed, in certain areas there is an attempt to accept as standard, from the standpoint of education, the local dialect, particularly since 90 percent of the people are often involved. However, as the percentage of people speaking the local dialect drops below 50 percent, demands are made by society from an educational, social, and economic standpoint, and as a result, acceptance of the local dialect is diminished.

The inhabitants of rural southern areas, inner cities, and certain other highly unified societies tend to perpetuate their pronunciation through majority usage.

185

Variation within the Standard. Still another difference arises from words for which there are two acceptable pronunciations. In this class are such words as *either* [iðɚ] or [aɪðɚ], *neither* [niðɚ] or [naɪðɚ], *isolate* [ɪsoleɪt] or [aɪsoleɪt], and so on. The best advice to a speaker is to employ the most common and accepted usage in his native community. Good pronunciation is largely a matter of adapting oneself to the cultured or most highly educated element of the environment.

ACQUIRING CORRECT PRONUNCIATION

The best advice that can be given to you is : Use the dictionary.[1] When you are not sure of a word, look it up. When you hear a word pronounced in a different manner to which you are accustomed, look it up. When you encounter a word in your reading with which you are not familiar, consult your dictionary. Always have it available. Learn the meaning of the pronunciation marks. *Use* the dictionary ! Of course, it may be easier to do what is commonly done, i.e., ask somebody how to pronounce the word, but the danger is that the person asked may have no more exact knowledge than the questioner. The safe rule is : Use the dictionary !

In order to understand pronunciation fully, a study of the vowels of American English is necessary. Before launching into a study of these sounds individually, we suggest you review them as classes of speech sounds and as differentiated from consonants, Chapter 7, pp. 128–129.

THE VOWELS

A vowel, as previously defined, is a speech sound in which the outgoing breath stream meets relatively little obstruction from the articulatory organs. The distinctive nature of each vowel is determined by the size, shape, and general nature (i.e., rigidity of the walls, size of the opening, etc.) of the resonance chambers of the head and neck. This fact is easily demonstrated in the following experiments :

1. Intone the vowel [u], as in *who*, for a few seconds, then slowly change the size and shape of your mouth opening. You will note that the vowel changes. Try several other vowels in the same manner ; other changes will be observed. The rounding and unrounding of the lips and the size of the mouth opening itself have much to do with the modification of vowel resonances.

[1] For regional standard speech ; within the context of the prescriptive-permissive argument, we suggest *Webster's Third New International Dictionary.*

2.   While the size and shape of the mouth opening have much to do with resultant clarity, quality, or, if you will, identifiableness of the vowel, it is primarily the position of the tongue within the mouth that forms the cavities, which, in turn, give rise to the specific appropriate vowel resonances. Try this experiment: Clench your teeth and spread your lips in a smile. Now without moving your lips or jaw, say the vowels [i, ɪ, e, ɛ, æ, ɑ, u, ʊ, o, ɔ, and ɑ] as best you can. Although the result will be somewhat muffled, you should be able to identify the different sounds.

3.   The position of the jaw facilitates the creation of the cavities in the mouth by making more or less space available, as the case may be. In this last experiment, let your tongue lie relaxed in the bottom of your mouth and make your lips flaccid. Now go through the same vowel sequence as before using a good jaw swing from high to low. The vowels this time should be more indistinct.

From these three experiments it becomes evident that: (a) the various positions of the tongue in the mouth form specific resonance cavities that account for vowel resonances each of which is slightly different from its nearest neighbor, (b) the cavities can be modified by the position of the lips, and (c) the cavities can be made relatively larger or smaller by the position of the jaw. Good vowel production is based upon all three factors working together for maximum effect. Reduction in the activity of any one of these factors can lessen the peak efficiency needed for best performance.

The fact that variation in any one of the above factors can change the vowel brings us to another consideration, namely, how pure are pure vowels ? The word *pure* refers to the fact that only one sound is discernible during production. In actual practice, the movement from one sound to another in speech requires the articulators to be in constant action, and the moment when the vowel is "stable" is very short, indeed. Therefore, as a sound is being formed the articulators are moving toward the appropriate position, and after achieving the appropriate position they move quickly toward the position of the next sound; it is during these transitions that we hear on-glides and off-glides, the tiny changes in resonance values that alter the so-called purity of the vowel. Research has shown that there is much information contained in these tiny transitional sounds.

The term *phoneme* is used to designate a group or family of very closely related sounds—so closely related that to the ear they sound almost the same and therefore are represented by only one symbol. The use of the word *phoneme* emphasizes the fact that no two persons make a given sound in exactly the same way and that the same person using the sound in different letter combinations—for example, [ɑ] in *father* [faðɚ] as contrasted with [ɑ] in *hearth* [hɑɚθ]—will make the sound in a slightly different manner in the various combinations.

The single (or pure) vowels are presented in the chart that follows:

THE SINGLE VOWELS

Phonetic Symbol	Diacritical Marking[1]	Key Word
[i]	ē	see [si]
[ɪ]	ĭ	pity ['pɪtɪ]
[e]	ā	rate [ret]
[ɛ]	ĕ	any ['ɛnɪ]
[æ]	ă	at [æt]
[a][2]	ȧ	bath (baθ)
[u]	o͞o	booth (buθ]
[ʊ]	o͝o	pull [pʊl]
[o]	ō	note [not]
[ɔ]	ô	jaw [dʒɔ]
[ɒ][3]	ŏ	stop [stɒp]
[ɑ]	ä	calm [kɑm]
[ɝ]	ûr	further ['fɝðɚ]
[ɜ][4]	ûr	further ['fɜðə]
[ɚ]	ər (ĕr)	ever ['ɛvɚ]
[ə]	[ə]	soda ['sodə]
[ʌ]	ŭ	above [ə'bʌv]

[1] *Dictionaries differ in their systems of diacritical markings: in general the markings here follow those used in* The American College Dictionary *(ACD).*
[2] *Heard principally in Eastern speech; [a] is between [æ] and [ɑ].*
[3] *Heard chiefly in Eastern Speech. In General American [ɑ] is commonly used in place of [ɒ].*
[4] *Heard chiefly in parts of the East and South. Both [ɝ] and [ɜ] occur only in accented syllables; [ɚ] and [ə] occur only in unaccented syllables.*

THE VOWEL [i]

The [i] is the vowel traditionally called long *e* (usual diacritical mark *ē*). It is the highest of the front vowels. In forming this sound, the front of the tongue is tensed a little and raised close to the hard palate behind the gum ridge. The lips are spread (as in a slight smile), and the sound issues through a comparatively narrow slit between them. [i] may be spelled *ae, ay, e, ea, ee, ei, eo, ey, i, ie,* and *oe* as in *Caesar, quay, equal, team, see, deceive, people, key, machine, field,* and *amoeba.* The [i] is often used in singing to develop a quality termed *brilliance.*

Common Errors

1. Since this vowel is formed with a degree of tension in the tongue and lips, there may be a tendency to extend the tension to the throat, thus impinging upon good tone production.

2. [i] has a tendency to become nasalized, especially when it occurs next to a nasal consonant, e.g., *seem, mean,* etc.

3. In common with the other vowels that are prolonged (called long vowels), there is a danger of adding what are known as on-glides or off-glides to [i] ; these tend to destroy the purity and stability of the vowel. Thus, *he* [hi] may become [hɪi] (on-glide), or [hiə] (off-glide).

EXERCISES

1. Practice the frames in the following operant conditioning exercise for [i] :

Initial				Medial				Final			
Frames		Frames		Frames		Frames		Frames		Frames	
1	i	7	i	13	i	19	i	25	i	31	
2	it	8	il	14	tit	20	lit	26	ti	32	li
3	i	9	i	15	i	21	i	27	i	33	i
4	ik	10	ib	16	kib	22	bik	28	ki	34	bi
5	i	11	i	17	i	23	i	29	i	35	i
6	if	12	im	18	fim	24	mif	30	fi	36	·mi

2. Practice the following words either individually or as frames in an operant conditioning sequence :

Initial				Medial				Final			
Frames		Frames		Frames		Frames		Frames		Frames	
1	eel	7	ego	13	beat	19	keen	25	see	31	me
2	each	8	edict	14	deal	20	peel	26	bee	32	flea
3	eagle	9	Edith	15	conceal	21	need	27	she	33	tree
4	Easter	10	eager	16	treat	22	steel	28	key	34	spree
5	eat	11	Egypt	17	complete	23	street	29	fee	35	knee
6	easy	12	equal	18	read	24	obese	30	pea	36	agree

3. Sentences :
- a. The beat of the hammer on the steel displeased the people in the street.
- b. Easter would not be complete without Edith's being here to eat with me.
- c. She tried to conceal her obesity.
- d. Eva agreed to keep the key to the green cottage.
- e. Maureen and Lee were eager to defeat Marie and me.

4. Repeat rapidly, in either singing or speaking tone, the syllable [mi-mi-mi-mi-mi]. Repeat this exercise on various pitch levels, working for a bright, clear tone.

5. Be careful not to insert an [ə] after [i] in the following words:

[i]—[pil] peel   [i]—[kil] keel
[i]—[sil] seal   [i]—[fil] feel
[i]—[mil] meal   [i]—[bil] beal
[i]—[til] teal   [i]—[stil] steel

6. In reading the following lines, form the [i] sound crisply:
   a. My Mary's asleep by thy murmuring stream,
      Flow gently, sweet Afton, disturb not her dream.
   b. Sand-strewn caverns, cool and deep,
      Where the winds are all asleep;
      Where the spent lights quiver and gleam;
      Where the salt weed sways in the stream;
      Where the sea-beasts, ranged all round,
      Feed in the ooze of their pasture ground.
   c. Over the ripening peach
      Buzzes the bee,
   Splash on the billowy beach
      Tumbles the sea.
      But the peach
      And the beach
      They are each
     Nothing to me.

THE VOWEL [ɪ]

The [ɪ] is commonly called short *i* (diacritical mark, ĭ). The apex of the tongue is high and forward in the mouth, but slightly lower than in [i]. Both the tongue and lips are less tense than in [i]. Other features include short duration, purity in production, and high frequency of occurrence. It is commonly spelled *e, ee, i, ie, o, u, ui,* and *y,* as in *England, been, if, sieve, women, busy, build,* and *hymn.*

Common Errors

1. [ɪ] is frequently made higher than it should be and takes on the quality of [i], e.g., *it* [ɪt] becomes [it], devoid [dɪvɔɪd] becomes [divɔɪd], city [sɪtɪ] becomes [sɪti].

2. [ɪ] is sometimes formed too far back in the mouth so that [ɪ] becomes [ə], for example, *smallest* [smɔlɪst], *shortest* ['ʃɔrtɪst], *tallest* ['tɔlɪst], *forfeit* ['fɔrfɪt], and *biscuit* ['bɪskɪt] become ['smɔləst], ['ʃɔrtəst], ['tɔləst], ['fɔrfət], and ['bɪskət]. Notice that in all these examples the shift of [ɪ]

to [ə] occurs in unstressed syllables; this is where the error is most likely to occur.

3. Persons who prolong the [ɪ] sound add an off-glide, so that words like *it* [ɪt], *hit* [hɪt], and *fit* [fɪt] become [ɪət], [hɪət], and [fɪət].

4. Several words that should employ the [ɪ] sound are pronounced as they are spelled, giving rise to an error; thus, *goodness*, *breeches*, and *women* are pronounced ['gʊdnɛs], ['britʃɪz], and ['wɪmɛn], instead of ['gʊdnɪs], ['brɪtʃɪz], and ['wɪmən].

EXERCISES

1. Practice the frames in the following operant conditioning exercise for [ɪ]:

Initial		Medial		Final	
Frames	Frames	Frames	Frames	Frames	Frames
1 ɪ	7 ɪ	13 ɪ	19 ɪ	25 ɪ	31 ɪ
2 ɪt	8 ɪl	14 tɪl	20 lɪt	26 tɪ	32 lɪ
3 ɪ	9 ɪ	15 ɪ	21 ɪ	27 ɪ	33 ɪ
4 ɪk	10 ɪb	16 kɪb	22 bɪk	28 kɪ	34 bɪ
5 ɪ	11 ɪ	17 ɪ	23 ɪ	29 ɪ	35 ɪ
6 ɪf	12 ɪm	18 fɪm	24 mɪf	30 fɪ	36 mɪ

2. Practice the following words either individually or as frames in an operant conditioning sequence:

Initial		Medial		Final	
Frames	Frames	Frames	Frames	Frames	Frames
1 it	7 enigma	13 bit	19 pretty	25 city	31 dizzy
2 inch	8 expend	14 crib	20 familiar	26 family	32 maybe
3 iniquity	9 inside	15 admit	21 inhibit	27 ability	33 canopy
4 imbue	10 invoice	16 exit	22 thing	28 apology	34 elegy
5 image	11 insult	17 knit	23 will	29 any	35 soapy
6 into	12 is	18 pit	24 sit	30 many	36 abbey

3. Practice the following sentences:

    a. The responsibility for splitting the electron fell upon the university physicists.

    b. The exhibition in the city was pretty, but was admittedly a fiasco.

    c. Don't give any apologies for Mr. Whipple; his activities are invariably enigmatic.

    d. The illiterate one in the family made millions as a financier.

    e. Milly administered pills to Billy and William when they were ill.

4. Distinguish clearly between [ɪ] and [i] sounds in the following pairs of words:

bit—beet	sin—seen
deem—dim	bean—bin
fit—feet	did—deed
peak—pick	reed—rid
pill—peal	hit—heat
seep—sip	meat—mitt

5. Study the following words in terms of [ɪ] and [ə]. Determine to what extent you want to weaken [ɪ] sounds to [ə].

inadvisability	congeniality	corruptibility
responsibility	proclivity	frivolity
gentility	conviviality	constitutionality
fragility	punctuality	compatibility

6. Work for good [ɪ] sounds in the following lines:

    a. Amidst the singing of the birds,
       Amidst the buzzing of the bees.

    b. A little learning is a dangerous thing;
       Drink deep, or taste not the Pierian spring.

    c. The Moving Finger writes; and having writ
       Moves on: nor all your Piety nor Wit
       Shall lure it back to cancel half a Line,
       Nor all your Tears wash out a Word of it.

    d. Gaily tripping,
       Lightly skipping,
       Flock the maidens to the shipping.
       Flags and guns and pennants dipping,
       All the ladies love the shipping.

THE VOWEL [e] AND DIPHTHONG [eɪ]

Because of the close relationship between the vowel [e] and the diphthong [eɪ], the two will be considered together. These sounds are usually called long *a* (diacritical mark, *ā*). The tongue is tense, forward, and half-high in the mouth, while the lips are spread slightly and the jaw is half-high. [e, eɪ] may be spelled *a, ai, ao, au, ay, ea, eh, ei,* and *ey* as in *ate, rain, gaol, gauge, ray, steak, eh, veil,* and *obey.*

192

If the sound [e] occurs under conditions of slight prolongation or stress, the diphthong usually occurs, e.g., [eɪ].

Common Errors

1. The second vowel of any diphthong should not be stressed; therefore, stressing the second element erroneously will result in the substitution of [i] for the [ɪ] in [eɪ]; for example, *pay* [peɪ] becomes [pei], *freight* [freɪt] becomes [freit], and so on.

2. In dialectal speech, prolongation gives rise to the addition of other sounds to the diphthong [eɪ]: *main* [meɪn] becomes [meɪən] or [meɪjən], *male* [meɪl] becomes [meɪəl] or [meɪjl̩], and possibly even [meɪjəl].

3. Substitution of another sound for [e, eɪ] can occur because of carelessness in the adjustment of the articulators or as a function of a local dialect. Therefore, *pay* [peɪ] might become [pɛɪ] or [paɪ], and so on.

EXERCISES

1. Practice the frames in the following operant conditioning exercise for [e] and [eɪ]:

Initial				Medial				Final			
Frames		Frames		Frames		Frames		Frames		Frames	
1	eɪ	7	eɪ	13	eɪ	19	eɪ	25	eɪ	31	eɪ
2	eɪt	8	eɪl	14	teɪl	20	leɪt	26	teɪ	32	leɪ
3	eɪ	9	eɪ	15	eɪ	21	eɪ	27	eɪ	33	eɪ
4	eɪk	10	eɪb	16	keɪb	22	beɪk	28	keɪ	34	beɪ
5	eɪ	11	eɪ	17	eɪ	23	eɪ	29	eɪ	35	eɪ
6	eɪf	12	eɪm	18	feɪm	24	meɪf	30	feɪ	36	meɪ

2. Practice the following words either individually or as frames in an operant conditioning sequence:

Initial				Medial				Final			
Frames		Frames		Frames		Frames		Frames		Frames	
1	ate	7	age	13	hail	19	bail	25	clay	31	spray
2	ape	8	aid	14	same	20	lame	26	hay	32	they
3	ache	9	apron	15	grade	21	came	27	stay	33	way
4	ace	10	eight	16	gave	22	blame	28	play	34	ray
5	aim	11	acre	17	faith	23	paper	29	may	35	pray
6	ale	12	ailment	18	station	24	played	30	bray	36	portray

193

3. Practice the following sentences:
   a. All day rain and hail fell on our eighty-eight acres of clay.
   b. The capable mate blamed the sailor for aiding the alien to escape.
   c. The nation's claim to fame lay in maintaining its great pace.
   d. The playwright's "angel" aided the failing play to stay on Broadway.
   e. The name of the maid who aided with the catering may be obtained by staying until after the fete.

4. In working with the following words, be sure that the diphthong [eɪ] does not become the triphthong [eɪə].

say	maiden	maybe
claim	alien	angel
same	grade	fame
vain	blame	raindrop

5. Work on the following lines of poetry:
   a. Gather ye rosebuds while ye may,
      Old time is still aflying;
      And that same flower that blooms today,
      Tomorrow will be dying.
   b. For he who fights and runs away
      May live to fight another day;
      But he who is in battle slain
      Can never rise and fight again.
   c. The glories of our blood and state
      Are shadows, not substantial things;
      There is no armor against fate;
      Death lays his icy hand on kings.
   d. Ere he alighted at Netherby gate,
      The bride had consented, the gallant came late. . . .
      So stately his form, and so lovely her face,
      That never a hall such a galliard did grace.

THE VOWEL [ɛ]

The [ɛ] is called short e (diacritical mark, ĕ). The tongue is lax, the apex of the tongue is forward, and both the tongue and jaw are lower than in [e]. The lips also are lax. [ɛ] may be spelled a, ae, ai, ay, e, ea, ei, eo, ie, oe, and u as in *any, aesthetic, said, says, ebb, leather, heifer, leopard, friend, foetid,* and *bury.*

Common Errors

1. Careless speakers sometimes substitute [ɪ] for [ɛ], so that a word like *many* [mɛnɪ] becomes ['mɪnɪ], and *get* [gɛt], *pen* [pɛn], and *hen* [hɛn], become [gɪt], [pɪn], and [hɪn].

2. The substitution of [eɪ] for [ɛ] also occurs, so that words like *beg, leg,* and *egg* are pronounced [beɪg], [leɪg], and [eɪg].

3. Speakers who habitually drawl their words are prone to diphthongize this sound, changing [ɛ] to [ɛə]. Thus, words like *said* [sɛd], *met* [mɛt], and *head* [hɛd] become [sɛəd], [mɛət], and [hɛəd].

4. It is even possible to open too much for [ɛ] and substitute [æ] in the process, e.g., *help* [hɛlp] becomes [hælp], etc.

EXERCISES

1. Practice the frames in the following operant conditioning exercise for [ɛ] :

Initial				Medial			
Frames		Frames		Frames		Frames	
1	ɛ	7	ɛ	13	ɛ	19	ɛ
2	ɛt	8	ɛl	14	tɛl	20	lɛt
3	ɛ	9	ɛ	15	ɛ	21	ɛ
4	ɛk	10	ɛb	16	kɛb	22	bɛk
5	ɛ	11	ɛ	17	ɛ	23	ɛ
6	ɛf	12	ɛm	18	fɛm	24	mɛf

2. Practice the following words either individually or as frames in an operant conditioning sequence:

Initial				Medial			
Frames		Frames		Frames		Frames	
1	ebb	7	exit	13	help	19	bent
2	end	8	exude	14	kelp	20	forever
3	elk	9	exquisite	15	center	21	together
4	edge	10	edible	16	never	22	penny
5	enter	11	entity	17	rent	23	set
6	ever	12	elf	18	bet	24	met

3. Practice the following sentences:
   a. Let us not forget that our friends are our best investment.
   b. Many forget to emphasize the direction of the breath stream in therapy for cleft-palate speech.
   c. The knell of the bell recalled unpleasant memories to the festive men.
   d. The fretful guest then asked a question about the genuine feather bed.
   e. He tested Fred with questions relative to Heaven and Hell.
4. Distinguish carefully between the words in the following groups:

   pen—pin—peek   set—sit—seat
   bet—bit—beet   neck—nick—neat
   red—rid—reed

5. Take care not to diphthongize the [ɛ] sound in the following words:

egg	led	pleasure
leg	fed	measure
beg	head	treasure
bell	wed	twelve
fell	said	shelve

6. Work for smoothness in reading the following lines:
   a. The bell invites me.
      Hear it not, Duncan, for it is a knell
      That summons thee to heaven or to hell.
   b. Oh, young Lochinvar is come out of the west:
      Through all the wide border his steed is the best.
   c. I do not love thee, Doctor Fell,
      The reason why I cannot tell;
      But this alone I know full well,
      I do not love thee, Dr. Fell.

THE VOWEL [æ]

The [æ] is a low, front vowel called short a (diacritical mark, ă). The jaw is half-low, the lips are retracted, and the mouth is open. The tongue is tense and the front portion is only slightly elevated. [æ] may be spelled a and ai as in hat and plaid.

Common Errors

1. Among careless speakers, substitutions for [æ] are common. Some of the most frequent substitutions are [ɛ], [ʌ], and [ɪ]. Thus for example, gather [gæðɚ] becomes ['gɛðɚ], rather ['ræðɚ] becomes ['rʌðɚ], and can becomes [kɪn].

2. Nasalization of this sound is common, so that words like *ask* [æsk], *half* [hæf], *bath* [bæθ], *bag* [bæg], and *lad* [læd] take on a sharp nasal quality which is unpleasant and should be eliminated. This fault is especially common in words in which the nasal consonants precede or follow the [æ], as in *can* [kæn], *man* [mæn], etc.

3. Often, in trying to avoid the above fault, people who are careful in their speech but untrained in pronunciation go to the opposite extreme. They "broaden" their [æ] sounds into [a], [a] or possibly even [ɔ]. Thus, *and* [ænd] becomes [and], *hand* [hænd] becomes [hand], and so forth. One making this substitution is often judged affected; therefore, the practice should be avoided.

EXERCISES

1. Practice the frames in the following operant conditioning exercise for [æ]:

Initial				Medial			
Frames		Frames		Frames		Frames	
1	æ	7	æ	13	æ	19	æ
2	æt	8	æl	14	tæl	20	læt
3	æ	9	æ	15	æ	21	æ
4	æk	10	æb	16	kæb	22	bæk
5	æ	11	æ	17	æ	23	æ
6	æf	12	æm	18	fæm	24	mæf

2. Practice the following words either individually or as frames in an operant conditioning sequence:

Initial				Medial			
Frames		Frames		Frames		Frames	
1	at	7	abduct	13	ham	19	patter
2	add	8	angle	14	rang	20	brass
3	act	9	agate	15	jam	21	mantle
4	am	10	apple	16	fan	22	manner
5	atom	11	ashes	17	fang	23	dash
6	ant	12	asterisk	18	mat	24	map

3. Practice the following sentences:
  a. The ham actor had a hankering to play Falstaff.
  b. Jams, yams, and hams are standard foods throughout the land.
  c. The sand on the bank of the river was damp, and camping was hazardous.
  d. The sacrilegious blasphemy of the crass blacksmith shattered dad's apathy.
  e. The damsel was glad that the handsome young man asked for her hand.

4. Distinguish between the vowel sounds in the following word groups:

axe—egg—it	sat—set—sit
big—beg—bag	pit—pet—pat
bat—bet—bit	pan—pen—pin
mitt—met—mat	dint—dense—dance

5. Avoid nasality on the [æ] in the following words:

ban	man	gnat	manna
can	mat	nab	banana
ran	mash	nag	manner
fan	mangle	nap	tanner

6. Work on the following lines:
  a. His hair is crisp, and black, and long,
     His face is like the tan;
     His brow is wet with honest sweat,
     He earns whate'er he can.
  b. Can storied urn or animated bust,
     Back to its mansion call the fleeting breath?
     Can honor's voice provoke the silent dust,
     Or flatt'ry soothe the dull cold ear of death?

THE VOWEL [a]

The [a] (diacritical mark, à) occurs chiefly in Eastern Standard speech. It is formed just slightly farther back in the mouth, the tongue is slightly lower, and the mouth slightly wider open than for [æ]. [a] is made midway between [æ] and [ɑ], the next vowel to be discussed.

[a] occurs in Eastern Standard Speech, as we have said, but it also occurs in most British dialects and in theatre speech. One reared in the General American dialectal area should not attempt to adopt [a] for his speech unless there is a good reason for doing so, i.e., professional purposes.

198

Common Errors

1. In attempting to produce [a], the speaker may produce [ɑ], [ɒ], or [ɔ]. In making this substitution, the speaker runs the risk of being considered affected by all English speaking groups.

2. Probably the greatest mistake in the misuse of [a] is to employ this phoneme for [æ], where [æ] is the only acceptable pronunciation. A careful study of the list below will identify [æ-a] distinctions:

[æ] words in all dialects		[æ] words in General American, but [a] in certain regional dialects	
at	hand	ask	advance
can	mantle	can't	demand
catch	band	calf	France
flat	bland	grass	chance
attic	fan	craft	bath

THE VOWEL [u]

The highest of the back vowels is [u]. It is identified by the words *who*, *tomb*, etc. (diacritical mark, $\overline{oo}$). The back of the tongue is raised high in relation to the hard palate, the jaw is high, and the lips are rounded in the production of this sound. [u] occurs frequently with [j] as in the [ju] combination in *you*, *few*, etc. [ju] will be treated separately as a diphthong later in this chapter. [u] is spelled *eu, ew, o, oe, oo, ou, u, ue,* and *ui* as in *maneuver, grew, move, canoe, ooze, troupe, rule, flue,* and *fruit*.

Common Errors

1. In common with most of the other vowels, there is danger of drawing out the vowel [u] into the diphthong [uə], as in words like *boon, moon*, etc.

2. Careless placement or inactive lip rounding can cause [u] to sound like [ʊ]; thus, words like *spoon* [spun], *soon* [sun], and *balloon* [bə'lun], become [spʊn], [sʊn], and [bə'lʊn].

3. The choice of whether to use [u], [ɪu], or [ju] has become a source of confusion among students of diction. In many cases, even within dialectal regions some variation is permissible. Note the direction of change in a word like *new*, e.g., from [nju] to [nɪu], and eventually [nu]. Words like *due, tune,* and *tumult* are also good examples of those words that receive a variety of pronunciations chiefly because they are in a process of change. Our only advice here is to be consistent in the prununication of similar words.

199

EXERCISES

1. Practice the frames in the following operant conditioning exercise for [u]:

Initial				Medial				Final			
Frames		Frames		Frames		Frames		Frames		Frames	
1	u	7	u	13	u	19	u	25	u	31	u
2	ut	8	ul	14	tul	20	lut	26	tu	32	lu
3	u	9	u	15	u	21	u	27	u	33	u
4	uk	10	ub	16	kub	22	buk	28	ku	34	bu
5	u	11	u	17	u	23	u	29	u	35	u
6	uf	12	um	18	fum	24	muf	30	fu	36	mu

2. Practice the following words either individually or as frames in an operant conditioning sequence:

Initial				Medial				Final			
Frames		Frames		Frames		Frames		Frames		Frames	
1	ooze	7	ouzel	13	rude	19	group	25	who	31	threw
2	oozy	8	Uhlan	14	moon	20	brood	26	do	32	true
3	oolong	9	ulema	15	loon	21	plume	27	shoe	33	Sioux
4	oorali	10	ulu	16	move	22	luminous	28	blue	34	through
5	Ubangi	11	umiak	17	whose	23	troup	29	drew	35	brew
6	oubliette	12	oodles	18	tool	24	booth	30	crew	36	flew

3. Practice the following sentences:
   a. It is rumored that the Sioux are moving their canoes at noon.
   b. The fool's buffoonery ended when his spoon overthrew his soup.
   c. The rooster was rudely crowing at noon.
   d. The supersititous booby's belief in spooks was lampooned at school.
   e. Lou's tooth was so loose that she couldn't eat her food.

4. Take special care in distinguishing between the following pairs of words:

ooze—use	choose—refuse	ewe—coo
too—few	woo—view	dispute—troop
ruse—abuse	beauty—booty	youth—tooth
snooze—accuse	buttes—boots	

5. Enunciate clearly the following sentences containing [u] or [ju], but be consistent:

      a. Please introduce me when you have the opportunity.

      b. Don't be a stupid nuisance.

      c. The tumult aroused the multitude.

      d. The tuba can do things with tunes that the flute can't do.

      e. Lucy seemed to deem it her duty to tell everything to Sue.

6. With respect to the following words, opinions and customs differ. Make your choice, based upon observation of the speech of educated persons with whom you associate; then try to maintain a reasonable degree of consistency.

new	student	multitude	introduce
due	assume	stupendous	tumult
tune	Tuesday	numerous	deuce
stupid	adieu	opportunity	neutral

7. Practice these selections:

      a. Death will come when thou art dead,

          Soon, too soon—

      Sleep will come when thou art fled;

      Of neither would I ask the boon

      I ask of thee, beloved Night—

      Swift be thine approaching flight,

          Come soon, soon!

      b. We sail the ocean blue,

      And our saucy ship's a beauty;

      We're sober men and true,

      And attentive to our duty.

THE VOWEL [ʊ]

The [ʊ] is the vowel sound found in the word *put* [pʊt] (diacritical mark, o͝o). In making this sound the lips are slightly less rounded and less tense than in forming the [u]. The back of the tongue is somewhat lower in the mouth for [u], though [ʊ] is also a high-back vowel.

Common Errors

1. Speakers are often inconsistent in their use of the phonemes [u] and [ʊ]. There is considerable difference of opinion regarding the preferred pronunciation of the following words. *The American College Dictionary*

for example, allows both sounds but prefers [u] for the words in the first column and [ʊ] for those in the second.

root	hoop
roof	hoof
room	hooves
coop	soot
broom	bosom

2. [ʌ] should not be substituted for [ʊ] in a stressed syllable. If this error is made, *took* [tʊk] becomes [tʌk], *book* [bʊk] becomes [bʌk], and so forth. [ʊ] often weakens to [ə] in the unstressed syllable, e.g., *should* [ʃʊd] becomes [ʃəd]. A typical example of weakening may be seen in the sentence, "He should go." ['hi ʃəd'goʊ], where the speaker has purposely weakened *should* to gain greater emphasis on *go*. However, the speaker would be in error if he weakened *should* (stressed) in the following sentence: "*Should* I?" ['ʃʊd aɪ], making it ['ʃəd aɪ].

EXERCISES

1. Inasmuch as [ʊ] occurs only in the medial position, a modified version of the operant conditioning sequence is offered:

<table>
<tr><th colspan="12" align="center">Medial Position Only</th></tr>
<tr><th colspan="2">Frames</th><th colspan="2">Frames</th><th colspan="2">Frames</th><th colspan="2">Frames</th><th colspan="2">Frames</th><th colspan="2">Frames</th></tr>
<tr><td>1</td><td>book</td><td>7</td><td>rook</td><td>13</td><td>push</td><td>19</td><td>could</td><td>25</td><td>Pullman</td><td>31</td><td>good</td></tr>
<tr><td>2</td><td>took</td><td>8</td><td>shook</td><td>14</td><td>hook</td><td>20</td><td>put</td><td>26</td><td>wool</td><td>32</td><td>hook</td></tr>
<tr><td>3</td><td>forsook</td><td>9</td><td>foot</td><td>15</td><td>should</td><td>21</td><td>pull</td><td>27</td><td>crook</td><td>33</td><td>nook</td></tr>
<tr><td>4</td><td>bull</td><td>10</td><td>wood</td><td>16</td><td>would</td><td>22</td><td>bush</td><td>28</td><td>pudding</td><td>34</td><td>bullion</td></tr>
<tr><td>5</td><td>pullet</td><td>11</td><td>stood</td><td>17</td><td>puss</td><td>23</td><td>wood</td><td>29</td><td>full</td><td>35</td><td>wolf</td></tr>
<tr><td>6</td><td>look</td><td>12</td><td>cook</td><td>18</td><td>sugar</td><td>24</td><td>bullet</td><td>30</td><td>brook</td><td>36</td><td>pulpit</td></tr>
</table>

2. The following sentences contain both [ʊ] words and [u] words. Enunciate them clearly, and be sure that you make the distinction between the two sounds.

    a. Susie said, "Soon, soon, too soon!"
    b. Some men seek good looks, others seek good cooks.
    c. The brook glimmered in the moonlight.
    d. She said she did not choose to cook the prunes.
    e. I understood that she took her poodle with her on her cruise.
    f. Cooper should have put the pullet in the coop.
    g. The cook made sugar cookies and pudding.
    h. She used worsted wool in making a hooked rug for her room.

    i. The woman knew that she was hoodwinked when she dis-
covered that the Buddha was made of wood.

    j. The preacher took the Good Book from the pulpit and stood
silently.

3. Make a clear distinction between [ʊ] and [u] in the following paired
words.

book—boot	wooed—would
look—loot	stool—stood
hook—hoot	crude—crook
shook—shoot	brood—brook
butcher—blucher	pooling—pulling

4. Practice the following selections:

    a. No solemn sanctimonious face I pull.

        My only books were women's looks.

    b. There is no friend so faithful as a good book,

        There is no worse robber than a bad book.

    c. "How," cried the Mayor, "d'ye think I'll brook

        Being worse treated than a cook?"

THE VOWEL [o] AND DIPHTHONG [oʊ]

The vowel [o] and the diphthong [oʊ] will be treated together at this time.
Both of these sounds are traditionally referred to as long *o* (diacritical mark, *o*).
Although this sound may occur as a single vowel [o], it is far more likely in
American speech to be diphthongized. As a pure vowel it appears primarily
in unaccented syllables, as in *obey* [o'beɪ], *hotel* [ho'tɛl], *omit* [o'mɪt],
and *rotund* [ro'tʌnd]; it also occurs in certain accented syllables, particularly
when it is followed by an unvoiced consonant as in *ocean* ['oʃən] and *motive*
['motɪv]. When it occurs as a diphthong, which is far more common, it
forms a glide with [ʊ], as in *go* [goʊ], *hoe* [hoʊ], *loath* [loʊθ], etc. The
[o, oʊ] are spelled *au, eau, eo, ew, o, oa, oe, oh, oo, ou, ow*, and *o* as in
hautboy, beau, yeoman, sew, note, road, toe, oh, brooch, soul, flow, and
omit (for [o]).

The pure vowel [o] is made by rounding the lips considerably more than
for [ʊ]. The lips, as well as the blade of the tongue, are also somewhat
more tense than in [ʊ]. The chief point of distinction of the [o] is the definite
rounding of the lips into a circle, as suggested by the shape of the printed
symbol. The diphthong [oʊ] is formed by gliding quickly from [o] to [ʊ]
in one continuous sound in the same syllable. The second elements of
most diphthongs are short and unstressed.

Common Errors

1. As is true with most pure vowels, failure to adjust the articulators
properly can cause [o] and [oʊ] to take on the quality of neighboring vowels

—neighboring in the sense that they are made in the same general place in the mouth, i.e., back, half-low, half-high, etc. Thus [o] and [oʊ] can begin to sound like [ʊ] above and [ɔ] below and [ʌ] in a mid-vowel position. If one does not give [o] proper lip rounding, it loses much of its identifying acoustic characteristics.

2. If drawled (prolonged), [oʊ] can easily become a triphthong; hence, *go* becomes [goʊə], and particularly before [l] as in *old* [oʊld] and *cold* [koʊld] becoming [oʊəld] and [koʊəld].

The [o] and [oʊ] will vary from speaker to speaker, depending upon the amount of duration one typically uses for these two sounds. Variation is normal and natural. The slow speaker inevitably will diphthongize them more than the rapid speaker. The common practice is to use the diphthong [oʊ] in accented syllables and in the final position of words, while in unaccented syllables or before unvoiced consonants it is often pronounced as the simple vowel [o].

EXERCISES

1. Practice the frames in the following operant conditioning exercise for [oʊ]:

Initial			Medial			Final		
Frames		Frames		Frames		Frames		Frames
1 oʊ	7 oʊ	13 oʊ	19 oʊ	25 oʊ	31 oʊ
2 oʊt	8 oʊl	14 toʊl	20 loʊt	26 toʊ	32 loʊ
3 oʊ	9 oʊ	15 oʊ	21 oʊ	27 oʊ	33 oʊ
4 oʊk	10 oʊb	16 koʊb	22 boʊk	28 koʊ	34 boʊ
5 oʊ	11 oʊ	17 oʊ	23 oʊ	29 oʊ	35 oʊ
6 oʊf	12 oʊm	18 foʊm	24 moʊf	30 foʊ	36 moʊ

2. Practice the following words either individually or as frames in an operant conditioning sequence:

Initial			Medial			Final		
Frames		Frames		Frames		Frames		Frames
1 old	7 opaque	13 soap	19 poetic	25 low	31 potato
2 oak	8 oaf	14 toad	20 lower	26 slow	32 bellow
3 ode	9 only	15 road	21 folder	27 grow	33 pillow
4 obey	10 over	16 hope	22 mold	28 flow	34 yellow
5 opal	11 own	17 shoal	23 code	29 blow	35 bureau
6 opiate	12 open	18 pony	24 boulder	30 crow	36 snow

3. Practice the following sentences:

    a. The low tones of the oboe told the story in melody.
    b. Most people know that Poe's poetry has moments of fine lyric quality.
    c. The hobo's motto was, "Follow the open road."
    d. The boat came home so heavily loaded with potatoes and oats that it could scarcely keep afloat.
    e. Hope lost her opal ring in the snow.

4. Practice the following series of carry-over exercises:

a. obey	you obey	you obey him.
b. open	I open	I open with Kings.
c. omit	don't omit	don't omit anything.
d. ode	Shelley's ode	I read Shelley's ode.
e. omen	good omen	that's a good omen.

5. Practice the following selections:

    a. I know a bank where the wild thyme blows,
      Where oxlips and the nodding violet grows.
    b. A song to the oak, the brave old oak,
      Who hath ruled in the greenwood long.
    c. Now gold hath sway, we all obey,
      And a ruthless king is he.
    d. This hand, to tyrants ever sworn the foe,
      For freedom only deals the deadly blow.
    e. . . . If I should chance to fall below
      Demosthenes or Cicero,
      Don't view me with a critic's eye,
      But pass my imperfections by.
      Large streams from little fountains flow,
      Tall oaks from little acorns grow.
    f. Young Obadias,
      David, Josias,—
      All were pious.
    g. As unto the bow the cord is,
      So unto man is woman;
      Though she bends him, she obeys him,
      Though she draws him, yet she follows:
      Useless each without the other.
    h. Banners yellow, glorious, golden,
      On its roof did float and flow;
      This, all this, was in the olden
      Time, long ago.

THE VOWEL [ɔ]

[ɔ] is the vowel sound in words like *raw* [rɔ] and *saw* [sɔ] (diacritical mark ô or ạ). In making this sound the tongue is lower in the mouth than for [o] ; also, the lips are wider apart and projected farther forward than for [o]. Both lips and the tongue are somewhat tense. The [ɔ] is a low back-vowel. It is spelled *a, ah, al, au, aw, o, oa,* and *ou* as in *tall, Utah, talk, fault, raw, order, broad,* and *fought.*

Common Errors

1. It is not uncommon for [ɔ] to be diphthonized into [ɔʊ], changing the word *talk*, for example, to [tɔʊk].

2. Occasionally the sound [ɑ] is substituted for [ɔ], as in a word like *auto*, which becomes [ɑtoʊ].

3. Regionally, sometimes an [ɚ] is incorrectly added, as in *wash* [wɔɚʃ].

4. In substandard speech, [æ] is sometimes substituted for [ɔ], as in a word like *gaunt*, which becomes [gænt].

EXERCISES

1. Practice the frames in the following operant conditioning exercise for [ɔ] :

Initial		Medial		Final	
Frames	Frames	Frames	Frames	Frames	Frames
1 ɔ	7 ɔ	13 ɔ	19 ɔ	25 ɔ	31. ɔ
2 ɔt	8 ɔl	14 tɔl	20 lɔt	26 tɔ	32 lɔ
3 ɔ	9 ɔ	15 ɔ	21 ɔ	27 ɔ	33 ɔ
4 ɔk	10 ɔb	16 kɔb	22 bɔk	28 kɔ	34 bɔ
5 ɔ	11 ɔ	17 ɔ	23 ɔ	29 ɔ	35 ɔ
6 ɔf	12 ɔm	18 fɔm	24 mɔf	30 fɔ	36 mɔ

2. Practice the following words either individually or as frames in an operant conditioning sequence :

Initial		Medial		Final	
Frames	Frames	Frames	Frames	Frames	Frames
1 all	7 auction	13 cause	19 lawn	25 saw	31 claw
2 awe	8 awning	14 sauce	20 sought	26 raw	32 pshaw
3 auto	9 autumn	15 hawk	21 scrawl	27 jaw	33 paw
4 ordeal	10 author	16 caught	22 fortune	28 law	34 gnaw
5 awful	11 always	17 falter	23 tall	29 flaw	35 squaw
6 ought	12 also	18 warm	24 dawn	30 straw	36 withdraw

3. Practice the following sentences :

    a. All of the author's possessions were auctioned last autumn.

    b. The hawk fought the dog over a piece of raw flesh.

    c. The Shawnee squaws often wore shawls to keep them warm.

    d. The outlaws fought the law all fall.

    e. The cost of hauling the straw almost brought disaster to Paul.

4. The exercise for distinguishing [ɔ] from [ɑ] is found under drill materials for [ɑ], p. 209.

5. Practice the following selections :

    a. Mourning when their leaders fall ;

      Warriors carry the warrior's pall,

      And sorrow darkens hamlet and hall.

    b. A song for our banner ! The watchword recall

      Which gave the Republic her station :

      "United we stand, divided we fall !"

      It made and preserves us a nation !

    c. Men use thought only as authority for their injustice, and employ speech only to conceal their thoughts.

    d. Where law ends, tyranny begins.

THE VOWEL [ɒ]

The vowel sound [ɒ] is sometimes heard in words like *wander* ['wɒndɚ], *box* [bɒks], and *John* [dʒɒn]. Its diacritical mark is ŏ. It is spelled *a* and *o*, as in the above words; it may also be spelled *au* as in *laurel* and *aw* as in *Lawrence* (second choice dictionary pronunciations in both cases). In forming this sound the tongue is nearly flat in the mouth, but the back of it is raised slightly. The mouth is a little less rounded and the lips a little less projected than for [ɔ], but the lips are definitely tensed. The [ɒ] is a shorter, crisper sound than [ɔ]. The [ɒ] is found most often in the speech of New Englanders and New Yorkers, and is often absent altogether in the speech of those from the General American area.

Some authorities feel that [ɒ] not only deserves separate classification, but is the preferred pronunciation in many words, such as the following :

Initial		Medial	
of	ocular	job	watch
on	oligarchy	hot	profit
odd	ominous	got	hospital
olive	oscillate	God	college
osprey	osculate	golf	column
omelet	Odyssey	flop	wander
Oliver	operatic	stop	progress
occupy	opposite	wash	prodigy

THE VOWEL [ɑ]

The [ɑ] is a low back-vowel found in words like *palm, calm,* and *arm* (diacritical mark, *ä*). In forming this sound the tongue is flat and relaxed on the floor of the mouth except for a very slight arching at the back; the lips are quite far apart and not rounded; the jaw is free from tension and the mouth is well opened. The [ɑ] is spelled *a, e,* and *ea* as in *father, sergeant,* and *hearth.*

Common Errors

1. Typically [ɑ] is easy for most speakers to make, and hence few errors occur per se on this sound. Also, there is a wider variation in production permitted before error is introduced in [ɑ] than on most of the other pure vowels. For example, an [a] or [ɒ] may be substituted for [ɑ] without introducing error, e.g., *hot* may be pronounced [hɑt] or [hɒt], and *father* may be pronounced both [faðɚ] and [faðɚ].

2. Occasionally a speaker may drawl [ɑ] and pick up an off-glide [ɑə] so that *father* [faðɚ] becomes [faəðɚ].

3. It is erroneous to substitute [ɔ] for [ɑ] in words like *palm, calm,* and others.

EXERCISES

1. Practice the frames in the following operant conditioning exercise for [ɑ]:

Initial				Medial				Final			
Frames		Frames		Frames		Frames		Frames		Frames	
1	ɑ	7	ɑ	13	ɑ	19	ɑ	25	ɑ	31	ɑ
2	ɑt	8	ɑl	14	tɑl	20	lɑt	26	tɑ	32	lɑ
3	ɑ	9	ɑ	15	ɑ	21	ɑ	27	ɑ	33	ɑ
4	ɑk	10	ɑb	16	kɑb	22	bɑk	28	kɑ	34	bɑ
5	ɑ	11	ɑ	17	ɑ	23	ɑ	29	ɑ	35	ɑ
6	ɑf	12	ɑm	18	fɑm	24	mɑf	30	fɑ	36	mɑ

2. Practice the following words either individually or as frames in an operant conditioning sequence:

Initial				Medial				Final			
Frames		Frames		Frames		Frames		Frames		Frames	
1	arm	7	ardent	13	hearth	19	psalm	25	pa	31	shah
2	ark	8	almond	14	cartoon	20	heart	26	ma	32	rah
3	alms	9	artist	15	father	21	bomb	27	fa	33	bra
4	arch	10	arson	16	barn	22	far	28	la	34	bah
5	arbor	11	arc	17	farm	23	want	29	schwa	35	grandpa
6	argue	12	army	18	calm	24	car	30	ha	36	grandma

3. Practice the following sentences:
   a. The Shah and the Rajah had qualms about the palmist's artistry.
   b. Mama kept her almond tarts in a large jar.
   c. The parson's knowledge of the psalms was marvelous.
   d. The shepherd guarded his flock from harm.
   e. The artist argued that it would be stark melodrama for him to plead for alms.

4. Practice the three vowels, [æ, ɑ, ɔ], to develop good placement. Reverse the order [ɔ, ɑ, æ], and finally practice them randomly, [ɑ, æ, ɔ, æ, ɑ, ɑ, ɔ, æ, ɑ, æ, ɔ]. Now say the following groups of words, attempting to get good placement of the vowel on each word:

at—art—ought	bat—balm—Boston
hat—ha—haw	cat—calm—cost
fast—farm—forest	damp—dark—daughter
calf—calm—coffee	lamb—lama—laundry
fat—father—fought	sand—psalm—saunter

5. Practice the following selections:
   a. There are maidens in Scotland more lovely by far,
      That would gladly be wed to the young Lochinvar.
   b. My spirit beats her mortal bars,
      As down dark tides the glory slides,
      And, star-like, mingles with the stars.
   c. To me more dear, congenial to my heart,
      One native charm than all the gloss of art.
   d. Twilight and evening bell,
      And after that the dark!
      And may there be no sadness of farewell
      When I embark.

209

THE VOWELS [ɝ] AND [ɜ]

The [ɝ] is the vowel sound in words like *fur* [fɝ], *earn* [ɝn], *fern* [fɝn], *world* [wɝld] (diacritical mark, *ɝr*). In General American speech [ɝ] represents this vowel sound, while [ɜ] represents the sound as pronounced in parts of New England, where people "drop their r's." In forming the sound [ɝ], the apex of the tongue is raised high in the middle position of the mouth. The lateral margins are against the adjacent upper gum ridges. The tongue tip, as in consonantal [r], is curled backward slightly (retroflexed), and the lips are unrounded. In [ɜ] the tongue tip is not retroflexed, nor is there the degree of tension one finds in [ɝ].

[ɝ] and [ɜ] occur only in stressed syllables; these sounds are spelled *er, ear, ir, or, our, ur,* and *yr,* as in *term, learn, thirst, worm, courage, hurt,* and *myrtle.*

Common Errors

1. Excessive retroflexion, which causes the [ɝ] to be made too far back in the mouth, alters the quality of the sound.

2. Too much tension in the tongue can cause [ɝ] to become too "hard" (the higher overtones have more amplitude) and sound unpleasant.

3. With both tension and marked retroflexion, [ɝ] can become identified with Midwestern "r," which is acceptable in that dialectal area but not elsewhere.

4. If prolonged, [ɝ] and [ɜ] can develop an off-glide, e.g., *bird* [bɝd] or [bɜd] becomes [bɝəd] or [bɜəd].

EXERCISES

1. Practice the frames in the following operant conditioning exercise for [ɝ]:

Initial		Medial		Final	
Frames	Frames	Frames	Frames	Frames	Frames
1 ɝ	7 ɝ	13 ɝ	19 ɝ	25 ɝ	31 ɝ
2 ɝt	8 ɝl	14 tɝl	20 lɝt	26 tɝ	32 lɝ
3 ɝ	9 ɝ	15 ɝ	21 ɝ	27 ɝ	33 ɝ
4 ɝk	10 ɝb	16 kɝb	22 bɝk	28 kɝ	34 bɝ
5 ɝ	11 ɝ	17 ɝ	23 ɝ	29 ɝ	35 ɝ
6 ɝf	12 ɝm	18 fɝm	24 mɝf	30 fɝ	36 mɝ

2. Practice the following words either individually or as frames in an operant conditioning sequence:

Initial						Medial						Final					
Frames		Frames		Frames		Frames		Frames		Frames	
1	earl	7	earnest	13	birth	19	alert	25	blur	31	recur
2	earn	8	urban	14	dirt	20	burden	26	cur	32	spur
3	urn	9	urchin	15	curl	21	swirl	27	err	33	were
4	early	10	irked	16	first	22	surface	28	fur	34	burr
5	earth	11	ergot	17	girt	23	mirth	29	deter	35	infer
6	urge	12	err	18	hurt	24	perfect	30	refer	36	stir

3. Practice the following sentences:
    a. Myrtle learned the first verse of the stirring song.
    b. Don't hurry, don't worry; learn to take your time.
    c. The colonel was irked when he heard that his shirts were dirty.
    d. The murder trial was adjourned pending further pertinent information.
    e. "Don't shirk work," chirped the bird to the turtle.
4. Read the following selection:

From SONG OF THE SHIRT

With fingers weary and worn,
    With eyelids heavy and red,
A woman sat in unwomanly rags,
    Plying her needle and thread—
        Stitch! stitch! stitch!
In poverty, hunger, and dirt,
    And still with a voice of dolorous pitch
She sang the "Song of the Shirt!"

"Work! work! work!
    While the cock is crowing aloof!
And work—work—work,
    Till the stars shine through the roof!
It's Oh! to be a slave
    Along with the barbarous Turk,
Where woman has never a soul to save,
    If this is Christian work!

"Work—work—work
   Till the brain begins to swim;
Work—work—work
   Till the eyes are heavy and dim.
Seam, and gusset, and band,
   Band, and gusset, and seam,
Till over the buttons I fall asleep,
   And sew them on in a dream!

—Thomas Hood

THE VOWEL [ɚ]

The [ɚ] is the counterpart of [ɜ]. Whereas [ɜ] always occurs in stressed syllables, [ɚ] always occurs in unstressed syllables. Its diacritical mark is *ər* (or *êr*).

The position of the tongue and the unrounded shape of the lips are similar in [ɚ] and [ɜ], both being mid-vowels. However, [ɚ] is much shorter in duration than [ɜ], and therefore weaker and less definite. The word *murmur* ['mɜmɚ] contains both sounds.

The vowel [ɚ] occurs only in General American speech. Persons using Eastern and Southern pronunication substitute [ə̂], to be considered shortly. The common errors listed for [ɜ] also apply to [ɚ].

EXERCISES

1. The [ɚ] occurs in the final syllable of the following words:

ever	other	picture	further	alter	foster
never	actor	fixture	brother	debtor	poster
sever	humor	sister	mother	weather	roster
better	tumor	similar	leisure	fisher	taper
heifer	glamour	pillar	pleasure	measure	cater

2. Practice the following sentences:
   a. The purser on the Clipper catered to the wealthier passengers.
   b. The dapper sailor thought his brother's humor odder than his own.
   c. Too much leisure and pleasure may adversely alter a worker's attitude.
   d. Greater numbers of red snappers than flounders are caught by fishermen in the harbor.
   e. The preacher married the actor and the glamour girl at the altar of the church.

3. Practice the following selection:

Somewhat back from the village street
Stands the old-fashioned country-seat.
Across its antique portico
Tall poplar-trees their shadows throw;
And from its station in the hall
An ancient timepiece says to all,—
　"Forever—never!
　Never—forever!"

Half-way up the stairs it stands,
And points and beckons with its hands
From its case of massive oak,
Like a monk, who, under his cloak,
Crosses, himself, and sighs, alas!
With sorrowful voice to all who pass,—
　"Forever—never!
　Never—forever!"

By day its voice is low and light;
But in the silent dead of night,
Distinct as a passing footstep's fall,
It echoes along the vacant hall,
Along the ceiling, along the floor,
And seems to say, at each chamber-door,—
　"Forever—never!
　Never—forever!"
　　　.　.　.　.　.　.　.　.

In that mansion used to be
Free-hearted Hospitality;
His great fires up the chimney roared;
The stranger feasted at his board;
But, like the skeleton at the feast,
That warning timepiece never ceased,—
　"Forever—never!
　Never—forever!"

　　　　　　　　　　—Henry Wadsworth Longfellow

THE VOWEL [ʌ]

The [ʌ] is the vowel that is usually called short *u* as in *up* [ʌp] (diacritical
mark, *ŭ*). This vowel is easily made, as the jaw is relaxed, the mouth open,
the lips unrounded, and the tongue at ease on the floor of the mouth. The
sound is a mid-vowel. [ʌ] is spelled *o*, *oe*, *oo*, *ou*, and *u* as in *son*, *does*,
flood, *couple*, and *cup*.

Because of its ease of production, [ʌ] offers no special difficulties to most persons. The following exercises will help to establish this sound in your mind.

EXERCISES

1. Practice the frames in the following operant conditioning exercise for [ʌ] :

Initial		Medial	
Frames	Frames	Frames	Frames
1 ʌ	7 ʌ	13 ʌ	19 ʌ
2 ʌt	8 ʌl	14 tʌl	20 lʌt
3 ʌ	9 ʌ	15 ʌ	21 ʌ
4 ʌk	10 ʌb	16 kʌb	22 bʌk
5 ʌ	11 ʌ	17 ʌ	23 ʌ
6 ʌf	12 ʌm	18 fʌm	24 mʌf

2. Practice the following words either individually or as frames in an operant conditioning sequence:

Initial		Medial	
Frames	Frames	Frames	Frames
1 up	7 other	13 bum	19 done
2 upper	8 umpire	14 brother	20 much
3 under	9 until	15 blood	21 trouble
4 usher	10 unable	16 asunder	22 mutton
5 uncle	11 oven	17 thunder	23 honey
6 ugly	12 onion	18 wonder	24 supper

3. Practice the following sentences:
   a. The unusual sled pulled in front in the slushy snow and finally won the race.
   b. Some said the prisoners should be hung at sunset.
   c. The assumption that the budget for the tall structure had to be doubled was judged incorrect.
   d. His uncle felt that Bud's brother should be punished for his blunder.
   e. The crowd unloaded its thunder of disapproval when the umpire was uncivil to the usher.

THE VOWEL [ə]

The [ə] is the neutral, indefinite, or schwa vowel (diacritical mark, ə). It always occurs in unstressed syllables such as the first vowel sound in *alone* [ə'loʊn], *above* [ə'bʌv], etc., and as the last vowel in *sofa* ['sofə], *postman* ['poʊstmən], etc.

This vowel is the counterpart of [ʌ], discussed earlier. In forming [ə], like [ʌ], the tongue lies flat on the floor of the mouth with the tip resting back of the lower front teeth; the jaw is relaxed, the mouth open, and the lips unrounded. The chief difference between [ʌ] and [ə] is that [ə] occurs only in unstressed syllables. Thus [ʌ] is both longer and stronger than [ə]. [ə] is the lowest of the mid-vowels.

In normal conversation this vowel occurs more frequently than any other; in fact it is the sound to which most vowels have a tendency to revert in unstressed syllables. It is also the vowel sound substituted for [ɚ] in the speech of those who "drop their r's."

Common Errors

1. In the discussion of strong and weak forms later in this chapter, we emphasize that most pure vowels in their weakest form become [ə]. If speakers insist on retaining strong forms in weak positions, the result may be speech that is considered affected. For example, in the sentence *I am ready to go* both *am* and *to* are in unstressed positions. To stress them would be injudicious, if not stilted.

2. Certain vowel sounds in American speech have resisted to some degree the general trend toward [ə] and retain much of their individuality even in unaccented syllables. This is especially true of the high front vowels like [i] and [ɪ], and the high back-vowels like [u] and [ʊ]. For example, when the accented first syllable of *mystery* becomes unaccented in *mysterious*, we do not shift from [ɪ] to [ə]; all that occurs is a shortening of the [ɪ] sound. However, the [ɪ] sound does not always retain its individuality in unaccented syllables. Few speakers, for example, retain [ɪ] in all the appropriate syllables in *responsibility*, e.g., [rɪ'spɑnsɪbɪlɪtɪ] can weaken to [rə'spɑnsəbɪlətɪ] and other pronunciations.

EXERCISES

1. The [ə] sound is acceptable in the position indicated by italics.

Initial	Medial	Final
about	secondary	boa
around	firmament	sofa
acquire	permanent	comma
adjourn	specimen	guerrilla
attest	portable	soda
abbreviate	prominence	area
announce	promontory	Canada
affairs	composition	America

215

2. It is better, in the opinion of most careful speakers, not to go all the way to the neutral vowel in the italicized unaccented syllables in the following words. Consult the dictionary for the "acceptable" pronunciation.

*be*fore	al*ways*	*mo*mentous
*be*lief	prin*cess*	*Mon*golian
*be*come	short*est*	*ac*ceptable
*de*cline	long*est*	dis*pu*tatious

3. Practice the following sentences:
   a. The area of Alabama is not comparable to the area of Montana.
   b. The quiet smile of the Mona Lisa has appealed to many.
   c. The notable explorer from America was found alive but alone in the jungle.
   d. The quality of the specimen of sedimentary rock was difficult to analyze.
   e. Civilian authority is more characteristic of domestic American life than is military authority.

THE DIPHTHONGS

A diphthong is a complex sound made by gliding continuously from the position of one vowel to that of another within the same syllable. In most diphthongs the first element is stressed while the second element is not, except for [ju]. This definition recognizes a wide range of diphthongs that actually exist in American speech. However, it is not within the scope of the present text to cover every possible diphthong in American English.

Two sets of sentences contain the majority of the most widely used diphthongs: (a) *Pay my bold boy now* [peɪ maɪ boʊɪd bɔɪ naʊ], and (b) *Here's their poor oar* [hiɚz ðɛɚ pʊɚ oɚ]. The first sentence reveals the most common and highly recognized diphthongs, while the latter sentence yields the type of diphthongs that are seldom given individual treatment in textbooks. The diphthong [ju] needs special attention, chiefly because of its high frequency of occurrence in speech. Authorities stress the difference between allophonic diphthongs [eɪ] and [oʊ], or those that do not distinguish meaning from the pure vowels of which they are allophones, and phonemic diphthongs such as [ɔɪ] and [ju], which do. In other words, if the second element of the diphthong is dropped in the first type of diphthong, the meaning of the word is not altered, e.g., if *pay* [peɪ] is altered to [pe], the meaning is not changed. However, if the second element is dropped in the phonemic diphthong, the word is changed, e.g., *boy* [bɔɪ] becomes [bɔ].

The allophonic diphthongs [oʊ] and [eɪ] have already been presented with [o] and [e], respectively. Only the four phonemic diphthongs [aɪ], [aʊ], [ɔɪ], and [ju] will be included in this section.

THE DIPHTHONG [aɪ]

The diphthong [aɪ] occurs in such words as *ride* [raɪd], *brine* [braɪn], *crime* [kraɪm], etc., and is indicated by the diacritical mark ī). It is spelled *ai*, *ay, ei, ey, i, ie, uy, y,* and *ye* as in *aisle, aye, height, eye, ice, tie, buy, sky,* and *lye.*

The first element of this diphthong is sometimes written [ɑ]. so that it appears [ɑɪ] instead of [aɪ]. There is, without doubt, a normal variation from one to the other of these sounds even by careful speakers, and both pronunciations may therefore be considered acceptable.

Common Errors

1. While dialectal speech may be totally acceptable for a given area, we should point out that in certain regions [aɪ] may become [ɑ] ; thus [aɪ] becomes [ɑ] in *tired, my, I, fine,* etc., [tɑd], [mɑ], [ɑ], [fɑn].

2. Some speakers stress the second elements of diphthongs, in which case [aɪ] becomes [ai], as in *fine* [faɪn] becoming [fain]. Shifting the stress to the first element of the diphthong while shortening and weakening the second element will eliminate this fault.

EXERCISES

1. Practice the frames in the following operant conditioning exercise for [aɪ] :

Initial		Medial		Final	
Frames	Frames	Frames	Frames	Frames	Frames
1 aɪ	7 aɪ	13 aɪ	19 aɪ	25 aɪ	31 aɪ
2 aɪt	8 aɪl	14 taɪl	20 laɪt	26 taɪ	32 laɪ
3 aɪ	9 aɪ	15 aɪ	21 aɪ	27 aɪ	33 aɪ
4 aɪk	10 aɪb	16 kaɪb	22 baɪk	28 kaɪ	34 baɪ
5 aɪ	11 aɪ	17 aɪ	23 aɪ	29 aɪ	35 aɪ
6 aɪf	12 aɪm	18 faɪm	24 maɪf	30 faɪ	36 maɪ

2. Practice the following words either individually or as frames in an operant conditioning sequence:

Initial				Medial				Final			
Frames		Frames		Frames		Frames		Frames		Frames	
1	idle	7	ivy	13	cries	19	strive	25	tie	31	die
2	item	8	iron	14	lies	20	prize	26	rye	32	high
3	eye	9	I'm	15	sighs	21	size	27	my	33	why
4	island	10	aye	16	bright	22	rhyme	28	shy	34	nigh
5	ice	11	aisle	17	light	23	slight	29	pie	35	guy
6	idea	12	ire	18	might	24	ride	30	sigh	36	buy

3. Practice the following sentences:
    a. Trial by fright is the idea of the totalitarians.
    b. Tired eyelids upon tired eyes is my plight.
    c. "Tiger, tiger, burning light," is a line from a poem by Blake.
    d. "Higher still and higher," and "Like a cloud of fire," are lines written by Shelley.
    e. "My suit you denied," "This lost love of mine," and "Drink one cup of wine," are not my lines.

4. Read the following selections:
    a. In winter I get up at night
    And dress by yellow candle-light.
    In summer, quite the other way,
    I have to go to bed by day.
    b. How fleet is a glance of the mind!
        Compared with the speed of its flight,
    The tempest itself lags behind,
        And the swift-winged arrows of light.
    c. She was a form of life and light,
    That seen, became a part of sight;
    And rose, wherever I turn'd my eye,
    The morning star of memory.
    d. In this college
    Useful knowledge
        Everywhere one finds,
    And already,
    Growing steady,
        We've enlarged our minds.

THE DIPHTHONG [aʊ]

The diphthong [aʊ] is found in the words *now* [naʊ] and *town* [taʊn]. Its diacritical mark is *ou*. It is made by quickly gliding from [a] to [ʊ] while emitting the sound. The [aʊ] is spelled *ou, ough*, and *ow* as in *out, bough*, and *brow*.

The first element in this diphthong is sometimes written [ɑ] instead of [a], which is a normal and acceptable substitution, for both [ɑ] and [a] are relaxed and open vowels and are closely related. In general [ɑʊ] is heard more frequently in Eastern speech and [aʊ] in General American, but both [ɑʊ] and [aʊ] are in good usage throughout the country.

Common Errors

1. Occasionally speakers are careless and do not form the second element of the diphthong or drop it entirely; therefore [aʊ] becomes the pure vowel [a] or [ɑ]. Thus the question, *How are you doing?*, is apt to become something like [hɑ jə ˈduən].

2. Probably no vowel combination in our language is so frequently mispronounced as this one. The most common substitution is [æ] for [a] as the first element of the diphthong. Thus, [aʊ] becomes [æʊ], or sometimes even the triphthong [æʊə], so that *now* [naʊ], *about* [əˈbaʊt], and *town* [taʊn], etc., become [næʊ], [əˈbæʊt], [tæʊn], and so forth. This substitution, although widespread and quite common throughout the country, is not considered acceptable by careful speakers.

3. One variation of the [æʊ] error is to compound the problem by nasalization so that the tone takes on an unpleasant quality which is below standard. This fault is most pronounced in words in which the nasal consonants occur next to the diphthong, as in *now, town, down, noun*, etc.

EXERCISES

1. Practice the frames in the following operant conditioning exercise for [aʊ]:

Initial		Medial		Final	
Frames	Frames	Frames	Frames	Frames	Frames
1 aʊ	7 aʊ	13 aʊ	19 aʊ	25 aʊ	31 aʊ
2 aʊt	8 aʊl	14 taʊl	20 laʊt	26 taʊ	32 laʊ
3 aʊ	9 aʊ	15 aʊ	21 aʊ	27 aʊ	33 aʊ
4 aʊk	10 aʊb	16 kaʊb	22 baʊk	28 kaʊ	34 baʊ
5 aʊ	11 aʊ	17 aʊ	23 aʊ	29 aʊ	35 aʊ
6 aʊf	12 aʊm	18 faʊm	24 maʊf	30 faʊ	36 maʊ

2. Practice the following words either individually or as frames in an operant conditioning sequence:

Initial				Medial				Final			
Frames		Frames		Frames		Frames		Frames		Frames	
1	our	7	outing	13	astound	19	about	25	allow	31	now
2	hour	8	outlet	14	round	20	town	26	bough	32	endow
3	ouch	9	outer	15	mound	21	flower	27	prow	33	lowbrow
4	out	10	outline	16	sound	22	crown	28	plow	34	cow
5	owl	11	oust	17	pounce	23	shower	29	thou	35	somehow
6	ounce	12	outside	18	rebound	24	carouse	30	how	36	powwow

3. Practice the following sentences:
   a. Howard plowed the ground carefully after the shower.
   b. Every clown in town must have his hour upon the stage.
   c. When you doubt, shout your doubt from the housetop.
   d. The outline of the mound could be seen at the boundary of the iron foundry.
   e. The owl looked down with his great round eyes.
4. Practice the following lines:
   a. Till like one in slumber bound,
      Borne to ocean, I float down, around,
      Into a sea profound of everlasting sound.
   b. There for my lady's bower
      Built I the lofty tower
      Which to this very hour,
         Stands looking seaward.
   c. There is a silence where has been no sound,
      There is a silence where no sound may be,
         In the cold grave—under the deep, deep sea,
         Or in wide desert where no life is found,
      Which has been mute, and still must sleep profound.
   d. The thrush sings high on the topmost bough,
      Low, louder, low again; and now
      He has changed his tree,—you know not how,
         For you saw no flitting wing.
         —a kingly cedar green with boughs
      Goes down with a great shout upon the hills.

THE DIPHTHONG [ɔɪ]

The [ɔɪ] is the diphthong found in words like *boy* [bɔɪ], *coin* [kɔɪn], *noise* [nɔɪz], etc. (diacritical mark, *oi*). As indicated by the symbol [ɔɪ], this diphthong is a blend of the vowels [ɔ] and [ɪ]. It is made by adjusting the articulators for [ɔ], then, while the sound is being emitted, quickly gliding to [ɪ]. [ɔɪ] is spelled *oi* and *oy*, as in *oil* and *toy*.

Common Errors

1. Occasionally speakers are careless and do not form the [ɔ] in [ɔɪ] properly and an adjacent vowel is substituted. Thus the word *oil* [ɔɪl] may become [oɪl], [ʌɪl], [ɒɪl], or even [ɝl].

2. The same fault as was listed for [aɪ] can occur on [ɔɪ], namely, that the unstressed [ɪ] can become stressed [i] and result in [ɔi]. Thus *noise* [nɔɪz] becomes [nɔiz].

EXERCISES

1. Operant conditioning exercise for [ɔɪ] :

Initial				Medial				Final			
Frames		Frames		Frames		Frames		Frames		Frames	
1	ɔɪ	7	ɔɪ	13	ɔɪ	19	ɔɪ	25	ɔɪ	31	ɔɪ
2	ɔɪt	8	ɔɪl	14	tɔɪl	20	lɔɪt	26	tɔɪ	32	lɔɪ
3	ɔɪ	9	ɔɪ	15	ɔɪ	21	ɔɪ	27	ɔɪ	33	ɔɪ
4	ɔɪk	10	ɔɪb	16	kɔɪb	22	bɔɪk	28	kɔɪ	34	bɔɪ
5	ɔɪ	11	ɔɪ	17	ɔɪ	23	ɔɪ	29	ɔɪ	35	ɔɪ
6	ɔɪf	12	ɔɪm	18	fɔɪm	24	mɔɪf	30	fɔɪ	36	mɔɪ

2. Practice the following words either individually or as frames in an operant conditioning sequence :

Initial				Medial				Final			
Frames		Frames		Frames		Frames		Frames		Frames	
1	oil	7	oily	13	boil	19	join	25	boy	31	annoy
2	oiler	8	oilstone	14	soil	20	poison	26	ahoy	32	toy
3	ointment	9	oilskin	15	recoil	21	turmoil	27	decoy	33	cloy
4	oyster	10	oilbird	16	noise	22	flamboyant	28	enjoy	34	coy
5	oilcloth	11	oilcup	17	choice	23	poignant	29	destroy	35	joy
6	oilcan	12	oiliness	18	sirloin	24	rejoice	30	deploy	36	envoy

3. Practice the following sentences:

    a. The choice decoys employed in the marsh fooled the ducks and overjoyed the hunters.

    b. The oyster made a hissing noise; the sandcrab recoiled in annoyance.

    c. Boil a sirloin if you would destroy it, but broil the sirloin if you would enjoy it.

    d. Rubbing ointment and oil on Roy destroyed pain but annoyed him.

    e. What choice have we but to recoil in dismay at his flamboyant and coy demeanor.

4. Practice the following lines:

    a. Year after year beheld the patient toil
       That built that lustrous coil.

    b. Ne'er a peevish boy
       Would break the bowl from which he drank in joy.

    c. Made to tread the mills of toil
       Up and down in ceaseless moil.

    d. The devil hath not, in all his quiver's choice,
       An arrow for the heart like a sweet voice.

THE DIPHTHONG [ju]

The diphthong [ju] occurs in such words as *usual, view, pew, few,* and *beautiful* (diacritical mark, *ū*). Many authorities prefer to call [ju] a consonant-vowel glide, yet the vowellike quality of [j] qualifies [ju] as a diphthong. If the [j] element is not made with precision and distinctiveness, which is needed for consonantal glides, [ju] can easily become [ɪu] as it so often does. The [ju] is made by assuming the articulatory position for [j] and gliding quickly to [u]. Unlike other diphthongs, the second element in [ju] is stressed.

EXERCISES

1. Consult the pure vowel [u] for the exercise to distinguish differences between [u], [ɪu], and [ju].

2. Practice the following words individually or as frames in an operant conditioning exercise:

Initial				Medial				Final			
Frames		Frames		Frames		Frames		Frames		Frames	
1	U-boat	6	unite	11	mute	16	spume	21	cue	26	debut
2	utopian	7	unique	12	pupil	17	mule	22	hue	27	review
3	union	8	utility	13	pewter	18	futile	23	skew	28	imbue
4	eulogy	9	useless	14	amuse	19	putrid	24	mew	29	askew
5	ukelele	10	usury	15	mutation	20	immune	25	view	30	miscue

3. Practice the following sentences:
   a. Youth and beauty are lovely to view, but last only a few years.
   b. Matthew was proud of his culinary acumen.
   c. Our puny world is mutilated by futile disputes.
   d. "Cute" pupils are not in good repute.
   e. He called upon the muse of music to amuse us.

STRONG AND WEAK FORMS OF WORDS

Words and syllables have strong and weak forms, depending upon the emphasis which is given to them, and on their relationship to other words and syllables that surround them. In order to have rhythm and flowing quality in our speech, it is essential that main words be given greater prominence and that less important ones be subordinated.

This process of changing words from a strong to a weak form or vice versa is largely a matter of changing the nature of the vowel sounds. Reducing a vowel from its strong (or normal) form to a weak form consists in changing it usually to the so-called neutral vowel [ə], but sometimes to another vowel such as [ɪ] or [ʊ] ; in some cases the vowel sound is eliminated altogether, as will be explained a little later.

Many students, striving to speak correctly, use strong forms to excess, thus giving their speech a stilted quality. As a first step in correcting this fault, one needs to know something about the effect of stress upon pronunciation. To make meaning clear, it is necessary that the words of the greatest importance in conveying meaning stand out from words of lesser importance. This can be accomplished by giving important words greater force or duration, or by using some other device that gives them emphasis. However, if some words are to be stressed other words should be unstressed, for when everything is stressed nothing stands out in bold relief.

In general, articles, prepositions, conjunctions, and sometimes pronouns are unstressed, while nouns, adjectives, verbs, and adverbs are typically stressed. Variations can occur when special meaning is required, as

223

in the sentence, "*That* is the man," when the speaker wishes to emphasize that *that* is, indeed, the man. Meaning should be our guide when determining the use of strong and weak forms. One word of caution is necessary at this point, namely, that it is possible to carry the weakening of sounds too far; if such is the case, substandard speech results.

The list below contains words that are commonly used in a weak form. The second column shows them as they are pronounced in isolation and in accented syllables; the third column shows them as they are frequently pronounced in connected speech.

Word	Strong Form	Weak Forms
am	[æm]	[m]
an	[æn]	[ən], [n]
and	[ænd]	[ənd], [nd], [n]
as	[æz]	[əz], [z]
at	[æt]	[ət]
but	[bʌt]	[bət], [bt]
can	[kæn]	[kən], [kn]
could	[kʊd]	[kəd], [kd]
for	[fɔɚ]	[fɚ]
from	[frʌm]	[frəm]
has	[hæz]	[həz], [əz], [z]
her	[hɝ]	[ɚ]
his	[hɪz]	[ɪz]
is	[ɪz]	[z]
nor	[nɔɚ]	[nɚ]
of	[ɒv], [ʌv]	[əv]
or	[ɔɚ]	[ɚ]
shall	[ʃæl]	[ʃəl], [ʃl]
she	[ʃi]	[ʃɪ]
than	[ðæn]	[ðən]
to	[tu]	[tə], [t]
you	[ju]	[jʊ], [jə]

The following sample sentences demonstrate how weak forms can lead to substandard speech:

       a. Did you eat? [dʒit]
       b. I am going. [amgoʊn]
       c. It came for you and me. [ət keɪm fɚ jun mi]
       d. I can understand it. [aɪ kṇ ʌnɚstæn ət]
       e. Shall I tell her? [ʃḷ aɪ tɛlɚ]

EXERCISES

1. Omission of one or more sounds sometimes occurs in the following words. Be sure to check the pronunciation of each of them in the dictionary.

224

belong	interesting	pumpkin
candidate	Italy	regular
cemetery	laboratory	superintendent
chocolate	library	suppose
couldn't	mirror	surprise
diamond	municipal	temperature
dictionary	particular	understand
figure	perhaps	usual
generally	poem	violent
geography	poinsettia	when
government	police	which
governor	privilege	why
intellectual	probably	wouldn't

2. Addition of sounds is rather common in the following words. Work with them as in Exercise 1.

across	elm	often
athlete	evening	parliament
athletics	film	pincers
attacked	grievous	salmon
column	height	statistics
draw	idea	subtle
drowned	law	sword

3. Substitution of sounds sometimes occurs in the following words. For a few of the words a choice is permissible; again, check the pronunciation of each of the words in your dictionary.

accept	experiment	larynx
accessories	futile	percolator
almond	genuine	persist
apparatus	gesture	perspiration
breeches	get	prelude
catch	guarantee	presentation
character	hearth	pronunciation
children	hero	ration
coupon	heroine	relevant
creek	horizon	spontaneity
culinary	hundred	status
cupola	instead	substantiate
data	iodine	syrup
discretion	irrelevant	tedious
docile	jubilant	vigilant

4. Accent is often a problem in the following words. Look them up in the dictionary, and when there is a choice decide which pronunciation is preferable in your community and cultural surroundings. Observe that in many words the vowel in the last syllable is properly [ə].

abdomen	comparable	irrefutable
acclimated	contractor	pretense
admirable	despicable	program
adult	dirigible	recess
allies	divan	research
Arab	exquisite	resources
aspirant	finance	robust
assiduity	grimace	romance
autopsy	hospitable	vagary
cement	inquiry	vehement

5. Distinguish between the pronunciations of the following pairs of words. Try to use the words in each pair in a single sentence, e.g., *Our* hopes *are* with you.

accept—except	hurtle—hurdle
access—excess	immorality—immortality
adapt—adopt	line—lion
affect—effect	lose—loose
amplitude—aptitude	Mongol—mongrel
are—our	morning—mourning
Arthur—author	our—or
ascent—accent	pictures—pitchers
climatic—climactic	practical—practicable
coating—quoting	precedence—precedents
comprise—compromise	proceed—precede
consecrate—confiscate	respectively—respectfully
consolation—consultation	sense—cents
detect—detest	sex—sects
disillusion—dissolution	sins—since
distrait—distraught	statue—statute
exit—exist	turbid—turgid
exult—exalt	vocation—vacation
garnered—garnished	wandered—wondered

6. Most of the following words are quite common, but they are frequently mispronounced. Look up their correct pronunciation. Observe that in some of them (as in *education* and *blackguard*) a certain amount of "elision" or "assimilation" is called for. Don't guess at the pronunciation. Make sure.

actually	cynosure	longevity
amateur	deaf	mischievous
Arctic	decade	neither
Arkansas	education	ocean
bade	either	pianist
been	envelope	piano
blackguard	era	precious
bouquet	err	pretty
brochure	forehead	quay
capsule	gesture	quixotic
chasm	Himalaya	route
charivari	Illinois	schism
chiropodist	Italian	sugar
comptroller	lichen	tomato
corps	literature	zoological

227

CHAPTER NINE

achieving vocal variety

THUS FAR WE have analyzed voice and articulation in detail without attempting to integrate all of the components studied into a unified whole. In short, we have not tackled the rather difficult task of achieving vocal variety, which is necessary to effective speech.

Several important aspects of speech involving the measurable dimensions of voice, i.e., rate, pitch, quality, and loudness, should now be systematically studied in order to increase our effectiveness in the total performance. It is possible to achieve mastery over tone production, resonance, and articulation, and still be judged dull and monotonous in performance. The key to success lies in the direction of achieving vocal variety. Before studying the factors of voice related to variety, it is important for us to understand the anatomy of monotony.

MONOTONY

Many speakers are monotonous, some to the point of boredom. Monotony in speech can be a real liability, because it can easily lose the speaker his audience. All too often we are subjected to boredom, since custom and courtesy decree that long-suffering members of an audience sit and take it. Even in conversation monotony of speech is not uncommon and may be directly responsible for a speaker losing the attention of his listener. Monotony of speech in actors on the stage is intolerable to audience members who themselves may be monotonous in their speech, but demand that the performers be lifelike and stimulating.

The word *monotony* is derived from the Greek word *monotonia*, which may be broken into the segments *mono* (Greek, single) and *tone* (Greek, sound). In a narrow sense, then, monotony means the sameness of tone. *Monotony* also has other connotations such as lack of variation or variety, tiresome sameness, and wearisome uniformity. From the definition we may surmise that monotony stems from a monotonous tone (pitch) and little or no variety of other vocal factors, such as rate, quality, or loudness.

Many of our most skillful teachers of voice are aware of a larger principle governing monotony of performance, namely, that excessive repetition of any component of speech creates boredom. This principle is based upon a rule of learning called *satiation*. If a stimulus is presented to a subject at regular and frequent intervals without reinforcement, the subject will decrease his response to that stimulus. If the stimulus continues to occur regularly over time without reinforcement, the response will extinguish (fail to occur). The principle holds true even when the stimulus is strong; for example, feeding ice cream at regular, short intervals to a child who likes ice cream eventually results in satiation and rejection by the child of his favorite food.

The various types of monotony that are listed below suggest both narrow and broad bases for monotony.

TYPES OF MONOTONY

Monotony of Voice

Rate. (a) Use of same overall rate throughout speech, (b) failure to use rate variation on given segments of speech, (c) use of too slow a delivery rate for the content of the material presented, (d) use of too fast a delivery rate for the content of the material presented, (e) failure to use rate change for given types of material ideally suited for a change of pace.

Pitch. (a) Lack of pitch variation, (b) persistence in remaining on the same habitual level throughout the performance, (c) ending each sentence with the same downglide, (d) using the same step intervals, (e) repeating any type of pitch pattern too often, and (f) using unusual pitch variation too often.

Quality. (a) Use of same vocal quality throughout the performance, (b) use of inappropriate voice quality throughout (i.e., harsh, nasal, hoarse, etc.), (c) failure to use voice quality change to suit material, (d) failure to use voice quality change on words, phrases, sentences, or a series of sentences, and (e) failure to use voice quality change for climax.

Loudness. (a) Use of same general level of loudness throughout performance, (b) use of inadequate level of loudness for audience size, (c) failure

229

to use change of loudness for larger segments of material, (d) failure to use change of loudness on phrases within sentences, (e) failure to use strong and weak forms for stress, and (f) failure to use loudness for climax.

Monotony of Content

An analysis of monotony due to content is beyond the scope of this book; however, the speaker is reminded that for an audience monotony can stem from (a) his failure to choose appropriate materials, (b) his failure to choose stimulating materials, (c) his failure to use an effective overall plan for the material selected, (d) his failure to use variety of material, (e) his failure to use variety of supporting materials, (f) his failure to use interesting, thoughtful, colorful, or unusual words, phrases, sentences, thought sequences, and entire sections, (g) his failure to capitalize on timing of ideas, (h) his failure to use climax in arranging material, and (i) his failure to conclude ideas satisfactorily and effectively.

CAUSES OF VOCAL MONOTONY

1. Undue tension or a rigid, unresponsive body set may cause monotony. Tension throughout the body can extend to the muscles of the larynx, causing them to be too restricted to permit the voice to respond to a person's thoughts and feelings. This condition may be temporary, the result of an attack of stage fright, timidity, anxiety, or other emotional stress; or it may be habitual, the result of persistent nervous tension.

2. Another cause of monotony is poor health. The condition may come from temporary exhaustion or illness, or it may be a manifestation of a longstanding ailment, such as anemia.

3. Mental dullness is another cause of monotony, for if one's thinking is ponderous and dull, the voice also is likely to be flat and dull. This may be true also if a person is mentally lazy. Vocal expressiveness is usually dependent upon clear and vigorous thinking.

4. Physical inertness, like mental inertness, is a common cause of vocal monotony. Whether the inactivity of the body results from physical laziness or from restraints induced by social fears and platform inhibitions, the results are likely to be similar—a monotonous voice. Bodily activity is necessary to give the needed energy to a speaker for a strong performance. Bodily activity may be subliminal, or may be seen only in posture and gesture, yet it is essential to animated speech.

5. Monotony may be closely linked to the personality characteristics of the speaker. Excessive modesty or shyness, for example, may cause vocal monotony, as the speaker literally withdraws from communicative situations that focus attention upon him. Personality characteristics are usually set early in life and often represent the sum total of our interactions with others. An

overly dominant parent, for example, could be responsible for the shy, with-drawing behavior of her child by her persistent demands for obedience, con-formity, and performance.

6. Environmental causes, other than the above, can also cause vocal monotony. Many early environmental influences may have had a direct bear-ing upon our present speech behavior. For example, our parents served as our earliest speech models,[1] and we readily acquired their speech habits in the first five years of our lives. The environment continues to interact with each of us, doing much to shape the speech behavior we eventually ex-hibit as adults. Adverse influences such as deprivation, illness, shock, etc., also play an important part in influencing one's speech behavior in adulthood.

7. Defective hearing takes its toll of vocal expressiveness. Those with severe hearing losses are susceptible to vocal monotony. We depend heavily upon auditory feedback to regulate our voices. The person with hearing loss has a breakdown in the feedback loop, which, if serious enough, can influence the entire speech process.

PRECAUTIONS IN ACHIEVING VOCAL VARIETY

While it is possible to manipulate all of the factors of voice (rate, pitch, quality, and loudness) in practice in order to break up monotonous patterns, a speaker must always concentrate upon the meaning and emotional content of the material presented during performance. In practice he can rehearse certain elements of what he wishes to say until a given effect is achieved ; but final rehearsals and the actual performance should be free of analytic methods of delivery. Therefore, in this chapter, rate pitch, quality, and loudness are broken down into their components in order to provide both insight and control, but the speaker is cautioned to be aware that he must incorporate these elements into his speech smoothly and naturally in actual performance.

VARIETY OF RATE

One of the factors of voice that may be manipulated easily for variety is rate. Rate, of course, is the time element involved in speaking and can be measured in a number of ways, depending upon the unit under consideration, i.e., sound, syllable, word, phrase, sentence, subdivision, or the entire reading or speech. Rates of speech units been analyzed in terms of milliseconds,

---

[1] A parent can be a poor model as well as a good one. A child may often be discouraged in talking at home with the admonition to "be quiet," often turning a lively, inquisitive child into a monotonous mumbler. We are particularly impressed with this because of a series of observations of family situations in which talk is not a common thing, where authoritarian statements are made by the senior male, and the concept of discussion is unknown. Children from such families seem not only to be poor talkers, and monotonous when they do talk, but they are consequently also poor readers.

seconds, minutes, and even hours. The overall rate of speech cannot be stated as a given number of words per minute, for variations occur among speakers. The average student reads nonemotional material at approximately 165 words per minute (wpm). In conversational speech, word rate fluctuates markedly from 80 to 135 wpm, depending upon several variables—content, emotion, familiarity with subject, and others. Naturally, our silent-reading rates are much faster. If you wish to time yourself for oral reading rate, select a prose passage of at least 300 words, and have a classmate signal you for a start and stop you after reading 60 seconds. Count the number of words read during the 60 second interval.

Rate is also related to nonspeech time elements such as pauses that contribute to the duration of individual units and the performance as a whole. The following section will analyze rate from the smallest component, the sound or phoneme, to the largest, the performance of the entire speech. To gain mastery over each time element of rate, complete successfully the exercises provided.

Duration of Sounds and Words

Duration refers to the amount of time given to individual sounds. On the whole, as we have seen in our study of articulation, vowels inherently have greater duration than consonants. Vowels, however, differ in the amount of time they require. In their short form ([æ] as in *cat*, [ɛ] as in *get*, [ɪ] as in *it*, [ɒ] as in *hot*, [ʊ] as in *cook*) they take less time than in their long form ([eɪ] as in *ate*, [i] as in *me*, [aɪ] as in *high*, [ou] as in *go*, [u] as in *tune*).

Although consonants, on the whole, take less time than vowels, there is considerable difference in the time they require. Fricatives, glides, nasals, and semivowels need more time for utterance than do the plosives. Practice the word lists in Chapters 7 and 8 for proper sound duration.

Likewise, stressed syllables in words require more time than do unstressed syllables. Take, for instance, the word *inherently*. Note how much more time is given to the stressed syllable *her* than to the other syllables. So it is with words like *con*-stant-ly, in-*quis*-i-tive, or-*nate*, *dai*-sies, *ro*-ses, *vi*-o-lets, and so forth.

In a similar fashion, certain words in a phrase or sentence require more time than other words. In general, nouns, verbs, adjectives, and adverbs naturally call for more duration than prepositions, articles, conjunctions, and the like. Such words as *the, a, or, but, and,* and *as* ordinarily play only a minor role in transmitting thought and therefore should remain unstressed.

The above facts pertaining to duration are standardized, determined by our best speakers, but there is another area in which there are no rules. That is the field of individual attitudes, where each one differs from everybody else. In this area each individual determines for himself how much duration to use. Here duration becomes an extremely important phase of emphasis.

Consider the sentence, "It was a cold day." The individual may hold the diphthong in *cold* almost at will; within limits, the longer he holds it, the colder he represents the day to be. Notice how quickly the comparatively unimportant words *it, was,* and *a* may be passed over. They receive only the shortest time required to make them distinct. Duration is given only to the last two words, and particularly to the qualifying word *cold*.

Syllables, words, phrases, and sentences which the speaker considers important may be emphasized by the amount of time he gives them. Note the emphasis added by prolonging the italicized syllables in the following:

> What do *you* think we should do now?
> What's the *good* of all this?
> Grant me just this *one* favor.
> No place to *hide*!
> She was *old,* and *gray,* and *wrinkled.*

It is in reading poetry that the skillful use of duration of sounds and words becomes most effective. A good poet is adept in using sonorous vowels in accented (prolonged) syllables to help create the effect he desires. Poetry should be read aloud to make these sound effects evident. In well-constructed poetry there is always a close relationship between the quantity of time given to the various syllables and the meaning of the lines. For example, if short sounds are used to express sentiments of solemnity, the effect is missed, as it is also if long sounds are used to portray gaiety and liveliness. Note how effectively quantity is employed to carry both meaning and feeling in the following excerpts:

> The road was a ribbon of moonlight over the purple moor,
> And the highwayman came riding, riding, riding,
> The highwayman came riding, up to the old inn door.[2]
>
> This is the forest primeval. The murmuring pines and the
>   hemlocks,
> Bearded with moss, and in garments green, indistinct in the
>   twilight,
> Stand like Druids of eld...
>
> Maid of Athens, ere we part,
> Give, oh, give me back my heart!

[2] Reprinted by permission of the publishers, J. B. Lippincott Company, from *Collected Poems in One Volume* by Alfred Noyes. Copyright, 1906, 1934, 1947, by Alfred Noyes.

To test the value of duration as a means of enriching the oral reading of poetry, hold the italicized words in the lines below beyond the normal time.

> I *love* thee, I love but *thee,*
> With a love that shall not *die*
> Till the *sun* grows *cold,*
> And the *stars* are *old,*
> And the *leaves* of the *Judgment Book unfold.*

> For *frantic boast* and *foolish word,*
> Thy *mercy* on thy *people* Lord !

> They rowed her in across the *rolling foam,*
> The *cruel crawling foam,*
> The *cruel hungry* foam.

> I like a *church* ; I like a *cowl* ;
> I like a prophet of the *soul* ;
> And on my heart monastic *aisles*
> Fall like *sweet strains,* or *pensive smiles.*

Phrase Length

How long is a well-turned phrase ? There is no categorical answer to this question. We are dealing with an art, not a science ; and art leaves plenty of room for the individual's creative tastes. The dictionary indicates how variable phrases are : "A word or group of spoken words which the mind focuses on momentarily as a meaningful unit and which is preceded and followed by pauses." A phrase, then, may be a single word, or "a group of words." How many words in a group ? Two ? Ten ? Twenty ? It depends upon the speaker's thoughts and intentions in communication. Let us look at the following two lines :

> Advice to the lean : don't eat fast.
> Advice to the fat : don't eat ! fast !

Now suppose we reversed the phrasing, advising the lean, "Don't eat ! fast !" If our advice were followed, we might have an anemic underfed invalid on our hands.

It is in reading poetry that college students are most likely to make such mistakes in phrasing. They often seem to have the impression that phrases should always coincide with lines, and that therefore the reader should pause at the end of every line. This problem is illustrated by two lines in the short poem by Leigh Hunt, "Cupid Swallowed."

> T'other day, as I was twining
> Roses for a crown to dine in . . .

Again and again students phrase these lines thus:

> T'other day as I was twining/
> Roses for a crown to dine in/

The slightest attention to thought grouping will make clear the need for combining *twining* and *roses*, so that the phrase will read *as I was twining roses*/.

Not only can meaning be altered by a change in phrasing, but the intended meaning can be completely lost. The following lines from the same poem illustrate our point:

> T'other day as I was twining
> Roses for a crown to dine in
> What, of all things, midst the heap,
> Should I light on, fast asleep,
> But the little desperate elf—
> The tiny traitor—Love, himself!

The narrator is saying that while twining a crown of roses he encountered the little elf, Love. Then for emphasis he uses the reflexive pronoun *himself*, as one might say, *He looked like the old devil himself*. But when students reading the poem include both *Love* and *himself* in one phrase, as they frequently do, the lines sound as if the reference were to someone who had a bad case of self-admiration. There is a lot of difference between *Love himself* and *Love/himself*.

Look for a minute at a poem that expresses a more serious sentiment, Milton's sonnet "On His Blindness." Note the following lines:

> And that one talent which is death to hide
> Lodged with me useless, though my soul more bent
> To serve therewith my Maker, and present
> My true account, lest he returning chide . . .

What a distortion of meaning would ensue if the lines were phrased thus:

> . . . though my soul more bent/
> To serve therewith my Maker and present/
> My true account/. . .

The meaning Milton intended obviously is:

> . . . though my soul/more bent to serve therewith my Maker/
> and present my true account/. . .

Two lines from Wordsworth's "She was a Phantom of Delight" illustrate the same point:

> But all things else about her drawn
> From May-time and the cheerful dawn...

It is obvious that if we would give any sense of logical meaning to a listener we must disregard the line endings. Therefore the phrasing would be:

> But all things else about her/drawn from May-time/
> and the cheerful dawn/...

Hence we may draw a rule, or rather a principle, for rules are too narrow and restrictive to be applicable to artistic endeavor: *In reading poetry, if the thought is important we should disregard line endings, rhyming, and any other factor that interferes with proper phrasing.*

In the above principle, the qualifying phrase *if the thought is important* must be included, because sometimes the poet is striving to create a mood rather than to impart a thought. In these cases the rhythmical beat is much more important than the thought grouping. This is the case in many of Poe's rhythmical poems such as "Annabel Lee."

But not all poor phrasing is associated with the oral reading of poetry. Almost equally bad is phrasing based upon the notion that the oral reader of prose should always follow the punctuation. Intelligent reading is impossible unless the reader realizes that punctuation in writing does not apply to speech. In the first place it is not necessary to pause at every punctuation mark. For example, in the phrase," Now, if I were in your place," we normally would not pause after *now*. Furthermore, the punctuation marks in written discourse are usually spaced much too far apart for good oral phrasing. If the oral reader phrases his reading according to the punctuation in his material, he is bound to try to express in one breath group long complex clauses, which are clearly beyond his breath capacity, and just as clearly beyond the capacity of his hearers' minds to focus on as meaningful units.

The punctuation of the printed page has become conventionalized. Note that the definition of phrasing on page 234 refers to speech. The dictionary also gives a series of definitions for writing, based on grammatical rules. These rules are designed to aid the eye, so that the mind can grasp the units of meaning quickly and easily. Sometimes punctuation for the ear (the pause) and eye is synonymous and sometimes it is not.

That brings us to another principle regarding phrasing for voice and speech: *The speaker or reader has to make his own phrasing as he goes along, according to the needs of the occasion.* Phrasing for speech cannot be standardized. Identical words, spoken in different surroundings and with different attendant circumstances, may call for entirely different phrasing.

Several factors may influence the length of phrases, including (a) breath control of the speaker, (b) the speaker's articulation (if poor, shorter phrasing), (c) lack of familiarity of material (both speaker and audience), (d) acoustics of the room (if very reverberant, shorter phrasing is needed), (e) emphasis desired by speaker, and (f) the size of the audience.

EXERCISES

1. Read the following exercises two ways. First, assume you are speaking to a small group (10 persons) in a small room, and second, assume you are speaking to 5000 people without a public address system:

    a. Materially we must strive to secure a broader economic opportunity for all men, so that each shall have a better chance to show the stuff of which he is made.

        Materially / we must strive / to secure / a broader / economic opportunity / for all men, / so that each / shall have / a better chance / to show / the stuff / of which / he / is made.

    b. Ladies and gentlemen. You will now see the greatest sensation of the age, the death defying slide for life.

        La/ dies and gen / tle / men./ You / will now / see / the greatest / sen / sa / tion / of / the age, / the / death / defying / slide / for life.

Phrase Rate

The overall phrase rate will vary according to both meaning and emotional details. Generally the more profound and complex the meaning of a speaker the slower the rate. On the other hand, many phrases are relatively meaningless and serve only as verbal fillers while the speaker is gaining time to formulate his next thought, e.g., "as I said before," "what I really mean is," and so on. Emotional content will greatly affect the rate of utterance of many phrases; for example, take the words spoken by Macbeth upon learning that Lady Macbeth was dead.

    She should have died hereafter;
    There would have been a time for such a word.
    To-morrow, and to-morrow, and to-morrow,
    Creeps in this petty pace from day to day,
    To the last syllable of recorded time;

Typically, lightheartedness, excitement, gaiety, etc., calls for a speeding up of tempo, while the more heavy, dull, and sad feelings are best reflected in reducing normal tempo—provided that the feelings are truly experienced. Practice the following materials according to the general principles discussed in this section.

237

1. Read the following italicized phrases with relatively no meaning:
    a. *As I mentioned before,* he is bound to come.
    b. Sally and Jim, *in the meantime,* began to prepare for dinner.
    c. Burnsides, *you understand,* didn't arrive at all.
    d. *It is interesting to note that* Shakespeare uses both prose and poetry in this love scene.

2. Make up a sentence with the following verbal fillers, which are often found at the beginning or within a sentence:

which is to say	as I said before	nevertheless
as is often the case	it is interesting to note	moreover
what I really mean is	mind you	well, that is
you can see	in the main	uh, uh, uh ...

3. Read the following sentences with a feeling of gaiety, lightheartedness, excitement, or happiness.
    a. Oh Ruth, I think that is absolutely beautiful!
    b. I don't know what happened, but the fire broke out very suddenly.
    c. I have never been so happy in all my life!
    d. Mary, Betty, Joe! How delighted I am to see you!
    e. Look out for that car!

4. Read the following lines for sadness, sombreness, or unhappiness.
    a. There is no way out of it, I am simply going to have to face it.
    b. That's the last of our money until the strike is over.
    c. I felt miserable when she told me that we were through.
    d. The rain, the fog, the dampness—every day, day after day— doesn't this place ever have any sunshine?
    e. I just don't feel very well.

CONTROLLING RATE BY MENTAL CONCENTRATION

The close relationship between mental concentration and rate of speaking may be demonstrated by the following experiment: Read aloud in an off-hand, indifferent manner Tennyson's brief poem, "Flower in the Crannied Wall." As you read, carefully observe your rate of speech.

Flower in the crannied wall,
I pluck you out of the crannies,
I hold you here, root and all, in my hand,
Little flower—but *if* I could understand
What you are, root and all, and all in all,
I should know what God and man is.

Now really study the poem. Picture in your mind a flower growing out of a crack in some crumbling old rock wall. Let your mind dwell for a bit on the marvelous characteristics of the growing plant, its power to push a rock apart with the prodigious strength of its slender roots.

When you have created that picture, let your thoughts turn to the next image, a man stepping up and nonchalantly plucking the flower out of the wall. Get the picture: man, the lord of creation, strong, dominating, ruthless; the little flower so unimportant and so feeble that it can offer no resistance when the man plucks it out of its home. There is deliberate significance in the choice of the word *pluck*; it suggests indifference, almost contemptuousness. From the flower's point of view there might be some dignity about being gathered, but not plucked; that's sheer effrontery.

The next idea makes that cumulative: "I hold you here, root and all, in my hand, little flower." The whole life process of the plant is lying helpless there in the man's hand. Big man, lord of creation; little, insignificant flower lying bruised and helpless in his hand.

But the next thought shows a change in mood, a change so deep, so fundamental, that it is colossal in its mental and emotional scope. "But *if* I could understand what you are." The word *understand* has a world of meaning. There is nothing superficial about it. Understanding is deep; it is something more than a glib recital of the botanical names of the parts of the flower, something more than a scientific classification of it. To *understand* is to know what force makes a dormant seed begin a new life; to know what power makes it grow into a chrysanthemum instead of a daisy; to know whence come its color and its fragrance. To know this would be to unlock the door to complete understanding, to unravel the master knot of human fate.

The next line gives this thought cumulative significance. "What you are, root and all, and all in all." Then comes the unfolding of the whole poem, "I should know what God and man is." God and man *is*. Plural subject, singular verb! Shame on Tennyson; a grammatical error? Or maybe it was just poetic license? Not at all! The word was deliberately chosen and there's no poetic license about it. In the choice of that word lies the key to Tennyson's religious philosophy. God and man *is*. To Tennyson, God and man are one.

Now read the poem again, thinking these thoughts, seeing these mental images, dwelling on this philosophizing. The rate will necessarily be slow—not the slow drawling of the phlegmatic mind, but the deliberateness, the prolonged pauses of the thinking person. Such a reading would perhaps be something like the following, though of course each individual will interpret according to his own past experience and his own mental habits, and there will be no absolute uniformity:

Flower / in the crannied wall, / I pluck you / out of the crannies, / I hold you here, / root and all / in my hand. / Little flower / but *if* I would understand / what you are / root and all, / and all in all, / I should know / what God and man *is*.

PAUSE

Long ago the great speaker and writer about speech, Cicero, stated, "There is an art in silence, and there is an eloquence in it too." In a similar vein an ancient proverb says, "Speech is silvern ; silence is golden."

Sometimes it seems that a speaker has to become both experienced and skillful before he learns that there is art and eloquence in a judicious bit of silence.

Trained actors use the pause with tremendous dramatic effect. Great speakers drive home their strongest points by pausing for emphasis. Most beginners fear silence and seldom pause for control and emphasis. Pauses seem so terribly long and frightening !

Lack of confidence, however, is not the only cause for failure to use pauses. Another cause is lack of thought. For example, when a speech student is reading Shakespeare's dramatic scene in which Macbeth challenges Macduff, and he reads it all in one phrase, thus :

Damned be he who first says hold enough

as if Macbeth were talking about some kind of eating contest or drinking bout, the student's mind is clearly not on what he is saying. This is by no means a far-fetched example of typical oral reading and speaking from memory.

Still another reason for the absence of effective pauses is that the student does not know how to pause. That is, he is so accustomed to speaking automatically, without any conscious thought of how normal, habitual speech really sounds, that when he faces a new and tense situation he does not have command of the techniques necessary for making his speech appear natural. Pauses sound unnatural. They are louder to his ears than speech, so he shuns them.

The Pause and Emphasis

Let us look at a few of the beneficial results that come through use of the pause for emphasis.

Pauses can indicate major thought transitions. As chapter and paragraph indentations in printing and writing call attention to changes of thought, so deliberate, meaningful speech stops can make evident the rounding out of one idea and the shifting to another one.

Look for a moment at part of the speech on football given by the famous football coach, the great Knute Rockne, before the Chicago Executives' Club.

When my good friend, Coach Thistlewaite, or any other high grade man in the coaching profession, looks over his squad in the fall trying to get tangible evidence as to whom he shall place on the first eleven, what does he look for?

The first thing he looks for is brains. . . . [followed by about 300 words on the need for intelligence in players].

Another thing the coach will insist upon from his men is concentration. Brains are no good if they rattle. . . . [followed by about 100 words on this theme].

The third thing we insist on is hard work. . . . [followed by about 150 words on the importance of hard work].

Transitional phrases like the following require deliberate meaningful pauses, somewhat as indicated. The slash (/) indicates a prolonged pause:

However / in spite of all that we have just said / the future / holds the light of promise.

But, that / is only one side of the picture. / Let us / for a few minutes / look at the other side.

That / in brief summary / gives you the heart / of Hayne's argument. / Now / listen to what Webster / said in reply /.

Pauses can give added significance to names of people and places. Frequently an inexperienced speaker will virtually bury the name of the poem he is going to recite, the title of the book he wants his audience to read, even the name of the person he is introducing. The names, titles, subjects, and places may be perfectly familiar to him; what he fails to realize is that they are not familiar to his listeners, and therefore need to be made especially distinct. Pauses rightly placed can relieve auditors of the uncertainty and the sense of frustration which such uncertainty induces. Try the following introductory remarks.

Ladies and Gentlemen / the President of the United States.

I'd like to introduce / the man who / believes in righting wrong/ the man who / believes in action / the man who / believes in woman's place in the world! Ladies and Gentlemen / Congressman William J. Olson.

Notice how the master of ceremonies on a television program builds up his guest artists. Usually it is something like this:

And / look who's h-e-r-e / *Ray Jones*!

241

Pauses can make an important idea stand out. Pauses can make an important idea stand out in bold relief against the background of the rest of the speech if handled properly. By pausing both before and after an idea we intensify the thought by giving it unique emphasis. The only precaution one must take is to deliver that idea with stress rather than to say it casually or without special treatment. The following examples illustrate this point.

Daniel Webster, defending his state from an attack by Hayne in the Senate, used the following words. Imagine how flat they would have sounded without pauses.

> Mr. President, / I shall enter on no encomium upon Massachusetts / she needs none. / There she is / behold her / and judge for yourselves.

Consider the following two Beatitudes ; how much more meaningful they become when solemn pauses are used, instead of being chanted as they so frequently are :

> Blessed are the meek / for they / shall inherit / the earth.

> Blessed are the merciful / for they / shall obtain / mercy.

Pauses can sharpen humor. A meaningful pause just before the point of a joke can heighten the comic effect immeasurably. Many a potentially good story is ruined by the storyteller's rushing at and over his climax.

Consider the added punch given the following by using a pause as indicated :

Bernard Shaw, it was reported, was standing on the sidelines at a social function, looking bored. A friend asked, "Aren't you enjoying yourself ?" Shaw replied, "Yes I am / but that's the only thing I'm enjoying."

Another example illustrative of a possible whimsical turn which may be given a phrase by means of a pause, is the following sentence from Ruskin's essay on the fly :

> He steps out of the way of your hand, and alights on the back of it.

Note how the whimsy is heightened by inserting a pause, thus :

> He steps out of the way of your hand, and / alights on the back of it.

Pauses can help to make reading sound conversational. One reason reading is often so dull is perhaps the format of the printed page—lines the same length, letters the same height, words on the same level, all the printing in the same degree of blackness, sentences packed in rows like sardines in a can. Every suggestion urges the reader to hurry along. How different these printed symbols of speech are from the ups and downs, the shading and coloring, and especially the speeding up and the slowing down of animated, thoughtful conversation! If there is a bit of advice the oral reader needs more often than any other, it is: S l o w   d o w n! if you have any hope of giving your listeners the full flavor of what you are reading, p a u s e and give them time to think! If you have any hope of having your reading sound like conversation, p a u s e and give *yourself* time to think!

The following excerpt is marked with pauses to indicate how it might be read. Use the pauses to intensify the meaning.

> I think / by far the most important bill / in our whole code / is that for the / diffusion of knowledge / among the people /.
>
> In a great crisis / it is thinking / so as to make others think / feeling / so as to make others feel / which tips the orator's tongue / with fire / that lights / as well as burns /.

The Pause Versus Hesitation

All the preceding discussion refers to deliberate, meaningful pauses for emphasis. Careful distinction must be made between a pause and hesitation. Pausing is strength; hesitation is weakness. And do not think that the audience does not recognize the difference. Even if the ever present *ah*'s and *uh*'s that so often accompany hesitation are absent, the shifting eye and general air of indecision give it away.

Pause to let the idea sink into the audience's mind! Pause to choose the fitting word to dress the idea for expression! But avoid those *er-* and *um-* bedecked hesitations. Get the idea so well in mind that the thoughts are there ready to be given utterance. Hesitation will lose the audience; judicious pauses will hold them to the speech.

SELECTIONS FOR RATE

PIPPA PASSES

The year's at the spring
And day's at the morn;
Morning's at seven;
The hillside's dew-pearled;
The lark's on the wing;
The snail's on the thorn:
God's in his heaven—
All's right with the world!

—Robert Browning

243

THE GATE

Scene I

A gate.
Two lovers.
A father mad.
The hour is late.
Two hearts are glad.

Scene II

A growl.
A leap.
A nip.
A tear.
A cry.
A sigh.
And then—
A swear.

Scene III

A gate.
No lovers.
A father glad.
A dog triumphant.
A maiden sad.

Epilogue

If it took two hours to say good-night,
It served him right if the dog did bite.

—Bessie Cahn

This City now doth, like a garment, wear
The beauty of the morning; silent, bare
Ships, towers, domes, theatres, and temples lie
Open upon the fields, and to the sky;
All bright and glittering in the smokeless air....
Ne'er saw I, never felt, a calm so deep!

—William Wordsworth

Tomorrow, and tomorrow, and tomorrow,
Creeps in this petty pace from day to day
To the last syllable of recorded time;
And all our yesterdays have lighted fools
The way to dusty death. Out, out, brief candle!

Life's but a walking shadow, a poor player
That struts and frets his hour upon the stage
And then is heard no more. It is a tale
Told by an idiot, full of sound and fury,
Signifying nothing.

—William Shakespeare

The following two selections of poetry are good for mastering the use of pause to heighten meaning.

MALCOLM X

Original
Ragged-round
Rich-robust.

He had the haw-man's eyes.
We gasped. We saw the maleness.
The maleness raking out and making guttural the air
and pushing us to walls.

And in a soft and fundamental hour
a sorcery devout and vertical
beguiled the world.

He opened to us—
who was a key.

who was a man.[3]   .

—Gwendolyn Brooks

MEDGAR EVERS

The man whose height his fear improved he
arranged to fear no further. The raw
intoxicated time was time for better birth or
a final death.

Old styles, old tempos, all the engagement of
the day—the sedate, the regulated fray—
the antique light, the Moral rose, old gusts,
tight whistlings from the past, the mothballs
in the Love at last our man forswore.

[3] From *In The Mecca* by Gwendolyn Brooks. Copyright ©, 1967, by Gwendolyn Brooks Blakely. Reprinted by permission of Harper & Row, Publishers, Inc.

Medgar Evers annoyed confetti and assorted
brands of businessmen's eyes.

The shows came down : to maxims and surprise.
And palsy.

Roaring no rapt arise-ye to the dead, he
leaned across tomorrow. People said that
he was holding clean globes in his hands.[4]

—Gwendolyn Brooks

THE SQUAW DANCE

Beat, beat, beat, beat, beat upon the tom-tom,
Beat, beat, beat, beat, beat upon the drum.
Hóy-eeeeeee-yáh ; Hóy-eeeeeee-yáh !
Shuffle to the left, shuffle to the left,
Shuffle, shuffle, shuffle to the left, to the left.
Fat squaws, lean squaws, gliding in a row,
Grunting, wheezing, laughing as they go ;
Bouncing up with a scuffle and a twirl,
Flouncing petticoat and hair in a whirl.
Rheumatic hags of gristle and brawn,
Rolling in like a ponderous billow :
Fair squaws lithe as the leaping fawn,
Swaying with the wind and bending with the willow ;
Bouncing buttock and shriveled shank,
Scuffling to the drumbeat, rank on rank ;
Stolid eye and laughing lip,
Buxom bosom and jiggling hip,
Weaving in and weaving out,
Hí ! Hi ! Hí ! with a laugh and a shout,
To the beat, beat, beat, beat, beat upon the tom-tom,
Beat, beat, beat, beat, beat upon the drum ;
Hóy-eeeeeee-yáh ! Hóy-eeeeeee-yáh !
Hí ! Hi ! Hí ! Hi ! Hóy-eeeeeeeeeeeeee-yáh ![5]

—Lew Sarett

[4] From *In The Mecca* by Gwendolyn Brooks. Copyright ©, 1964, by Gwendolyn Brooks Blakely. Reprinted by permission of Harper & Row Publishers, Inc.

[5] From *Covenant with Earth* by Lew Sarett. Edited and copyrighted, 1956, by Alma Johnson Sarett, and published, 1956, by University of Florida Press. Reprinted by permission of Mrs. Sarett.

ANNABEL LEE

It was many and many a year ago,
    In a kingdom by the sea,
That a maiden there lived whom you may know
    By the name of Annabel Lee;
And this maiden she lived with no other thought
    Than to love and be loved by me.

I was a child and she was a child,
    In this kingdom by the sea,
But we loved with a love that was more than love—
    I and my Annabel Lee;
With a love that the wingèd seraphs of heaven
    Coveted her and me.

And this is the reason that, long ago,
    In this kindgom by the sea,
A wind blew out of a cloud, chilling
    My beautiful Annabel Lee;
So that her highborn kinsmen came
    And bore her away from me,
To shut her up in a sepulchre
    In this kingdom by the sea.

                                        —Edgar Allan Poe

Break, break, break,
    On thy cold gray stones, O Sea!
And I would that my tongue could utter
    The thoughts that arise in me.

O, well for the fisherman's boy,
    That he shouts with his sister at play!
O, well for the sailor lad,
    That he sings in his boat on the bay!

And the stately ships go on
    To their haven under the hill;
But O for the touch of a vanish'd hand,
    And the sound of a voice that is still!

Break, break, break,
    At the foot of thy crags, O Sea!
But the tender grace of a day that is dead
    Will never come back to me.

                                        —Alfred, Lord Tennyson

The wind was a torrent of darkness among the gusty trees,
The moon was a ghostly galleon tossed upon cloudy seas,
The road was a ribbon of moonlight over the purple moor,
And the highwayman came riding—
    Riding—Riding—
The highwayman came riding, up to the old inn-door.

.   .   .   .

Over the cobbles he clattered and clashed in the dark inn-yard,
And he tapped with his whip on the shutters, but all was
                                                locked and barred;
He whistled a tune at the window, and who should be waiting
                                                         there
But the landlord's black-eyed daughter, Bess, the landlord's
                                                      daughter,
Plaiting a dark red love-knot into her long black hair.[6]

—Alfred Noyes

CONCORD RIVER

It is worth the while to make a voyage up this stream . . . .
Many waves are there agitated by the wind, keeping nature
fresh, the spray blowing in your face, reeds and rushes waving;
ducks by the hundred, all uneasy in the surf, in the raw wind,
just ready to rise, and now going off with a clatter and a
whistling like riggers straight for Labrador, flying against the
stiff gale with reefed wings, or else circling around first, with all
their paddles briskly moving, just over the surf, to reconnoiter
you before they leave these parts; gulls wheeling overhead,
muskrats swimming for dear life, wet and cold, with no fire to
warm them by that you know of, their labored homes rising
here and there like haystacks; and countless mice and moles
and winged titmice along the sunny, windy shore; cranberries
tossed on the waves and heaving up on the beach, their little
red skiffs beating about among the alders—such healthy
natural tumult as proves the last day is not yet at hand. And
there stand all around the alders, and birches, and oaks, and
maples, full of glee and sap, holding in their buds until the
waters subside.

—Henry David Thoreau

Suddenly the waters around them slowly swelled in broad circles; then quickly unheaved, as if sideways sliding from a submerged berg of ice, swiftly rising to the surface. A low rumbling sound was heard; a subterraneous hum; and then all held their breaths; as bedraggled with trailing ropes, and harpoons, and lances, a vast form shot lengthwise, but obliquely from the sea. Shrouded in a thin drooping veil of mist, it hovered for a moment in the rainbowed air; and then fell swamping back into the deep. Crushed thirty feet upwards, the waters flashed for an instant like heaps of fountains, then brokenly sank in a shower of flakes, leaving the circling surface creamed like new milk round the marble trunk of the whale.

—Herman Melville

From PYGMALION

(ELIZA, *who is exquisitely dressed, produces an impression of such remarkable distinction and beauty as she enters that they all rise, quite flustered. Guided by* HIGGIN'S *signals, she comes to* MRS. HIGGINS *with studied grace.*)

LIZA (*Speaking with pedantic correctness of pronunciation and great beauty of tone.*): How do you do, Mrs. Higgins? (*She gasps slightly in making sure of the H in Higgins, but is quite successful.*) Mr. Higgins told me I might come.

MRS. HIGGINS (*Cordially*): Quite right: I'm very glad indeed to see you.

PICKERING: How do you do, Miss Doolittle?

LIZA (*Shaking hands with him*): Colonel Pickering, is it not?

MRS. EYNSFORD HILL: I feel sure we have met before, Miss Doolittle. I remember your eyes.

LIZA: How do you do? (*She sits down on the ottoman gracefully in the place just left vacant by* HIGGINS.)

MRS. EYNSFORD HILL (*Introducing*): My daughter Clara.

LIZA: How do you do?

CLARA (*Impulsively*): How do you do? (*She sits down on the ottoman beside* ELIZA, *devouring her with her eyes.*)

FREDDY (*Coming to their side of the ottoman*): I've certainly had the pleasure.

MRS. EYNSFORD HILL (*Introducing*): My son Freddy.

LIZA: How do you do?

(FREDDY *bows and sits down in the Elizabethan chair, infatuated.*)

HIGGINS (*Suddenly*) : By George, yes : it all comes back to me ! (*They stare at him.*) Covent Garden ! (*Lamentably*) What a damned thing !

MRS. HIGGINS : Henry, please ! (*He is about to sit on the edge of the table.*) Don't sit on my writing-table : you'll break it.

HIGGINS (*Sulkily*) : Sorry.

(*He goes to the divan, stumbling into the fender and over the fire-irons on his way; extricating himself with muttered imprecations; and finishing his disastrous journey by throwing himself so impatiently on the divan that he almost breaks it.* MRS. HIGGINS *looks at him, but controls herself and says nothing.*)

(*A long and painful pause ensues.*)

MRS. HIGGINS (*At last, conversationally*) : Will it rain, do you think ?

LIZA : The shallow depression in the west of these islands is likely to move slowly in an easterly direction. There are no indications of any great change in the barometrical situation.

FREDDY : Ha ! ha ! how awfully funny !

LIZA : What is wrong with that, young man ? I bet I got it right.

FREDDY : Killing !

MRS. EYNSFORD HILL : I'm sure. I hope it won't turn cold. There's so much influenza about. It runs right through our whole family regularly every spring.

LIZA (*Darkly*) : My aunt died of influenza : so they said.

MRS. EYNSFORD HILL (*Clicks her tongue sympathetically*) : ! ! ! !

LIZA (*In the same tragic tone*) : But it's my belief they done the old woman in.

MRS. HIGGINS (*Puzzled*) : Done her in ?

LIZA : Y-e-e-e-es, Lord love you ! Why should she die of influenza ? She come through diphtheria right enough the year before. I saw her with my own eyes. Fairly blue with it, she was. They all thought she was dead ; but my father he kept ladling gin down her throat til she came to so sudden that she bit the bowl off the spoon.

MRS. EYNSFORD HILL (*Startled*) : Dear me !

LIZA (*Piling up the indictment*) : What call would a woman with that strength in her have to die of influenza ? What become of her new straw hat that should have come to me ? Somebody pinched it ; and what I say is, them as pinched it done her in.

MRS. EYNSFORD HILL : What does doing her in mean ?

HIGGINS (*Hastily*) : Oh, thats the new small talk. To do a person in means to kill them.

MRS. EYNSFORD HILL (*To* ELIZA, *horrified*) : You surely don't believe that your aunt was killed?

LIZA : Do I not! Them she lived with would have killed her for a hat-pin, let alone a hat.

MRS. EYNSFORD HILL : But it can't have been right for your father to pour spirits down her throat like that. It might have killed her.

LIZA : Not her. Gin was mother's milk to her. Besides, he'd poured so much down his own throat that he knew the good of it.

MRS. EYNSFORD HILL : Do you mean that he drank?

LIZA : Drank! My word! Something chronic.

MRS. EYNSFORD HILL : How dreadful for you!

LIZA : Not a bit. It never did him no harm what I could see. But then he did not keep it up regular. (*Cheerfully*) On the burst, as you might say, from time to time. And always more agreeable when he had a drop in. When he was out of work, my mother used to give him fourpence and tell him to go out and not come back until he'd drunk himself cheerful and loving-like. There's lots of women has to make their husbands drunk to make them fit to live with. (*Now quite at her ease*) You see, it's like this. If a man has a bit of a conscience, it always takes him when he's sober; and then it makes him low-spirited. A drop of booze just takes that off and makes him happy. (*To* FREDDY, *who is in convulsions of suppressed laughter*) Here! what are you sniggering at?

FREDDY : The new small talk. You do it so awfully well.

LIZA : If I was doing it proper, what was you laughing at? (*To* HIGGINS) Have I said anything I oughn't?

MRS. HIGGINS (*Interposing*) : Not at all, Miss Doolittle.

LIZA : Well, that's a mercy, anyhow. (*Expansively*) What I always say is—

HIGGINS (*Rising and looking at his watch*) : Ahem!

LIZA (*Looking round at him; taking the hint; and rising*) : Well: I must go. (*They all rise.* FREDDY *goes to the door*) So pleased to have met you. Goodbye. (*She shakes hands with* MRS. HIGGINS.)

MRS. HIGGINS : Goodbye.

LIZA : Goodbye, Colonel Pickering.

PICKERING : Goodbye, Miss Doolittle. (*They shake hands.*)

LIZA (*Nodding to the others*) : Goodbye, all.

FREDDY (*Opening the door for her*) : Are you walking across the Park, Miss Doolittle? If so—

LIZA: Walk! Not bloody likely. (*Sensation*) I am going in a taxi. (*She goes out.*)

(PICKERING *gasps and sits down.* FREDDY *goes out on the balcony to catch another glimpse of* ELIZA.)

—George Bernard Shaw

PITCH

In Chapters 4 and 5 we discussed several important aspects of pitch, principally the physiology of pitch change, how to determine optimum pitch and habitual (or modal) pitch, and how to analzye pitch range. It would be wise to review these sections before attempting the exercises for obtaining variety in pitch.

In our efforts to achieve expressiveness in the speaking voice, few things are of more importance than developing skill in the use of pitch variation. Pitch is more effective than either rate or force in expressing delicate shades of meaning. Modulation of quality, rate, and force are more closely related to total emotional states; pitch variation is primarily the instrument of fine discriminations of thought. Consequently, its wise use indicates a high order of mental development.

While it is true that pitch is essentially the instrument of thought expression, it also plays a role in the expression of emotion. As a matter of fact no one is capable of establishing a clear line of distinction between thinking and feeling. Consequently, it cannot be denied that the pitch of the voice is related to a person's feelings. If the voice is free and uninhibited, excitement will produce a heightened pitch and sorrow a lowered pitch, almost as inevitably as the rising and setting of the sun produce daylight and darkness.

Before attempting to vary pitch to suit both meaning and emotional content, it is necessary to achieve control over the three ways of changing pitch, namely, *step*, *inflection* (or *glide*), and *key*.

METHODS OF CHANGING PITCH

Step

Pitch may be changed by stepping from one pitch level to another without an intermediate glide. Typically, we use step to change our voice level from low to high or high to low. In order to achieve step there is a perceptible, momentary cessation of tone between the two pitch levels involved. If the vocal tone is not terminated for an instant, a glide would inevitably follow when moving from one pitch level to another. Step is also integrally related to force, as we shall see in the drill material that follows.

A well-trained and sensitive speaker will utilize many different step levels in both reading and conversation. Monotonous speakers tend to employ the same step levels over and over again.

EXERCISES

1. Attempt to achieve at least five different upward steps on the sentence below:

know

know

know

know

I *know* him. I   him. I   him. I   him. I   him.

Use the same procedure for:

    a. The *last* boy came in.

    b. She said, *"no."*

    c. *Who's* there?

    d. *Red* roses are pretty.

    e. I *love* you.

2. A downward step may be employed after a speaker has used a high pitch level for the preceding word or phrase:

    a. The red [highest], orange [medium], and yellow [lowest] of autumn were everywhere.

    b. Don't ever [highest] see [medium] him [lowest].

3. Steps may be used to vary the pitch level of phrases within the sentence; the direction of the step is the speaker's option:

    a. First, he took out his keys [highest], then he opened the door [medium], and he quietly tiptoed in [lowest].

    b. First, he took out his keys [lowest], then he opened the door [medium], and he quietly tiptoed in [highest].

    c. First, he took out his keyes [medium], then he opened the door [highest], and he quietly tiptoed in [lowest].

4. Vary the pitch level on the phrases of these sentences:

    a. Eldon is the tallest, Mark is the next tallest, and Allen is the shortest of our three sons.

    b. The forest was alive with the sounds of nature—the bubbling of the brook, the lazy buzzing of the bees, the gentle wafting of the breezes, and the multitudinous songs of the birds.

    c. The model was built around several concepts: (a) ability to measure attitudes, (b) use with all groups, (c) simplicity in administration, and (d) ease in scoring.

Inflection

Inflection, or glide, means change in pitch *on* the tone, chiefly on vowels, diphthongs, and to some extent, syllabic consonants. The voice glides up and down the scale to express changing thoughts and emotions. In general, upward glides on individual words express questions, indecision, or incomplete thoughts; downward glides express complete thoughts and degrees of emphasis. Use of both an upward and downward glide on the stressed syllable of a word, called *circumflex*, expresses uncertainty, irony, or double meaning.

EXERCISES

1. Practice the following words, using rising, falling, and circumflex inflections:

yes	alarmed	divorced	poor
no	courageous	honest	amusing
always	brave	dishonest	boring
never	smart	careful	licentious
happy	married	rich	parsimonious
sad	separated	wealthy	conglomerate

2. After mastering control of inflection, use the above words in a short sentence, demonstrating rising, falling, and circumflex inflections on each.

3. Attempt to achieve different levels of pitch change (either up or down) on the italicized words in the following sentences:

    a. The *curl* of the *wave extended* for at least a *quarter* of a *mile parallel* to the *shore*.

    b. *Smoke poured* through the *broken windows* on the *second floor* of the *house*.

    c. The *new moon* could be *seen* through the *rising mists* on the *western horizon*.

    d. *Sam accelerated quickly*, but *couldn't escape* the *madly careening car* to his *left*.

    e. The *president slowly rose* from his *chair* and *approached* the *podium*.

Key

Key is the general level (modal level) selected by the speaker for each given segment of material communicated. In an oral reading key is the predominant pitch level used by the speaker. It is also possible and often desirable to shift the general pitch level during a given performance. The following experiments will be helpful in understanding key better.

EXERCISES

1. Hum a given pitch level that is close to your optimum pitch. Now chant (on a monotone) the following sentence: "What do you want me to do?" Without changing the modal level, develop a pitch pattern in keeping with the meaning of the sentence. Be sure to keep each successive trial the same, using the same steps and glides. Now, hum a pitch level one whole note above the one you started with. Try to simulate the same pitch pattern. If you are able to do so, you have shifted key. You may key the same sentence below the first pitch level, which will substantially lower your voice without changing the overall pitch pattern.

2. Experiment with the following sentences, using at least three keys for each (high, medium, and low) ; be sure that you do not alter the pitch pattern established on the first reading for the subsequent reading.

      a. Rachel seldom used her expensive China.

      b. She sat poring over her accounts wondering how to make ends meet.

      c. Ralph played tight end in all ten games.

      d. The zoo was known for its large collection of flamingos.

      e. Choose at least two of the four cards in my hand.

INFLECTIONAL DIFFERENCES BETWEEN EMOTIONAL AND NONEMOTIONAL MATERIALS

Generally speaking, if the emotion expressed is one of happiness, excitement, exhilaration, or happy surprise, the number or degree of pitch changes will increase from a normal baseline. On the other hand, if the emotion expressed is sadness, dejection, deep feelings, etc., the number and degree of pitch changes are likely to decrease. Take, for example, the sentence, "I never saw anything like it." and read it two ways ; first, with the excitement of receiving an unusual, beautiful gift from a friend, then second, with the dejection of finding out that your car has another flat tire.

Deeply emotional and elevated passages often require very few glides. To express these deep sentiments in the frequent glides of ordinary conversation would be to remove them from the serenity of the temple to the give-and-take of the market place. The following lines taken from the Twenty-Third Psalm, read in two different ways, illustrate our point. Read them with the thought and feeling of announcing that you are going to a football game, then read them again, attempting to communicate the full meaning and emotional impact intended by the psalmist.

> The Lord is my shepherd ; I shall not want.
> He maketh me to lie down in green pastures :
> He leadeth me beside the still waters.
> He restoreth my soul :

PITCH FAULTS

1. Probably the greatest error associated with pitch is monotony due to an absence (or near absence) of pitch variation. The droning effect of a speaker using a monotone has lulled many an audience to sleep. Whether the cause of the fault is lack of enthusiasm, reaction of the speaker to his material, or physical inability to change pitch, the person with this problem should work diligently to solve it. Probably the best way to correct this error is to work harder to bring out the meaning of the text and to become more responsive to its emotional details. Experiment with the following passage

on Daniel Webster by reading the sentences three different ways: (a) first attempt to obtain a baseline reading of extreme monotony to identify the problem, (b) then read the passage attempting to bring out all the shades of meaning you can by varying the pitch patterns, and (c) attempt to add all the emotional details you can by sensing the imagery, grasping the quality of the man, and capturing the subtle differences in the emotional content of each phrase.

DANIEL WEBSTER

Everyone had heard him on the platform, every boy and girl had seen his picture, the dark brow that looked like Mount Monadnock, the wide-brimmed hat and the knee-high boots, the linsey-woolsey coat and the flowing necktie, the walking stick that was said to be ten feet long. There was something elemental in his composition, something large and lavish. Even his faults were ample. Webster despised the traditional virtues. He spent money in a grand way, borrowing and lending with equal freedom. He was far from sober, or would have been if two tumblers of brandy had been enough to put him under the table. He could be surly enough, when he had his moods of God-Almightiness, or when he wished to insult some sycophant. The thunderclouds would gather on his brow and the lightning flash from his eye, and he would tell a committee that their town was the dullest place on earth. No one could be more truculent, especially in the hay-fever season; but he was always good-natured with the farmers, who liked to think of him as their man. They knew what Webster meant when he said that his oxen were better company than the men in the Senate. They knew all his ways and the names of his guns and animals, as the Jews of old knew the weapons of Nimrod, or Abraham's flocks and herds—his great ram Goliath, his shotguns, "Mrs. Patrick" and "Wilmot Proviso," his trout rod, "Old Killall." They knew he had written the Bunker Hill oration, composed it word by word, with Old Killall in his hand, wading in the Marshfield River. They had heard of his tens of thousands of swine and sheep, his herds of Peruvian llamas and blooded cattle, the hundreds of thousands of trees he had raised from seed. They knew that while his guests were still asleep—the scores of guests who were always visiting Marshfield—he rose at four o'clock and lighted the fires, roused the cocks with his early-morning candles, milked and fed the stock, and chatted in the kitchen with his farm hands, quoting Mr. Virgil, the Roman farmer. And at Marshfield, as everyone knew, his horses were buried in a special graveyard, with all the honors of war, standing upright, with their shoes and halters.

—Van Wyck Brooks

2. Another pitch fault that is commonly associated with ineffective speakers is the repeated use of an indefinite glide on the last words in phrases and sentences. The indefinite glide may vary all the way from an absence of any degree of downward (or upward) pitch change to a pitch change that is so slight that it is inappropriate to the meaning. Use the following lines to identify the problem by reading with little or no downglides at the ends of phrases and sentences, then read it again with pronounced downglides. The difference should be remarkable.

Anyone who has visited Grand Teton National Park and camped by Jenny Lake knows what I mean. A lake that is perfectly calm, with not a ripple to mar the smooth surface of the water. And what a beautiful sky-blue water it is, surrounded by mountains that soar thousands of feet into the sky, snow-crowned and magnificent! The mirrored images of the lake are indescribable.

—Harold Kassarjian

3. One may unwittingly fall into a pitch fault by not varying step or glide in reading or speaking. Read the passage in the foregoing exercise using the same step and pitch level for the words: *anyone, Grand, camped, lake, not, smooth, what, surrounded, soar, snow-crowned, mirrored,* and *indescribable.* Now, read the passage a second time and glide up to the same pitch level on the chosen words. If you are able to read the passage under these conditions, you will have achieved a unique monotony.

4. Any pitch pattern repeated too often can lead to monotony. Read the selection below, "The Caterpillar," by Ogden Nash, under the following conditions: (a) all lines are to be read with an identical pitch pattern, (b) every other line is to be read with the same pitch pattern, and (c) every third line is to be read with the same pitch pattern. You will note that as you interpose two lines between the lines with identical patterns in (c) that the patterning becomes more obscure, provided, of course that you have not introduced a new monotonous pattern into the other two lines.

THE CATERPILLAR

I find among the poems of Schiller
No mention of the caterpillar,
Nor can I find one anywhere
In Petrarch or in Baudelaire,
So here I sit in extra session
To give my personal impression.
The caterpillar, as it's called,
Is often hairy, seldom bald;
It looks as if it never shaves;
When as it walks, it walks in waves;
And from the cradle to the chrysalis
It's utterly speechless, songless, whistleless. [7]

—Ogden Nash

5. Excessive variation in pitch, which is the opposite extreme from droning, suggests, variously, talking down to an audience, pedantic speech, the "eager beaver" approach, the overemphasis of the effeminate man, the attention-getting trick of a designing female, and childishness, all of which are an offense to good taste. The corrective lies in working on material that requires strength and power in rendition such as is found in some of the selections provided at the end of this chapter.

SELECTIONS FOR PITCH

From THE RIVALS

MRS. MALAPROP: Observe me, Sir Anthony. I would by no means wish a daughter of mine to be a progeny of learning; I don't think so much learning becomes a young woman; for instance, I would never let her meddle with Greek, or Hebrew, or algebra, or simony, or fluxions, or paradoxes, or such inflammatory branches of learning—neither would it be necessary for her to handle any of your mathematical, astronomical, diabolical instruments.—But, Sir Anthony, I would send her, at nine years old to a boarding-school, in order to learn a little ingenuity and artifice. Then, sir, she should have a supercilious knowledge in account;—and as she grew up, I would have her instructed in geometry, that she might know some-

258

thing of the contagious countries ;—but above all, Sir Anthony, she should be mistress of orthodoxy, that she might not misspell and mispronounce words so shamefully as girls usually do ; and likewise that she might reprehend the true meaning of what she is saying. This, Sir Anthony, is what I would have a woman know ;—and I don't think there is a superstitious article in it.

—Richard B. Sheridan

FOOLISH ABOUT WINDOWS

I was foolish about windows.
The house was an old one and the windows were small.
I asked a carpenter to come and open the walls and put in
bigger windows.
"The bigger the window the more it costs," he said.
"The bigger the cheaper," I said.
So he tore off siding and plaster and laths
And put in a big window and bigger windows.
I was hungry for windows.

One neighbor said, "If you keep on you'll be able to see everything there is."
I answered, "That'll be all right, that'll be classy enough for me."

Another neighbor said, "Pretty soon your house will be all
windows."
And I said, "Who would the joke be on then ?"
And still another, "Those who live in glass houses gather no
moss."
And I said, "Birds of a feather should not throw stones and a
soft answer turneth away rats."[8]

—Carl Sandburg

O WHERE ARE YOU GOING?

"O where are you going ?" said reader to rider,
"That valley is fatal when furnaces burn,
Yonder's the midden whose odours will madden,
That gap is the grave where the tall return."

---

[8] From *Good Morning, America*, copyright, 1928, 1956, by Carl Sandburg. Reprinted by permission of Harcourt Brace Jovanoich, Inc.

"O do you imagine," said fearer to farer,
"That dusk will delay on your path to the pass,
Your diligent looking discover the lacking
Your footsteps feel from granite to grass?"

"O what was that bird," said horror to hearer,
"Did you see that shape in the twisted trees?
Behind you swiftly the figure comes softly,
The spot on your skin is a shocking disease?"

"Out of this house"—said rider to reader,
"Yours never will"—said farer to fearer,
"They're looking for you"—said hearer to horror,
As he left them there, as he left them there.[9]

—W. H. Auden

From DON JUAN

The Coast—I think it was the coast that I
    Was just describing—Yes, it *was* the coast—
Lay at this period quiet as the sky,
    The sands untumbled, the blue waves untost,
And all was stillness, save the sea-bird's cry,
    And dolphin's leap, and little billow crost
By some low rock or shelve, that made it fret
Against the boundary it scarcely wet.

—George Gordon, Lord Byron

'Tis the last rose of summer,
    Left blooming alone;
All her lovely companions
    Are faded and gone;
No flower of her kindred,
    No rose bud is nigh,
To reflect back her blushes
    Or give sigh for sigh.

—Thomas Moore

[9] Copyright 1934 renewed 1962 by W. H. Auden. Reprinted from *Collected Shorter Poems 1927–1957*, by W. H. Auden, by permission of Random House, Inc.

RONDEAU

Jenny kiss'd me when we met,
Jumping from the chair she sat in ;
Time, you thief, who love to get
Sweets into your list, put that in.
Say I'm weary, say I'm sad,
Say that health and wealth have missed me,
Say I'm growing old, but add,
Jenny kissed me.

—Leigh Hunt

From VAGABOND'S HOUSE

When I have a house—as I sometime may—
I'll suit my fancy in every way.
I'll fill it with things that have caught my eye
In drifting from Iceland to Molokai.
It won't be correct or in period style
But . . . oh, I've thought for a long, long while
Of all the corners and all the nooks,
Of all the bookshelves and all the books,
The great big table, the deep soft chairs
And the Chinese rug at the foot of the stairs,
(It's an old, old rug from far Chow Wan
That a Chinese princess once walked on).
My house will stand on the side of a hill
By a slow broad river, deep and still,
With a tall lone pine on guard nearby
Where the birds can sing and the storm winds cry.
A flagstone walk with lazy curves
Will lead to the door where a Pan's head serves
As a knocker there like a vibrant drum
To let me know that a friend has come,
And the door will squeak as I swing it wide
To welcome you to the cheer inside.
For I'll have good friends who can sit and chat
Or simply sit, when it comes to that,
By the fireplace where the fir logs blaze
And the smoke rolls up in a weaving haze.

I'll want a wood-box, scarred and rough,
For leaves and bark and odorous stuff
Like resinous knots and cones and gums
To chuck on the flames when winter comes.
And I hope a cricket will stay around
For I love its creaky lonesome sound....[10]

—Don Blanding

"AH, ARE YOU DIGGING ON MY GRAVE?"

"Ah, are you digging on my grave
    My beloved one?—planting rue?"
—"No; yesterday he went to wed
One of the brightest wealth has bred.
'It cannot hurt her now,' he said,
    'That I should not be true.'"

"Then who is digging on my grave?
    My nearest dearest kin?"
—"Ah, no; they sit and think, 'What use!
What good will planting flowers produce?
No tendance of her mound can loose
    Her spirit from Death's gin.'"

"But some one digs upon my grave?
    My enemy?—prodding sly?"
—"Nay; when she heard you had passed the Gate
That shuts on all flesh soon or late,
She thought you no more worth her hate,
    And cares not where you lie."

"Then, who is digging on my grave?
    Say—since I have not guessed!"
—"O it is I, my mistress dear,
Your little dog, who still lives near,
And much I hope my movements here
    Have not disturbed your rest?"

"Ah, yes! *You* dig upon my grave...
    Why flashed it not on me
That one true friend was left behind!
What feeling do we ever find
To equal among human kind
    A dog's fideltiy!"

[10] Reprinted by permission of Dodd, Mead & Company from *Vagabond's House* by Don Blanding. Copyright 1928 by Don Blanding.

"Mistress, I dug upon your grave
  To bury a bone, in case
I should be hungry near this spot
When passing on my daily trot.
I am sorry, but I quite forgot
  It was your resting place."

—Thomas Hardy

O CAPTAIN! MY CAPTAIN!

O Captain! my Captain! our fearful trip is done,
The ship has weathered every rack, the prize we sought is won,
The port is near, the bells I hear, the people all exulting,
While follow eyes the steady keel, the vessel grim and daring;
But O heart! heart! heart!
  O the bleeding drops of red,
Where on the deck my Captain lies,
  Fallen cold and dead.

O Captain! my Captain! rise up and hear the bells;
Rise up—for you the flag is flung—for you the bugle trills,
For you bouquets and ribboned wreaths—for you the shores
                                        a-crowding,
For you they call, the swaying mass, their eager faces turning;
Here, Captain! dear father!
  This arm beneath your head!
It is some dream that on the deck
  You've fallen cold and dead.

My Captain does not answer, his lips are pale and still,
My father does not feel my arm, he has no pulse nor will,
The ship is anchored safe and sound, its voyage closed and
                                        done,
From fearful trip the victor ship comes in with object won;
  Exult O shores, and ring O bells!
    But I, with mournful tread,
  Walk the deck my Captain lies,
    Fallen cold and dead.

—Walt Whitman

From JULIUS CAESAR

MARK ANTONY: Friends, Romans, countrymen,
Lend me your ears;
I come to bury Caesar, not to praise him.
The evil that men do lives after them;

263

The good is oft interred with their bones;
So let it be with Caesar. The noble Brutus
Hath told you Caesar was ambitious;
If it were so, it was a grievous fault,
And grievously hath Caesar answer'd it.
Here, under leave of Brutus, and the rest—
For Brutus is an honourable man;
So are they all, all honourable men—
Come I to speak in Caesar's funeral.
He was my friend, faithful and just to me;
But Brutus says he was ambitious,
And Brutus is an honourable man.
He hath brought many captives home to Rome,
Whose ransoms did the general coffers fill;
Did this in Caesar seem ambitious?
When that the poor have cried, Caesar hath wept;
Ambition should be made of sterner stuff:
Yet Brutus says he was ambitious,
And Brutus is an honourable man.
You all did see that on the Lupercal
I thrice presented him a kingly crown,
Which he did thrice refuse. Was this ambition?
Yet Brutus says he was ambitious,
And, sure, he is an honourable man.
I speak not to disprove what Brutus spoke,
But here I am to speak what I do know.
You all did love him once, not without cause;
What cause withholds you then to mourn for him?
O judgment! thou art fled to brutish beasts,
And men have lost their reason. Bear with me;
My heart is in the coffin there with Caesar,
And I must pause, till it come back to me.

—William Shakespeare

From ROMEO AND JULIET

ROMEO: He jests at scars that never felt a wound—
But, soft! what light through yonder window breaks?
It is the east, and Juliet is the sun!—
Arise, fair sun, and kill the envious moon,
Who is already sick and pale with grief,
That thou her maid art far more fair than she:
Be not her maid, since she is envious;
Her vestal livery is but sick and green,

And none but fools do wear it; cast it off.—
It is my lady; O, it is my love!
O, that she knew she were!—
She speaks, yet she says nothing: what of that?
Her eye discourses, I will answer it.—
I am too bold, 'tis not to me she speaks:
Two of the fairest stars in all the heaven,
Having some business, do entreat her eyes
To twinkle in their spheres till they return.
What if her eyes were there, they in her head?
The brightness of her cheek would shame those stars,
As daylight doth a lamp; her eyes in heaven
Would through the airy region stream so bright
That birds would sing, and think it were not night.—
See how she leans her cheek upon her hand!
O, that I were a glove upon that hand,
That I might touch that cheek!
JULIET: Ay me!
ROMEO: She speaks:—
O, speak again, bright angel! for thou art
As glorious to this night, being o'er my head,
As is a winged messenger of heaven
Unto the white-upturned wondering eyes
Of mortals that fall back to gaze on him
When he bestrides the lazy-pacing clouds
And sails upon the bosom of the air.
JULIET: O Romeo, Romeo! wherefore art thou Romeo?
Deny thy father, and refuse thy name;
Or, if thou wilt not, be but sworn my love,
And I'll no longer be a Capulet.
ROMEO: Shall I hear more, or shall I speak at this?
JULIET: 'Tis but thy name that is my enemy;—
Thou art thyself though, not a Montague.
What's Montague? It is not hand, nor foot,
Nor arm, nor face, nor any other part
Belonging to a man. O, be some other name!
What's in a name? That which we call a rose,
By any other name would smell as sweet;
So Romeo would, were he not Romeo call'd,
Retain that dear perfection which he owes
Without that title. Romeo, doff thy name;
And for that name, which is no part of thee,
Take all myself.

       —William Shakespeare

From OTHELLO

IAGO : My noble lord,—
OTHELLO : What dost thou say, Iago ?
IAGO : Did Michael Cassio, when you woo'd my lady,
Know of your love ?
OTHELLO : He did, from first to last ; why dost thou ask ?
IAGO : But for a satisfaction of my thought ;
No further harm.
OTHELLO : Why of thy thought, Iago ?
IAGO : I did not think he had been acquainted with her.
OTHELLO : O, yes ; and went between us very oft.
IAGO : Indeed !
OTHELLO : Indeed ! ay, indeed ; discern'st thou aught in that ?
Is he not honest ?
IAGO : Honest, my lord ?
OTHELLO : Honest ! ay, honest.
IAGO : My lord, for aught I know.
OTHELLO : What dost thou think ?
IAGO : Think, my lord !
OTHELLO : Think, my lord !
By heavens, he echoes me,
As if there were some monster in his thought
Too hideous to be shown.

—William Shakespeare

SONNET XLIII

How do I love thee ? Let me count the ways.
I love thee to the depth and breadth and height
My soul can reach, when feeling out of sight
For the end of Being and ideal Grace.
I love thee to the level of everyday's
Most quiet need, by sun and candle-light.
I love thee freely, as men strive for Right ;
I love thee purely, as they turn from Praise.
I love thee with the passion put to use
In my old griefs, and with my childhood's faith.
I love thee with a love I seemed to lose
With my lost saints,—I love thee with the breath,
Smiles, tears, of all my life !—and, if God choose,
I shall but love thee better after death.

—Elizabeth Barrett Browning

EDUCATION

When a man teaches something he does not know to somebody else who has no aptitude for it, and gives him a certificate of proficiency, the latter has completed the education of a gentleman.

A fool's brain digests philosophy into folly, science into superstition, and art into pedantry. Hence University education. The best brought-up children are those who have seen their parents as they are. Hypocrisy is not the parent's first duty.
The vilest abortionist is he who attempts to mould a child's character.

At the University every great treatise is postponed until its author attains impartial judgment and perfect knowledge. If a horse could wait as long for its shoes and would pay for them in advance, our blacksmiths would all be college dons.
He who can, does. He who cannot, teaches.

A learned man is an idler who kills time with study. Beware of his false knowledge: it is more dangerous than ignorance.

Activity is the only road to knowledge.

Every fool believes what his teachers tell him, and calls his credulity science or morality as confidently as his father called it divine revelation.

No man fully capable of his own language ever masters another. No man can be a pure specialist without being in the strict sense an idiot.

Do not give your children moral and religious instruction unless you are quite sure they will not take it too seriously. Better be the mother of Henri Quatre and Nell Gwynne than of Robespierre and Queen Mary Tudor.

—George Bernard Shaw

From TOM SAWYER

. . . By and by Tom said:
"Looky-here, Huck, there's footprints and some candle grease on the clay about one side of this rock, but not on the other sides. Now, what's that for? I bet you the money *is* under the rock. I'm going to dig in the clay."
"That ain't no bad notion, Tom!" said Huck with animation.
Tom's "real barlow" was out at once, and he had not dug four inches before he struck wood.

267

"Hey, Huck!—you hear that?"

Huck began to dig and scratch now. Some boards were soon uncovered and removed. They had concealed a natural chasm which led under the rock. Tom got into this and held his candle as far under the rock as he could, but said he could not see to the end of the rift. He proposed to explore. He stooped and passed under; the narrow way descended gradually. He followed its winding course, first to the right, then to the left, Huck at his heels. Tom turned a short curve, by and by, and exclaimed:

"My goodness, Huck, looky-here!"

It was the treasure box, sure enough, occupying a snug little cavern, along with an empty powder keg, a couple of guns in leather cases, two or three pairs of old moccasins, a leather belt, and some other rubbish well soaked with the water-drip.

—Mark Twain

From SCHOOL FOR SCANDAL

(*Scene 1:* LADY SNEERWELL'S *dressing-room*
LADY SNEERWELL *discovered at her toilet;* SNAKE *drinking chocolate.*)

LADY SNEERWELL: The paragraphs, you say, Mr. Snake, were all inserted?

SNAKE: They were, madam; and, as I copied them myself in a feigned hand, there can be no suspicion whence they came.

LADY SNEERWELL: Did you circulate the report of Lady Brittle's intrigue with Captain Boastall?

SNAKE: That's in as fine a train as your ladyship could wish. In the common course of things, I think it must reach Mrs. Clackitt's ears within four-and-twenty hours; and then, you know, the business is as good as done.

LADY SNEERWELL: Why, truly, Mrs. Clackitt has a very pretty talent, and a great deal of industry.

SNAKE: True, madam, and has been tolerably successful in her day. To my knowledge, she has been the cause of six matches being broken off, and three sons being disinherited; of four forced elopements, and as many close confinements; nine separate maintenances, and two divorces. Nay, I have more than once traced her causing a *tête-à-tête* in the "Town and Country Magazine," when the parties, perhaps, had never seen each other's face before in the course of their lives.

268

LADY SNEERWELL: She certainly has talents, but her manner is gross.

SNAKE: 'Tis very true. She generally designs well, has a free tongue and a bold invention; but her colouring is too dark, and her outlines often extravagant. She wants that delicacy of tint, and mellowness of sneer, which distinguish your ladyship's scandal.

LADY SNEERWELL: You are partial, Snake.

SNAKE: Not in the least; everybody allows that Lady Sneerwell can do more with a word or look than many can with the most labored detail, even when they happen to have a little truth on their side to support it.

LADY SNEERWELL: Yes, my dear Snake; and I am no hypocrite to deny the satisfaction I reap from the success of my efforts. Wounded myself, in the early part of my life, by the envenomed tongue of slander, I confess I have since known no pleasure equal to the reducing others to the level of my own injured reputation.

SNAKE: Nothing can be more natural. But, Lady Sneerwell, there is one affair in which you have lately employed me, wherein, I confess, I am at a loss to guess your motives.

LADY SNEERWELL: I conceive you mean with respect to my neighbour, Sir Peter Teazle, and his family?

SNAKE: I do. Here are two young men, to whom Sir Peter has acted as a kind of guardian since their father's death; the eldest possessing the most amiable character, and universally well spoken of—the youngest, the most dissipated and extravagant young fellow in the kingdom, without friends or character: the former an avowed admirer of your ladyship, and apparently your favourite; the latter attached to Maria, Sir Peter's ward, and confessedly beloved by her. Now, on the face of these circumstances, it is utterly unaccountable to me, why you, the widow of a city knight, with a good jointure, should not close with the passion of a man of such character and expectations as Mr. Surface; and more so why you should be so uncommonly earnest to destroy the mutual attachment subsisting between his brother Charles and Maria.

LADY SNEERWELL: Then, at once to unravel this mystery, I must inform you that love has no share whatever in the intercourse between Mr. Surface and me.

SNAKE: No!

LADY SNEERWELL: His real attachment is to Maria or her fortune; but, finding in his brother a favoured rival, he has been obliged to mask his pretensions, and profit by my assistance.

SNAKE: Yet still I am more puzzled why you should interest yourself in his success.

LADY SNEERWELL: Heavens! how dull you are! Cannot you surmise the weakness which I hitherto, through shame, have concealed even from you? Must I confess that Charles—that libertine, that extravagant, that bankrupt in fortune and reputation—that he it is for whom I am thus anxious and malicious, and to gain whom I would sacrifice everything?

SNAKE: Now, indeed, your conduct appears consistent; but how came you and Mr. Surface so confidential?

LADY SNEERWELL: For our mutual interest. I have found him out a long time since. I know him to be artful, selfish, and malicious—in short, a sentimental knave; while with Sir Peter, and indeed with all his acquaintance, he passes for a youthful miracle of prudence, good sense, and benevolence.

SNAKE: Yes; yet Sir Peter vows he has not his equal in England; and, above all, he praises him as a man of sentiment.

LADY SNEERWELL: True; and with the assistance of his sentiment and hypocrisy he has brought Sir Peter entirely into his interest with regard to Maria; while poor Charles has no friend in the house—though, I fear, he has a powerful one in Maria's heart, against whom we must direct our schemes.

—Richard B. Sheridan

GUNGA DIN

You may talk o' gin and beer
When you're quartered safe out 'ere,
An' you're sent to penny-fights an' Aldershot it;
But when it comes to slaughter
You will do your work on water,
An' you'll lick the bloomin' boots of 'im that's got it.
Now in Injia's sunny clime,
Where I used to spend my time
A-servin' of 'Er Majesty the Queen,
Of all them black-faced crew
The finest man I knew
Was our regimental bhisti, Gunga Din.
    He was "Din! Din! Din!
   You limpin' lump o' brick-dust, Gunga Din!
      Hi! *Slippy hitherao*!
      Water, get it! *Panee lao*!
   You squidgy-nosed old idol, Gunga Din!"

The uniform 'e wore
Was nothin' much before,
An' rather less than 'arf o' that be'ind,
For a piece 'o twisty rag
An' a goatskin water-bag
Was all the field-equipment 'e could find.
When the sweatin' troop-train lay
In a sidin' through the day,
Where the 'eat would make your bloomin' eyebrows crawl,
We shouted "Harry By!"
Till your throats were bricky-dry,
Then we wopped 'im 'cause 'e couldn't serve us all.
    It was "Din! Din! Din!
  You 'eathen, where the mischief 'ave you been?
    You put some *juldee* in it
    Or I'll *marrow* you this minute
  If you don't fill up my helmet, Gunga Din!"

—Rudyard Kipling

FORCE

The third means of achieving vocal expressiveness which we shall consider is variation in the degree of force.

There are several other terms that express the same concept, such as amplitude, energy, intensity, loudness, and volume. These terms are alike in that they have some relationship to the degree of loudness of the tone, but they are not exact synonyms. The reason we have chosen the term *force* is that at this time we are interested in several aspects of voice in relation to both intensity and loudness. Intensity refers to the physical energy of the voice as measured by scientific instruments, and loudness refers to the sensing, perceiving, and interpreting of sound as it is heard. The former is a physical term, while the latter is a psychological term.

Force, then, in the sense in which the term is used here, implies several concepts when effectively employed as a means of achieving vocal expressiveness; they are as follows:

1. The speaker initiates his voice with enough energy to suggest a strong and thoroughly alive personality.

2. He makes his voice loud enough to be heard without strain or effort on the part of his listeners.

3. He adjusts his voice to the needs of the material and the occasion.

4. He uses his voice as a means of emphasizing syllables, words, and phrases for a special purpose.

For the student to acquire command of force in these various areas requires that he approach the study in an intelligent, thoughtful, and analytical way. Because vocal force is more suited to emotion and the broader aspects of meaning than to fine intellectual discriminations, it does not lend itself to the portrayal of fine shades of meaning as does pitch. It nevertheless does provide a revealing clue to the speakers' personality. People often instinctively judge a person according to his ability to adjust vocal force to the occasion.

"BIG" VOICE NOT NECESSARY

It is not possible for everyone to acquire the stentorian tones of a Webster, an O'Connell, or a Demosthenes, nor is it necessary. Science through the medium of the public address system has obviated the necessity for the shouting that was required of those who addressed huge gatherings in the past. Today a speaker, with the aid of an amplification system, can be heard with equal distinctness in all parts of a large auditorium or outdoor assemblage. We also want to stress the point that in acting, projecting the voice is not a function of force alone, as so many neophytes in theatre discover. Many good directors patiently try to demonstrate to their actors how projection may be achieved by means other than simply "turning up the volume."

While the average man is seldom called upon to speak before large audiences, he is often called upon to converse in conferences, committees, business groups, or in fraternal or religious gatherings, all of which are comparatively small assemblies. To be sure, this is not always the case. Great public meetings where thousands gather to hear a speaker are still held and probably always will be. It is likewise true that these meetings are not always equipped with modern public address systems, but the exceptions do not alter the fact that most speeches today are made before smaller groups where thunderous volume is quite unnecessary.

DEGREE OF FORCE TO USE

Hamlet said to the players, " Let your own discretion be your tutor." Hamlet must have thought that their discretion could be improved, or at least awakened by a little judicious prodding, or he would not have bothered to emphasize that his players suit the action to the word and the word to the action.

There is no doubt that our judgment with respect to the use of vocal force can be improved by heeding certain principles. Let us summarize some of these principles which should influence our "discretion" in the use of vocal force.

1. There is the obvious fact that conflicting noises—the rumble of traffic, coughing, flapping curtains, and so forth—must be overcome; it is an obvious fact, yet one frequently ignored by inexperienced and indifferent speakers.

2. The size of the audience, acoustic properties of the auditorium, and similar considerations constitute another obvious but not always observed

factor which should influence our judgment. Discretion and good taste should instruct the speaker regarding his responsibility for keeping his audience awake. To do this, he must first of all make them hear.

3. The nature of the audience has a bearing. In intellectual circles quiet speaking may be appropriate ; in certain other circles, however, especially among people who do not hear much public speaking and are therefore unskilled in listening, a strong, virile tone may pay much bigger dividends. Indeed, some audiences consider noise practically tantamount to eloquence, and a quiet voice a badge of weakness or indicative of lack of sureness. Without doubt certain politicians derive a large share of their great influence from their vocal force.

4. The nature of the subject being discussed and the type of occasion must not be ignored. For extreme examples which will demonstrate the point, consider the difference in the vocal force requirements of a funeral eulogy and a noisy Fourth of July celebration, or a classroom lecture and an outdoor rally on campus.

5. The limitations of the speaker's vocal powers constitute a significant factor. If one can use good strong tones without straining, that is one thing ; for a person to attempt to use loud tones when his effort results only in a rasping, ineffective vocal quality is another thing entirely. If you have conscientiously practiced vocal exercises in respiration, phonation, and resonation, you have launched upon a program which will ultimately help you to meet the demand of using greater vocal power. If you are unable to project your voice without strain, you must stay within your range or suffer the consequences.

CONVERSATIONAL SPEECH REQUIRES VARIETY IN VOCAL FORCE

Monotony may be of the full-voiced, leather-lunged type or it may be of the frail and mouselike variety, or it may be, and usually is, of the innocuous, medium-range, commonplace type, which, in the words of Holy Writ, being " neither hot nor cold, is fit only to be spewed out of the mouth." Any degree of force, if too long sustained, becomes an invitation to mental drowsiness on the part of the auditor.

Listen to an animated conversation—you will note a natural ebb and flow of force that is closely associated with the thought and emotional content of the material being presented.

TYPES OF VOCAL FORCE

There are at least three types of vocal force which we should understand in order to make the most efficient use of our voices.

The first type is centered in individual words, the second in climax sentences, and the third in sustained passages.

273

Individual Word Force

This type of force is used typically in animated conversation and is characterized by a significant change in power on key syllables and words. Listen to a lively conversation and you will quickly identify the frequent and rather pronounced use of individual word force by effective speakers. We hear it clearly exemplified in such conversation around the campus as the following:

> Just *where* do you think *you're* going?
> I didn't get a *low* grade on that test, I got a *high* grade.
> He didn't say he *had* called home; he said he *meant* to call home.
> I'll *never ever* go out with him again.

Climax Sentences

Sentence force is more extreme. As the concept implies, it is more explosive in nature. Important words and syllables are stressed by an abrupt explosion of force, giving tremendous emphasis. This is often the vehicle for expressing strong emotions. It is not adaptable to polite and dignified occasions. Used to excess it readily becomes unsettling to an audience; under proper conditions and with proper timing it is undeniably useful. It often stirs a lethargic audience to attention when all other devices fail. There are also times when no other kind of force gives adequate release to the speaker's feelings. Give explosive force to such emotion-charged expressions as:

> *Give me liberty or give me death.*
> *This is no time for debate—this is the time for action*!
> *You say honor? What honor is there?*

Sustained Force

Sustained force is the smooth regular flow of certain types of speech, which may (if rightly used) express calmness, serenity, submissiveness, assurance; it may also suggest debility and senility. It may be either loud or soft as the sentiment requires. It seldom shifts abruptly from loud to soft or vice versa, but changes gradually and by long sweeping gradations. Sustained force is chiefly used in poetry, poetic prose, and highly emotionalized expression of the calm placid variety.

Sustained force is the natural form for expressing such smooth-flowing lines as the following:

> Roll on, thou deep and dark blue ocean, roll!
> If the British Commonwealth and Empire last for a thousand years, men will say, "This was their finest hour."
> O, my love is like a red, red rose!

Errors in the use of Vocal Force

Let us quickly review some of the most common faults that arise from improper use of vocal force:

1. Probably the most common of all the errors of vocal force is lack of variety giving rise to monotony. The constant use of any level of loudness without variation will result in a monotonous performance.

2. *Too little force* can become a vocal fault if used as a habitual speaking level. The weak voice can suggest lack of vigor, health, or conviction, as well as indicating such negative psychological factors as excessive shyness, withdrawal tendencies, undue fear, or anxiety. We should also point out that the person who chronically uses less force than is appropriate to the situation forces his auditors to expend more energy than is usually required to listen, which can give rise to inattentiveness, boredom, and fatigue. A few speakers might adopt a stereotyped voice such as speaking in hushed tones or using a small babyish voice, both of which have limited or questionable value as general styles and may suggest insincerity or immaturity.

3. Speaking with *too much force* can be a liability if employed as a base level. While this fault does not occur too often it does arise on occasion. Underlying causes may range from a desire on the part of the speaker to *overpower* his audience to nervousness that causes the speaker to overcompensate by using too much force. The fault might also be traced to the personality structure of the individual, i.e., blustering, brash, boorish, etc.

4. *Any force pattern which is repeated too often,* that is, to the point of becoming an obvious device, can be listed as a fault. For example, a speaker's utilizing a high-to-low force pattern on sentences may be directly related to breath control rather than decreasing conviction in an idea. Usually such a person is not aware that he has fallen into a force pattern and needs to be corrected. One is always aware of stereotyped climax patterns often employed by professional speakers to achieve a heightened effect in concluding ideas. If thought and emotion are not closely linked to the material presented, a mechanical insincere performance will result.

SHADING OR TOUCH

Shading or *touch* is the artistic use of degrees of force. It implies an intimate sense of a wide range of values. It recognizes the effectiveness of quiet intensity when the occasion is appropriate, and it likewise recognizes the power of voice strength when emotional content justifies it, but never offends good taste.

Not all ideas contained in our speech are of equal importance, nor are all words in a sentence. Any reasonably good conversationalist varies the force of his voice according to his meaning. Unimportant words such as articles, prepositions, and conjunctions are properly subordinated. Likewise, certain complete sentences stand out in bold relief when the thought or emotion demands emphasis. All too often this pleasant and interesting variation is suppressed into a dead level of monotony, with no lights and shadows, no hills and valleys, no relief.

Emphasis can be gained by force after quietness, and by quietness after force. The lull after the storm is as impressive as the sudden thunder after clear weather. Cultivate, even in more formal speaking situations, a sense of touch comparable to the variety in vocal force which characterizes brilliant, scintillating conversation.

EXERCISES

1. Emphasize the italicized words by added force:
   a. I want *you* to do it.
   b. *Never darken* my *doorway* again!
   c. What *new tricks* has he been up to?
   d. Did you say a *dollar?*
   e. *Wow!* Did you see *that?*

2. In the following sentences, stress the indicated word and note the changing meanings:
   a. *I* said he was a scoundrel.
   b. I *said* he was a scroundrel.
   c. I said *he* was a scoundrel.
   d. I said he *was* a scoundrel.
   e. I said he was a *scoundrel.*

3. Study the following selection. Hunt for the key words and underscore them. Now read the selection aloud, emphasizing the underscored words with added force and subordinating those that are not underscored. Give the latter only such force as is necessary for distinctness. Do this solely as an exercise and for practice. To follow such a plan in actual speaking might make your speech sound mechanical.

> The man who enjoys marching in line and file to the strains of martial music falls below my contempt; he received his great brain by mistake—the spinal cord would have been amply sufficient. This heroism at command, this senseless violence, this accursed bombast of patriotism—how intensely I despise them!
>
> —Albert Einstein

276

SELECTIONS FOR FORCE

From THE MAN WITH THE HOE

Bowed by the weight of centuries, he leans
Upon his hoe and gazes on the ground,
The emptiness of ages in his face,
And on his back the burden of the world.
Who made him dead to rapture and despair,
A thing that grieves not and that never hopes,
Stolid and stunned, a brother to the ox?
Who loosened and let down this brutal jaw?
Whose was the hand that slanted back this brow?
Whose breath blew out the light within this brain?
Is this the thing the Lord God made and gave
To have dominion over sea and land?[11]

—Edwin Markham

From MACBETH

Awake! Awake!
Ring the alarum bell! Murder and treason!
Banquo and Donalbain! Malcolm! awake!
Shake off this drowsy sleep, death's counterfeit,
And look on death itself! up, up, and see
The great doom's image! Malcolm! Banquo!
As from your graves rise up, and walk like sprites,
To countenance this horror! Ring the bell!

—William Shakespeare

Out of the North the wild news came,
Far flashing on its wings of flame,
Swift as the boreal light which flies
At midnight through the startled skies.
And there was tumult in the air,
    The fife's shrill note, the drum's loud beat,
And through the wide land everywhere
    The answering tread of hurrying feet;
While the first oath of Freedom's gun
Came on the blast from Lexington;

[11] Reprinted by permission of Virgil Markham.

277

And Concord roused, no longer tame
Forgot her old baptismal name,
Made bare her patriot arm of power,
And swelled the discord of the hour.
And there the startling drum and fife
Fired the living with fiercer life ;
While overhead, with wild increase,
Forgetting its ancient toll of peace,
    The great bell swung as ne'er before :
It seemed as it would never cease ;
And every word its ardor flung
From off its jubilant iron tongue
    Was "War ! War ! WAR !"

                    —Thomas B. Read

YE CRAGS AND PEAKS

Ye crags and peaks, I'm with you once again !
I hold you to the hands you first beheld,
To show they still are free. Methinks I hear
A spirit in your echoes answer me,
And bid your tenant welcome to his home
Again ! O, sacred forms, how proud you look !
How high you lift your heads into the sky !
How huge you are ! how mighty and how free !
Ye are the things that tower, that shine, whose smile
Makes glad, whose frown is terrible, whose forms,
Robed or unrobed, do all the impress wear
Of awe divine. Ye guards of liberty !
I'm with you once again !—I call to you
With all my voice ! I hold my hands to you
To show they still are free. I rush to you,
As though I could embrace you !

                    —Sheridan Knowles

From CYRANO DE BERGERAC

                  Ah, no, young sir !
You are too simple. Why, you might have said—
Oh, a great many things ! Mon dieu, why waste
Your opportunity ? For example, thus :—
(*Aggressive*)   I, sir, if that nose were mine,
I'd have it amputated—on the spot !

278

(*Friendly*)   How do you drink with such a nose?
You ought to have a cup made specially.
(*Descriptive*)   'Tis a rock—a crag—a cape—
A cape? say rather, a peninsula!
(*Inquisitive*)   What is that receptacle—
A razor-case or a portfolio?
(*Kindly*)   Ah, do you love the little birds
So much that when they come and sing to you,
You give them this to perch on?   (*Insolent*)
Sir, when you smoke, the neighbors must suppose
Your chimney is on fire.   (*Cautious*)   Take care—
A weight like that might make you topheavy.
(*Thoughtful*)   Somebody fetch my parasol—
Those delicate colors fade so in the sun!
(*Pedantic*)   Does not Aristophanes
Mention a mythologic monster called
Hippocampelephantocamelos?
Surely we have here the original!
(*Familiar*)   Well, old torchlight! Hang your hat
Over that chandelier—it hurts my eyes.
(*Eloquent*)   When it blows, the typhoon howls,
And the clouds darken.   (*Dramatic*)   When it bleeds—
The Red Sea!   (*Enterprising*)   What a sign⁻
For some perfumer!   (*Lyric*)   Hark—the horn
Of Roland calls to summon Charlemagne!—
(*Simple*)   When do they unveil the monument?
(*Respectful*)   Sir, I recognize in you
A man of parts, a man of prominence—
(*Rustic*)   Hey? What? Call that a nose? Na, na—
I be no fool like what you think I be—
That there's a blue cucumber!   (*Military*)
Point against cavalry!   (*Practical*)   Why not
A lottery with this for the grand prize?
Or—parodying Faustus in the play—
"Was this the nose that launched a thousand ships
And burned the topless towers of Ilium?"
These, my dear sir, are things you might have said
Had you some tinge of letters, or of wit
To color your discourse. But wit,—not so,
You never had an atom—and of letters,
You have just those that are needed
To spell, "Fool!"

—Edmund Rostand

From JULIUS CAESAR

Wherefore rejoice? What conquest brings he home?
What tributaries follow him to Rome
To grace in captive bonds his chariot-wheels?
You blocks, you stones, you worse than senseless things!
O you hard hearts, you cruel men of Rome,
Knew you not Pompey? Many a time and oft
Have you climbed up to walls and battlements,
To towers and windows, yea, to chimney-tops,
Your infants in your arms, and there have sat
The live-long day, with patient expectation
To see great Pompey pass the streets of Rome:
And when you saw his chariot but appear,
Have you not made an universal shout,
That Tiber trembled underneath her banks,
To hear the replication of your sounds
Made in her concave shores?
And do you now put on your best attire?
And do you now cull out a holiday?
And do you now strew flowers in his way
That comes in triumph over Pompey's blood?
Be gone!
Run to your houses, fall upon your knees,
Pray to the gods to intermit the plague
That needs must light on this ingratitude.

—William Shakespeare

From KING LEAR

Blow, winds, and crack your cheeks! rage! blow!
You cataracts and hurricanes, spout
Till you have drench'd our steeples, drown'd the cocks!
You sulphurous and thought-executing fires,
Vaunt-couriers of oak-cleaving thunderbolts,
Singe my white head! And thou, all-shaking thunder,
Strike flat the thick rotundity o' the world!
Crack nature's moulds, all germins spill at once,
That make ingrateful man! . . .
Rumble thy bellyful! Spit, fire! spout, rain!
Nor rain, wind, thunder, fire, are my daughters:
I tax not you, you elements, with unkindness;

I never gave you kingdom, call'd you children,
You owe me no subscription : then let fall
Your horrible pleasure ; here I stand, your slave,
A poor, infirm, weak, and despis'd old man ;
But yet I call you servile ministers,
That will with two pernicious daughters join
Your high engender'd battles 'gainst a head
So old and white as this. O ! O ! 'tis foul !

—William Shakespeare

I have nothing to offer but blood, toil, tears, and sweat. . . . You ask, what is our policy ? I will say, it is to wage war, by sea, land, and air, with all our might and with all the strength that God can give us ; to wage war against a monstrous tyranny, never surpassed in the dark, lamentable catalogue of human crime. That is our policy. You ask, what is our aim ? I can answer in one word : it is victory, victory at all costs, victory in spite of terror, victory, however long and hard the road may be ; for without victory there is no survival.

—Winston Churchill

We shall not flag or fail. We shall go on to the end. We shall fight in France, we shall fight on the seas and oceans, we shall fight with growing strength in the air, we shall defend our Island, whatever the cost may be. We shall fight on the beaches, we shall fight on the landing grounds, we shall fight in the fields and in the streets, we shall fight in the hills ; we shall never surrender, and even if, which I do not for a moment believe, this Island or a large part of it were subjugated and starving, then our empire beyond the seas, armed and guarded by the British Fleet, would carry on the struggle, until, in God's good time, the New World, with all its power and might, steps forth to the rescue and the liberation of the old.

—Winston Churchill

If we wish to be free—if we mean to preserve inviolate those inestimable privileges for which we have been so long contending—if we mean not basely to abandon the noble struggle in which we have been so long engaged, and which we have pledged ourselves never to abandon, until the glorious object of our contest shall be obtained—we must fight ! I repeat it, sir, we must fight ! An appeal to arms and to the God of Hosts is all that is left us !

They tell us, sir, that we are weak—unable to cope with so formidable an adversary. But when shall we be stronger? Will it be the next week, or the next year? Will it be when we are totally disarmed, and when a British guard shall be stationed in every house? Shall we gather strength by irresolution and inaction? Shall we acquire the means of effectual resistance by lying supinely on our backs and hugging the delusive phantom of hope, until our enemies shall have bound us hand and foot?

Sir, we are not weak if we make a proper use of those means of people armed in the holy cause of liberty, and in such a country as that which we possess, are invincible by any force which our enemy can send against us. Besides, sir, we shall not fight our battles alone. There is a just God who presides over the destinies of nations, and who will raise up friends to fight our battles for us. The battle, sir, is not to the strong alone; it is to the vigilant, the active, the brave. Besides, sir, we have no election. If we were base enough to desire it, it is now too late to retire from the contest. There is no retreat but in submission and slavery! Our chains are forged! Their clanking may be heard on the plains of Boston! The war is inevitable—and let it come! I repeat it, sir, let it come.

It is vain, sir, to extenuate the matter. Gentlemen may cry, Peace, peace—but there is no peace. The war is actually begun! The next gale that sweeps from the North will bring to our ears the clash of resounding arms! Our brethren are already in the field! Why stand we here idle? What is it that gentlemen wish? Is life so dear, or peace so sweet, as to be purchased at the price of chains and slavery? Forbid it, Almighty God! I know not what course others may take; but as for me, give me liberty, or give me death!

—Patrick Henry

SUPPLEMENTARY SELECTIONS FOR CLASS PRESENTATION

RATE

The Black Horse Troop Returns to War, Stephen Vincent Benet, *poetry.*
The Congo, Vachel Lindsay, *poetry.*
I'm Nobody, Emily Dickinson, *poetry.*
On His Blindness, John Milton, *poetry.*
The Raven, Edgar Allan Poe, *poetry.*
Tarantella, Hilaire Belloc, *poetry.*

282

PITCH

The Importance of Being Earnest, Oscar Wilde (any of the long speeches), *prose.*

Piazza Piece, John Crowe, Ransom, *poetry.*

The Tell-Tale Heart, Edgar Allan Poe, *prose.*

FORCE

General William Booth Enters Into Heaven, Vachel Lindsay, *poetry.*

Invictus, William Ernest Henley, *poetry.*

Petrified Man, Eudora Welty, *prose.*

Why I Burned the City, Lawrence Benford, in Clarence Major's *The New Black Poetry.*

integrating vocal skills

THUS FAR WE have concentrated upon achieving skills in voice, articulation, pronunciation, and vocal variety. In performance it is essential to concentrate on conveying both the meaning and emotional content of what we wish to communicate to our auditors. All of the skills we have studied in the many areas—breath control, tone production, resonation, and articulation—must be automatic in actual performance. Therefore, in the final chapter we shall be concerned with integrating vocal skills into the communicative process.

In order to accomplish this goal, it is important to study (a) meaning and speech, (b) the use of imagery, (c) emotion and voice, and (d) the use of physical activity.

MEANING AND SPEECH

A speaker becomes effective when he knows his subject, is stimulated by its content, and is motivated to communicate his ideas to others. The authors have worked with many college students whose classroom performances have been characterized by listlessness and monotonous speech.

Some of the underlying reasons for dull performances can be traced to: (a) lack of interest in the subject, (b) failure to choose material of common interest to the audience, (c) colorless treatment of the subject, and (d) lack of understanding of the material presented. The first two reasons for a dull performance can be remedied easily since they involve a choice. However, the latter two reasons for poor performance are not so easily overcome, since they require greater study and imagination on the part of the student.

The preparation of speeches for public performance belongs to courses in public speaking and will not be discussed here. However, a rudimentary study of the thought content of prose and poetry is necessary in order to show the relationship between meaning and the voice.

THOUGHT CONTENT IN PUBLIC READING

The average person does not read aloud effectively. He is often guilty of reading so monotonously that his auditors are bored. We find this kind of reading in performances involving secretaries' reports, papers read at conventions, materials read in the classroom, and in most other situations in which people read publicly.

The principle reason for this inadequacy is that people read words rather than ideas. The basis of this problem probably lies in our childhood training in reading. The average youngster is more concerned in reading one word at a time when he first starts to read, e.g., " John / sees / the / ball. The / ball / is / red," and so on. He continues in this form of reading behavior long enough to establish a pattern that is quite unlike his oral speaking behavior. Furthermore, the average person has had comparatively little training or actual experience in reading aloud throughout his formative years.

In order to read effectively it is necessary to extract the meaning intended by the author. In many works the intended meaning is not always apparent, particularly in poetry. In order to expedite the process of acquiring meaning from difficult or obscure materials, a method of literary analysis is needed.

METHOD OF LITERARY ANALYSIS

Read the passage through without stopping to study difficult words, phrases, or sentences. Attempt to grasp the central idea or theme of the work. After you have completed your reading, close the book and attempt to write a statement that is sufficiently comprehensive to serve as the theme for the passage.

Read the selection a second time. Try to determine the method by which the author develops his theme. Is the work divided into sections ? If so, how do they differ one from the other ? In what way are the sections related to each other ? Does the author use a sequence to tie the various parts of the work together ?

Read the selection a third time, noting all words, phrases, and sentences that you do not fully understand. Reread each of these carefully. Decide upon the best interpretation you can make for the difficult phrases and sentences. Further research in the library on the selection and author may yield the answer you seek. If not, discuss the difficult lines with your instructor. Be sure to look up in the dictionary all words that you do not fully understand.

Before reading the passage again, ask youself who is speaking. Is it the author, a character created by the author, the voice of universal truth, or yourself? If the speaker is someone other than yourself, try to determine what he is like in terms of age, personality, and experience. What is the relationship of the time, place, and nature of the situation depicted to the person speaking?

Now read the passage again for enjoyment. Your analysis should have deepened your understanding and heightened your appreciation. Give yourself over to the passage with abandonment. As a consequence your oral reading should be both discriminating and interesting.

As an illustration, let us try this suggested procedure for literary analysis on the following poem by George Meredith that is usually considered difficult to understand.

1. First, we'll read the poem over rapidly to get the central idea:

IS LOVE DIVINE?

Ask, Is Love Divine?
Voices all are *ay*.
Question for the sign:
Would we through our years
Love forego,
Quit of scars and tears?
Ah, but no, no, no!

Chances are that the first reading does not produce a great deal of meaning. The poet seems to be talking about love, but there is nothing unusual about that—most poets do. Why does the author bring up the concept of scars and tears? What do they have to do with love? If you do not know the author's intention, you had better read the poem again.

The first sentence is clear enough; the poet is asking whether or not love is divine, but what does he mean by *divine*? That word, we see by the dictionary, has several meanings. There is one that seems to fit: " proceeding from God." Meredith seems to be inquiring whether or not love comes from God.

2. Since we are not concerned with sections of the poem, let us move on to the next step.

3. *Voices*! What does Meredith mean by *voices*? Here is another word with many meanings, but the one that seems most applicable is: "Any sound likened to vocal utterance: *the voice of the wind*." Meredith must

mean, then, that all the voices of nature say—what? What is the meaning of that *ay*? We go to the dictionary again and find that there are a series of *ays* and *ayes*, the two spellings being used interchangeably, at least in part of the meanings. This is unusual. Here is a word whose meaning is determined not by the spelling, as in *beech* (a hardwood timber tree) versus *beach* (the shore of the sea or of a lake), but by the pronunciation. Both *aye* and *ay* may be pronounced [eɪ], and when so pronounced they mean "ever, always" (an archaic meaning, but that would not stop a poet). Also, both *aye* and *ay* may be pronounced [aɪ], and when so pronounced they mean *yes*. It must be, then, that Meredith is answering his question with an affirmative: Voices of nature all say *yes, love is divine*!

Now, analyse the next line, *Question for the sign*: The individual words are clear enough, but together they may not seem to mean much. What is that colon doing at the end of the line? We remember that a colon is often used after an introductory statement to indicate that an explanation follows. Meredith must be saying: "Do you want proof? All right, I'll give it to you. And here it is:" Now we will be on the lookout for his proof that love comes from God.

The meaning of the next two lines is simple enough: Would we be willing to get along without love? However, the next line is not clear. What does he mean by *quit*? The dictionary gives as one meaning: "released from obligation, penalty." So now we have it: Would we be willing to give up love, if by so doing we could be free of the penalties that love entails?

The final line is a negation, made emphatic by three repetitions of the word *no*.

We may want to spend a little more time musing over the implications of "scars and tears." We may think of the sickness, accidents, and even death that have come to persons we have loved. Because of our love for the afflicted ones, we suffered—scars and tears. We may reflect upon the "sweet sorrow" that has come to us from lovers' quarrels—scars and tears. We may reluctantly dwell upon the perfidy of a friend whom we had come to love and trust—scars and tears. But we may decide that in spite of the sorrow and suffering we will cling to love, along with Meredith.

4. Now read the poem again for artistic enjoyment. Enjoy the poet's skill in saying so much in a few words. Enjoy his architectural craftsmanship in building so symmetrical a structure from such carefully chiseled building blocks.

Enjoy it, perhaps, because the poet has said what you believe to be true and would like to have said yourself if you possessed the skill.

EXERCISES

1. The following brief excerpts from poems and prose poems, although out of context, are worthy of study in their own right. Each exemplifies the poet's flashing insight and power of concise expression. Be sure you grasp

the author's full meaning, and add your own reaction to his concept, before you attempt to read the lines aloud.

      a. Wilt thou not open thy heart to know
         What rainbows teach, and sunsets show !

      b. What is this life if, full of care,
         We have no time to stand and stare !

      c. The Devil was sick—the Devil a monk would be ;
         The Devil was well—the devil a monk was he ![1]

      d. Eternal Spirit of the chainless mind !
         Brightest in dungeons, Liberty ! thou art,
         For there thy habitation is the heart—

      e. Beauty is truth, truth beauty—That is all
         Ye know on earth, and all ye need to know.

      f. I warmed both my hands against the fire of Life ;
         It sinks, and I am ready to depart.

      g. And Thought leapt out to wed with Thought,
         Ere Thought could wed with Speech.

      h. Some books are to be tasted, others to be swallowed, and some few to be chewed and digested.

      i. Life is a narrow vale between the cold and barren peaks of two eternities.

      j. ... in this batter'd Caravanserai
         Whose Portals are alternate Night and Day.[2]

2. There is good vocal drill in trying to present the full significance of such balanced expressions as the following :

      a. I come to bury Caesar, not to praise him.

      b. The evil that men do lives after them.
         The good is oft interred with their bones.

      c. Destroy our cities and leave our broad farms and cities will spring up anew—Destroy our farms and grass will grow in the streets of every city.

      d. Oh, East is East, and West is West,
         And never the twain shall meet.

      e. As you are old and reverend, you should be wise.

      f. Striving to better, oft we mar what's well.

      g. We live in deeds, not years ; in thoughts, not breaths ;
         In feelings, not in figures on a dial.

      h. You have been brave, but not brutal ; confident, but not arrogant ; and you have welded the tremendous military poten-

---

[1] Do not overlook the significance of the change to a small *d* in *devil* in the second line which makes the word simply part of a slang phrase.
[2] Observe the similarity in the philosophical concepts of this and the preceding selection. Also note the significance of the word *caravanserai* (or *caravansary*) in this context, i.e., a sort of inn, a brief stopping place for a caravan as it comes out of the desert and goes back into the desert.

tial of this country into a great fighting machine without having sacrificed the rights of the individual.

i. The machine can free man or enslave him; it can make of this world something resembling a paradise or a purgatory. Men have it within their power to achieve a security hitherto dreamed of only by philosophers, or they may go the way of the dinosaurs, actually disappearing from the earth because they fail to develop the social and political intelligence to adjust to the world their mechanical intelligence has created. Right now the outcome is doubtful and the issue hangs in balance.

3. Study the following poem. First, read it perfunctorily, as a task to be performed without enthusiasm—read it as the secretary usually reads the minutes of the last meeting. Then study it to understand Browning's philosophy of death. Feel the surging courage—the daring to face death as he had faced life, chest forward, head high, undaunted by the dread specter. Now read it aloud; give your voice over to the thought and feeling of it.

PROSPICE

Fear death?—to feel the fog in my throat,
    The mist in my face,
When the snows begin, and the blasts denote
    I am nearing the place,
The power of the night, the press of the storm,
    The post of the foe;
Where he stands, the Arch Fear in a visible form,
    Yet the strong man must go:
For the journey is done and the summit attained,
    And the barriers fall,
Though the battle's to fight ere the guerdon be gained,
    The reward of it all.
I was ever a fighter, so—one fight more,
    The best and the last!
I would hate that death bandaged my eyes, and forebore,
    And bade me creep past.
No! let me taste the whole of it, fare like my peers,
    The heroes of old,
Bear the brunt, in a minute pay glad life's arrears
    Of pain, darkness, and cold.
For sudden the worse turns the best to the brave,
    The black minute's at end,
And the elements' rage, the fiend-voices that rave,
    Shall dwindle, shall blend,

Shall change, shall become first a peace out of pain,
    Then a light, then thy breast,
O thou soul of my soul! I shall clasp thee again,
    And with God be the rest!

                          —Robert Browning

4. Figure out the meaning of the following poem. The mental pictures Mrs. Browning presents are as clear as spring water, but her *meaning* bears closer resemblance to the turbid river she describes in the poem. Quite obviously she wants to impress a message; but what is it? Do you consider it possible that she deliberately made the message somewhat obscure, on the theory that we appreciate most those things which we have to struggle hardest to get? Look closely at the last stanza for the key thought.

After you have the thought, see if you can give it vocally.

A MUSICAL INSTRUMENT

What was he doing, the great god Pan,
    Down in the reeds by the river?
Spreading ruin and scattering ban,
Splashing and paddling with hoofs of a goat,
And breaking the golden lilies afloat
    With the dragon-fly on the river?

He tore out a reed, the great god Pan,
    From the deep cool bed of the river:
The limpid water turbidly ran,
And the broken lilies a-dying lay,
And the dragon-fly had fled away,
    Ere he brought it out of the river.

High on the shore sat the great god Pan,
    While turbidly flow'd the river;
And hack'd and hew'd as a great god can,
With his hard bleak steel at the patient reed,
Till there was not a sign of a leaf indeed
    To prove it fresh from the river.

He cut it short, did the great god Pan,
    (How tall it stood in the river!)
Then drew the pith, like the heart of a man,
Steadily from the outside ring.
And notch'd the poor dry empty thing
    In holes, as he sat by the river.

" This· is the way," laugh'd the great god Pan,
    (Laugh'd while he sat by the river)
" The only way, since gods began
To make sweet music, they could succeed."
Then, dropping his mouth to a hole in the reed,
    He blew in power by the river.

Sweet, sweet, sweet, O Pan !
    Piercing sweet by the river !
Blinding sweet, O great god Pan !
The sun on the hill forgot to die,
And the lilies revived and the dragon-fly
    Came back to dream on the river.

Yet half a beast is the great god Pan,
    To laugh as he sits by the river,
Making a poet out of a man :
The true gods sigh for the cost and pain—
For the reed which grows never more again
    As a reed with the reeds in the river.

                    —Elizabeth Barrett Browning

5. In the following selection, distinguish between a hazy grasp of the general meaning and complete realization of all the significant implications. Express the detailed meanings in your voice shadings.

From PRELUDE TO THE VISION OF SIR LAUNFAL

And what is so rare as a day in June ?
    Then, if ever, come perfect days ;
Then Heaven tries earth if it be in tune ;
    And over it softly her warm ear lays ;
Whether we look, or whether we listen,
We hear life murmur, or see it glisten ;
Every clod feels a stir of might,
    An instinct within it that reaches and towers,
And, groping blindly above it for light,
    Climbs to a soul in grass and flowers ;
The flush of life may well be seen
    Thrilling back over hills and valleys ;
The cowslip startles in meadows green,
    The buttercup catches the sun in its chalice,
And there's never a leaf nor a blade too mean
    To be some happy creature's palace ;

The little bird sits at his door in the sun,
    Atilt like a blossom among the leaves,
And lets his illumined being o'errun
    With the deluge of summer it receives;
His mate feels the eggs beneath her wings,
And the heart in her dumb breast flutters and sings;
He sings to the wide world, and she to her nest,—
In the nice ear of Nature which song is the best?

                      —James Russell Lowell

6. In this exercise you will find two contrasting attitudes toward old age, each expressed by a major poet. Studying the two together will help you to appreciate the full implication of each. After you are thoroughly conversant with both poems, read them aloud. Read each so well that you do full justice to the author's meaning. But in reading the poem which comes closer to your own belief about old age, give it the added emphasis that will show your agreement with it.

From RABBI BEN EZRA

Grow old along with me!
The best is yet to be,
The last of life, for which the first was made:
Our times are in his hand
Who saith, "A whole I planned,
Youth shows but half; trust God: see all, nor be afraid!"
          . . . . . .

Therefore I summon age
To grant youth's heritage,
Life's struggle having so far reached its term:
Thence shall I pass, approved
A man, for aye removed
From the developed brute; a god though in the germ.
          . . . . . .

Youth ended, I shall try
My gain or loss thereby;
Leave the fire ashes, what survives is gold:
And I shall weigh the same,
Give life its praise or blame:
Young, all lay in dispute; I shall know, being old.
          . . . . . .

So, still within this life,
Though lifted o'er its strife,
Let me discern, compare, pronounce at last,
"This rage was right i' the main,
That acquiescence vain :
The Future I may face now I have proved the Past."

—Robert Browning

GROWING OLD

What is it to grow old?
Is it to lose the glory of the form,
The luster of the eye?
Is it for beauty to forego the wreath?
—Yes, but not this alone.

Is it to feel our strength—
Not our bloom only, but our strength—decay?
Is it to feel each limb
Grow stiffer, every function less exact,
Each nerve more loosely strung?

Yes, this, and more; but not,
Ah! 'tis not what in youth we dreamed 'twould be.
Tis not to have our life
Mellowed and softened as with sunset-glow—
A golden day's decline.

'Tis not to see the world
As from a height, with rapt prophetic eyes,
And heart profoundly stirred;
And weep, and feel the fullness of the past,
The years that are no more.

It is to spend long days,
And not once feel that we were ever young;
It is to add, immured
In the hot prison of the present, month
To month with weary pain.

It is to suffer this,
And feel but half, and feebly, what we feel.
Deep in our hidden heart
Festers the dull rememberence of a change,
But no emotion—none.

It is—last stage of all—
When we are frozen up within, and quite
The phantom of ourselves,
To hear the world applaud the hollow ghost,
Which blamed the living man.

—Matthew Arnold

7. The following exercise is similar to Exercise 6 except that the theme pertains to personal habits of industry, and the medium is prose instead of poetry.

From AN APOLOGY FOR IDLERS

It is certain that much may be judiciously argued in favor of diligence; only there is something to be said against it, and that is what, on the present occasion, I have to say . . . .

I have attended a good many lectures in my time. I still remember that the spinning of a top is a case of Kinetic Stability. I still remember that Emphyteusis is not a disease, nor Stillicide a crime. But though I would not willingly part with such scraps of science, I do not set the same store by them as by certain other odds and ends that I came by in the open street while I was playing truant . . . .

Suffice it to say this: if a lad does not learn in the streets, it is because he has no faculty of learning. Nor is the truant always in the streets, for if he prefers, he may go out by the gardened suburbs into the country. He may pitch on some tuft of lilacs over a burn, and smoke estimable pipes to the tune of the water on the stones. A bird will sing in the thicket. And there he may fall into a vein of kindly thought, and see things in a new perspective. Why, if this be not education, what is? We may conceive Mr. Worldly Wiseman accosting such a one, and the conversation that should thereupon ensue:

" How now, young fellow, what doest thou here?"

" Truly sir, I take mine ease."

" Is not this the hour of the class? And should'st thou not be plying thy Book with diligence, to the end thou mayest obtain knowledge?"

" Nay, but thus also I follow after Learning, by your leave."

" Learning, quotha! After what fashion, I pray thee? Is it mathematics?"

" No, to be sure."

" Is it metaphysics ?"

" Nor that."

" Is it some language ?"

" Nay, it is no language."

" Is it a trade ?"

" Nor a trade neither."

" Why, then, what is't ?"

" Indeed, sir . . . I lie here, by this water, to learn by root-of-heart a lesson which my master teaches me to call Peace, or Contentment. . . ."

Look at one of your industrious fellows for a moment, I beseech you. He sows hurry and reaps indigestion ; he puts a vast deal of activity out to interest, and receives a large measure of nervous derangement in return. Either he absents himself entirely from all fellowship, and lives a recluse in a garret, with carpet slippers and a leaden inkpot ; or he comes among people swiftly and bitterly, in a contraction of his whole nervous system, to discharge some temper before he returns to work. I do not care how much or how well he works, this fellow is an evil feature in other people's lives. They would be happier if he were dead.

—Robert Louis Stevenson

8. Browning has always been known as very dramatic and at times obscure. *My Last Duchess* provides excellent material as a difficult exercise in the interpretation of meaning.

MY LAST DUCHESS

That's my last Duchess painted on the wall,
Looking as if she were alive. I call
That piece a wonder, now ; Frà Pandolf's hands
Worked busily a day, and there she stands.
Will 't please you sit and look at her ? I said
" Frà Pandolf " by design, for never read
Strangers like you that pictured countenance,
The depth and passion of its earnest glance,
But to myself they turned (since none puts by
The curtain I have drawn for you, but I)
And seemed as they would ask me, if they durst,
How such a glance came there ; so, not the first
Are you to turn and ask thus. Sir, 'twas not
Her husband's presence only, called that spot

Of joy into the Duchess' cheek; perhaps
Frà Pandolf chanced to say, "Her mantle laps
Over my lady's wrist too much," or "Paint
Must never hope to reproduce the faint
Half-flush that dies along her throat." Such stuff
Was courtesy, she thought, and cause enough
For calling up that spot of joy. She had
A heart—how shall I say?—too soon made glad,
Too easily impressed; she liked whate'er
She looked on, and her looks went everywhere.
Sir, 'twas all one! My favor at her breast,
The dropping of the daylight in the West,
The bough of cherries some officious fool
Broke in the orchard for her, the white mule
She rode with round the terrace—all and each
Would draw from her alike the approving speech,
Or blush, at least. She thanked men—good! but thanked
Somehow—I know not how—as if she ranked
My gift of a nine-hundred-years-old name
With anybody's gift. Who'd stoop to blame
This sort of trifling? Even had you skill
In speech—which I have not—to make your will
Quite clear to such an one, and say, "Just this
Or that in you disgusts me; here you miss,
Or there exceed the mark"—and if she let
Herself be lessoned so, nor plainly set
Her wits to yours, forsooth, and made excuse—
E'en then would be some stooping; and I choose
Never to stoop. Oh sir, she smiled, no doubt,
Whene'er I passed her; but who passed without
Much the same smile? This grew; I gave Commands
Then all smiles stopped together. There she Stands
As if alive. Will't please you rise? We'll meet
The company below, then. I repeat,
The Count your master's known munificence
Is ample warrant that no just pretense
Of mine for dowry will be disallowed;
Though his fair daughter's self, as I avowed
At starting, is my object. Nay, we'll go
Together down, sir. Notice Neptune, though,
Taming a sea-horse, thought a rarity,
Which Claus of Innsbruck cast in bronze for me!

—Robert Browning

THE USE OF IMAGERY

The use of imagery by writers and speakers has been universal since the beginning of human communication, and should be studied and mastered by students of voice and diction. The value of mental imagery was stressed by the great orator Quintilian almost two thousand years ago when he discussed "images by which the presentation of absent objects are so distinctly represented to the mind that we seem to see them with our eyes and to have them before us. Whoever shall best conceive such images will have the greatest power in moving the feelings."

Imagery may be defined as "mental images as produced by memory or imagination;" this definition also includes descriptions and figures of speech. Mental images drawn from memory are sensory in nature, i.e., sight, hearing, smell, touch, taste; and they evoke a definite response in the one recalling the images. For example, try to remember the last time you answered the telephone. If you can concentrate for a moment, the experience will begin to emerge in your mind. You will begin to see the room where the telephone is located (visual). You will recall the telephone bell and the sound of the other person's voice (auditory). Perhaps you were seated in a comfortable chair and reached over to pick up the telephone (tactile and kinesthetic). Let us also assume that you were drinking a cup of hot coffee and took a sip before answering the bell (olfactory and gustatory). Such sensory events definitely make an experience more vivid and actually do much to help one recall the experience as a whole. Chances are one may not readily remember all of the features of an experience, but there is a strong stimulus from mental processes in all areas when one concentrates upon recreating the event, particularly if it has occurred just a short time before.

The response to imagery is extremely important, since it is this response that determines the subtle nuances that are heard in the voice when orally recalling the details of an experience. Suppose the telephone call in the preceding example had been from an old friend that you hadn't seen for a long time? Your surprise and joy would probably be evident in your voice immediately. Now, imagine what your response might be if the call were from a stranger telling you that a dear friend was critically injured in an automobile accident. All factors of voice, i.e., pitch, rate, quality, and force, would undoubtedly be affected.

In interpreting the works of others, one can only imagine what the author or the character he created has experienced and what his reaction might be. Can one respond in a like manner? Probably not in an exact manner, but the sensitive and imaginative person will create what *he thinks* the author has intended, and thereby give his personal interpretation to the material. It is very important, then, to study the imagery occurring in any of the selections to be performed for others. Think not only in terms of how you feel, but how the character that the author has created feels. What clues are there in the lines that give insight into the feelings involved? The author's use of imagery is the best source to which one can turn to recreate the sensory details of the work.

On the other hand, if one is asked to give a speech and is responsible for developing the material presented, the skillful use of imagery will do much to enhance his performance.

EXERCISES

1. In the following excerpts, observe the skill with which the authors support their general statements by giving significant details that create mental images. Reproduce the sensory details of the pictures clearly yourself, then express them orally.

a. In the following paragraph, note how Garland uses the senses of sight, hearing, smell, and feeling to support his statement about a corn field:

A corn field in July is a sultry place. The soil is hot and dry, the wind comes across the lazily-murmuring leaves laden with a warm, sickening smell drawn from the rapidly growing broad-flung banners of the corn. The sun, nearly vertical, drops a flood of dazzling light upon the field over which the cool shadows run, only to make the heat seem more intense.

b. In "Tam o'Shanter," the Scottish poet Burns exemplifies the abstract thought of the ephemeral nature of pleasures thus:

But pleasures are like poppies spread,
You seize the flow'r, its bloom is shed!
Or like the snow-falls in the river,
A moment white—then melts for ever;
Or like the borealis race,
That flit ere you can point their place;
Or like the rainbow's lovely form
Evanishing amid the storm.—

c. Note how few details Keats uses to create the desired picture in the following stanza:

I met a lady in the meads,
    Full beautiful—a faery's child;
Her hair was long, her foot was light,
    And her eyes were wild.

d. Here in Browning's portrait of Napoleon is another quick picture made up of significant details:

On a little mound, Napoleon
　　Stood on our storming-day:
With neck out-thrust, you fancy how,
　　Legs wide, arms lock'd behind,
As if to balance the prone brow
　　Oppressive with its mind.

e. Here is another rapidly drawn picture from the same Browning poem, this one involving action. Note how few details are needed:

Out 'twixt the battery smokes there flew
　　A rider, bound on bound
Full galloping; or bridle drew
　　Until he reached the mound.

f. Note how quickly Sandburg creates a picture of a particular city:

Hog Butcher for the world,
Stormy, husky, brawling,
City of the Big Shoulders.

g. Observe how another author, Bryant, creates a mood by presenting a few image-stirring details:

. . . approach thy grave
Like one who wraps the drapery of his couch
About him, and lies down to pleasant dreams.

2. In the following selection the ancient Greek dramatist Aeschylus is exhibiting a barren, mole-like type of existence. Study it for meaning and for mental imagery. Then express the thought vocally:

First of all, though they had eyes to see, they saw to no avail; they had ears, but understood not; but, like to shapes in dreams, throughout their length of days, without purpose they wrought all things in confusion. Knowledge had they neither of houses built of bricks and turned to face the sun, nor yet of work in wood; but dwelt beneath the ground like swarming ants, in sunless caves. They had no sign either of winter or of flowery spring or of fruitful summer, whereon they could depend.

3. Recreate mentally the pictures in the following stirring attack on capital punishment:

> A man, a convict, a sentenced wretch, is dragged, on a certain morning, to one of our public squares. There he finds the scaffold! He shudders, he struggles, he refuses to die. He is young yet—only twenty-nine. Ah! I know what you will say—'He is a murderer!' But hear me. Two officers seize him. His hands, his feet, are tied. He throws off the two officers. A frightful struggle ensues. His feet, bound as they are, become entangled in the ladder. He uses the scaffold against the scaffold! The struggle is prolonged. Horror seizes on the crowd. The officers—sweat and shame on their brows,—pale, panting, terrified... strive savagely. The victim clings to the scaffold, and shrieks for pardon. His clothes are torn,—his shoulders bloody,—still he resists. At length, after three-quarters of an hour of this monstrous effort, of this spectacle without a name, of this agony,—agony for all, be it understood,—agony for the assembled spectators as well as for the condemned man—after this age of anguish, Gentlemen of the Jury, they take back the poor wretch to his prison.
>
> The People breathe again. The People, naturally merciful, hope that the man will be spared. But no,—the guillotine, though vanquished, remains standing. There it frowns all day, in the midst of a sickened population. And at night, the officers, reinforced, drag forth the wretch again, so bound that he is but an inert weight,—they drag him forth, haggard, bloody, weeping, pleading, howling for life,—calling upon God, calling upon his father and mother,—for like a very child had this man become in the prospect of death—they drag him forth to execution. He is hoisted on the scaffold, and his head falls!— And then through every conscience runs a shudder.
>
> —Victor Hugo

4. Catch the spirit of a child's imagination as pictured in Stevenson's charming poem, then try it orally.

WHERE GO THE BOATS?

Dark brown is the river,
  Golden is the sand,
It flows along forever,
  With trees on every hand.

Green leaves a-floating,
    Castles on the foam,
Boats of mine a-boating—
    Where will all come home?

On goes the river
    And out past the mill,
Away down the valley,
    Away down the hill.

Away down the river,
    A hundred miles or more,
Other little children
    Shall bring my boats ashore.

                —Robert Louis Stevenson

5. Imagine youself on some quiet hidden lake, far from the paths of mankind: dwell upon the auditory images presented by Tennyson in the following poem. When you have given yourself over completely to the mood of it, let your voice try to express the feeling. Imagine your own voice sounding pure and clear like a bugle note, across the calm lake.

BUGLE SONG

The splendour falls on castle walls
    And snowy summits old in story:
The long light shakes across the lakes,
    And the wild cataract leaps in glory.
Blow, bugle, blow, set the wild echoes flying,
Blow, bugle; answer, echoes, dying, dying, dying.

O hark, O hear! how thin and clear,
    And thinner, clearer, farther going!
O sweet and far from cliff and scar
    The horns of Elfland faintly blowing!
Blow, let us hear the purple glens replying:
Blow, bugle; answer, echoes, dying, dying, dying.

O love, they die in yon rich sky,
    They faint on hill or field or river:
Our echoes roll from soul to soul,
    And, grow forever and forever.
Blow, bugle, blow, set the wild echoes flying,
And answer, echoes, answer, dying, dying, dying.

                —Alfred, Lord Tennyson

6. Concentrate upon the sensory details in the following selections:

A WISH

Mine be a cot beside the hill;
A bee-hive's hum shall soothe my ear;
A willowy brook that turns a mill,
With many a fall shall linger near.

The swallow, oft, beneath my thatch
Shall twitter from her clay-built nest;
Oft shall the pilgrim lift the latch,
And share my meal, a welcome guest.

Around my ivied porch shall spring
Each fragrant flower that drinks the dew;
And Lucy, at her wheel, shall sing
In russet gown and apron blue.

The village church among the trees,
Where first our marriage vows were given,
With merry peals shall swell the breeze
And point with taper spire to Heaven.

—Samuel Rogers

I waited in the little sunny room:
The cool breeze waves the window lace, at play,
The white rose on the porch was all in bloom,
And out upon the bay,
I watched the wheeling sea-birds go and come.

—Edward Rowland Sill

If upon this earth we ever have a glimpse of heaven, it is when
we pass a home in winter, at night, and through the windows,
the curtains drawn aside, we see the family about the pleasant
hearth; the old lady knitting, the cat playing with the yarn, the
children wishing they had as many dolls or dollars or knives or
something as there are sparks going out to join the roaring blast;
the father reading and smoking, and the clouds rising like
incense from the altar of domestic joy. I never pass such a house
without feeling that I have received a benediction.

—Robert G. Ingersoll

302

I remember, I remember
The house where I was born,
The little window where the sun
Came peeping in at morn ;
He never came a wink too soon
Nor brought too long a day ;
But now, I often wish the night
Had borne my breath away.

I remember, I remember
The roses, red and white,
The violets, and the lily-cups—
Those flowers made of light !
The lilacs where the robin built,
And where my brother set
The laburnum on his birthday,—
The tree is living yet.

I remember, I remember
Where I was used to swing—
And thought the air must rush as fresh
To swallows on the wing ;
My spirit flew in feathers then
That is so heavy now,
And summer pools could hardly cool
The fever on my brow.

I remember, I remember
The fir trees dark and high ;
I used to think their slender tops
Were close against the sky :
It was a childish ignorance,
But now 'tis little joy
To know I'm farther off from Heaven
Than when I was a boy.

—Thomas Hood

From A SOUTH-SEA BRIDAL

I saw that island first when it was neither night nor morning. The moon was to the west, setting, but still broad and bright. To the east, and right amidships of the dawn, which was all pink, the day-star sparkled like a diamond. The land breeze blew in our faces, and smelt strong of wild lime and vanilla ; other things besides, but these were the most plain ; and the chill of it set me sneezing. I should say I had been for years on a low island near the line, living for the most part solitary among natives. Here was a fresh experience; even the tongue would be quite strange to me; and the look of these woods and mountains, and the rare smell of them, renewed my blood.

The beginning of the desert was marked off by a wall, to call it so, for it was more of a long mound of stones. They say it reaches right across the island, but how they know it is another question, for I doubt if any one has made the journey in a hundred years, the natives sticking chiefly to the sea and their little colonies along the coast, and that part being mortal high and steep and full of cliffs. Up to the west side of the wall the ground has been cleared, and there are cocoa-palms and mummy-apples and guavas, and lots of sensitive. Just across, the bush begins outright; high bush at that, trees going up like the masts of ships, and ropes of liana hanging down like a ship's rigging, and nasty orchids growing in the forks like funguses. The ground where there was no underwood looked to be a heap of boulders. I saw many green pigeons which I might have shot, only I was there with a different idea.

—Robert Louis Stevenson

From THE JUNGLE BOOKS

Then Mowgli picked out a shady place, and lay down and slept while the buffaloes grazed round him. Herding in India is one of the laziest things in the world. The cattle move and crunch, and lie down, and move on again, and they do not even low. They only grunt, and the buffaloes very seldom say anything, but get down into the muddy pools one after another, and work their way into the mud till only their noses and staring china-blue eyes show above the surface, and there they lie like logs. The sun makes the rocks dance in the heat, and the herd-children hear one kite (never any more) whistling almost out of sight overhead, and they know that if they died, or a cow died, that kite would sweep down, and the next kite miles away would see him drop and would follow, and the next, and the next, and almost before they were dead there would be a score of hungry kites come out of nowhere. Then they sleep and wake and sleep again, and weave little baskets of dried grass and put grasshoppers in them; or catch two praying-mantises and make them fight; or string a necklace of red and black jungle-nuts; or watch a lizard basking on a rock, or a snake hunting a frog near the wallows. Then they sing long, long songs with odd native quavers at the end of them, and the day seems longer than most people's whole lives, and perhaps they make a mud castle with mud figures of men and horses and buffaloes, and put reeds into the men's hands, and pretend that they are kings and the figures are their armies, or that they are gods to be worshipped. Then evening comes, and the children call, and the buffaloes lumber up out of the sticky mud with noises like gunshots going off one after the other, and they all string across the gray plain back to the twinkling village lights.

—Rudyard Kipling

EMOTION AND VOICE

For many years the question has been debated whether or not an actor feels the emotion he portrays. Articles and books have been written on both sides of the argument. Many prominent stage people say yes, but about as many say no.

It undoubtedly is true that actors cannot feel the *full extent* of the emotion they depict; the constant repetition of the play, week after week, and sometimes year after year, would be too much of a drain on their emotional resources. This is especially true in some of the great tragedies.

Furthermore, it is doubtful whether an actor could safely depend upon feeling just the right degree of sorrow every time he reproduced a sorrowful line, or be sure of feeling hilarious whenever he came to a line that required laughter, or hate, even to the point of murder, whenever the script called for it. No, the actor must substitute some degree of artistic technique for intense emotional experience on the stage.

Nevertheless, the work of even a master artist would be a cold and life-less exhibition were he devoid of emotional response. It is a case, probably, of memorized emotions only partially revived—something like Wordsworth's definition of poetry: "Passion recollected in tranquillity." It would seem that the actor must identify himself with the emotion, understanding it so deeply and sympathetically that he can portray it realistically *with the aid of a trained technique.*

Caruso said that the requisites for a great singer are "a big chest, a big mouth, ninety percent memory, ten percent intelligence, lots of hard work, and something in the heart,"

THE RELATIONSHIP OF VOICE TO EMOTION

Man's emotional nature is exceedingly complex. To attempt to explain the exact neurological process by which voice quality changes in response to our varying emotional states is beyond the purpose of this book. Students desiring to investigate this field will find statements of current thinking of researchers along these lines in speech books by Eisenson, Auer, and Irwin; Gray and Wise; Judson and Weaver; and others, as well as in general textbooks on physiology and psychology.

The central nervous system and the autonomic nervous system interact during emotional states. The interaction has a definite effect upon control over the muscles of the larynx. The more intense the emotional state becomes, the greater the problem of controlling phonation. For example, when a person becomes angry his voice generally rises in pitch because of increased tension, and his voice quality has a tendency to become strident or harsh; in moments of grief, pitch tends to be lower and phonation, in extreme cases, may be interrupted by spasms. These are the grosser, more obvious changes; minor variations of vocal quality are constantly taking place. Many of these smaller changes are subliminal, that is, they are below the threshold of consciousness. Cicero once said:

> Every emotion of the mind has from nature its own peculiar look, tone, and gesture; and the whole frame of man, and his whole countenance, and the variations of his voice, sound like strings in a musical instrument, just as they are moved by the affections of the mind.

Cicero's utilization of emotion as a means of communicating more effectively may be seen in his statement:

> Never, I assure you, have I endeavored to excite in the judges the emotions of grief, commiseration, envy or hatred, without becoming sensibly touched myself with the passion I wished to communicate to them.

EMOTION MUST BE CONTROLLED

Close as the relationship is, however, between emotion and voice, emotion must at all times be controlled. Extreme emotions master us. They are essentially chaotic in nature. Refusing to be used for either intellectual or practical purposes, they lead to confusion and awkwardness. In some of his early studies on the effect of emotion upon human action, Charles Darwin analyzed the effect of rage thus: "The paralyzed lips refuse to obey the will, and the voice sticks in the throat; or it is rendered loud, harsh, and discordant." Overanxiety, extreme excitement, rage, fear, and other accentuated forms of emotionalism often cause the speaker to lose control of his voice.

Stage Fright

Closely related to this uncontrolled emotionalism is a malady which affects not only voice quality but the rest of the personality as well—stage fright. The shaking knees, dry tongue, quickened pulse, general perspiration, spasmodic breathing, and peculiar feeling in the pit of the stomach are all symptoms of this strange malady. Most authorities are in agreement that stage fright has as its basis the attempt by man to face a crisis. The body is literally preparing for "fight or flight," as man had to do so often in primitive life. The causes of stage fright are many and complex. For a detailed treatment of this topic, we refer you to two well-known sources.[3]

In connection with stage fright we should note that teachers of singing and speaking have long recognized that a reasonable degree of nervousness is a valuable asset before a performance. This anticipatory nervousness is nature's conditioner. It lifts us above the commonplace and stimulates us to meet the occasion. Persons entirely lacking in this type of nervousness are apt to be less effective in performance than those who do experience it.

SINCERITY AND EMOTION

Before finishing our consideration of emotion and its basic relationship to voice, we must deal specifically with a concept that is of primary importance in voice work—sincerity. This word, like so many others in our language, has many meanings. Sincerity with regard to voice means genuineness, honesty, unaffectedness, and earnestness. People are quick to sense insincerity in speech and will distrust the speaker who appears to be insincere. No tricks of oratory can substitute for sincerity. In a recent survey college students chose sincerity as the most desirable attribute that a speaker could possess.

EXERCISES

1. The following lines are charged with emotion. Before attempting to read them, study the lines. Determine who it is that is speaking and why. Then, attempt to charge yourself with a feeling similar to that suggested by the passage and then speak. Go through this process with each short outburst.

      a. Oh, World, I cannot hold thee close enough!

      b. On with the dance! Let joy be unconfined!

      c. Each age is a dream that is dying, or one that is coming to birth.

      d. Ye blocks, ye stones, ye worse than senseless things!

      e. Methought I heard a voice cry, "Sleep no more! Macbeth doth murder sleep. . . . Macbeth shall sleep no more!"

[3] Theodore Clevenger, Jr., "A Synthesis of Experimental Research in Stage Fright," *Quarterly Journal of Speech*, 45 : 134–145. D. E. Watkins, and H. M. Karr, *Stage Fright and What to Do About It*, Expression Co., 1940.

f. Alone, alone, all, all, alone,
   Alone on a wide, wide sea!

g. It matters not how straight the gate,
       How charged with punishment the scroll,
   I am the master of my fate;
       I am the captain of my soul.

h. Great God! I'd rather be
   A pagan suckled in a creed outworn,
   So might I, standing on this pleasant lea,
   Have glimpses that would make me less forlorn.

i. Fool! All that is, at all,
   Lasts ever, past recall:
   Earth changes, but thy soul and God stand sure;
   What entered into thee,
   That was, is, and shall be:
   Time's wheel runs back or stops: Potter and clay endure.

j. Ne'er saw I, never felt, a calm so deep!
   The river glideth at his own sweet will;
   Dear God! the very houses seem asleep.

2. In the following poem you will find moods within a mood; that is, three distinct emotional states are incorporated within the dominant emotion. They are like the three acts of a drama. Find the changing moods and depict them in your voice.

THE THREE FISHERS

Three fishers went sailing out into the West,
Out into the West as the sun went down;
Each thought on the woman who loved him the best;
   And the children stood watching them out of the town;
For men must work, and women must weep,
And there's little to earn, and many to keep,
   Though the harbour bar be moaning.

Three wives sat up in the light-house tower,
   And they trimm'd the lamps as the sun went down;
They look'd at the squall, and they look'd at the shower,
   And the night rack came rolling up ragged and brown!
But men must work, and women must weep,
Though storms be sudden, and waters deep,
   And the harbour bar be moaning.

Three corpses lay out on the shining sands
  In the morning gleam as the tide went down,
And the women are weeping and wringing their hands
  For those who will never come back to the town;
For men must work, and women must weep,
And the sooner it's over, the sooner to sleep—
  And good-bye to the bar and its moaning.

—Charles Kingsley

3. Attempt to capture the emotional details of the following poem.

THE SEA
———————

The sea! the sea! the open sea!
The blue, the fresh, the ever free!
Without a mark, without a bound,
It runneth the earth's wide regions round;
It plays with the clouds; it mocks the skies;
Or like a cradled creature lies.

I'm on the sea! I'm on the sea!
I am where I would ever be;
With the blue above and the blue below,
And silence wheresoe'er I go;
If a storm should come and awake the deep,
What matter? I shall ride and sleep.

I love, O how I love to ride
On the fierce, foaming, bursting tide,
When every mad wave drowns the moon
Or whistles aloft his tempest tune,
And tells how goeth the world below,
And why the sou'west blasts do blow.

—Bryan Waller Proctor

4. Here are three poems pertaining to duty. Before undertaking to read them aloud, analyze them briefly. Wordsworth's and Browning's poems are entirely serious. The fact that the third poem treats the theme playfully should not blind us to the sublime truth of these poems. Approach them in the spirit that the authors intended.

From ODE TO DUTY

Stern Daughter of the Voice of God!
O Duty! if that name thou love
Who art a light to guide, a rod
To check the erring, and reprove;
Thou, who art victory and law
When empty terrors overawe,
From vain temptations dost set free,
And calm'st the weary strife of frail humanity!

. . . .

Stern Lawgiver! yet thou dost wear
The Godhead's most benignant grace;
Nor know we anything so fair
As is the smile upon thy face:
Flowers laugh before thee on their beds,
And fragrance in thy footing treads;
Thou dost preserve the stars from wrong;
And the most ancient heavens, through thee, are fresh and
strong.

To humbler functions, awful Power!
I call thee: I myself commend
Unto thy guidance from this hour;
O let my weakness have an end!
Give unto me, made lowly wise,
The spirit of self-sacrifice;
The confidence of reason give;
And in the light of Truth thy bondman let me live!

—William Wordsworth

DUTY

The sweetest lives are those to duty wed,
Whose deeds, both great and small,
Are close-knit strands of an unbroken thread,
Whose love ennobles all.
The world may sound no trumpet, ring no bells;
The book of life the shining record tells.
Thy love shall chant its own beatitudes,
After its own life-working. A child's kiss

Set on thy singing lips shall make thee glad;
A poor man served by thee shall make thee rich;
A sick man helped by thee shall make thee strong;
Thou shalt be served thyself by every sense
Of service thou renderest.

—Robert Browning

Ogden Nash is chiefly known as a writer of humorous verse. Several features of the following poem should be noted in preparation for its oral delivery:

Note the "coined" words, and show by your voice inflection that you recognize them for what they are: such words as, "abominously" and "forbiddinger." The deliberate misspellings for rhyming effect such as "Ortumn" for Autumn and the highly unique grammatical constructions have to be treated with a light and whimsical touch or they become absurd. The poem will be enriched for you, and for your listeners, if you appreciate the literary allusions in the piece. There are direct allusions to passages in Greek mythology, the Bible, Emerson, the short stories of the popular English writer, P. G. Wodehouse, and one of Coleridge's poems. See if you can locate them.

KIND OF AN ODE TO DUTY

O Duty,
Why hast thou not the visage of a sweetie or a cutie?

.   .   .   .

Why glitter thy spectacles so ominously?
Why art thou clad so abominously?
Why art thou so different from Venus?
And why do thou and I have so few interests mutually in
                          common between us?
Why art thou fifty percent martyr
And fifty-one percent Tartar?
Why is it thy unfortunate wont
To attract people by calling on them either to leave undone the
                          deeds they like, or to do the deeds they don't?
Why art thou so like an April post-mortem
Or something that died in the Ortumn?
Above all, why dost thou continue to hound me?
Why art thou always albatrossly hanging round me?
Thou so ubiquitous,
And I so iniquitous.

I seem to be the one person in the world thou art perpetually
preaching at who or to who;
Whatever looks like fun, there are thou standing between me
and it, calling yoo-hoo.
O Duty, Duty!
How noble a man should I be, hadst thou the visage of a
sweetie or cutie!

.   .   .   .

But as it is thou art so much forbiddinger than a Wodehouse
hero's forbiddingest aunt,
That in the words of the poet, When Duty whispers low, Thou
must, this erstwhile youth replies, I just can't.[4]

—Ogden Nash

5. Here is a group of selections which are rather pessimistic in tone,
followed in the next exercise by selections in a more optimistic vein. Study
the two groups together to get the contrast. In fairness to the authors, we
should say that some of these excerpts are taken out of context and do not
express the spirit of the poem or article as a whole. They do, however,
serve our purpose here.

We are not sure of sorrow,
And joy was never sure;
Today will die tomorrow;
Time stoops to no man's lure;
And love, grown faint and fretful,
With lips but half regretful
Sighs, and with eyes forgetful
Weeps that no loves endure.

—Algernon Charles Swinburne

This is the curse of life! that not
A nobler, calmer train
Of wiser thoughts and feelings blot
Our passions from our brain:

But each day brings its petty dust
Our soon-choked souls to fill,
And we forget because we must
And not because we will.

—Matthew Arnold

[4] From *I'm a Stranger Here Myself*, copyright 1938, by Ogden Nash; by permission of
Little, Brown & Co.

Come, fill the Cup, and in the fire of Spring
Your Winter-garment of Repentance fling:
The Bird of Time has but a little way
To flutter—and the Bird is on the Wing.

    .   .   .   .

O threats of Hell and Hopes of Paradise!
One thing at least is certain—*This* Life flies;
One thing is certain and the rest is Lies—
The Flower that once has blown for ever dies.

    .   .   .   .

And that inverted Bowl they call the sky,
Whereunder crawling cooped we live and die,
Lift not your hands to *It* for help—for It
As impotently moves as you or I.

                                   —Edward Fitzgerald

Oppress'd with grief, oppress'd with care,
A burden more than I can bear,
    I sit me down and sigh:
O lift! thou art a galling load,
Along a rough, a weary road,
    To wretches such as I!
Dim backward as I cast my view,
    What sick'ning scenes appear!
What sorrows yet may pierce me through
    Too justly I may fear!

                                   —Robert Burns

6. These selections are in a different vein from those in the preceding group. Study the two groups together.

A merry heart is a good medicine:
But a broken spirit drieth up the bones.

From AS YOU LIKE IT

It was a lover and his lass,
    With a hey, and a ho, and a hey nonino,
That o'er the green corn-field did pass
    In the spring time, the only pretty ring time,
    When birds do sing, hey ding a ding, ding;
Sweet lovers love the spring.

313

This carol they began that hour,
    With a hey, and a ho, and a hey nonino,
How that a life was but a flower
    In the spring time, the only pretty ring time,
    When birds do sing, hey ding a ding, ding;
Sweet lovers love the spring.

And therefore take the present time,
    With a hey, and a ho, and a hey nonino,
For love is crowned with the prime
    In the spring time, the only pretty ring time,
    When birds do sing, hey ding a ding, ding;
Sweet lovers love the spring.

                             —William Shakespeare

For, lo, the winter is past,
    The rain is over and gone;
The flowers appear on the earth;
    The time of the singing of birds is come,
And the voice of the turtle is heard in our land;
The fig tree putteth forth her green figs,
    And the vines with the tender grape
    Give a good smell.

                             —The Bible

Oh, the wild joys of living! the leaping from rock up to rock,
The strong rending of boughs from the fir-tree, the cool silver
                                 shock
Of the plunge in a pool's living water, the hunt of the bear,
And the sultriness showing the lion is couched in his lair.
And the meal, the rich dates yellowed over with gold dust
                               divine,
And the locust-flesh steeped in the pitcher, the full draft of wine,
And the sleep in the dried river-channel where bulrushes tell
That the water was wont to go warbling so softly and well.
How good is man's life, the mere living! How fit to employ
All the heart and the soul and the senses forever in joy!

                             —Robert Browning

Joy comes, grief goes, we know not how;
Everything is happy now,
    Everything is upward striving;
'Tis as easy now for the heart to be true
As for grass to be green or skies to be blue,—
    'Tis the natural way of living:

Who knows whither the clouds have fled?
    In the unscarred heaven they leave no wake;
And the eyes forget the tears they have shed,
    The heart forgets its sorrow and ache;
The soul partakes the season's youth,
    And the sulphurous rifts of passion and woe
Lie deep 'neath a silence pure and smooth,
    Like burnt-out craters healed with snow.

                        —James Russell Lowell

BARTER

Life has loveliness to sell,
All beautiful and splendid things,
Blue waves whitened on a cliff,
    Soaring fire that sways and sings,
And children's faces looking up
Holding wonder like a cup.
Life has loveliness to sell,
Music like a curve of gold,
Scent of pine trees in the rain,
    Eyes that love you, arms that fold,
And for your spirit's still delight,
Holy thoughts that star the night.
Spend all you have for loveliness,
Buy it and never count the cost;
For one white singing hour of peace
    Count many a year of strife well lost,
And for a breath of ecstasy
Give all you have been or could be.[5]

                          —Sara Teasdale

TO A SKYLARK

Hail to thee, blithe spirit!
    Bird thou never wert,
That from heaven, or near it,
    Pourest thy full heart
In profuse strains of unpremeditated art.

[5] From Sara Teasdale, *Collected Poems*, copyright 1937 by The Macmillan Company and used with their permission.

Higher still and higher
    From the earth thou springest
Like a cloud of fire;
    The blue deep thou wingest,
And singing still dost soar, and soaring ever singest.

In the golden light'ning
    Of the sunken sun,
O'er which clouds are bright'ning,
    Thou dost float and run;
Like an unbodied joy whose race is just begun.

The pale purple even
    Melts around thy flight;
Like a star of heaven,
    In the broad daylight
Thou art unseen,—but yet I hear thy shrill delight,
    . . . .

Better than all measures
    Of delightful sound—
Better than all treasures
    That in books are found—
Thy skill to poet were, thou scorner of the ground!

Teach me half the gladness
    That thy brain must know,
Such harmonious madness
    From my lips would flow,
The world would listen then—as I am listening now.

                    —Percy Bysshe Shelley

7. A sense of mystery is a mood. To interpret it vocally requires a sensitive understanding. Before you attempt to read the following poems aloud, be sure that you know the meaning of all the words and that you see the pictures.

From ULALUME
_____

The skies they were ashen and sober;
    The leaves they were crispèd and sere—
    The leaves they were withering and sere:
It was night in the lonesome October
    Of my most immemorial year;

It was hard by the dim lake of Auber,
    In the misty mid region of Weir—
It was down by the dank tarn of Auber,
    In the ghoul-haunted woodland of Weir.
       .   .   .   .

Then my heart it grew ashen and sober
    As the leaves that were crispèd and sere—
    As the leaves that were withering and sere;
And I cried: "It was surely October
    On *this* very night of last year
    That I journeyed—I journeyed down here!—
    That I brought a dread burden down here—
    On this night of all nights in the year,
    Ah, what demon has tempted me here?
Well I know, now, this dim lake of Auber—
    This misty mid region of Weir—
Well I know, now, this dank tarn of Auber,
    This ghoul-haunted woodland of Weir."

—Edgar Allan Poe

From THE FALL OF THE HOUSE OF USHER

From that chamber, and from that mansion, I fled aghast. The storm was still abroad in all its wrath as I found myself crossing the old causeway. Suddenly there shot along the path a wild light, and I turned to see whence a gleam so unusual could have issued; for the vast house and its shadows were alone behind me. The radiance was that of the full, setting, and blood-red moon, which now shone vividly through that once barely discernible fissure, of which I have before spoken as extending from the roof of the building, in a zig-zag direction, to the base. While I gazed, this fissure rapidly widened—there came a fierce breath of the whirlwind—the entire orb of the satellite burst at once upon my sight—my brain reeled as I saw the mighty walls rushing asunder—there was a long tumultuous shouting sound like the voice of a thousand waters—and the deep and dank tarn at my feet closed sullenly and silently over the fragments of the "*House of Usher.*"

—Edgar Allan Poe

8. The following selections are provided for the further study of emotion:

From HEDDA GABLER

LÖVBORG: Suppose now, Hedda, that a man—in the small hours of the morning—came home to his child's mother after a night of riot and debauchery, and said: "Listen—I have been here and there—in this place and in that. And I have taken our child with me—to this place and to that. And I have lost the child—utterly lost it. The devil knows into what hands it may have fallen—who may have had their clutches on it."

HEDDA: Well—but when all is said and done, you know—this was only a book—

LÖVBORG: Thea's pure soul was in that book.

HEDDA: Yes, so I understand.

LÖVBORG: And you can understand, too, that for her and me together no future is possible.

HEDDA: What path do you mean to take then?

LÖVBORG: None. I will only try to make an end of it all—the sooner the better.

HEDDA (*a step nearer him*): Eilert Lövborg—listen to me.— Will you not try to—to do it beautifully?

LÖVBORG: Beautifully? (*Smiling*). With vine-leaves in my hair, as you used to dream in the old days—?

HEDDA: No, no. I have lost my faith in the vine-leaves. But beautifully nevertheless! For once in a way!—Goodbye! You must go now—and do not come here any more.

LÖVBORG: Good-bye, Mrs. Tesman. And give George Tesman my love. (*He is on the point of going.*)

HEDDA: No, wait! I must give you a memento to take with you. (*She goes to the writing-table and opens the drawer and the pistol-case; then returns to* LÖVBORG *with one of the pistols.*)

LÖVBORG (*looks at her*): This? Is this the memento?

HEDDA (*nodding slowly*): Do you recognise it? It was aimed at you once.

LÖVBORG: You should have used it then.

HEDDA: Take it—and do you use it now.

LÖVBORG (*puts the pistol in his breast pocket*): Thanks!

HEDDA: And beautifully, Eilert Lövborg. Promise me that?

LÖVBORG: Good-bye, Hedda Gabler. (*He goes out by the hall door.*)

(HEDDA *listens for a moment at the door. Then she goes up to the writing-table, takes out the packet of manuscript, peeps under the cover, draws a few of the sheets half out, and looks at them. Next she goes over and seats herself in the arm-chair beside the stove, with the packet in her lap. Presently she opens the stove door, and then the packet.*)

HEDDA (*throws one of the quires into the fire and whispers to herself*): Now I am burning your child, Thea!—Burning it, curly-locks! (*Throwing one or two more quires into the stove.*) Your child and Eilert Lövborg's. (*Throws the rest in.*) I am burning—I am burning your child.

—Henrik Ibsen

From THE TELL-TALE HEART

. . . They sat, and while I answered cheerily, they chatted familiar things. But, ere long, I felt myself getting pale and wished them gone. My head ached, and I fancied a ringing in my ears: but still they sat and still chatted. The ringing became more distinct:—it continued and became more distinct: I talked more freely to get rid of the feeling: but it continued and gained definitiveness—until, at length, I found that the noise was *not* within my ears.

No doubt I now grew *very* pale;—but I talked more fluently, and with a heightened voice. Yet the sound increased—and what could I do? It was *a low dull, quick sound—much such a sound as a watch makes when enveloped in cotton*. I gasped for breath—and yet the officers heard it not. I talked more quickly—more vehemently; but the noise steadily increased. I arose and argued about trifles, in a high key and with violent gesticulations, but the noise steadily increased. Why *would* they not be gone? I paced the floor to and fro with heavy strides, as if excited to fury by the observation of the men—but the noise steadily increased. Oh God! what *could* I do? I foamed—I raved—I swore! I swung the chair upon which I had been sitting, and grated it upon the boards, but the noise arose over all and continually increased. It grew louder—louder—*louder*! And still the men chatted pleasantly, and smiled. Was it possible they heard not? Almighty God!—no, no! They heard!—they suspected!—they *knew*!—they were making a mockery of my horror!—this I thought, and this I think. But any thing was better than this agony! Any thing was more tolerable than this derision. I could bear those hypocritical smiles no longer! I felt that I must scream or die!—and now—again!—hark! louder! louder! louder! *louder*!—

"Villains!" I shrieked, "dissemble no more! I admit the deed!—tear up the planks!—here, here!—it is the beating of his hideous heart!"

—Edgar Allan Poe

I HAVE A DREAM

Five score years ago, a great American, in whose symbolic shadow we stand, signed the Emancipation Proclamation. This momentous decree came as a great beacon light of hope to millions of Negro slaves who had been seared in the flames of withering injustice. It came as a joyous daybreak to end the long night of captivity.

But one hundred years later, we must face the tragic fact that the Negro is still not free. One hundred years later, the life of the Negro is still sadly crippled by the manacles of segregation and the chains of discrimination. One hundred years later, the Negro lives on a lonely island of poverty in the midst of a vast ocean of material prosperity. One hundred years later, the Negro is still languished in the corners of American society and finds himself an exile in his own land. So we have come here today to dramatize an appalling condition.

In a sense we have come to our nation's Capital to cash a check. When the architects of our republic wrote the magnificent words of the Constitution and the Declaration of Independence, they were signing a promissory note to which every American was to fall heir. This note was a promise that all men would be guaranteed the inalienable rights of life, liberty, and the pursuit of happiness.

It is obvious today that America has defaulted on this promissory note insofar as her citizens of color are concerned. Instead of honoring this sacred obligation, America has given the Negro people a bad check; a check which has come back marked "insufficient funds." But we refuse to believe that the bank of justice is bankrupt. We refuse to believe that there are insufficient funds in the great vaults of opportunity of this nation, So we have come to cash this check—a check that will give us upon demand the riches of freedom and the security of justice. We have also come to this hallowed spot to remind America of the fierce urgency of *now*. This is no time to engage in the luxury of cooling off or to take the tranquilizing drug of gradualism. *Now* is the time to make real the promises of Democracy. *Now* is the time to rise from the dark and desolate valley of segregation to the sunlit path of racial justice. *Now* is the time to open the doors of opportunity to all of God's children. *Now* is the time to lift our nation from the quicksands of racial injustice to the solid rock of brotherhood.

It would be fatal for the nation to overlook the urgency of the moment and to underestimate the determination of the Negro. This sweltering summer of the Negro's legitimate discontent will not pass until there is an invigorating autumn of freedom and equality. 1963 is not an end, but a beginning. Those who hope that the Negro needed to blow off steam and will now be content will have a rude awakening if the nation returns to business as usual. There will be neither rest nor tranquillity in America until the Negro is granted his citizenship rights. The whirlwinds of revolt will continue to shake the foundations of our nation until the bright day of justice emerges.

But there is something that I must say to my people who stand on the warm threshold which leads into the palace of justice. In the process of gaining our rightful place we must not be guilty of wrongful deeds. Let us not seek to satisfy our thirst for freedom by drinking from the cup of bitterness and hatred. We must forever conduct our struggle on the high plane of dignity and discipline. We must not allow our creative protest to degenerate into physical violence. Again and again we must rise to the majestic heights of meeting physical force with soul force. The marvelous new militancy which has engulfed the Negro community must not lead us to a distrust of all white people, for many of our white brothers, as evidenced by their presence here today, have come to realize that their destiny is tied up with our destiny, and their freedom is inextricably bound to our freedom. We cannot walk alone.

And as we walk, we must make the pledge that we shall march ahead. We cannot turn back. There are those who are asking the devotees of civil rights, "When will you be satisfied?" We can never be satisfied as long as the Negro is the victim of the unspeakable horrors of police brutality. We can never be satisfied as long as our bodies, heavy with the fatigue of travel, cannot gain lodging in the motels of the highways and the hotels of the cities. We cannot be satisfied as long as the Negro's basic mobility is from a smaller ghetto to a larger one. We can never be satisfied as long as a Negro in Mississippi cannot vote and a Negro in New York believes he has nothing for which to vote. No, no, we are not satisfied, and we will not be satisfied until justice rolls down like waters and righteousness like a mighty stream.

321

I am not unmindful that some of you have come here out of great trials and tribulations. Some of you have come fresh from narrow jail cells. Some of you have come from areas where your quest for freedom left you battered by the storms of persecution and staggered by the winds of police brutality. You have been the veterans of creative suffering. Continue to work with the faith that unearned suffering is redemptive.

Go back to Mississippi, go back to Alabama, go back to South Carolina, go back to Georgia, go back to Louisiana, go back to the slums and ghettos of our northern cities, knowing that somehow this situation can and will be changed. Let us not wallow in the valley of despair.

I say to you today, my friends, that in spite of the difficulties and frustrations of the moment I still have a dream. It is a dream deeply rooted in the American dream.

I have a dream that one day this nation will rise up and live out the true meaning of its creed: "We hold these truths to be self-evident; that all men are created equal."

I have a dream that one day on the red hills of Georgia the sons of former slaves and the sons of former slaveowners will be able to sit down together at the table of brotherhood.

I have a dream that one day even the state of Mississippi, a desert state sweltering with the heat of injustice and oppression, will be transformed into an oasis of freedom and justice.

I have a dream that my four little children will one day live in a nation where they will not be judged by the color of their skin but by the content of their character.

I have a dream today.

I have a dream that one day the state of Alabama, whose governor's lips are presently dripping with the words of interposition and nullification, will be transformed into a situation where little black boys and black girls will be able to join hands with little white boys and white girls and walk together as sisters and brothers.

I have a dream today.

I have a dream that one day every valley shall be exalted, every hill and mountain shall be made low, the rough places will be made plains, and the crooked places will be made straight, and the glory of the Lord shall be revealed, and all flesh shall see it together.

This is our hope. This is the faith with which I return to the South. With this faith we will be able to hew out of the mountain of despair a stone of hope. With this faith we will be able to transform the jangling discords of our nation into a beautiful symphony of brotherhood. With this faith we will be able to work together, to pray together, to struggle together, to go to jail together, to stand up for freedom together, knowing that we will be free one day.

This will be the day when all of God's children will be able to sing with new meaning

> My country, 'tis of thee,
> Sweet land of liberty,
>   Of thee I sing:
> Land where my fathers died,
> Land of the pilgrims' pride,
> From every mountain-side
>   Let freedom ring.

And if America is to be a great nation this must become true. So let freedom ring from the prodigious hilltops of New Hampshire. Let freedom ring from the mighty mountains of New York. Let freedom ring from the heightening Alleghenies of Pennsylvania!

Let freedom ring from the snowcapped Rockies of Colorado!

Let freedom ring from the curvacious peaks of California!

But not only that; let freedom ring from Stone Mountain of Georgia!

Let freedom ring from Lookout Mountain of Tennessee!

Let freedom ring from every hill and molehill of Mississippi. From every mountainside, let freedom ring.

When we let freedom ring, when we let it ring from every village and every hamlet, from every state and every city, we will be able to speed up that day when all of God's children, black men and white men, Jews and Gentiles, Protestants and Catholics, will be able to join hands and sing in the words of the old Negro spiritual, "Free at last! free at last! thank God almighty, we are free at last!"[6]

—Martin Luther King, Jr.

THE USE OF PHYSICAL ACTIVITY

There are several factors related to physical activity that can contribute to greater vocal expressiveness. These are: (a) the use of empathy, (b) the release from physical inhibition, and (c) the use of gestures.

[6] Reprinted by permission of Joan Daves, Copyright ©, 1963, by Martin Luther King, Jr.

THE USE OF EMPATHY

Empathy may be defined as "mentally entering into the feeling or spirit of a person or thing; appreciative perception; motor mimicry." In entering into the feelings of another person, we often take on some of the tension of that person. For example, imagine that you are at a football game and your team is making a goal-line stand at a critical stage in the contest. As your team musters all the determination and muscle it can to meet the situation, you likewise develop muscular tensions to physically throw back the attack. When the attack comes, you literally push the oncoming ballcarrier back in sympathy with your team. The muscles of your arms, legs, and torso are literally involved in a reduced version of the action on the field.

In interpreting prose and poetry of various authors you may be able to put the principle of empathy to good use. The example above is an extreme form of bodily activity, but there are many opportunities to "become one" with the character you are interpreting by assuming, to a degree, some of the body states that are appropriate to the author's creation. In the banquet scene in *Macbeth* the vision of a bloody dagger appears before Macbeth and fills his soul with terror. Attempt to experience some of the bodily tension that must have been created by the vision as you read the lines:

> Is this a dagger which I see before me,
> The handle toward my hand? Come, let me clutch thee.
> I have thee not, and yet I see thee still.

In the exercises that complete this section of physical activity, attempt to make good use of bodily activity in interpreting the selections.

THE RELEASE FROM PHYSICAL RESTRAINT

Our society is paradoxial in that it expects males to be aggressive men of action on the one hand but demands restraint, order, and obedience on the other. The observation has been made that man is an animal in motion, that he thrives on activity. Yet early in life he is told to sit still, stop wiggling, stop getting into closets, etc. Man is disciplined for showing the same aggressive forms of behavior early in life that are rewarded at maturity, when he is expected to drive hard and persevere in order to succeed in a highly competitive society.

The many restraints placed upon us as children undoubtedly have contributed to the inhibitory forms of behavior we display as adults. Inhibition usually means curtailment, and in vocal expression it is manifested in lifelessness of performance. One method of combating physical restriction due to inhibition or stage fright is to engage in physical activity in performing. Suggestions for developing increased bodily action are included at the conclusion of this section.

THE USE OF GESTURE

Gesture in the sense intended here means any movement of the body, head, arms, hands, or face expressive of an idea or emotion. Gestures are the externalized manifestations of internal processes and should be entirely natural in origin and execution. One must avoid superficial or mechanical use of gesture.

Gestures are sometimes used to communicate in and of themselves. For example, the extended arm and hand, palm up, mean acceptance or "you may come closer," while the overturned, upheld hand and arm mean, "halt, do not come closer.' Many other common gestures are directly related to action, e.g., pointing, beckoning, etc.

The use of gesture is one way of releasing physical inhibition, which we described previously. If one habitually does not use gestures but feels physically restricted, he might attempt a few basic gestures, judiciously done, in his next performance.

The use of gesture in conversation and in public speaking is natural and is to be encouraged, with one precaution—that it is not overdone. However, in reading, particularly in formal oral interpretation, the use of gesture must be more circumspect and appropriate to the situation of reading. In oral interpretation the performer is not acting, and therefore full gestures and movements are inappropriate. However, facial expressions and small movements based upon inner thoughts and feelings are entirely appropriate.

There are two additional precautions that all speakers should observe with regard to gesture : (a) gestures should not be artificial in any way, and (b) gestures must be congruous with the spoken word.

The actor must be facile in his use of gesture, particularly since he must portray a wide range of people in the roles he assumes. A careful study of the use of gesture by people of all ages and descriptions should prove rewarding to the professional actor. Before attempting physical action in the reading of selected passages, try the following exercises :

EXERCISES

1. Say the following lines with appropriate movements :
    a. Hold up your arms and hands, palms up, and say, "Stop."
    b. Extend both arms out, palms up, and say, "But I don't have any more."
    c. Hold your hand out, palm up, and say, "Give me all the pennies you have—right now."
    d. Beckon with your arms and hands (and torso) and say, "I want all of you, every one, right over here. Hurry up."
    e. Use your hands and arms as you say, "But I'll never get over it, never."
2. Do examples (a) through (e) as though you were very angry.

325

3. Use your hands, arms, face, head, and torso to say the following lines. Be versatile in varying your gestures.

  a. It's in that direction.

  b. It's way, way over there.

  c. It's under the box.

  d. It's on the chair, over there.

  e. It's on the top shelf in the back room.

4. Use appropriate descriptive gestures to suit the following lines:

  a. The rock fell from that cliff up there all the way down to the path over there.

  b. Oh, it was a great big, soft, fluffy pillow with a little embroidery on it.

  c. First, you take the thread, then you roll it between your thumb and forefinger, like this; then, carefully put it through the eye of the needle, like this.

  d. I want to emphasize this point: *Never back away.*

  e. Oh, it's so sour I can't stand it.

  f. I want to welcome everyone here with open arms.

  g. I got so mad I could have punched him in the nose.

  h. I said, "open your books"; don't you understand?

5. Pantomime can be very useful in developing greater bodily expressiveness.

  a. Pretend you are putting on a sweater.

  b. Pretend you are washing your hands and face with warm water and drying them with a hand towel.

  c. Pretend you are going to the garage to get tools. Open the door; pick up the hoe, the shovel, and the hedge clippers; drop the hoe and pick it up again; set the tools down outside the door and close the garage door; pick up the tools and leave.

6. Give yourself over to the following passages with abandon. Replace repression with freedom. Let your imagination have full sway.

  a. Imagine you are Macbeth:

  Lay on, MacDuff, and damn'd be him who first cries, " Hold, enough ! "

  b. Imagine you are Othello:

  Now, by heaven,
  My blood begins my safer guides to rule.

  c. Imagine you are Marmion defying Douglas:

  And 'twere not for thy hoary beard,
  Such hand as Marmion's had not spared
  To cleave the Douglas head !

d. Imagine you are Lorenzo:

   Sit, Jessica. Look how the floor of heaven
   Is thick inlaid with patines of bright gold.

e. Imagine you are Spartacus trying to foment an uprising among the gladiators:

   If ye be beasts, then stand there like fat oxen, waiting for the butcher's knife.

f. Imagine you are Mark Antony striving to quiet the restless throng:

   "Friends!"
   (You get very little response; the crowd keeps milling around. You try again.)
   "Romans!"
   (A few of the excited crowd listen, but the confusion is still great. You make your strongest appeal, with vigor and power.)
   "Countrymen!"
   (You have their attention now, and you continue.)
   "Lend me your ears!"

g. Imagine you are Warren trying to hearten your soldiers at Bunker Hill:

   Stand! The ground's your own, my braves!
   Will ye give it up to slaves?

h. Imagine yourself Patrick Henry before the Virginia House of Burgesses:

   I know not what course others may take, but as for me, give me liberty or give me death!

i. Imagine you are Lord Chatham before the English House of Lords during the American Revolution:

   If I were an American, as I am an Englishman, while a foreign troop were landed in my country, I would never lay down my arms, never, *never*, NEVER!

7. Here is a good selection to induce physical release. Feel the courage and vitality of the old adventurer, Ulysses. Although old, he keeps thinking back to his earlier exploits (remember the one-eyed Cyclops, Circe, Scylla and Charybdis!) and he longs for one more adventure. He calls his old comrades around him and says:

> There lies the port; the vessel puffs her sail:
> There gloom the dark, broad seas. My mariners,
> Souls that have toil'd, and wrought, and thought, with me—
> That ever with a frolic welcome took
> The thunder and the sunshine, and opposed
> Free hearts, free foreheads—you and I are old;
> Old age hath yet his honor and his toil;
> Death closes all: but something ere the end,
> Some work of noble note, may yet be done,
> Not unbecoming men that strove with gods.
> The lights begin to twinkle from the rocks:
> The long day wanes: the slow moon climbs: the deep
> Moans round with many voices. Come, my friends,
> 'Tis not too late to seek a newer world.
> Push off, and sitting well in order smite
> The sounding furrows; for my purpose holds
> To sail beyond the sunset, and the baths
> Of all the western stars, until I die.
> It may be that the gulfs will wash us down:
> It may be we shall touch the Happy Isles,
> And see the great Achilles, whom we knew.
> Though much is taken, much abides; and though
> We are not now that strength which in old days
> Moved earth and heaven, that which we are, we are—
> One equal temper of heroic hearts,
> Made weak by time and fate, but strong in will
> To strive, to seek, to find, and not to yield.

—Alfred, Lord Tennyson

8. Below is part of a speech which should stir your emotions and heighten bodily activity. In 1837, when pro- and anti-slavery feeling was approaching the climax which resulted in the Civil War, an event occurred which brought the brilliant orator, Wendell Phillips, into the public eye. Twenty-six years old and recently graduated from Harvard Law School, Phillips attended a public indignation meeting in Faneuil Hall that was called to denounce a pro-slavery mob which had destroyed the printing press of an abolitionist editor, Elijah P. Lovejoy, in Alton, Illinois. Feeling was especially strong

because in attempting to defend his press Lovejoy had lost his life. One speaker, Attorney General Austin, opposed the resolution about to be passed ; he accused Lovejoy of being a troublemaker and said that he "died as the fool dieth." He also compared the mob to the Boston citizens who destroyed the British tea at the Boston Tea Party. Phillips sprang to the platform :

> Mr. Chairman . . . I hope I shall be permitted to express my surprise at the sentiments of the last speaker, surprise not only at such sentiments from such a man, but at the applause they have received within these walls. A comparison has been drawn between the events of the Revolution and the tragedy at Alton . . . and we have heard the mob at Alton, the drunken murderers of Lovejoy, compared to those patriot fathers who threw the tea overboard. . . .

> Sir, when I heard the gentleman lay down the principles which place the murderers of Alton side by side with Otis and Hancock, with Quincy and Adams (*pointing to their pictures on the wall*), I thought those pictured lips would have broken into voice to rebuke the recreant American, the slanderer of the dead.
>
> The gentleman says Lovejoy was presumptuous and imprudent, he "died as the fool dieth." . . . Imprudent to defend the liberty of the press ! Why ? Because the defense was unsuccessful ? Does success gild crime into patriotism, and the want of it change heroic self-devotion into imprudence ? Was Hampden imprudent when he drew the sword and threw away the scabbard ? Yet he, judged by that single hour, was unsuccessful. After a short exile the race he hated sat again upon the throne.
>
> Imagine yourself present when the first news of Bunker Hill battle reached a New England town. The tale would have run thus : "The patriots are routed, the redcoats victorious, Warren lies dead upon the field." With what scorn would that Tory have been received who should have charged Warren with imprudence, who should have said that bred as a physician, he was "out of place" in the battle, and "died as a fool dieth." . . .
>
> Presumptuous to assert the freedom of the press upon American ground ? . . . Who invents this libel on his country ? It is the very thing which entitles Lovejoy to greater praise. The disputed right which provoked the Revolution—taxation without representation—is far beneath that for which he died. As

much as thought is better than money, so much is the cause in which Lovejoy died nobler than a mere question of taxes. James Otis thundered in this hall when the king did but touch his pocket. Imagine if you can his indignant eloquence had England offered to put a gag upon his lips.

9. Following are parts of two speeches by American Indians. Catch the spirit of strength and simple dignity which pervades their words.

Friends and Brothers:—You say that you are sent to instruct us how to worship the Great Spirit agreeably to His mind; and, if we do not take hold of the religion which you white people teach, we shall be unhappy hereafter. You say that you are right and we are lost. How do we know this to be true? We understand that your religion is written in a Book. If it was intended for us, as well as you, why has not the Great Spirit given to us, and not only to us, but why did not the Great Spirit give to our forefathers the knowledge of that Book, with the means of understanding it rightly? We only know what you tell us about it. How shall we know when to believe, being so often deceived by the white people?

Brother, you say that there is but one way to worship and serve the Great Spirit. If there is but one religion, why do you white people differ so much about it? Why not all agreed, as you can all read the Book?

Brother, we do not understand these things. We are told that your religion was given to your forefathers and has been handed down from father to son. We also have a religion which was given to our forefathers and has been handed down to us, their children. We worship in that way. It teaches us to be thankful for all the favors we receive, to love each other, and to be united. We never quarrel about religion.

Brother, the Great Spirit had made us all, but He has made a great difference between His white and His red children. He has given us different complexions and different customs.... Since He has made so great a difference between us in other things, why may we not conclude that He has given us a different religion according to our understanding? The Great Spirit does right. He knows what is best for his children; we are satisfied.

Brother, we do not wish to destroy your religion or take it from you. We only want to enjoy our own....

Brother, we are told that you have been preaching to the white people in this place. These people are our neighbors. We are acquainted with them. We will wait a little while and see what effect your preaching has upon them. If we find it does them good, makes them honest, and less disposed to cheat Indians, we will then consider again of what you have said.

—Red Jacket

You have taken me prisoner, with all my warriors. I am much grieved ; for I expected, if I did not defeat you, to hold out much longer, and give you more trouble, before I surrendered. I tried hard to bring you into ambush, but your last general understood Indian fighting. I determined to rush on you, and fight you face to face. I fought hard. But your guns were well aimed. The bullets flew like birds in the air, and whizzed by our ears like the wind through the trees in winter. My warriors fell around me ; it began to look dismal.

I saw my evil day at hand. The sun rose dim on us in the morning, and at night it sank in a dark cloud, and looked like a ball of fire. That was the last sun that shone on Black Hawk. His heart is dead, and no longer beats quick in his bosom. He is now a prisoner of the white men ; they will do with him as they wish. But he can stand torture, and is not afraid of death. He is no coward. Black Hawk is an Indian. He has done nothing for which an Indian ought to be ashamed. He has fought for his countrymen, against white men, who came, year after year, to cheat them and take away their lands. . . .

The spirits of our fathers arose, and spoke to us to avenge our wrongs or die. We set up the war-whoop, and dug up the toma-hawk ; our knives were ready and the heart of Black Hawk swelled high in his bosom, when he led his warriors to battle. He is satisfied. He will go to the world of spirits contented. He has done his duty. His father will meet him there and commend him.

Black Hawk is a true Indian, and disdains to cry like a woman. He feels for his wife, his children, and his friends. But he does not care for himself. He cares for the Nation and the Indians. They will suffer. He laments their fate. Farewell, my Nation ! Black Hawk tried to save you, and avenge your wrongs. He drank the blood of some of the whites. He has been taken prisoner, and his plans are crushed. He can do no more. He is near his end. His sun is setting and he will rise no more. Farewell to Black Hawk.

—Black Hawk

10. The following scene may be read by a young man and a young woman or by a single individual reading both parts.

If one person takes both parts, a certain principle of voice control should be kept in mind : A boy should not attempt to imitate a woman's voice by forcing his pitch up into the falsetto range, nor should a girl imitate a man by pushing her voice down into an unnatural guttural. There should be no imitation at all. If the boy simply lightens his voice a little, i.e., uses a little less volume and a slightly higher pitch, in its natural quality, he is likely to get the desired contrast. And if the girl relaxes her throat and lets her natural voice sink a little lower in pitch, she too is likely to get the contrast she desires. At any rate, there must be no imitation of someone else's tone; that kind of training is injurious to the student's voice, and it sounds artifical to the audience. Bodily activity should be different for the two parts.

From MACBETH

MACBETH: I have done the deed. Didst thou not hear a noise?
LADY M: I heard the owl scream and the crickets cry.
    Did not you speak?
MACBETH: When?
LADY M: Now.
MACBETH: As I descended?
LADY M: Ay.
MACBETH: Hark!
    Who lies i' the second chamber?
LADY M: Donalbain.
MACBETH (*Looking on his hands*): This is a sorry sight.
LADY M: A foolish thought to say a sorry sight.
MACBETH: There's one did laugh in 's sleep, and one cried
                "Murder!"
    That they did wake each other: I stood and heard them:
    But they did say their prayers, and address'd them
    Again to sleep.
LADY M: There are two lodg'd together.
MACBETH: One cried "God bless us!" and "Amen" the other,
    As they had seen me with these hangman's hands.
    Listening their fear, I could not say "Amen,"
    When they did say "God bless us!"
LADY M: Consider it not so deeply.
MACBETH: But wherefore could not I pronounce "Amen?"
    I had most need of blessing, and "Amen"
    Stuck in my throat.
LADY M: These deeds must not be thought
    After these ways; so, it will make us mad.
MACBETH: Methought I heard a voice cry "Sleep no more!
    Macbeth does murder sleep"—the innocent sleep,

Sleep that knits up the ravell'd sleave of care,
The death of each day's life, sore labour's bath,
Balm of hurt minds, great nature's second course,
Chief nourisher in life's feast,—

LADY M: What do you mean?

MACBETH: Still it cried "Sleep no more!" to all the house:
"Glamis hath murder'd sleep, and therefore Cawdor
Shall sleep no more; Macbeth shall sleep no more."

LADY M: Who was it that thus cried? Why, worthy thane,
You do unbend your noble strength, to think
So brainsickly of things. Go get some water,
And wash this filthy witness from your hand.
Why did you bring these daggers from the place?
They must lie there; go carry them, and smear
The sleepy grooms with blood.

MACBETH: I'll go no more.
I am afraid to think what I have done;
Look on't again I dare not.

LADY M: Infirm of purpose!
Give me the daggers. The sleeping and the dead
Are but as pictures; 'tis the eye of childhood
That fears a painted devil. If he do bleed,
I'll gild the faces of the grooms withal,
For it must seem their guilt.

(Exit Knocking within.)

MACBETH: Whence is that knocking?
How is't with me, when every noise appals me?
What hands are here? Ha! they pluck out mine eyes.
Will all great Neptune's ocean wash this blood
Clean from my hand? No, this my hand will rather
The multitudinous seas incarnadine,
Making the green one red.

(Enter LADY MACBETH.)

LADY M: My hands are of your color; but I shame
To wear a heart so white. (Knocking within.) I hear a
knocking
At the south entry: retire we to our chamber.
A little water clears us of this deed:
How easy is it, then! Your constancy
Hath left you unattended. Hark! more knocking.
Get on your nightgown, lest occasion call us,
And show us to be watchers. Be not lost
So poorly in your thoughts.

MACBETH : To know my deed, 'twere best not know myself.
(*Knocking within.*)
Wake Duncan with thy knocking ! I would thou couldst !

—William Shakespeare

11. Further selections follow :

From LOCHINVAR

So boldly he entered the Netherby Hall,
Among bride's-men, and kinsmen, and brothers, and all :
Then spoke the bride's father, his hand on his sword
(For the poor craven bridegroom said never a word),
" O come ye in peace here, or come ye in war,
Or to dance at our bridal, young Lord Lochinvar ? "—

" I long wooed your daughter, my suit you denied ;—
Love swells like the Solway, but ebbs like its tide !
And now am I come, with this lost love of mine,
To lead but one measure, drink one cup of wine ;
There are maidens in Scotland more lovely by far,
That would gladly be bride to the young Lochinvar."

The bride kissed the goblet : the knight took it up.
He quaffed off the wine, and he threw down the cup.
She looked down to blush, and she looked up to sigh,
With a smile on her lips, and a tear in her eye.
He took her soft hand, ere her mother could bar,—
" Now tread we a measure ! " said young Lochinvar.

. . . .

One touch to her hand, and one word in her ear,
When they reached the hall door, and the charger stood near ;
So light to the croupe the fair lady he swung !
So light to the saddle before her he sprung !
" She is won ! we are gone, over bank, bush and scaur :
They'll have fleet steeds that follow," quoth young Lochinvar.
There was mounting 'mong Graemes of the Netherby clan :
Forsters, Fenwicks, and Musgraves, they rode and they ran ;
There was racing and chasing on Canobie Lee,
But the lost bride of Netherby ne'er did they see.

—Sir Walter Scott

MACBETH : Is this a dagger which I see before me,
The handle toward my hand ? Come, let me clutch thee.
I have thee not, and yet I see thee still.
Art thou not, fatal vision, sensible
To feeling as to sight ? Or art thou but
A dagger of the mind, a false creation,
Proceeding from the heat-oppressed brain ?
I see thee yet, in form as palpable
As this which now I draw.
Thou marshall'st me the way that I was going ;
And such an instrument I was to use.
Mine eyes are made the fools o' the other senses,
Or else worth all the rest. I see thee still ;
And on thy blade and dudgeon gouts of blood,
Which was not so before. There's no such thing ;
It is the bloody business which informs
Thus to mine eyes. . . .

       —William Shakespeare

The whole fury and might of the enemy must very soon be
turned on us. Hitler knows that he will have to break us in this
Island or lose the war. If we can stand up to him all Europe may
be free, and the life of the world may move forward into broad,
sunlit uplands. But if we fail, then the whole world, including
the United States, and all that we have known and cared for,
will sink into the abyss of a new Dark Age made more sinister,
and perhaps more prolonged, by the lights of a perverted
science.

 Let us therefore brace ourselves to our duty and so bear
ourselves that, if the British Commonwealth and Empire last
for a thousand years, men will still say, " This was their finest
hour."

       —Winston Churchill

Deep sleep had fallen on the destined victim, and on all beneath his roof. A healthful old man to whom sleep was sweet,
the first sound slumbers of the night held him in their soft
but strong embrace. The assassin enters, through the window,
already prepared, into an unoccupied apartment. With noiseless
foot he paces the lonely hall, half lighted by the moon. He winds
up the ascent of the stairs and reaches the door of the chamber.
Of this he moves the lock, by soft and continued pressure, till
it turns on its hinges without noise, and he enters, and beholds
his victim before him. The room is uncommonly open to the

admission of light. The face of the innocent sleeper is turned from the murderer, and the beams of the moon, resting on the grey locks of his aged temple, show him where to strike. The fatal blow is given and the victim passes without a struggle or a motion, from the repose of sleep to the repose of death! It is the assassin's purpose to make sure work; and he plies the dagger, though it is obvious that life has been destroyed by the blow of the bludgeon. He even raises the aged arm, that he may not fail in his aim at the heart, and replaces it again over the wounds of the poniard. To finish the picture, he explores the wrist for the pulse! He feels for it and ascertains that it beats no longer! It is accomplished. The deed is done. He retreats, retraces his steps to the window; passes out through it as he came in and escapes. The secret is his own and it is safe! Ah, gentlemen, that was a dreadful mistake.

—Daniel Webster

SPECIAL MESSAGE TO THE CONGRESS ON EDUCATION
January 29, 1963

To the Congress of the United States:

Education is the keystone in the arch of freedom and progress. Nothing has contributed more to the enlargement of this nation's strength and opportunities than our traditional system of free, universal elementary and secondary education, coupled with widespread availability of college education.

For the individual, the doors to the school-house, to the library and to the college lead to the richest treasures of our open society: to the power of knowledge—to the training and skills necessary for productive employment—to the wisdom, the ideals, and the culture which enrich life—and to the creative, self-disciplined understanding of society needed for good citizenship in today's changing and challenging world.

For the nation, increasing the quality and availability of education is vital to both our national security and our domestic well-being. A free Nation can rise no higher than the standard of excellence set in its schools and colleges. Ignorance and illiteracy, unskilled workers and school dropouts—these and other failures of our educational system breed failures in our social and economic system: delinquency, unemployment, chronic dependence, a waste of human resources, a loss of productive power and purchasing power and an increase in tax-supported

336

benefits. The loss of only one year's income due to unemployment is more than the total cost of twelve years of education through high school. Failure to improve educational performance is thus not only poor social policy, it is poor economics.

This nation is committed to greater investment in economic growth; and recent research has shown that one of the most beneficial of all such investments is education, accounting for some 40 percent of the nation's growth and productivity in recent years. It is an investment which yields a substantial return in the higher wages and purchasing power of trained workers, in the new products and techniques which come from skilled minds and in the constant expansion of this nation's storehouse of useful knowledge.

In the new age of science and space, improved education is essential to give new meaning to our national purpose and power. In the last 20 years, mankind has acquired more scientific information than in all of previous history. Ninety percent of all the scientists that ever lived are alive and working today. Vast stretches of the unknown are being explored every day for military, medical, commercial, and other reasons. And finally, the twisting course of the cold war requires a citizenry that understands our principles and problems. It requires skilled manpower and brainpower to match the power of totalitarian discipline. It requires a scientific effort which demonstrates the superiority of freedom. And it requires an electorate in every state with sufficiently broad horizons and sufficient maturity of judgement to guide this nation safely through whatever lies ahead.

—John F. Kennedy

SUPPLEMENTARY SELECTIONS FOR CLASS PRESENTATION

MEANING

Acquainted with the Night, Robert Frost, *poetry*.
Ash Wednesday, T. S. Eliot, *poetry*.
I Heard a Fly Buzz When I Died, Emily Dickinson, *poetry*.
Saul, Robert Browning, *poetry*.
We Wear the Mask, Laurence Dunbar, *poetry*.

IMAGERY

Flight, John Steinbeck, *prose*.
The Jungle Book, Rudyard Kipling, *prose*.
Maude Martha, Gwendolyn Brooks, *poetry*.
Renascence and other poetry of Edna St. Vincent Millay.
Treasure Island, Robert Louis Stevenson, *prose*.

337

EMOTION

Dirge, Kenneth Fearing, *poetry.*
Fiddler Jones, Edgar Lee Masters, *poetry.*
The Primitive, Don L. Lee, *poetry.*
Sonnett III, Conrad Aiken, *poetry.*
Tract, William Carlos Williams, *poetry.*

PHYSICAL ACTIVITY

King Henry V's speech, " Once more into the breach, dear
friends, . . . "
King Henry V William Shakespeare, *prose.*

338

bibliography

Anderson, V. A. (1961) *Training the Speaking Voice*. New York: Oxford University Press.

Bronstein, A. J., and Jacoby, F. (1967) *Your Speech and Voice*. New York: Random House.

Fairbanks, G. (1960) *Voice and Articulation Drillbook*, 2nd Edition. New York: Harper & Row.

Fisher, H. B. (1966) *Improving Voice and Articulation*. Boston: Houghton Mifflin.

Fletcher, H. (1953) *Speech Communication in Hearing*, 2nd Edition. New York: Van Nostrand Reinhold.

Gagne, R. M. (1965) *The Conditions of Learning*. New York: Holt, Rinehart & Winston.

Gray, G. W., and Wise, C. M. (1959) *The Bases of Speech*, 3rd Edition. New York: Harper & Row.

Greene, M. C. L. (1964) *The Voice and Its Disorders*, 2nd Edition. Philadelphia: Lippincott.

Jacobson, E. (1934) *You Must Relax*. New York: McGraw-Hill.

Jacobson, E. (1938) *Progressive Relaxation*, Rev. Ed. Chicago: University of Chicago Press.

Krasner, L., and Ullman, L. P. (1965) *Research in Behavior Modification.* New York: Holt, Rinehart & Winston.

Mager, R. F. (1962) *Preparing Instructional Objectives.* Palo Alto, Calif. Fearon.

Miller, G. A. (1951) *Language and Communication.* New York: McGraw-Hill.

Moore, G. P. (1971) *Organic Voice Disorders.* Englewood Cliffs, N. J.: Foundations of Speech Pathology Series by Prentice-Hall.

Mowrer, O. H. (1960) *Learning Theory and Behavior.* New York: John Wiley.

Palmer, M., and LaRusso, D. A. (1965) *Anatomy for Speech and Hearing.* New York: Harper & Row.

Potter, R. K., Kopp, G., and Green, H. (1947) *Visible Speech.* New York: Van Nostrand Reinhold.

Skinner, B. F. (1953) *Science and Human Behavior.* New York: Macmillan.

Sloane, H. N., Jr., and MacAulay, D. (1968) *Operant Procedures in Remedial Speech and Language Training.* Boston: Houghton Mifflin.

Spence, K. W. (1956) *Behavior Theory and Conditioning.* New Haven, Conn.: Yale University Press.

Thomas, C. K. (1958) *The Phonetics of American English*, 2nd Edition. New York: Ronald Press.

Van Riper, C. and Irwin, J. (1958) *Voice and Articulation.* Englewood Cliffs, N.J.: Prentice-Hall.

Watkins, D. E., and Karr, H. M. (1940) *Stage Fright and What to Do About It.* Boston: Expression.

Winitz, H. (1969) *Articulatory Acquisition and Behavior.* New York: Meredith Corp.

Zemlin, W. R. (1968) *Speech and Hearing Science.* Englewood Cliffs, N.J.: Prentice-Hall.

INDEXES

index
of
selections
and
authors

index
of
topics